Penguin Education

**Penguin Education Specials**
*General Editor:* Willem van der Eyken

D0183110

**Counter Course**
**A Handbook for Course Criticism**
Edited by Trevor Pateman

# Counter Course
## A Handbook for Course Criticism
Edited by Trevor Pateman

Penguin Books

Penguin Books Ltd, Harmondsworth,
Middlesex, England
Penguin Books Inc, 7110 Ambassador Road,
Baltimore, Md 21207, USA
Penguin Books Australia Ltd,
Ringwood, Victoria, Australia

First published 1972
Copyright © Trevor Pateman and contributors, 1972

Made and printed in Great Britain by
Hazell Watson & Viney Ltd,
Aylesbury, Bucks
Set in Monotype Times

# Contents

# Preface

We have produced this handbook for the use of students in higher education who find their courses boring, cramped by exams, methodologically unsound or with a content politically obnoxious in its only possible real-world uses. In short, for students who find that their education consists in being processed for a particular niche in the class structure of society.

The book has been produced by individuals who do not have a shared political position, though their common denominator is that of being students or recent ex-students engaged in radical and revolutionary political activity. Each of them proposes, implicitly or explicitly, his own strategy for students.

Of course, what we say cannot determine what is done with our work. It may be put to use more or less politically. Less politically, it could be used as source material to articulate the shouts that challenge the lecturer's monopologue. Or it could simply serve as a stimulus to further counter-ideological theoretical work. Or it could be treated as just another book, presenting alternative knowledge, parallel to, at peace with, and probably on the reading lists for the existing courses: the only contradiction then would be the mental one of dual knowledge.

More politically, our ideas, in so far as they show the mechanisms of production of ideology and the social functioning of higher education, could inform a wider struggle which does not accept to fight on a terrain defined by the boundaries of the higher educational institution, but rather aims at a society in which that boundary will itself be destroyed – which implies the destruction of the institution.

These are some of the possibilities. We would like to know of and participate in what actually happens. We would like to know how the book has been used by groups of students, what they think wrong with it. The contributors are available to talk about their articles and about countering courses. All correspondence to Trevor Pateman, c/o Penguin Education, Horton Road, West Drayton, Middlesex.

The help of Gay Best and Jane Lawrence has been indispensable in completing this project, and in thanking them by name I hope that many others who helped in different ways will not feel forgotten. They are not.

# Introduction

Each form is the frozen temporary image of a process. Thus, any work merely represents a staging point in the process of becoming, not a fixed goal. (Lissitsky)

To the police mind it may appear that the student movement flared up in 1968, and has since died down because there was no real basis for it in England. The truth is that unrest is spreading into new areas of the education system – science students, the 'second sector' of the binary system, the schools – whereas before it centred on the universities.

Within education, the discontent shows at present in largely negative terms which, however, it would be wrong to identify as political integration. Certainly we have not been deceived by reformist–authoritarian plans for pseudo-'participation' in the management of our own alienation. On the campus, we experience widespread resentment, boredom, anxiety, disaffection from syllabus and exams, sporadic indiscipline, and dropping out, rather than performing coordinated and dramatic action.

But off the campus, our dissaffection increasingly takes the positive form of serious political work in the communities and at the factory gate – in the rank-and-file politics of resistance to the Industrial Relations Bill and immigration laws, to imperialism in Ireland, and to the police repression of immigrant, political and youth culture groups. Some indication of this tendency is the present growth in membership of every political group left of the Communist Party.

Meanwhile, the conventional option offered to students – the gradual ascent of a professional employment ladder – seems less and less attractive or plausible. There is heavy unemployment of graduates even in the high-technology industries where growth was supposed to be 'self-sustaining'. The work conditions of mental workers increasingly approximates to those of the mass of the working class, a fact which is registered by the growth of white-collar trade-union militancy. There is nothing whatever in all this to support the idea that the English ruling class need expect no more 'trouble' from its young mental workers. The social roots of student unrest have not withered – rather they have deepened, and their political flowering will survive the spring frost to which it was exposed by the international movement which was based on the more advanced conditions of other countries.

Even if there were not these influences from our immediate economic situation, in the sense of our work conditions and rewards, we would still find ourselves in a state of crisis because of our position as students and academics in the system of production. As 'intellectuals', as producers and reproducers of knowledge, our consciousness reflects the general state of society. When a class successfully dominates society, as did the bourgeoisie in its progressive stage, its ideology is an almost perfect crime – people are hardly aware that anything is being stolen from them. But when the rule of a class enters a stage of crisis, as we see in the present chaotic state of British capital, then its ideas no longer seem to represent natural necessity. (Just look at the international monetary system and think of teaching the classical elegancies of economics, at Ireland and think of teaching the consistency of the British Constitution, at the crisis of personal relations and identity and think of teaching that linguistic philosophy is important.) The intellectuals whose task it is to put over the rulers' view of the world are sensitive to the changing climate, and show all the strains and uncertainties of life on the edge of the weather. As Herzen put it in pre-revolutionary Russia, 'We are living on the boundary between two worlds – which makes life for thinking people especially oppressive and difficult.' Such conditions naturally give rise to a body of intellectuals who would rather express the ideas of the working class who are moving towards the seizure of social power, than those of the decaying rulers who, apart from anything else become in this period increasingly banal, trivial and unilluminating.

Placed in the context of the present economic situation of mental workers, these historically general remarks about radical intellectuals acquire a particular modern significance. For the intellectual element in society is now greatly expanded in numbers, recruited from lower social groups, and more directly linked with the productive process – an aspect of the increasing role in advanced economies for delegated technical and control functions. A radical intellectual element is no longer, therefore, condemned to the isolation of detached critical consciousness, but is increasingly a substantive force in the primary contradictions in society. The criticism of courses is not purely intellectual, but a development in a substantive economic element. It represents a change in the formation of a particular industrial input, that of skilled manpower, and a challenge to that formation. It is the resistance of a productive force against the relations of production. So even in those cases where the ideas in the course critiques, formally speaking, do not as yet exceed the most radical ideas developed by the orthodox academic world, they still represent an entirely new movement when seen in context. They have been developed not in order to pass an exam, to conform to orthodox definitions of subject boundaries and qualifications, to ascend the academic profession, to publish or perish – nor even in fact to be purely intellectual contributions – but to discover a new and more radical mode of thought and action, disjoined from the academic world and part, as we ourselves are becoming, of the working class forces of our time: they could not have been written without telling teacher to stand out of the light.

The revolution is our university. It is the world revolution that both discovers new forms of knowledge and necessitates their discovery. Official society is hidebound by forms of learning and discovery that do not even meet the needs of its own most advanced productive sectors. Planning and research for modern industry require that knowledge is fluid wherever education is frozen. It innovates where education copies the obsolete, subverts where education obeys, integrates and generalizes where education specializes, applies where education abstracts, internationalizes where education is parochial, collectivizes where education sets individual against individual in a meaningless competitive and professional race.

Yet capitalism cannot break with its own ossified education system, not only because it lacks resources for development and makes cuts, but also because it actually depends on this old regime to maintain its own *social* preconditions. Education's very resistance to the growth of objective knowledge suits it for the production of pseudo-knowledge, of ideology which makes out that capitalist society is just and natural. The very rigidity of its hierarchies suits it for the fractional distillation of the student mass into the grades of the capitalist labour force; for the very authoritarianism which restricts development is the only possible social basis for production where the fruits of labour go to a minority which must therefore repress the majority.

The development of the productive forces is therefore contradicted by the fixed social relations of capitalism. It is only the revolutionary working class who can completely identify with social progress, and within education it is only the radical students who completely identify with the modern forms of knowledge.

The more advanced and confident sectors of capitalism would like to use our futurism up to a certain point, against their own old regime: it is of no use to ICI that the set books are out of date. They are happy if students 'protest' about obvious archaisms. Up to now, though, they have been able to rely on students being a relatively privileged stratum of the labour force and so not prepared to oppose the system totally. But as our 'privileges' turn stale and are anyway diminished, our radicalism cannot be limited. Capital *itself* is exposed as the limit on productive forces which its own logic has forced it to bring into being. But the productive forces develop relentlessly: science, the skills and culture which are embodied in a modern labour force, the understanding of production which is gained by an organized working class, these forces – let us say, we ourselves – continually batter at the social relations of the capitalist system which restricts our development.

Part One
**The Institutional Context**

# The Changing Role of the Bourgeois University[1]
## Ernest Mandel

Over the past twenty-five years the function of the university in the West has gradually altered. In this process the university has been in large measure the subject and not the object of a programmed social change which can be summed up in the formula '*transition from the second to the third phase in the history of the capitalist mode of production*', or, in fewer words, '*the rise of neocapitalism*'.

The function of the university during the two preceding phases of capitalism was primarily to give the brightest sons – and, to a lesser extent, also the daughters – of the ruling class the required classical education and to equip them to administer industry, the nation, the colonies and the army efficiently.

Training in orderly thinking, fostering methods for independent scholarship, laying down a common cultural background and the informal ties based on this background between 'elites' in all areas of social life (the 'old school tie' system) – that was the primary role of the university education for the great majority of students.

Specialized professional training was only a by-product. Even in the natural sciences the stress was generally put on pure theory. The way in which higher education was financed in practice gave the ruling class a 'monopoly of knowledge'. Most university graduates were in fact professionally independent – members of the liberal professions and businessmen – or directly associated with people in an independent position.

Neocapitalism has changed all that fundamentally. Two features of neocapitalism alike have produced the change:

1. The demand for technically specialized labour in industry and in the swelling state apparatus.

2. The need to respond to the increasing quest for higher education, which, in consequence of the rising standard of living, the middle class,

1. This article was originally given as a speech at Rijks University, Leiden in 1970. It was first published in England by the Spartacus League with whose permission it is now reprinted. It can be obtained from them as a pamphlet at 182 Pentonville Road, London, N1.

government functionaries, white-collar workers, and – to a lesser extent – even skilled blue-collar workers, began to seek as a means of social advancement.

The university explosion which we are still experiencing has thus reflected a strongly increased demand for, and a no less strongly increased supply of, intellectual labour.

The university was not prepared for this, neither in the content itself of higher education nor in its material infrastructure and its administrative organization. This failure of the university to adjust to the demands of neocapitalism has been regarded not incorrectly as one of the causes of the worldwide student revolt. But it is in the nature of our society that it can force the universities to adapt to these needs of the ruling class.

In the context of neocapitalism, technocratic reform of the university – transformation from the classical to the technocratic university – is inevitable.

The student revolt is not only a reaction to the failure of today's universities to adapt; it is at the same time a reaction against the so far too successful attempt to make this adaptation on the basis of almost total subordination to the demands and the interests of neocapitalism.

The connection between this third industrial revolution – often called the 'technical-scientific revolution' – the growing demand for intellectual labour, and technocratic university reform is obvious. The third industrial revolution is to a certain extent distinguished by a massive reintegration of intellectual labour into industry, production, and even the work process, symbolized by the electronics specialist who runs and watches over automated production operations.

Thus a real 'labour market' for university graduates is developing. Talent scouts pick through every new class graduating from the important universities in the United States, Great Britain and Japan, and the same procedure is increasingly being introduced into the West European countries. The law of supply and demand determines the wages of intellectual workers as it has those of manual workers for two hundred years.

*Thus a process is under way of proletarianization of intellectual labour. Proletarianization does not mean primarily (or in some circumstances at all) limited consumption or a low standard of living, but increasing alienation, increasing subordination of labour to demands that no longer have any correspondence to the special talents or fulfilment of the inner needs of men.*

If the university is to fulfil the function of training the specialists wanted by the big corporations, higher education must be reformed in a functional direction. Specialists on economic growth have 'discovered' that one of the reasons for the slow growth of the gross national product in Great Britain has been the overstressing of theoretical science in the universities at the expense of applied science.

The drive to adapt higher education to meeting practical needs is being promoted by every means – at the same time that the most intelligent masters of the big monopolies concede that in the long run pure theoretical research is more fruitful than research along predetermined lines, even in the 'purely economic' realm.

Functionalization of the university is pushed to the extreme when education and academic research are subordinated to specific projects of private companies or government departments (the tying of certain British and American schools into research on biological weapons comes to mind, as well as the *war games* of some American schools dealing with civil conflicts in one or another colonial country).

But these ultimate cases must be seen for what they are – extreme examples and by no means the quintessence of functionalization, which is the substance of the technocratically reformed university.

Overspecialization, functionalization and proletarianization of intellectual labour are the objective manifestation of the growing alienation of labour and they lead inevitably to a growing subjective awareness of alienation. The feeling of losing control over the content and development of your own work is as widespread today among so-called specialists, including university graduates, as among manual workers.

The anticipation of this alienation among the students themselves, in conjunction with unrest over the authoritarian structure of the university, plays an important role as a driving force of the student revolt.

Sixty years ago the conservative or liberal apologies for the existing social order were all the more convincing because the stability of the system was hardly questioned, even by its most radical critics. At best, social revolution was on the agenda only for the underdeveloped countries. For the West itself it was a vague future goal.

Two world wars, innumerable social and economic crises, and various revolutions have since greatly altered this view. Precisely because the existing social order is much less stable than before the First World War, the function of bourgeois scholarship is no longer primarily theoretical apology but practical reform and intervention in order to overcome certain crises.

*But for these very reasons, it has become much easier to challenge the capitalist system from both the theoretical and practical standpoints in the universities than it was in the past. This system is seen as only one of several possible variants and not as a self-evident reality.*

And so we have the peculiar three-pronged situation which gave rise to the student movement. From one angle, there is a growing dissatisfaction with the existing society, which virtually no one can deny is in crisis. Neocapitalist reform of the university carried out in an authoritarian way, and in large measure forced on the students, can only increase this malaise.

From another angle, the traditional critical structures, that is, the left political parties and, above all, the workers' movement have stopped playing their role of radical opposition to the existing society, for reasons I cannot dwell on here.

Since the critical students find no possibility for radical opposition and confrontation within these structures, they try to achieve this *outside* the parties, the parliament, and the manipulated mass media. But because they do not have the mass or the social weight to transform society themselves, their activity is limited to imitating such a social revolution in order to set an example that is limited to a kind of show.

For some student radicals this show is transformed from a means to an end in itself. In this way, despite their radical verbiage, they become victims of one of the most typical phenomena of a society based on an extreme division of labour, the phenomenon of partial and therefore false consciousness.

Other student radicals make an attempt to operate rationally, that is, they attempt to function as an example in a different way for the working class, as a detonator that can set off an explosion among these broader masses. The events of May 1968 in France have proved that this is not unrealistic.

*But these events also showed that a student revolt as such cannot substitute for a politically educated and organizationally consolidated revolutionary vanguard of the working class.*

Thus it seems that today's universities are caught between two conflicting pressures. On the one hand, technocratic reform is being driven through from the outside in the interest of the ruling class. On the other, a radical challenge is emerging from within the universities but, in the absence of support in other sectors of society, it gets bogged down in utopianism and impotence.

Is there any way out of this dilemma? Are students – and 'intellectuals' in general – condemned to the choice of integrating themselves into the existing irrational and inhuman social order – disorder it might better be called! – or engaging in hopeless gestures of revolt by individuals or small groups?

An answer to this question presupposes an opinion on the capacity of neocapitalist society to overcome its most important inner contradictions. In opposition to Marcuse and others, we start from the position that the most important contradiction in capitalist society – in its neo-capitalist as well as its preceding stages – is the contradiction between capital and labour in the production process.

*We are convinced, therefore, that in the long run the workers cannot be coopted into neocapitalism, because the fundamental contradiction between capital and labour will always reappear, whether or not this occurs in the realm of consumption.*

*Furthermore, many signs indicate that in the industrialized Western countries the centre of gravity of the class struggle is slowly but surely shifting from questions of dividing the national income between wages and profits to the question of who determines what is produced, how it should be produced and how labour should be organized to produce it.*

If our position is confirmed by events – and much of what has been happening in the recent two or three years in the plants of three major Western countries (France, Italy and Great Britain) seems in fact to confirm it – then the dilemma referred to does not say all that can be said on the question of the role of the university in programmed social change.

There is a way out of this dilemma because a force still exists which has the potential to bring about a radical transformation of society. When it does not let itself be trapped by neocapitalist functionalization, the contemporary university can also escape the other side of the dilemma – quixotic rebellion. *The university can be the cradle of a real revolution.*

We must immediately include a warning in the argument. Whenever we speak of 'the university', we mean the people of the university collectively, that is, the teachers and the students. We do not mean the university as an institution.

As an institution, the university is incorporated in the existing social structure. Students, professors and workers cannot finance and maintain any universities in the final analysis as long as the social surplus value is not collectivized, that is, as long as we live in a capitalist society.

In the long run the university as an institution remains bound with golden chains to the power of the ruling class. Without a radical trans-formation of society itself the university cannot undergo any *lasting* radical transformation.

But what is impossible for the university as an institution is possible for students as individuals and in groups. And what is possible for students as individuals and groups can, on the collective level, temporarily emerge as a possibility for the university as a whole.

The role of students as a driving and initiating force for the renewal of society is not new. Marx, Lenin and Fidel Castro after all must be rated as intellectual and not manual workers.

To begin once more like the pioneers of the modern workers' movement, spreading anti-capitalist revolutionary socialist consciousness in the working class, is as possible today for students and intellectuals as it was three quarters of a century ago. The task is more difficult because this is not the first time it has been attempted and because a mountain of failures and disappointments weighs on the consciousness of the broad masses.

There are, however, many indications that the young generation of blue- and white-collar workers suffers less from this scepticism than the older generation. Moreover, ties can be developed between the students and young workers, as they have been in several Western countries. Once the initial difficulty is surmounted, the task automatically becomes easier than in the nineteenth century, because the objective conditions are much riper.

What the university must offer the young workers is first of all the product of theoretical production, that is, scientific knowledge, nothing so sterile as the masochistic populism of some students who want to go '*to the workers*' with empty hands and empty heads to offer them their muscles and vocal cords. What the workers need most of all is knowledge, a radical critique of the existing society, systematic exposure of all the lies and half-truths projected by the mass media.

It is not easy to put this knowledge into words that can be understood by the masses. Rhetoric and academic jargon are as sterile as populism. But the job of popularization comes after that of assimilating real knowledge. And it is in this latter realm that a really critical university can make its prime contribution today to transforming society. It can offer a critique of the existing society as a whole and of its parts that is all the more radical and relevant for being serious, scholarly and incorporating a large amount of factual material.

The basic data for such a task are a thousand times more easily accessible to students and academics than to those who are faced with making a living in the day-to-day professional world. Collecting and processing the basic data is a practical step towards self-criticism and social change on the part of the contemporary university.

We have all said that the most important contribution, at least as a starting point, that the university can make towards the radical transformation of society lies in the area of theoretical production. But it need not limit itself to pure theoretical production. It can serve as a bridge to practical experimental application, or experimental practical research.

The larger the number of students, and the broader the student challenge, the more extensive become the possibilities for uniting theory and practice. We have a rich storehouse of literature on the problem of alienated labour – 90 per cent of it written by learned philosophers, sociologists or economists; 10 per cent by self-educated workers themselves. A few priests and ministers have tried to supplement previous theoretical knowledge of this problem with practical experience in the factories.

Why shouldn't working students in medicine, physiology and psychology begin to apply such experiments on a large scale to their own experiences in a modern enterprise, above all to description and analysis of the experiences of their fellow workers? Critical medical students will be able to analyse the problem of fatigue, of frustration caused by alienated mechanical labour, by a steadily rising intensity of labour, better than positivist doctors – if they combine real professional expertise with a grasp of social phenomena in their full context, and enrich this with personal experience.

But this is only one example out of many. Converting the mass media from instruments for producing conformity to instruments for criticizing the society can be tested out with precision and can prove very effective. The police use films of demonstrations to facilitate repression. Amateur radical films – which tens of thousands of people have the potential for producing – can be used just as well to train demonstrators in self-defence against repression.

Today's technology can be used at innumerable different points as a means for exposing the existing repressive structures and as a means for speeding the self-emancipation of the masses. Here is an unexploited, challenging area of work for students and academics of all scholarly disciplines, in which the first requisite is: *Begin yourself to overcome the contradiction between theory and practice.*

Here emerges another important contribution that the university can make to the radical transformation of society. As a permanent institution, the university remains subject to the control of the ruling class. But wherever the struggle of the university collective for self-management assumes such scope that a temporary breakthrough in this area occurs, then for a short period the university becomes a 'school of self-management' for the entire people. This was what happened in the Sorbonne in Paris in May 1968; this is what happened, among other places, in Chicago in May 1970. These examples were extremely limited in scope and duration. But under favourable circumstances the attraction of such examples for the broad masses can be very promising.

In a certain sense this is the central problem of 'programmed social change'. Programming for whom and by whom? That is the question.

The argument advanced by the opponents of democratic self-management in the universities as well as in the plants deals with competence. Society is divided into 'competent' bosses and 'incompetent' workers, as they see it. Let us leave aside the question of whether the 'competence' of the bosses is such as to justify their retaining the function of decision-making. Whenever we compare this proclaimed competence with the results, at least in so far as society is concerned, then there are at least a few reasons for doubt.

The decisive argument against this concept, however, is not affected by such a value judgement. With the development of computers and the functionalized university, a system is emerging in which the control of levers of economic power, the concentration of economic power goes hand in hand with a growing monopolization of access to a no less horrible concentration of information.

Because the same social minority keeps a tight grip on power and information while scientific knowledge becomes more and more specialized and fragmented, a growing hiatus is developing between detailed professional competence and the concentration of information that makes it possible to make centralized strategic decisions.

The members of the board of directors of a multi-national corporation can leave thousands of small decisions to 'competent professionals'. But since the directors alone have the final outcome of the information-gathering process at their disposal, they alone are 'competent' to make the central strategic decisions.

Self-management overcomes this hiatus by giving the masses the necessary information to equip them to understand what is involved in the strategic central decisions. Any member of the mass who is 'competent' in this or that detail plays a participating role in making these decisions whenever cooperation and not competition among individuals is the social norm.

If the capitalist system survives, despite the tremendous crisis of capitalist production relations caused by technological progress, the growing alienation of 'competent professionals' from 'incompetent masses' is inevitable. If, however, the system of private ownership of the means of production, independent investment decisions by firms, and generalized commodity production, is replaced by democratically centralized, planned self-management of all the producers and workers, a universal social interest arises in eliminating 'incompetence' in general. And this social interest will be reflected in a tendency towards universalized higher education.

The increasing exclusion of unskilled labour from the productive process – its exclusion from the tertiary sector as well is only a question of time – makes such universal higher education in fact an absolute necessity, since a growing sector of the population will be condemned to the status of unemployable drop-outs in the midst of great social wealth.

Furthermore, technocratic university reform, functionalization of the university – debasement of higher education to fragmented, overspecialized, and unintegrated professionalism – what the radical German students call '*Fachidiotismus*' ('Professional Cretinism') – has developed increasingly into organized incompetence.

One of the sharpest accusations that can be lodged against the existing social disorder is that in a period when scientific knowledge is expanding at explosive speed the level of university education is steadily declining instead of rising. Higher education is thus incapable of fully exploiting the rich potential of scientific productive power. Moreover, it is producing incompetent labour power, not in the absolute sense, of course, but in comparison to the possibilities created by science.

Some neocapitalist spokesmen say openly what they want, like the authors of the West German university reform programme. It is in the order of things therefore for them to cynically assail the too liberal character of the old Humboldtian university. They admit that from their point of view, that is, from the standpoint of neocapitalism, the freedom of students to read, to study and to attend lectures as they choose must be curtailed.

Subordinating – not production to human needs but human needs to production – that is the very essence of capitalism.

*Self-management, therefore, is the key to full development of both scientific competence and the potential productive power of science. The future of the university and of the society intersect here and finally converge. When it is said that many people are not suited to a university education, that is doubtless a truism . . . in the context of our present society. But this is not a matter of physiologically or genetically determined unsuitability but of a long process of preselection by the home and social environment.*

When, however, we consider that a society that subordinates the development of men to the production of things stands the real hierarchy of values on its head, we can assume that, with the exception of marginal cases, there is nothing inevitable about this unsuitability.

When society is reorganized in such a way that it puts the education of people before the accumulation of things and pushes in the opposite direction from today's preselection and competition – that is, surrounds every less gifted child with so much care that he can overcome his 'natural handicap' then the achievement of universal higher education does not seem impossible.

Thus, universal higher education, cutting the workday in half, and all-embracing self-management of the economy and society based on an abundance of consumer goods is the answer to the problem of the twentieth century – what shall the teachers teach? 'Who will watch the police?' Then social development would become a fundamental process of self-education for everyone. Then the word 'progress' will have real meaning – when humanity has the competence to determine its own social fate consciously and relying only on itself.

# The Institute, the Ministry and the State Corporation[1]
## Henry Bernstein

### Institute of Development Studies (Seminar)

*Sir R. Russell* asked the Minister of Overseas Development if he will make a statement on a study course sponsored by his Department to be held by the Institute of Development Studies at the University of Sussex, for civil servants from developing countries, at which it is planned to hold a session on methods for nationalizing externally-owned companies.

*Mr Richard Wood:* I assume that my Hon. Friend is referring to the Study Seminar on the State Corporation to be held next month. The Institute is organizing this Seminar as part of its teaching programme, but it is not being sponsored by my Department.

*Sir R. Russell:* Is my Right Hon. Friend aware that this will relieve the anxiety of thousands of investors who strongly object to public money being spent on teaching developing countries how to seize their assets, and can he give an assurance that no public moneys are involved in this?

*Mr Wood:* I can assure my Hon. Friend that I share his anxiety about this. It did cause me disquiet to see how this Seminar was presented. Certain steps have been taken. I hope that we shall not see this particular matter in this form again.

*Mrs Hart:* I am sure the Right Hon. Gentleman would wish to make it clear that on this particular course decisions were made some time ago – the decisions to which he referred; but would he agree that it is of some considerable importance that he should arrive at some new understanding with the Institute, on the one hand to protect the rights of Government in deciding how public money is wisely spent and, on the other hand, to protect the academic freedom of the Institute?

*Mr Wood:* I should like to discuss with the Right Hon. Lady the understanding which I hope my Department has reached with the Institute, because I think it is very important for its future administration (Hansard, Col. 828, 1970).[2]

1. For more than a little help, I would like to thank my friends George Irvin, David Lehmann and Brian Van Arkadie. The views expressed are, however, the responsibility of the writer alone.
2. Sir Roland Russell is Conservative M.P. for Wimbledon South; Mr Richard Wood was appointed Minister of Overseas Development in the Conservative Government which came into office in June 1970; Mrs Judith Hart held the same post in the preceding Labour government.

Development studies, i.e. research directed to promoting the 'economic, political and social development' of 'poor' countries, shares certain features with other areas of applied social science like race relations, urban studies and industrial relations. Social scientists are recruited to these various fields to collect and analyse data, and to advise on the formulation and implementation of policy. Who sponsors and finances such research, and for what reasons? How does this affect its terms of reference, and what kind of ideology does it operate with?

To answer these questions we need to locate applied social science in an institutionalization of academic life under corporate capitalism that is unprecedented in both the extent and the directness of its involvement with government and big business.[3] This precludes any simple separation of the applied and the 'pure', as the latter, traditionally more academic activity, provides theoretical resources and philosophical justifications for the former. Applied social science assumes the prevailing ideology of 'piecemeal social engineering'. Racialism, poverty, labour 'unrest' or underdevelopment are not seen as the expressions of basic social contradictions but as 'problems' which can be solved by appropriate reforms. Moreover, this ideology entails the view that it is in the interests of all social groups (with the exception of 'extremist minorities' pursuing their own devious and disruptive ends) to subscribe to this form of 'conflict-resolution' which precludes any fundamental changes in the unequal distribution of power. This is not to presume that the motivations and attitudes of social scientists are either simple or homogeneous. Alongside careerism, and probably combined with it in varying degrees, there is often a genuine desire to help those who constitute the subject of study, whether immigrants, drop-outs and other 'deviants', or underdeveloped countries. Indeed, the participation of those with attested liberal credentials has an important function in legitimating the enterprise; on the other hand, the liberal soon encounters situations which bring out the tension between the stated humanitarian purpose of his work and the interests of those who finance and ultimately direct it.

Since 1945 as the great majority of former colonies attained political independence and were incorporated in the United Nations, a concern for their 'development' became a major theme in Western foreign policy and gave rise to a host of international agencies and research bodies.

3. Private corporations are the dominant institutions in contemporary Western society, and their functional needs for security, control and expansion determine the broad outlines of the social structure, government policy, beliefs and values (Szymanski, 1970, p. 3). See also the speech of Martin Nicolaus at the 1968 Convention of the American Sociological Association (reprinted in this volume).

In one view, this intense interest in the Third World may be seen as an aspect of the strategy of the former colonial powers and those countries which did not have an empire in the classic sense, for example, the United States and West Germany, namely, to maintain and extend 'imperialism without colonies'. However, conventionally the underlying justification of development studies is found in the liberal sentiment that this interest in – and ostensible contribution to – development derives from a concern to alleviate human deprivation or some combination of altruism and enlightened self-interest. The possibility of fundamental contradictions between viable development in the Third World and the security of Western economic and political power is mostly ignored.[4] In so far as conflicts are recognized they are usually treated as the result of infringements of the game of capitalist development, and therefore avoidable. This is illustrated in a recent publication of Cornell University's South-East Asia Program:

Economic development is concerned with the size of the 'pie' without regard to its racial dimensions; economic nationalism is concerned with the racial and ethnic distribution of the 'pie' rather than its size. . . . Economic nationalism is a fact of life which, if ignored, will upset the most careful economic calculations. It is not an attractive phenomenon and our intention is not to gloss over the basic inhumanity it propagates (Golay *et al.*, 1969, pp. vii, viii, ix).[5]

Such 'basic inhumanity' apart, the conventional wisdom holds that the relationship between the development of the Third World and the future of the capitalist 'free world' should and can be one of mutual benefit. This is often evoked in the notion of 'partnership' – itself evocative of earlier catch-phrases of colonial rule – as, for example, in the titles of a collection of essays on international agencies and development *The Global Partnership* (Gardner and Millikan, 1968), and of the World Bank sponsored report *Partners in Development* (Pearson, 1969).[6]

4. Compare the argument in Susan Vickery's contribution to this book (p. 140).

5. One element of the ideological distortion in this statement is the implication that economic nationalism is an aberration practised only by some underdeveloped countries, whereas economic nationalism was crucial in the early development of the advanced capitalist countries – and continues to be so. For a recent study of the United States with a lot of useful data see Magdoff (1969).

6. It is no more surprising that many Third World elites subscribe to this developmentist ideology than to find a leading British trade-union official addressing an employers' federation on 'the problems that face *us*', i.e. in getting 'rid of the power of the unauthorized Shop Stewards and the militants inside *our* factories' (quoted in Cliff, 1970, p. 97). [My emphasis.]

The conventional use of the developed–underdeveloped countries classification helps obscure the necessity of class analysis of the latter.

In this country critical comment on the conventional notion of development in the Third World has been conspicuous by its absence – in contrast to the United States where research on the Third World has been under attack from the mid-1960s. America's leadership of world capitalism and the war in Indo-China have resulted in a searching examination of the activities of American social science, and its many links with the State Department, the CIA, the Pentagon, and the business corporations have been exposed (Irving Louis Horowitz, 1967; Africa Research Group, 1969; Gough, 1969; David Horowitz, 1970; Wolf and Jorgenson, 1970).[7] The events at the Institute of Development Studies (IDS) discussed here appear less dramatic and less obvious compared with what has been revealed in the United States. This is partly due to differences in the scale, intensity and visibility of imperialist activity between the two countries. However, our understanding of the general phenomenon is enhanced by examining a situation which is less transparent and which lacks villains more familiar to the demonology of the Left, such as the social scientists involved in planning the war in Vietnam. Most of the senior staff of IDS hold strong liberal convictions and are often critical of the government. For example, in a private capacity Fellows of IDS supplied no fewer than three of the seven contributors to the Penguin Special *Matters of Principle: Labour's Last Chance* (Burgess, 1968).[8] On the other hand, their institutional role entails a working relationship with government based on the characteristic British compound of tacit understanding, euphemism and compromise. When this balance was temporarily disturbed, the contradiction between the preferred ideology and the permitted practice of liberal social science was exposed.

The Ministry of Overseas Development (ODM) was set up by the Labour Government elected in 1964 as 'one of its first acts' (HMSO, 1965, p. 27). In the White Paper on the work of the new Ministry, the establishment of an Institute of Development Studies was announced as 'a major initiative':

144. The Institute will fill several needs. Its main function will be to organize courses of advanced study on the problems of overseas development in all aspects of economics, social studies and administration. The courses will cover modern theories of development, but will pay special attention to the practical

7. Examples in this country include a report on the Centre for Middle Eastern Studies at the University of Durham in the Durham underground newspaper *Ferret* (1970); and the case of the Overseas Development Institute in Hayter (1971) (see p. 36).

8. An article by the Director of IDS has been reprinted recently in a book of readings on imperialism (Seers, 1970), and there is no doubt that from the standpoint of most American development studies IDS is 'radical'.

experience of developing countries. Three types of people will be catered for: senior administrators from overseas countries especially those working in or destined for senior places in planning offices and economic departments; British graduates who want to specialize in problems of overseas development; and British government officials who will be working on the problems of developing countries, whether at home or overseas.

145. A small, but highly qualified and experienced, staff will conduct the courses and will also carry out research, so that the Institute may play a leading part in advancing our knowledge of development and working out a development strategy. The permanent staff will be supplemented by distinguished visitors from developing and other countries who are experts in development problems (pp. 48–9).

To clarify the relationship of the Institute to the Ministry, an appendix was included in the Institute's Third Annual Report which stressed:

The Institute's staff are *not*, however, civil servants. There are, of course, many informal contacts and we naturally keep ourselves informed of the Ministry's views on priorities. *The Ministry has never, however, in any way dictated to us what research we should do, what we should teach in our Study Seminars, nor how we should recruit staff or run the Institute* (IDS, 1969, p. 65). [Last sentence – my emphasis.]

At least this was the case until Dr Brian Van Arkadie, a Fellow of IDS, proposed *The State Corporation* as the theme of Study Seminar 15.[9] The Ministry began to send out the brochure for the course in the normal way when, at the beginning of April 1970, it was learned that further distribution had been stopped in what amounted to a crisis move. Presumably someone at the Ministry had actually read the brochure by that time and had raised an objection to some of its wording, above all to one sentence which read:

There is now an increasing body of evidence from a number of developing countries regarding satisfactory methods of nationalization; the problems involved are administrative (taking over control and tackling the short-term problems of management in the initial period), financial (problems involved in minimizing compensation), and political (handling the problems of international political pressures).

The reasons for the Ministry's objection was that its enemies would make political capital of the proposed Seminar through an embarrassing

9. Study Seminars constitute the main teaching function of the Institute – see paragraph 144 of the White Paper above. They are residential courses on various aspects of development policy and planning for officials from underdeveloped countries. The fees of Study Fellows are paid by Technical Assistance grants (part of the British aid budget) and provide an important source of revenue for IDS – a consideration which did nothing to lessen the tension over Study Seminar 15.

question in the House of Commons. Accordingly, the Ministry refused to finance the Seminar unless the brochure was rewritten. This supposedly left the autonomy of the Institute intact but clearly the Ministry tried to prevent the Seminar taking place by using its financial control as a means of veto, against all previous practice as the statement quoted above shows. This action led to a crisis in the Institute the specific features and more general implications of which are summarily analysed in what follows.

The politics at IDS over Study Seminar 15 are best understood in terms of two groups I shall call radicals and institutionists. The radicals consisting mainly of junior members of the Institute, took the initiative in two ways.[10] First, they sought entry to a meeting called by the Director, to discuss the issue, to which only Fellows then present at the Institute had been invited. After this, discussion took place in a series of open meetings in which all academic and administrative staff were able to participate. Second, the radicals from the start argued against giving in to the Ministry's coercion and for holding the Seminar as planned. They maintained this stand against other suggestions involving postponement of the Seminar pending negotiations with the Ministry, or self-censorship in changing the brochure. Their position was summed up in a note circulated by Dr Van Arkadie which related the question of principle at stake to the necessity of analysing – *and taking sides in* – the conflicts that effective development policy presupposes, in this case the conflict between certain economic needs of underdeveloped countries and British overseas interests. The note went on to argue against the traditional practice of 'settling' such matters behind closed doors:

If the work of the Institute is to be subject to the veto of one or another pressure group, then better that this be public for all to see, than for us to hide behind liberal myths.

However, the desire to avoid publicity at all costs was common to all the institutionists – so termed because their primary concern was to defend the institution and its prospects of further expansion and prestige. This is not surprising as the institutionists consisted of the senior members of the Institute – those whose careers and self-image are intimately identified with the Institute's standing. Different institutionists subscribed initially to different defensive strategies. Some simply urged acquiescence with the Ministry's demand because of the danger to the Institute's future that resistance might entail. The possibility of the approaching

10. The term radicals is used relatively here – few of the group in this context were radical in the broader political sense.

General Election resulting in a Conservative government to which the forthcoming quinquennial plan of the Institute would have to be submitted added to their sense of desperation. For them the question of principle was effectively removed by being on the wrong side in a situation of unequal power – 'Who will get hurt in a clash between the pressure of overseas investors and a handful of academics down in Sussex?' This rhetorical question was sufficient to seal the matter.

Other institutionists recognized the principle but suggested negotiations with the Ministry, the Seminar to be postponed until a mutually satisfactory compromise had been reached. Some of the tactics advocated carried the curious flavour of life, if that is the right word, in a C. P. Snow novel. Suggestions were advanced of soliciting support among officials of the Ministry on the basis of various, sometimes contradictory, interpretations of the internal politics of the ODM bureaucracy. This devious elitism was rejected by the radicals, in any case precluded from such a game by their lack of 'informal' contacts.

The starkness of the case for 'pragmatism' was at times masked with rationalizations also advanced by the Ministry after it had first stated the most honest reason of its political sensitivity. For example, that the 'one-sided' presentation of the Seminar's theme offended against pedagogic impartiality; and that the hitherto equable relationship between Institute and Ministry was based on an implicit understanding concerning the 'rules of the game' now gratuitously violated by the brochure for Study Seminar 15. Obviously it was the side in question that pained the Ministry and not any generalized concern for impartiality – would ODM have withdrawn finance from a Seminar on means of *attracting* foreign private investment? And the 'rules of the game' had prevailed in a political vacuum, in the absence of any challenge to the unspoken gentlemen's agreement that the Institute would not do anything of possible harm to British interests in the Third World. This basis of harmony between politicians, civil servants and academics was upset by naming the game as manipulative politics and by reversing the customary rules – i.e. *by proposing to explore the possibilities of manipulation by the governments of underdeveloped countries:*

If you are training trade-union leaders, you teach them how to get the most out of an employer. In the same way, underdeveloped countries must get the best they can out of their relationships with developed countries.[11]

11. Dr Van Arkadie quoted in the *Sunday Times*, 14 June 1970. On the first page of a symposium on development written by Fellows of the Institute several dimensions of the IDS brand of the poverty of liberalism relevant to this discussion are brought together:

A debate on the politics of its work had thus been made possible after four years of the Institute's existence, as a result of (1) a political initiative – the proposal of Study Seminar 15; (2) the incompetence of the Ministry in distributing the Seminar brochure and its subsequent reaction in stopping distribution and attempting to veto the Seminar; (3) the campaign of the radicals to hold the Seminar as planned. In a letter sent to the Minister, Mrs Judith Hart, on 1 May 1970 the Director of IDS pointed out that:

The Ministry's change of attitude provoked a lengthy debate within the Institute on the wider issues involved, and has led us to state our position *for the first time* on a number of points which we consider basic to the operation of the Institute. [My emphasis.]

This letter which asked the Minister to reconsider her decision was the outcome of a general meeting of the Institute on 28 April 1970. That the request was made at all was a victory for the radicals but the letter was conciliatory and went on to suggest early consultation on alternative means of financing Study Seminars so as to avoid future embarrassment to the Ministry.

The Minister's reply was far from conciliatory. It accused the Director of trying to force a confrontation, and stated that the correct procedure for dealing with the matter was for it to go to the Governing Body of the Institute, the Chairman of which (the Vice-Chancellor of the University of Sussex) could then approach the Ministry – thus denying those who actually work at IDS any effective voice. The Ministry's right to be interested in the Institute's teaching programme was mentioned, and its position on Study Seminar 15 reiterated – the Ministry would finance it if the brochure were changed. At the meeting to hear the Minister's reply it was decided that the Seminar should take place. The governments of Study Fellows were asked to pay their fees and other expenses, which of course

[The] world of the end of the twentieth century . . . is a world of very big inequalities, where the great majority of the capital and professional resources are in the hands of a small minority of countries, which also hold dominant positions in international trade, enjoy the preponderance of military power and exercise strong cultural influence. These imbalances create special problems (as well as special opportunities) for poor countries and special responsibilities for the rich (Seers, 1971, p. 7).

The inadequacy of the second sentence in the light of the first, which points to a description of imperialism, is staggering. What possible analytical meaning can be given to the concept of the 'responsibilities of the rich'? As for the opportunities open to the poor countries, it was precisely one kind of opportunity indicated in the brochure for Study Seminar 15, namely, minimal cost nationalization of foreign assets, that caused all the trouble.

had never been necessary before, and IDS offered to help in cases where this was impossible.

Study Seminar 15 on *The State Corporation* was held as planned from 16 August to 26 September 1970 without the financial assistance of the British government – to the relief of the overseas investor as given voice by Sir Ronald Russell, and for which Mrs Hart, no longer in office, was anxious to claim credit (see the extract from Hansard above).

The question of autonomy was clarified by one of the Study Seminars last year (15, *The State Corporation*). The issue was at first focused on part of the brochure advertising the seminar (referring to the nationalization of foreign companies), since the Ministry's position was that they would be prepared to sponsor a course on this subject if the programme were somewhat different. But the issue was really rather more fundamental, since our budget is constructed in such a way that makes us heavily dependent on fees paid by the Ministry of Overseas Development (ODM), in respect of seminar participants from overseas.

In the event we did hold the Seminar. Fifteen officials took part from eight countries, with overseas governments paying the fees of eleven of them. Moreover, an agreement was reached with the Ministry which should secure our position for the future. We will tighten our procedures for sponsoring courses and issuing material; but once our Board of Studies has approved the teaching programme, the Ministry (which appoints two members of the Board) will finance it as a whole. With willingness on both sides, the new procedures should be workable. We appreciate that ODM is accountable to Parliament for the funds it spends on training awards. I trust that any British Minister would also accept that, in this inevitably controversial field, we could hardly treat as an over-riding constraint the need to avoid embarrassing the government of the day (IDS, 1970, p. 5).[12]

Thus was the epitaph of the politics of Study Seminar 15 announced in the *Director's Introduction* to the *Fourth Annual Report* of IDS in two paragraphs which are cryptic but rich in significance. The last sentence of the statement is an act of window-dressing – such standard expressions of liberal faith ('academic freedom' and all that) are either vindicated or belied by practice. Negotiations on new arrangements for Study Seminars were already under way in May before the dust had settled. This expressed the policy of the institutionists of IDS and their counterparts at the Ministry to cut their losses, finalized in a new 'agreement' which 'should be workable' with the Institute's pledge to 'tighten' its procedures, and given 'willingness on both sides'. Whether this will result in a new form of self-censorship in IDS to prevent future 'trouble'

12. Ironically the Institute's Annual Report in 1970 carried a new title – *Development Studies in a Divided World*.

remains to be seen, but certainly the formula of 'responsibility' is the salient feature of the Director's statement.

The hypersensitivity of the IDS institutions and ODM bureaucrats to a certain kind of publicity is evident. This was reflected in the decision (before the case of Study Seminar 15 arose) to stage the official opening of the Institute on 30 June 1970, in the summer vacation, instead of during term-time as originally planned. All the same, when the ceremony was performed by the new Conservative Minister, Mr Wood, amidst potted flowers and glossy ODM publicity stands illustrating the splendours of British aid, a temporary fence appeared between the lawn of the Institutes and a Sussex campus ludicrously bare of students.[13] It was the opportunity open to the radicals to make public the dispute with the Ministry that produced the most violent fears in the institutionists, who tried desperately but unsuccessfully to prevent a letter being sent to *The Times* on 29 May 1970. (In the event the letter was not published.) By then the radicals, having ensured that the Seminar would go ahead as planned, felt things slipping from their grasp. The immediate objective gained, they were left standing in the wings as the Ministry and the Institute establishment began to plaster over the cracks that had appeared.

The feeling that very little had changed was intensified by the subsequent beneficence of the Government in granting funds for the Institute's programme of expansion over the next five years. The senior members of IDS shared a similar liberal outlook with a number of 'left-wing' Labour Ministers of Overseas Development – Barbara Castle, Reg Prentice and Judith Hart herself – but what is one to make of this act of generosity to the cause of the welfare of the Third World by a Conservative government then embarking on a series of savage and repressive domestic policies? The answer is that institutions like IDS are used to publicize the image of capitalism 'with a human face'. The Institute *is* sponsored and financed by the British government and its existence serves to legitimize the government's claims of concern and integrity in its policies towards underdeveloped countries. In this way the Institute has an important propaganda function. On one hand, its more technical research and teaching is unlikely to benefit or harm anyone directly.[14] On the other

13. It is only fair to point out that some consternation had been caused the year before by an article on IDS in a Maoist paper which ended 'DEATH TO ALL LACKEYS!' (*Sussex Student*, 1969).

14. Much of this work is of the type C. Wright Mills termed 'abstracted empiricism' by which he meant research directed by an obsession with techniques at the expense of a desire to answer relevant questions (Mills, 1967, ch. 3). One aspect of this kind of social science is particularly relevant here: '[The] economics of truth – the cost of research – seem to conflict with the politics of truth – the use of research to clarify significant issues and to bring political controversy closer to reality' (p. 64).

hand, the thousands of brochures it distributes and the activities of its members in the international round of development conferences, commissions of 'experts', and government consultancies, help maintain the present system. The basic contradictions of the relationship between development and underdevelopment are obscured by the busy activities of this 'developmentism'. The attendance of Study Fellows at the Institute's seminars has the dual function of demonstrating the generosity of the British government which pays for them, and of providing part of the training process of Third World elites.[15]

Applied social science is academic big business, sponsored and controlled by the big business of industry, finance and government. The liberal social scientist, however he sees his role, functions to provide the sugar on the pill administered by the corporation executives, the agencies of the state, the institutions of international finance. The 'liberal dilemma' intensifies with the changing tactics of those who employ intellectuals to help the system run more smoothly or to ward off crisis, and the position of the liberal becomes increasingly untenable. He survives by a constant adjustment to the rules laid down by his employers. As these rules embody priorities contrary to the avowed welfare and social justice principles of liberal social science, the latter deteriorates as the gap between its ideology and its practice widens. To continue to work in these conditions necessitates a cumulative – and tortuous – process of self-deception or a more simple dishonesty.

What happened at the Institute is an example of a general phenomenon and was not an isolated case. Another recent, and related, example in this country is provided by the experience of Teresa Hayter at the Overseas Development Institute (ODI) in London. ODI is not government-financed like IDS but is an 'independent non-government body aiming to ensure wise action in the field of overseas development' (Hayter, 1971, p. 7). Miss Hayter was commissioned by ODI and financed by the World Bank to prepare a report for publication on the policies in Latin America of the World Bank, the International Monetary Fund and the United States Agency for International Development. She proved to be critical of the uses made of the funds administered by these institutions and ODI did not publish her report, which was written on the *genuine liberal assumption* that 'the well-being of the peoples of the Third World was, or at least could become, the primary consideration in aid policies' (p. 11). This again stresses the general point – when, where and how liberal social science can be critical is beyond the control of its practitioners . Criticism

15. In this sense Study Seminar 15 was almost as limited as other Study Seminars as far as the Third World is concerned. Its importance lies in the way it pierced the liberal façade of O D M and made clear the limits of tolerance of I D S activity.

is permitted when it is harmless and helps preserve the pretence of open-mindedness.[16] When criticism might be dangerous it is censored even though the assumptions on which it is based are limited or invalid, as Miss Hayter now recognizes to have been the case with her view of aid.

Finally, a few comments on the radical role in IDS are necessary. Up to a certain stage the radicals made most of the running on Study Seminar 15, after which the politics they had set in motion were buried with the reestablishment of the customary ritual of committees and compromise. This was partly due to their failure to promote the issue outside the Institute, particularly, to begin with, on the Sussex campus. Sending a letter to *The Times*, while nearly inducing heart attacks among some of the institutionists, was a traditional and highly limited expedient. However, neither the immediate victory of the radicals nor their failure in broader political terms should be allowed to obscure the other's significance. The most important point in conclusion is that in this – and many comparable situations in the various institutions of higher education – opportunities exist, or can be created, to demonstrate *the poverty of liberalism*. To destroy the claims of liberalism to relevance and effectiveness in contemporary society, to expose the ideological oppression it embodies and the material exploitation it obscures is a fundamental task in clarifying the basis of revolutionary alternatives.

16. 'The World Bank has been happy to publicize the friendly reservations about international aid made by the Pearson Commission. By contrast, it has tried very hard to suppress Teresa Hayter's study' (R. B. Sutcliffe, Foreword to Hayter, 1971, p. 6).

*References*

Africa Research Group (1969), *African Studies in America: the Extended Family*, Cambridge, Mass.

BURGESS, T. (ed.) (1968), *Matters of Principle: Labour's Last Chance*, Penguin.

CLIFF, T. (1970), *The Employers' Offensive. Productivity Deals and How to Fight Them*, Pluto Press.

*Ferret No. 5* (1970), 'Durham and the Middle East', Durham University.

GARDNER, R. N., and MILLIKAN, M. F. (eds.) (1968), *The Global Partnership: International Agencies and Economic Development*, Praeger.

GOLAY, F. H. *et al.* (1969), *Underdevelopment and Economic Nationalism in Southeast Asia*, Cornell University Press.

GOUGH, K. (1969), 'World revolution and the science of man' in Theodore Roszak (ed.), *The Dissenting Academy*, Penguin.

HAYTER, T. (1971), *Aid as Imperialism*, Penguin.

HMSO (1965), *Overseas Development: the Work of the New Ministry*, Cmnd 2736.

HMSO (1970), *Weekly Hansard, Issue No. 832, 3 July–9 July, 1970.*

HOROWITZ, D. (1970), 'Sinews of empire' and 'Billion-dollar brains' in Ramparts (ed.), *Divided We Stand*, Harper & Row.

HOROWITZ, I. L. (1967), *The Rise and Fall of Project Camelot: Studies in the Relationship between Social Science and Practical Politics*, MIT Press.

Institute of Development Studies (1969), *Third Annual Report 1968–9*, HMSO.

Institute of Development Studies (1970), *Fourth Annual Report 1969–70: Development Studies in a Divided World*, HMSO.

MAGDOFF, H. (1969), *The Age of Imperialism: The Economics of US Foreign Policy*, Monthly Review Press.

MILLS, C. W. (1967), *The Sociological Imagination*, Oxford University Press.

PEARSON, L. B. (1969), (Commission on International Development), *Partners in Development*, Pall Mall Press.

SEERS, D. (1970), 'The stages of economic development of a primary producer in the middle of the twentieth century', in Robert I. Rhodes (ed.), *Imperialism and Underdevelopment*, Monthly Review Press.

SEERS, D. (1971), 'Preface' in D. Seers and L. Joy (eds.), *Development in a Divided World*, Penguin.

*Sussex Student* (1969), 'IDS – centre for reactionary training and research', vol. 3, no. 3.

SZYMANSKI, A. (1970), 'Toward a radical sociology' *Sociological Inquiry*, vol. 40, no. 1.

WOLF, E., and JORGENSON, J. (1970), 'Anthropology on the warpath in Thailand', *New York Review of Books*, vol. 15, no. 9.

# Sociology Liberation Movement[1]
## Martin Nicolaus

These remarks are not addressed to the Secretary of Health, Education and Welfare. This man has agreed voluntarily to serve as a member of a government establishment, which is presently fighting a war for survival on two fronts. Imperial wars such as the one against Vietnam are usually two-front wars, one against the foreign subject population, one against the domestic subject population. The Secretary of Health, Education and Welfare is a military officer in the domestic front of the war against people. Experience in the Vietnam teach-ins has shown that dialogue between the subject population and its rulers is an exercise in repressive tolerance. It is, in Robert S. Lynd's words, dialogue between chickens and elephants. He holds some power over me; therefore, even if he is wrong in his arguments he is right, even if I'm right, I'm wrong. I do address myself to the Secretary's audience. There is some hope – even though the hour is very late – that among the members and sympathizers of the sociological profession gathered here there will be some whose life is not so sold and compromised as to be out of their own control to change or amend.

The ruling elite within your profession has invited a speaker who is in charge of what is called Health, Education and Welfare. Those of you who listened passively to what he had to say presumably agreed that this definition, this description of what the man did carried an accurate message. Yet among you are many, including the hard researchers, who do know better or should know better. The department of which the man is head is more accurately described as the agency which watches over the inequitable distribution of preventable disease, over the funding of domestic propaganda and indoctrination, and over the preservation of a cheap and docile reserve labour force to keep everybody else's wages down. He is Secretary of Disease, Propaganda and Scabbing.

This may be put too strongly for you, but it all depends on where you look from, where you stand. If you stand inside the Sheraton Hotel these terms are offensive, but if you gentlemen and ladies would care to step across the street into Roxbury you might get a different perspective and a different vocabulary. If you will look at the social world through

1. A speech made to the 1968 convention of the American Sociological Association.

the eyes of those who are at the bottom of it, through the eyes of your subject population, and if you will endow those eyes with the same degree of clearsightedness you profess to encourage among yourselves, then you will get a different conception of the social science to which you are devoted. That is to say that this assembly here tonight is a kind lie. It is not a coming together of those who study and know, or promote study and knowledge of social reality. It is a conclave of high and low priests, scribes, intellectual valets and their innocent victims engaged in the mutual affirmation of a falsehood, in common consecration of a myth.

Sociology is not now and never has been any kind of objective seeking out of social truth or reality. Historically, the profession is an outgrowth of nineteenth-century European traditionalism and conservatism, wedded to twentieth-century American corporation liberalism.

That is to say that the eyes of sociologists, with few but honourable (or: honourable but few) exceptions, have been turned downwards, and their palms upwards.

Eyes down, to study the activities of the lower classes, of the subject population – those activities which created problems for the smooth exercise of governmental hegemony. Since the class of rulers in this society identifies itself as the society itself – in the same way that Davis and Moore in their infamous 1945 propaganda article identified the society with those who run it – therefore the problems of the ruling class get defined as social problems. The profession has moved beyond the tear-jerking stage today; 'social problems' is no longer the preferred term, but the underlying perspective is the same. The things that are sociologically 'interesting' are the things that are interesting to those who stand at the top of the mountain and feel the tremors of an earthquake.

Sociologists stand guard in the garrison and report to its masters on the movement of the occupied populace. The more adventurous sociologists don the disguise of the people and go out to mix with the peasants in the 'field', returning with books and articles that break the protective secrecy in which a subjugated population wraps itself, and make it more accessible to manipulation and control.

The sociologist as researcher in the employ of his employers is precisely a kind of spy. The proper exercise of the profession is all too often different from the proper exercise of espionage only in the relatively greater electronic sophistication of the latter's techniques.

Is it an accident that industrial sociology arose in a context of rising 'labour troubles', that political sociology grew when elections became less predictable, or that the sociology of race relations is now flourishing – to name only a few examples here?

As sociologists you owe your jobs to the union organizers who got beat up, to the voters who got fed up, to the black people who got shot up. Sociology has risen to its present prosperity and eminence on the blood and bones of the poor and oppressed; it owes its prestige in this society to its putative ability to give information and advice to the ruling class of this society about ways and means to keep the people down.

The professional eyes of the sociologists are on the down people, and the professional palm of the sociologist is stretched towards the up people. It is no secret and no original discovery to take public note of the fact that the major and dominant sectors of sociology today are sold, computer codes and questionnaires, to the people who have enough money to afford this ornament, and who see a useful purpose being served by keeping hundreds of intelligent men and women occupied in the pursuit of harmless trivia and off the streets. I am not asserting that the individual researcher sells his brains for a bribe – although many of us know of research projects where that has happened – but merely that the dominant structure of the profession, in which all of its members are to some extent socialized, is a structure in which service to the ruling class of this society is the highest form of honour and achievement. (The speaker's table today is an illustration.) The honoured sociologist, the big-status sociologist, the fat-contract sociologist, the jet-set sociologist, the book-a-year sociologist, the sociologist who always wears the livery, the suit and tie, of his masters – this is the type of sociologist who sets the tone and the ethic of the profession and it is this type of sociologist who is nothing more nor less than a house servant in the corporate establishment, a white intellectual Uncle Tom not only for this government and ruling class but for any government and ruling class, which explains to my mind why Soviet sociologists and American sociologists are finding after so many years of isolation that, after all, they have something in common.

To raise and educate and train generation after generation of the brightest minds whom this country's so-called educational system has let survive in this sociological ethic of servility, to socialize them into this sociocracy, is a criminal undertaking, one of the many felonies against youth committed by those who set themselves up in a *loco parentis* situation that is usually far more oppressive than any real parental relation. The crime which graduate schools perpetrate against the minds and morals of young people is all the more inexcusable because of the enormous liberating potential of knowledge about people which directly affects what we do, what we may hope for. The corporate rulers of this society would not be spending as much money as they do for knowledge if knowledge did not confer power. So far, sociologists have been schlepping this knowledge that confers power along a one-way chain, taking knowledge from the people, giving knowledge to the rulers.

What if that machinery were reversed? What if the habits, problems, actions and decisions of the wealthy and powerful were daily scrutinized by a thousand systematic researchers, were hourly pried into, analysed, and cross-referenced, tabulated and published in a hundred inexpensive mass-circulation journals and written so that even the fifteen-year-old high school drop-outs could understand it and predict the actions of their parents' landlord, manipulate and control him?

Would the war in Vietnam have been possible if the structure, function and motion of the US imperial establishment had been a matter of detailed public knowledge ten years ago?

Sociology has worked to create and increase the inequitable distribution of knowledge; it has worked to make the power structure relatively more powerful and knowledgeable, and thereby to make the subject population relatively more impotent and ignorant.

In the late summer of 1968, while the political party currently in power is convening amidst barbed wire and armoured cars, the sociological profession ought to consider itself especially graced and blessed that its own deliberations can still be carried on with a police-to-participant ratio smaller than one-to-one. This may be because the people of the USA do not know how much of their current troubles stem – to borrow Lord Keynes's phrase – from the almost forgotten scribblings of an obscure professor of sociology. Or it may be that sociology is still so crude that it represents no clear and present danger.

In 1968, it is late, very late, too late, to say once again what Robert S. Lynd and C. Wright Mills and hundreds of others have long said, that the profession must reform itself. In view of the forces and the money that stand behind sociology as an exercise in intellectual servility, it is unrealistic to expect the body of the profession to make an about-face.

If and when the barbed wire goes around the ASA convention in a future year, most of its members will still not know why.

# The Politics of Academic Freedom[1]
## Dick Atkinson

'Academic freedom' is a term in frequent and current use in higher education circles, and hit the national headlines in the wake of the Warwick files incident. It's been there ever since. Yet its meaning is obscure, for quite different and opposing groups use it – politicians, professors students, etc. Do they all mean the same thing by it – is it the one common plank in their otherwise opposed views – or, does the same term apply to, yet cloak, quite different meanings and intentions?

Tradition has it that academic freedom means two things. Firstly, it means that universities are autonomous and should be completely free from any external constraint and political pressure. Secondly, it means that internal decisions such as government research or staff appointments should not be influenced by political considerations – all should be free to have any belief, so long as they live within the university by the accepted academic standards.

This article will try to show how the first part of this formula does not fit – universities are a part of society and are inevitably influenced by it. The article then seeks to show that the second part of the formula is not correct either – a rather vicious, though often hidden, struggle for power and control on the part of several internal groupings distorts the educational process of all students, and robs them (and most staff) of the right to academic freedom.

For historical reasons, which are connected with the origin of the traditional formula, universities in Britain are formally self-governing. Despite this, we can, today, distinguish three main areas of external constraint by which opinion and activity is limited within universities.

Firstly, the social areas from which universities recruit students, staff and administrators constitutes one way in which they have never been and can never be fully free. Thus, say, the student's home and school background, his general experience and beliefs, will influence and shape preconceptions with which he will come to university. The same applies to staff and administrators. But their preconceptions and degrees of

1. This essay is based on a feature article which first appeared in *The Times*, 4 October 1970.

flexibility are radically different from the students'. Such externally derived ideas and consequent activity limit the exercise of freedom in the university. In particular, the attitudes of members of committees governing staff appointments and student admissions are crucial factors which further determine the composition of assumptions and shape what can be freely said or done. Such committees are now rigidly defended and criticized by, respectively, administrators and students, for they have different conceptions of who should come to university and what a university should be like.

The second area of constraint involves the activity of industry and commerce. Seventy years ago these pressures were vital factors in the creation of the red brick universities. The notorious courts of governors and their powerful working committee, the university councils (at LSE it is called the standing committee of the court) owe their existence to the original source of university power and finance: local men of industry and commerce. Such individuals, acting within the form of university decision-making, are now, perhaps, less prominent. Certainly their contribution to the typical university budget has dropped from 90 per cent to less than 5 per cent. But the part which organized industry and commerce plays remains important. Research grants for particular projects, the employment of staff, even the creation of departments and, often, grants to students, all crucially affect a range of formal and informal decisions within the university. Industry, after all, has an interest in certain areas of knowledge, and the kind of person which it requires to develop and employ. It therefore attempts to exercise a discrete control over these factors.

A third area of constraint has been steadily expanding during this century and has proceeded apace since the recent expansion of higher education, and its redefinition as a national, economic and technological asset. Each succeeding wave of politicians and governments has sought to increase control over all levels of education. It has done so with the purpose, amongst others, of relating education to economic and technological development. This has met with some resistance within the universities. We must widen our scope and refer to the state sector of higher education, before we can see how the government is countering this resistance.

Technological colleges and colleges of art, including the proposed new polytechnic, are not automatons. For, unlike the universities, the government controls these colleges directly through the DES and the LEAs.

The reasoning behind the new polytechnics, which the government has proposed, and the binary system, by which the government formally segregated the previously informal distinction between the colleges and universities, seems to be the creation of an even more powerful, state-controlled, sector of education. This would be capable of diminishing the traditional educational dominance and autonomy of the universities. Meanwhile, the UGC, the opening of university finance to the Auditor-General, and, say, the raising of overseas students' fees, constitute a frontal attack on the 'autonomy' of the universities. Similarly, those academics who thought the PIB report on their salaries was instituting a threat from student control must think again. The reasoning of the report was clear. In an attempt to tie salaries to a particular conception of productivity, the threat came not from student power, but from governmental and technocratic state power.

So the freedom of the university is restricted by pressure external to it. Its freedom is limited, not absolute. The question now becomes, how is the remaining freedom distributed within the university? Are all equally free? Why do different groups within the university define freedom differently? We must ask why some groups see students, and not the three external constraints mentioned, as the main threat to their freedom.

We have already said that the titular heads of the universities are the courts of governors. They predominantly comprise outsiders: the nobility, industrialists, and so on. Their active power lies in their main working committee, the council, which takes major financial and developmental decisions. Here again, the lay representatives usually comprise the large majority. Strictly academic control, though limited by the control of council, is dispensed by senate. This body normally contains most, if not all, professors. Through these bodies – court, council and senate – the senior professional and academic administrators exercise a fourth and, often, decisive constraining force on the freedom of the majority in the university – the staff and students. That is to say, the students and staff have no formal means of controlling or shaping their teaching and learning environment. They are only sparsely represented in a hierarchial structure dominated by others.

Partly because of this power structure, and the experience of those whose lives and activity give it the form it takes, there exist at least four different definitions of the same term: academic freedom. Equally, there are at least four kinds of activity and power which relate to these different definitions of freedom.

Firstly, most governors, councillors and senior administrators see themselves as reflecting the traditional interests and pursuits of the university. The decisions taken by this small group of men is, they feel, just, if undemocratic, and their power to take them is rationalized in traditional, authoritarian terms. Any attack on their power or control, therefore, is defined as a general attack on 'academic freedom' itself. They do recognize government, though usually not industry, as a threat to that freedom. Increasingly, however, they tend to use the students' activity alone as a scapegoat, and as a far more dangerous threat. Academic freedom does not encompass them. So, if they try to exercise it they merely abuse what is not rightfully theirs.

Secondly, professors have traditionally seen both the council and non-professional staff as a danger to their own 'academic freedom' to take academic decisions. These are defined as what they themselves practise and do as heads of departments, and, collectively, as senators. But students are now seen in terms of the same scapegoat picture which the administrators have. When facing students these two groups usually form an unwritten alliance in an attempt to preserve their own traditional rights.

Thirdly, the non-professorial staff, recognizing that most real power lies with council, senate and the heads of their departments, see the student as a final threat to what little control is traditionally left to them. This resides in the lecture hall and examination room. This fact partly accounts for outbursts against, and misunderstanding of student claims for reform of teaching methods, course content and examinations. So, the students are again a scapegoat, and the main source of the non-professorial staff's lack of control (the professors, etc.) goes unacknowledged.

Fourthly, students have a totally different definition from the three previous ones, each of which precludes students from the right to 'academic freedom'. One dimension of the students' concept is consequently defined negatively, in terms of freedom from those external constraints which have been indicated. The present university power structure is seen as an additional, internal, constraint. All constraints (both external and internal) are seen as educationally destructive, serving non-education group interests. As students have no constitutional means to assert their negative freedom they are driven to direct action to achieve results. On another dimension, students define freedom positively, as the freedom to enlarge and shape their educational experience. In the process they hope to build a democratic alternative structure through which all, staff and students together, may gain control over their joint work situation, so making it relevant to contemporary educational needs.

They further feel that such an alternative organization would be able to curtail the extension of governmental and industrial control which the present structure has been powerless or unwilling to curtail. This not only implies totally reshaping the existing oligarchical power-structure, but by the same principle, democratizing tertiary education itself, merging the educationally meaningless divisions of the binary system into a single comprehensive education system.

This concept involves integrating the 'pure' (university) with the 'applied' (college); replacing cultured amateurism (Oxbridge and universities' arts faculties) and narrow technical expertise (applied science faculties and colleges), with theoretically informed and socially committed professionalism; an expansion beyond the upper middle class (university) and lower middle and skilled working class (college) to include all social strata.

Such changes entail the extension of the revolution in primary schools (in teaching methods, course content, child centred education) to the tertiary level, so linking participation at departmental level with democracy at central level. When fully spelt out, such dramatic changes are at once relevant to the individual needs and aspirations of students, in tune with advanced educational theory, and are flexible enough to create and critize the various needs of a society undergoing rapid technological change.

Only such institutions as these could recognize the full implications of the three external constraints (bureaucratic state, industrial, home and school), develop the determination to resist them politically and, at the same time, be socially responsive and responsible enough to discharge their democratic obligations within society. Such freedom is quite rightly recognized as a threat to the freedom of governors, administrators and professors. They oppose it by political means, in order to defend their own positions. 'Academic freedom' should therefore, more properly be called academic power, or control. As such, it resides, with different meanings, in a rigidly hierarchical structure. A person's definition of it depends, in part, on his place in that structure, on whether he does or does not control his work situation, and on which group he identifies as a threat to his control, or the cause of his lack of it.

Each definition is regarded by its advocates as having universal validity. They consequently attempt to get the other groups to agree that their definition is the only legitimate one, and any challenge to their concept becomes an attack on 'academic freedom' in general. As all other groups agree that student activity is a threat to their particular control, they argue in tacit alliance that students violate general freedom. This blanket condemnation (by everyone from Mr Short, Mrs Thatcher, the vice-chancellors and professors, to leader writers) means that we should not be surprised that the 'public' has largely accepted this view.

Two years ago it was sufficient to denounce the students verbally in this way. Since then the argument for student power has gained in strength and it has, in quick succession, become necessary for Mr Short and Mrs Thatcher to suggest marginal reform before threatening students with the withdrawal of grants. Administrators have tightened control over admissions, recognized the NUS and agreed to minor reforms in an attempt to capture the moderate students, before using writs, police discipline and the sacking of two sympathetic staff at the LSE. All these stages in control and repression – and there have been many others – have clearly been taken in step with the growth in the student power movement. At first merely an inconvenience, it has become a serious challenge to those who occupy and intend to retain positions of real control. Simply, the time has been reached when the student movement can no longer be tolerated. It has to be attacked. In the process we can see more clearly who means what by the use of the term 'academic freedom'.

Part Two
**Two Attempts at a Theory of Ideology**

# Ideology and the Human Sciences:
## Some Comments on the Role of Reification in Psychology and Psychiatry[1]
David Ingleby

### Current consciousness and the possibility of an ideological critique[2]

The contention of this paper can be expressed very briefly: that the ideological ends which psychologists (and other human scientists) unconsciously accept lead them to present a model of man which dehumanizes him in the same ways that their own society does; obscures rather than clarifies the way in which that society's goals are mediated by the individual; and attempts to reify its values under the disguise of a spurious objectivity.

My first task is to understand the situation in which the majority of human scientists who read these by now familiar charges will find it hard to recognize any connection between them and their own experience of science – if indeed they perceive any meaning in the words at all; for (they will say) what are 'ideological ends'? How can objective science be politically partisan? What does 'de-humanizing' mean? What concept of 'human' does it assume, and how can we posit *a priori* any such concept? It must be admitted that the pivotal concepts in the above statements are quite inadequate to carry the burden of communication being imposed on them; and this is because we are groping in an area about which we are only just beginning to learn to speak. Until these concepts are more adequately clothed with meaning, therefore, an ideological critique will be doomed to incoherence.

Fortunately, there are moments when it becomes possible to say things which could not be said before.

Some of the influences which are now beginning to make a coherent critique possible are obvious. On the one hand, student consciousness of the underlying issues (which is largely experiential and inarticulate) has learned to express itself in ways which force even the most complacent

1. This article is an abridged and revised version of one which originally appeared in the *Human Context*, vol. 2, no. 2, July 1970, in English and in French.
2. The terms 'ideological' and 'political' critique are used throughout this paper, although 'cultural analysis' is perhaps a more familiar label for the activity referred to. None of these adjectives are satisfactory, but 'cultural' is least so, for the same reason that 'cultural revolution' is a somewhat bizarre rendering of the original Maoist concept.

to wonder what possible grounds for complaint there can be, and has encouraged the less confident to explore their suspicions further; at the same time, there have appeared a handful of works from which the language and the paradigm of new critiques can be extracted. Of the works I happen to have come across, apart from certain of Marcuse's writings, I would mention such attempts as the essays by Blackburn (1969), and Anderson (1969), and particularly the recently translated monograph of Lucien Goldmann (1969) – whose calm lucidity has given me as a psychologist the same gloomy satisfaction that asylum inmates derive from a reading of Goffman. But the influence of these obvious events itself needs explaining in terms of deeper factors: without attempting the no doubt primary historico-economic interpretation, I suggest that for the present purpose, the most important event to take note of is the profound shift in the nature of our conception of how social values are mediated by the individual, which has at last begun to do justice to the opacity of social institutions and the obliqueness of human action.

A good way to start understanding the nature of this shift is by examining the enlarged connotation of the word 'political'. The best illustration of its former usage, and perhaps the quaintest to us nowadays, is Harold Wilson's famous ascription of the 1966 Seamen's strike to 'a tightly-knit group of politically motivated men' (in Foot, 1968). 'Politics', here, is the conscious and organized action of an identifiable group of people, and it is concerned with a fairly circumscribed set of issues (those over which a government overtly governs). The contemporary usage of 'politics' not only calls that definition into question on every point: it even implies that the definition itself is 'political'. One reason for this expanded referent is that a greater awareness of the degrees of freedom in human action facilitates our perception of the value-choices it implies: we have also learned to identify the sorts of ideological schemata which might provide the key to the patterns relating a multitude of value-choices.

But as well as an extended content, the new concept of politics also embraces different *styles* of action: here, perhaps, we are applying to the behaviour of societies lessons acquired from our knowledge of individuals. We do not expect that political goals will operate with the conscious connivance of their individual mediators, any more than we expect a person to be aware of his own life-style or the games he plays. Moreover, we are used not only to unconscious motivation, but also to highly resistant forms of repression and mystification; people not only fail to recognize and acknowledge what they are up to, but often contrive quite strenuously to give the impression (to themselves as well as others) that they are doing the exact opposite. Freud spoke of 'reaction-formation' in the generosity that conceals meanness, or the type of philanthropy which disguises contempt for those it aids: the Orwellian devices of newspeak and doublethink are the most obvious social counterparts. It is no accident that Freud and Marx should both have encountered these defence mechanisms, since they are probably dictated by the logistics of the situation in which one conscious agent acts upon the interests of another. In other words, it may be quite convenient for the right hand that the left hand should not know what it is doing, if the two hands are in conflict about ultimate aims: for Freud the two agents are Unconscious and Ego, for Marx the ruling class and the proletariat. After all, the first rule of public relations is that if you want to get away with something that somebody else might not approve of, you shouldn't tell them what you are up to. Industrial firms find a 'free offer' the most effective form of robbery: likewise, the most successful religions label self-denial as fulfilment, subservience as freedom, death as life. If we want to understand why it is that the individual in society is taught to repress or deny his pursuit of certain political goals, we have only to reflect on the fact that as in war, many of them may be in simple conflict with his own interests – or with rationality itself.

One could characterize this change in our concept of political action as being a shift away from the obvious; and it follows that any critique of science as political action will have to forgo the pleasures of pointing out the obvious. A 'conspiracy theory' of science will be no more viable than a conspiracy theory of history (though rather more so than a non-conspiracy theory): to search for boardroom plots in the corridors of scientific power would be to credit the denizens of those corridors with an insight into their own activities which they all too plainly do not possess. The *Private Eye* approach to journalism has its uses, but we are not primarily interested in outrages – in scientists who tell lies, in rigged experiments, or in mental hospitals which institutionalize the sort of violence against patients about which you can set up a government inquiry. Generally, such behaviour turns out to be an act of deviance, a violation of accepted norms: more important, and more difficult, is the task of showing how these norms themselves serve or reflect political aims.

This addiction to what is morally and factually obvious weakens much contemporary polemic which would like to regard itself as political. To the extent that it is conducted within the framework of accepted criteria, such criticism abdicates the possibility of attacking those criteria. Perry Anderson (1969), for example, attacks Eysenck's psychology by showing, essentially, that Eysenck is a bad psychologist; the targets of Jules Henry

(1966) appear much of the time to be bad parents, bad schools and bad geriatric institutions, while Cooper (1967, p. 24) actually adduces *in support* of his critique of psychiatry the fact that many psychiatrists are bad doctors. Indicative as these phenomena may be, they tend to divert attention from what must surely be the author's real targets – 'good' psychologists, parents, schools, and 'good' geriatrics or psychiatry. The cry of 'put your house in order' must be resisted if it is going to be taken to mean that the house itself is structurally sound. Actually, the tactics of these authors are perfectly appropriate: dialogue proceeds from a recognition of common ground, and the exposure of internal contradictions may at least sow the seeds of doubt in one's opponent. Ultimately, however, dialogue and truth become irreconcilable goals, for to adopt moral outrage as the target of criticism only strengthens the moral norms being appealed to: one must not imagine for a moment that the *News of the World*, in attacking corrupt clergymen, teachers, councillors and policemen is challenging established authority, or that the *Sunday Times*, in exposing shady businessmen and savage colonialists is mounting an onslaught on capitalism.

A similar trap for the unwary user lies in the concept of violence, as applied to the imposition of one group's interests on another. The lay connotation of this term specifically denies mystification: violence is not only done, but seen to be done, if by no one else then at least by the agent and recipient. In modern practice, this is increasingly not so – perhaps simply for the logistic reasons outlined earlier: to describe the exercise of political power in colonialism, industrialism, family life, education or psychiatry as 'violent' will therefore be misleading to the precise extent that its workings are successfuly mystified in those areas. In the psychiatric methods of control to be described later, for example, the psychiatrist (and, slightly less often, the patient) may sincerely believe the familiar phrases 'it's all for your own good' ,'we're only trying to help you', and so on.

There is another reason, apart from the existence of mystification, why the term 'violence' may be unhelpful when describing methods of limiting freedom. This is that the means of control may be cognitive rather than physical. Just as Goffman ascribes social power to those who control 'the definition of the situation' (1959), so we have learned to think in terms of political power being vested in the 'managers of reality'. The term 'brain-washing' suffers from the same limitations as a name for this process as 'violence' did above: we have, in fact, no vocabulary to describe the ways in which by controlling information input, an individual's concept of himself and reality may be moulded in practically any direction – by non-verbal as much as verbal means, and by medium as much as message.

Thus, although this section has attempted to display some ways in which our unfolding consciousness of social action facilitates an ideological critique of science, it also reveals some pitfalls. The necessary condition of such a critique is the simultaneous ability to analyse and comment on a society's activities while eschewing many of its own concepts and norms: only to a limited degree will occupants of that society attain this condition, and then only in exceptional circumstances.

## How can ideology penetrate the 'objective' activity of science?

Just as the traditional concept of 'politics' must be rejected before political realities can come into view with sharp focus, so a new understanding of the nature of science is required before its own politics can be discovered. The key question could be put thus: what is bias? Once again there is a range of 'direct' and 'indirect' forms of bias, 'strong' or 'weak', of which the so-called weakest turn out to be the most potent, because most effectively concealed. (Much of what follows is relevant to the understanding of ideological bias in other 'truth-media' – art, journalism, etc.)

The strongest sense of the word is that in which most allegations of 'political bias' are made: this involves neglecting or even falsifying the results of empirical observation. Stock examples of this are Lysenko's biological forgeries, or the reaction of scientists at the time to Galileo's observations, in both of which the ideological significance is self-evident: in the human sciences, numerous examples can no doubt be found of a reluctance to reach conclusions which might challenge a particular ideology's model of man. However, there are two reasons why this level of criticism will not get us very far. Firstly, of all areas, the human sciences seem to attract a fair sprinkling of ideological non-conformists and malcontents, so that in many topics the bias is away from, rather than towards, the politically 'safe' (most investigators of the social environment, for instance, are quite keen to believe in its effects); and secondly, criticism in terms of undue bias is made from within the particular framework of scientific principles accepted at a particular time or place, and reinforces rather than undermines those principles themselves. We need instead to become aware of the extent to which the prevailing ideology dominates even the apparently 'nonconformist' researcher, and (which turns out to be the same thing) the sense in which 'good' scientific practice, rather than 'bad', is prey to ideological influences.

We might refine the concept of 'bias' a little further by treating it as a process of selection rather than distortion, 'ideological bias' being the selection of 'safe' topics for research (i.e. those which are unlikely to yield politically disturbing results). This concept seems much more fruitful, and the prevalence of ideologically acceptable conclusions about man, to be discussed below, can be largely accounted for in terms of the research which has *not* been done, rather than that which has. However, as the history of the subject shows, this tendency too is corrected by normal scientific pressures: what we are left having to explain is how the most controversial research work, scrupulously rigorous and totally fearless in its choice of issues, can still appear to be imprisoned inside a cage of ideologically determined pre-conceptions. As Goldmann puts it:

In the human sciences . . . it does not suffice, as Durkheim believed, to apply the Cartesian method, to call into question acquired truths and to open one's mind entirely to the facts, because the researcher generally approaches the facts with categories and implicit and unconscious preconceptions which close off to him in advance the way to an objective understanding (1969, p. 41).

Clearly then, we must talk about methodology, about the techniques and concepts of the science rather than any instance of their application: and much of what is relevant about methodology is summarized in Kuhn's (1962) concept of scientific 'paradigms'. The 'paradigm' of a science is the tradition which defines what sort of work shall be regarded as scientific or unscientific: as Kuhn points out, this is not always so much a matter of rigour and honesty as of the language used, the sources of evidence adduced, the criteria of debate accepted, and so on.

We must also consider, however, a dimension which is ignored in Kuhn's analysis – itself representative of a contemporary 'paradigm' of history and philosophy of science; namely, a recognition of the socio-political context of scientists and their enterprises. A new paradigm of paradigms, in other words, is demanded for understanding the human sciences: and the resulting study turns out to be a branch of nothing less than the fundamental relationship between consciousness and its socio-historical context. We need to understand the social psychology of the process whereby the institutions in which science is conducted, by embodying a certain culture, mortify any attempts to question that culture: undoubtedly the key to this lies in the ritualization of research, teaching and communication, by which each experiment, investigation, lecture, tutorial and conference becomes a tacit celebration of the ethic of normality.

## Psychology as a vehicle of ideology

From the opening discussion of power in terms of 'management of reality' rather than (or as well as) coercion, it follows that we should look for the ideological significance of human sciences in terms of the model of man they put forward rather than in their direct application to the furtherance of such goals. Thus we are not primarily concerned with the way psychology is used in the service of 'the military-industrial complex' – an issue which bulks large in sociology – because opposition to these activities is a straightforward matter of opposing the ends that are being sought, and does not necessarily reflect on the validity of the scientific means being used. It is through its potency as myth that the psychological model of man can be seen as serving ideological interests: to the extent that the human sciences are taking over from religion the function of providing man with a self-image, they should be seen in the same light as religious myths.

The search for a central motif in psychology, in which its ideological significance may be found, is hindered first of all by the totally mystifying front under which psychologists work, which disguises by straightforwardly contradicting the true nature of their work. In the first place, we are led to suppose that the psychologist is the guardian of everything which must be understood in terms of the acting human subject: from this material he endeavours to build up a concept of what it is to be, specifically, a human being. In practice the psychologist appears to be more anxious to sell out to some other variety of science, and to reduce human realities to some other, non-human, reality. Secondly, we are led to think of the psychologist as an idealistic, even subversive kind of scientist, engaged in analysing our way of life with a view to suggesting the key to a better one: yet if one examines this idealism it turns out to be largely a matter of pursuing our existing way of life slightly more efficiently. Psychologists claim to be social engineers, but turn out to be really maintenance men: in this, perhaps, they are only sharing in the fond aspirations of all skilled mechanics.

Thus, we might sum up the whole of our theme by saying that psychology manages to *lose sight of man*, with the effect (politically) that having been lost sight of, he cannot assert the demands of his nature against the social system that encloses him. This conjuring trick is achieved by the process of *reification*, that is, the reduction of human realities to the order of things: in the rest of this paper we will attempt to observe the process at close quarters. First, however, it is clear that more needs to be said about the opposition implied between the human and the material, and it is equally clear that none of this will be found in the Anglo-American tradition of psychology, which mentions the opposition only to stigmatize it as meaningless, dualistic, pre-scientific, etc. This tradition, in fact, maintains a rigid fragmentation from such philosophical issues, being a classic instance of Goldmann's 'illiterate scholarship': we learn there that philosophy is 'sterile', 'speculative' (note the wickedness of speculators) and a lazy substitute for empirical work – not, as happens to be the case, a difficult and exacting prerequisite. Consequently it is to continental psychology and philosophy, which have never allowed themselves to be split in this way, that we must turn for any useful discussion of what it is that is lost sight of when psychology 'loses sight of man'.

One concept from the continental tradition (specifically, from Sartre – see Laing and Cooper, 1964) will be taken as the key to the present discussion: namely, the concept of *praxis*. While *process* describes the behaviour of inanimate objects, accounted for wholly by causes, praxis is the medium of the specifically human: it implies behaviour which is purposive and accountable for only in terms of its meaningfulness (whatever may be said about its 'causes'). Moreover, human behaviour is based on human experience, through which it is related to an external context: and such experience, as the phenomenologists have emphasized, is itself praxis rather than process, being an active selection and structuring of sensory information. Praxis is thus a composite notion, referring to the activities of perception as well as behaviour, and bringing together the ideas of purposive (goal-directed) activity as well as communication.

What constitutes a person is here defined as a collection of meaningful actions (or 'projects') and experiences: to depersonalize or dehumanize, therefore, is to reduce this praxis to process, in other words to reify it. To the extent that the logic of communication resembles that of purpose, we can generalize about the components of praxis and from this generalization anticipate the strategies of reification.

A piece of praxis is defined in terms of its intended end, the end being a project achieved or a message communicated: the means to this end (movements or symbols) are always determined by the context (a situation and/or a code), and cannot be seen as meaningful without reference to this context. As Sommerhof (1951) showed, it is possible to distinguish between goals of behaviour and mere consequences, without suggesting that causality works backwards: the effect of behaviour can be said to be its goal only to the extent that, had the context demanded different behaviour to achieve the same effect, the behaviour would have changed appropriately. Ascriptions of purpose thus become 'counterfactual conditional' statements: they state what would have happened, had a situation been different from what it was. (An analogous criterion may be defined to distinguish symbols from signs.)

From this analysis the nature of reification follows clearly. If the components of praxis are regarded atomistically, ignoring their relation to a context, then the project or message they constitute will be lost sight of. The example of a wink illustrates several aspects of praxis: the particular muscular contraction constituting this gesture is determined by a context which involves both the presence of another person and the existence of a code. If we can see only the muscles involved, their contraction will never be intelligible. Reification, i.e. the misrepresentation of praxis as process, will thus be the inevitable consequence of the failure to study contexts; even when justice is done to the context, the intelligibility of praxis may still escape the observer who fails to look for the right meanings in the right places. The aim of this essay is to show how many different fallacies in psychology and psychiatry can be subsumed under the concept of 'reification' as outlined above: the same process is involved in 'the methodological denial of any historical dimension to social facts' which Goldmann attacked in his contemporaries. The denial is methodological, because it occurs in the concepts and observational methods used, rather than in their application: and Goldmann's 'historical dimension' is not just a time factor, but that larger perspective in which alone the patterns to which social facts belong can be perceived. The recognition of these patterns necessarily involves awareness of praxis: thus Lenin writes of Marx's work, 'Where the bourgeois economists saw a relation between things (the exchange of one commodity for another), Marx revealed *a relation between people*' (quoted in Blackburn, 1969).

At the same time as examining *how* the reduction of praxis to process occurs, I am also trying to explore the question of *why* it occurs; in other words, what is the psychological or historical *meaning* of reification? It is possible, in fact, to argue that reification was an inescapable result of the 'influences' lying behind the human sciences – indeed, the argument that a science of persons built out of a science of things will inevitably tend to reduce persons to things is an attractive one: but we shall attempt to show that this argument fails in the same way as most appeals to 'influences', i.e. that it does not explain why some ideas of natural science were accepted and others fairly strenuously rejected; and it does not even begin to ask in what frame of mind thing-sciences were applied to man in the first place. Thus we are left with the question: what sense does it make to deny sense in human behaviour and experience? Three initial possibilities suggest themselves.

Firstly, a reifying model of human nature, by definition, presents men as less than they really are (or could be): to the extent that a society requires men (or a certain proportion of them) to be thing-like in their work, orientation, thinking and experiencing, such a model will constitute both a reflection and a reinforcement of that society (reinforcing because men tend to become what they are told they *are*). If labour is mechanical, it is convenient that those who have to do it, should think of themselves as a species of machine: if freedom of choice, imagination, the pursuit of untried goals and experiences, are seen as threats to a sacrosanct 'social structure', then man should learn he is a species of simple computer, a 'limited capacity information channel', incapable by definition of creating such goals and meanings.

This model of alienated man, in which science reifies aspects of humanity which have already become reified by society, has a certain ironical truth-value: but the political process is aided as much by the omissions of this model as by its inclusions. Inasmuch as alienation is achieved by praxis, the methodological denial of praxis in the scientific model will guarantee our continued blindness to the intricate and subtly mystified means by which in education, mass-media and the family, as well as in psychology and psychiatry, the elimination of human possibilities is carried out.

For there are also elements of reality essential to the existence of a class which it is not in the interests of that class to have subjected to public, or even scientific, scrutiny. Anyone seeking to study such elements will encounter powerful internal and external resistances (Goldmann, 1969, p. 43).

So far, we have identified two of what might be termed the mythic functions of the positivistic view of man – regarding it as a picture whose subtle emphases and omissions each serve to reinforce the sponsoring political system. There is a third, and perhaps more obvious, way in which such a science can prop up the system, and that is by introducing value judgements under the guise of objective descriptions ('persuasive definitions'). Once we have taken the step of applying one of these labels (e.g. sickness–health) to a human phenomenon, we will have – implicitly and unsuspectingly – adopted an attitude to the phenomenon which cannot then be abandoned without self-contradiction. In such concepts there is always an attempt to replace the logic of 'good' and 'bad' by the logic of 'correct' and 'incorrect'; this confounding of imperative and indicative, however subtly achieved, is always fallacious and, one might add, always ideologically determined.

The occurrence of 'persuasive definitions' in psychology and psychiatry is so common as to call for more detailed analysis; philosophy, however, to which we might turn for this analysis, has long been aware of the fallacy (Hume, Poincaré, Moore), but seldom of the ideological motive. Moore, for example, in his monumental attack on ethical naturalism (1903), accepted all along the now conventional definition of analytical philosophy: recognizing, quite correctly, that the motivation of a statement has no logical bearing on its truth or falsity, this philosophy proceeds to fragment questions of validity so disastrously from questions of motive that the refutation of ethical naturalism becomes no more than a logical pastime (the Sunday afternoon brain-twister: what is wrong with this statement?). Thus, when Moore (somewhat unprofessionally) paused to ask himself how any intelligent being could possibly accept the crudest interpretation of Mill's belief – that moral principles can be deduced from human preferences – he confessed himself at a total loss: but once the ideological uses of utilitarianism are perceived (as, for instance, in the contemporary politics of 'pragmatism'), the reasons for its acceptance become obvious. (The belief that accepted goals define what is right, is after all, the simplest form of conservatism.) To show up the sterility of the purely analytic approach to naturalism we need only turn to Sartre's treatment of the same phenomenon under the name of 'bad faith': through novels as well as theoretical works, Sartre shows in detail how the premiss 'I must act according to my (socially defined) nature' is the very foundation of the bourgeois ethic, which since it serves interests other than its own is obliged to be, in Sartre's own words (1967), 'sham from beginning to end'.

As in sociology, naturalism in psychology resides in hypostasized concepts of the ideal, natural, healthy state of man, from which deviations are, as we have already noted, not merely wrong but 'incorrect'. These concepts involve something slightly more than merely reducing praxis to process, which I would call 'normative reification': they assimilate human choices and actions to a special realm of material processes where the concepts of correctness–incorrectness, maturation–retardation, naturalness–unnaturalness apply. The place where these concepts are most at home, of course, is in biology: hence 'normative reification' in psychology can usually be spotted wherever biological or medical concepts are applied to behaviour. Obvious usages are sickness–health, adaptation, efficient 'functioning', integration, adjustment–maladjustment, maturity, development, etc., all of which imply an ideal state from which deviations are 'incorrect': even the term 'socialization', which might be thought a fairly neutral description of what must happen for a human being to become really human, always begs the question of which society the child should socialize into. The concepts of 'illness' and 'symptom' are even more heavily loaded (see below): they not only imply that behaviour is 'incorrect', but also provide a highly theoretical interpretation of its causes and properties. This interpretation is deeply concealed: it takes a long time to see, for example, that the report of 'an epidemic of drug-taking' is a moral pronouncement, not a statistical one.

We should recognize that the infiltration of value judgements into 'objective' terminology is not just loose talk, a psychological weakness of scientists; to classify actions which are seen as a threat to society as malignant process is a means of repression more final and devastating in its effects than any overt condemnation. Consider the power of the two norms which such a classification invokes. Firstly, action characterized as 'process' immediately forfeits the degree of respect and indemnity enjoyed by actions credited to human personalities – even 'bad 'ones; it becomes subject to the absolute right of control we exercise over the world of things (a value judgement which is universally embodied in the natural sciences – so universally, in fact, that as Goldmann points out, we sometimes imagine that since all natural sciences occupy the same point on the value dimension, the dimension of value is not present in them at all). Secondly, the classification as process having invoked an absolute right of control over deviating praxis, the classification as 'malignant' process establishes that control must take the form of correction; thus, from the effects of being classified as 'sick', 'immature', 'degenerate', etc., there can be no appeal.

### Ideology and the history of behaviour theory

I must now consider how one might support the claim that the science of behaviour has been biased towards the presentation of ideologically acceptable models of man, specifically via the reduction of human qualities to the order of things. It is not as inappropriate as it seems that much of the time I shall be dealing with theories originally put forward to account for animal behaviour: for firstly, the implicit justification for this research has always been that it will somehow serve as a basis for understanding man, and secondly, the fact that behavioural science has attempted to lose sight even of the limited degree of mind that animals possess, reveals the underlying motivation even more sharply. Nor is it entirely misleading that I speak of the many conflicting schools of thought on behaviour as one theory: it makes little difference that many of the defects I shall describe have been pointed out by people calling themselves behaviour theorists, because however much the dominant model of stimulus–response psychology has been bent or adapted to accommodate these criticisms, their full implications have never been acted on – nor could they be, in fact, since they are so central to the whole approach – and the mainstream has gone on flowing in the same direction.

Our guide is the notion that wherever the distinctive properties of mind have called for recognition in the study of behaviour, behaviourists have been biased (in all of the senses of 'bias' defined earlier) against acknowledging them. They have attempted to produce a theory in which the areas where praxis operates – perception, understanding, reasoning, thinking, purpose and communication of meaning – have either been left out altogether, or treated in such a way that praxis is denied; we shall argue later that much of this antagonism to mind could be explained as the result of a philosophical misunderstanding, i.e. that the nature of these mental concepts was misunderstood at the time when the behaviourist project was launched, but it will also be seen that this explanation by itself cannot account for the zeal with which mind has been eliminated from theoretical psychology. Hence, it will emerge that nearly all the crucial weaknesses of behaviour theory arise in cases where mentalistic concepts have demanded to be instantiated but have been rejected. Most of the credit for exposing these weaknesses goes to two schools of thought: the continental tradition of phenomenology (e.g. Merleau-Ponty, 1962, 1965, or Gurwitsch, 1966), and American psychologists drawing from cybernetics and linguistics (e.g. Miller, Galanter and Pribram 1960, or Chomsky 1957, 1959, 1968).

The first and most obvious instances of reification in behaviour theory are the two fundamental concepts of 'stimulus' and 'response'. Moreover, the falsifying nature of this reification emerges in the discovery that no stable predictions can be made about behaviour as long as stimulus and response are defined in terms denying praxis. To start with the concept of a stimulus: initially, following Pavlov, behaviourists sought to define stimuli entirely in terms of particular receptor excitations, and thereby to abolish the perceptual process altogether. This could not work, however, as the response of an animal appeared to be more invariant in terms of the object presented than in terms of the physiological impression it left (the phenomenon of Constancy); behaviourism thus found itself at a choice point, obliged either to adopt externalized definitions of the stimulus (tables, chairs, etc.), as Skinner has tended to do (1938), or to work on a theory of how the many-to-one mapping of impressions on to perceptions is accomplished (see, e.g. Hebb, 1949). In fact, open commitment to either point of view is rare: more commonly we find stimuli spoken of in behaviour theory as if they were atomistic physiological events (so that perceptual mechanisms can be ignored), but actually defined in terms of external realities. Methodologically, this blurring is encouraged by the behaviourist's preference for stimuli (lights or sounds) which make a fairly constant physiological impression, and can thus be described equally accurately as external objects or physiological events.

But even if the animal's response to an external object is more invariant than its response to a physiological event, there is still some variability which it seems more satisfactory to accommodate by changing our notion of what a stimulus is than by saying that the mapping of stimuli onto responses has altered (i.e. that learning has occurred). Firstly, there is the simple problem of whether the impinging excitation is registered by the animal: Broadbent (1958) clearly showed that in humans at least, a concept of 'attention' is required, which involves speaking about incoming information passing or not passing through a perceptual mechanism: so as well as the praxis involved in achieving constancy, there is praxis in what the organism chooses to pay attention to. (Even Pavlov's dogs would not salivate to order if they were distracted by irrelevant events.) Secondly, there is another sort of attention, concerning the particular dimensions along which the subject classifies the object displayed, or the particular interpretations he puts on it; in discrimination learning experiments it has been shown (Sutherland, 1964; Broadbent, 1961) that we must talk about the way an animal learns to analyse the input, as well as what he learns to do about it. Thus, the 'stimulus' of a square object may be totally ineffectual to a rat trained to make choices according to the colour of things: so either stimuli are something other than square objects, or else learning does not consist in a connection between stimuli and responses.

The problem of defining the stimulus becomes even more acute when we consider language behaviour, but even from these animal studies it is clear that a behaviour theory which ignores the praxis involved in perception, and tries to substitute a fixed mapping of connections from receptors to whatever actuates a response, cannot be regarded as scientifically respectable. It seems, in fact, that a return to concepts such as experience, awareness or consciousness is dictated if we are to find what it is that humans – or animals – base their actions on. At the same time, a great deal of philosophical clarification of these concepts is required in order that we should not fall again into old Cartesian pseudo-questions about the unverifiability and non-material 'substance' of experience: no analysis as indifferent to psychological fact as Ryle's (1949) will do, though nothing less rigorous will do either.

When we return to the question of 'what is a response?' or 'what is learned?' – still ignoring the issue of *how* learning occurs – the same diagnosis is inescapable. The phenomena of 'place learning', and the flexibility of behavioural strategies (Watson, 1961), do not exist only in a few contrived experiments (still less are they peculiar to language behaviour), but are central to the nature of responses: as Hinde points out (1966), what remains invariant in a learned response is usually an achievement, rather than a particular set of movements. As we noted with stimuli, behaviourist methodology helps to sweep this problem under the carpet, by singling out for observation responses like the pressing or pecking of levers, which can be defined more or less equally well in terms of movements or achievements. If 'response' itself is a teleological concept, we are clearly taking for granted a conscious, goal-directed system in the production of responses: and how can we isolate this system from the very mechanism which behaviour theory sets out to discover? It will not do to assume a repertoire of 'tropisms' or 'subroutines', programmed to organize an appropriate set of movements given a certain intention: for how are we to draw the line between this faculty and the learning mechanism itself? If it is given in the definition of the response acquired that an animal that can walk from A to B can also run from A to B, on what grounds do we decide that (say) building a helicopter and flying from A to B is a 'new response', representing learning which must be explained? It is obvious that criteria can be set up, but before we bother to do so it is worth asking whether there is any practicable concept of 'response' on which a connectionist theory could legitimately be based: only by pretending that the observed praxis could be reduced to muscular process have behaviourists managed to sustain the project for so long.

Thus, moving on to consider the question of how learning takes place, we see that so far from being the *only* question of psychology – as s–r theory implies – it is already overshadowed by complex questions concerning the way in which incoming information is processed and responses are organized, and ought perhaps never to have been separated from these issues. But even if we put on one side the problem of defining stimulus and response, and discuss the circumstances under which s–r connections are formed, we find in behaviour theory the same stultifying resistance to acknowledging and analysing the distinctively 'mindful' features of human and animal learning. In large areas of behaviour, we may concede that the acquisition of 'sensible', adaptive responses can be accounted for by the psychological equivalent of natural selection – trial-and-error followed by reinforcement; and, in fact, many criticisms of the 'law of effect' (e.g. much of Watson's (1961), penetrating analysis) would be removed if appropriate adjustments could be made to the concepts of stimulus and response, and to the definition of reinforcers. In contrast to the evolution of species, however, the development of behaviour frequently shows forward leaps which cannot be accounted for as the preservation of successful mutations. This, of course, is the problem of reasoning and insight, and at this choice-point, behaviourists who attempted to cling to the law of effect as the sole explanatory principle left themselves with only two equally futile options: either deny the phenomena altogether, as Skinnerians have done, or (starting with Hull) to construct an elaborate mythology of *internal* 'stimuli and responses', which, unless it adopts totally *ad hoc* assumptions, never succeeds in predicting the behaviour it sets out to explain (Deutsch, 1956; Triesman, 1960).

Thus, we see that by adopting the superficial attributes of established sciences, behaviourists succeeded in constructing a theory which violated practically all the deeper canons of science, and in almost every case this can be traced to their insistence on reducing praxis to process, i.e. their reification of mental processes. It still remains to be considered, however, to what extent this failure was inevitable, and to what extent over-determined by the motive, fundamentally political in origin, to present man as a thing. We must not deny the many factors which made this conclusion an almost (but not quite) inevitable result of the climate of ideas in which behaviourism was conceived; and in this climate three strong pressures towards reification can be discerned. Firstly, as we have noted, the predominantly dualistic philosophy of mind had loaded all mental concepts with connotations that truly made mind an 'impossible object': with each of the crucial concepts of experience, reasoning, intention and purpose were associated dilemmas which, if not pseudo-problems in the first place, became such through the terms in which they were discussed (non-material substance, will, final causes, and so on). The fault in these concepts, however, lay in the fact that they suggested certain models and theories about the mind which simply did not work (if they had worked, psychology would not have been necessary): the psychologists were right to reject the implicit theories, but instead of throwing away along with these concepts of mind all the phenomena they embraced, they should have retained the phenomena and accepted as their unique task the provision of an appropriate descriptive and explanatory framework for them. (Even today, Skinnerians use the word 'mentalistic' as a term of abuse, showing their inability to progress beyond a nineteenth-century concept of mind.)

A second reason for avoiding accounts in terms of praxis stems from the strict criteria of inference which were brought into psychology from the physical sciences. Ockham's razor found a place early on in psychology, as 'Lloyd Morgan's Canon' – the principle that one should not attribute to organisms faculties more complex than were strictly needed to explain their behaviour. Since one could get away without praxis in describing fairly large areas of behaviour – particularly if one adhered to the orthodox styles of experimental observation – the pressure to ignore or falsify those areas where one could not was always strong. Moreover, ascriptions of purpose and meaning, although not unverifiable, are always difficult to be certain of: this is obvious when one considers that validating a counterfactual condition proposition (cf. above, p. 58) involves making a practically infinite array of hypothetical statements, most of which can only be known inductively. Similar concern is also beginning to be expressed about the validation of linguistic structures such as Chomsky's (1957), even by those who accept their necessity.

But the third, and most crucial, reason for the dismissal of mental phenomena was the sheer dearth of hard, intelligible concepts with which to theorize about them. Hull saw his attempts to explain insight in terms of 'the modern theory of conditioning' as 'the only alternative to an explanation in terms of a non-physical, psychic agent called mind or consciousness' (1935), and when we consider the vapidity of early cognitive and Gestalt theory (Miller, Galanter and Pribram, 1960), which Hull called 'a mere tautological gesture', this conclusion is understandable. Only now can we appreciate the enormity of the task psychology had undertaken: in the end it was the theoretical work that underlay the second industrial revolution – the creation of machines in the image of man – that made it possible to understand man himself, and we now see that to produce an authentic science of mind on its own, psychology would have had to anticipate the enormous theoretical achievements in the field of artificial intelligence, perception and language associated with Wiener, von Neumann and Chomsky.

Given these three factors, it seems almost gratuitous to see any particular motive in the exclusion of mental phenomena from behaviour theory: but certain facts of history call for further explanation. Why, for example, was the behaviourist project not abandoned sooner? How is it that its totally discredited and outdated conceptual framework not only survives, but flourishes as the basis of new 'revolutions' in education and psychiatry? We may of course say that Skinner's work, for example, can be accounted for on his own principles, as the untiring emission of responses which continue to be rewarded with a succession of honours and salary increments (as the graph of his *Cumulative Record* (1959) ironically implies): but why do the reinforcements still keep on arriving for Skinner and the rest of his persuasion? More to the point (for we know that Skinnerian principles can only be applied to Skinnerians in jest) how can we explain the rise of this mindless intelligentsia? Here it is hard to resist a political interpretation, for the Skinnerian model of man provides an almost comical parody of the ideology of 'organized capitalism': in the lever-pressing rat we may see a rodent parable of the profit motive and the incentive principle, or Jules Henry's 'virtuoso consumer' epitomized.

To rest one's interpretation on this one case, however, would be to fall into the trap mentioned earlier – for Skinner is, by present-day standards, a bad psychologist. The strategies of reification in contemporary psychology are harder to see. Miller (Galanter and Miller, 1960) has pointed out, however, how the fallacies of the connectionist model are incorporated in the new systems of mathematical learning theory and psychophysics: and through all contemporary experimental work runs the same pattern of losing sight of those aspects of behaviour that are distinctively human. Cybernetic models are used which credit the human mind with mechanisms of a crudity which would be an insult to the cheapest computers on the market: this might be defended on heuristic grounds – for while the computer engineer can give his imagination full rein, the psychologist working in the opposite direction can only choose between small numbers of simple alternative designs. However, it is significant that the methodology of experimental psychology seems almost designed to perpetuate these oversimplifications; in few laboratory experiments nowadays does the subject perform a task which could not be better done by an extension of the apparatus. (Indeed, the joke is frequently made that human subjects will soon disappear completely from the laboratory, having been made redundant by the arrival of the small computer.) By this method it is easy to confirm that man is adequately described as a 'limited capacity information-processing channel' – and the benefits to industrial society of such a conclusion are obvious: but the costs to science and humanity may not be so easily reckoned.

## The politics of psychiatry

In the theory and practice of psychiatry we encounter forms of reification not only more highly-developed than any of the cases considered so far, but also more straightforwardly related to social values. Almost within the last ten years, a mere handful of thinkers (in conjunction of course with other changes in our consciousness) have so transformed our awareness of the social meaning of psychiatry as to seal off, virtually, the historical era they describe; after being spoken of in such terms, psychiatry ceases to be, politically speaking, an invisible agency.

All forms of psychiatry have this hallmark: that they transform the conceptual elimination of human praxis into a practical achievement. At the mythic level we are describing, the diverse procedures of psychiatry reduce to a single technique, which we shall call 'amputation by reification'. Thus, behaviour therapy, medical psychiatry and psychoanalysis all display the following schema: firstly, they take those portions of an individual's praxis which it is desired to eliminate, and present them as malignant process, i.e. as manifestations of aberrations in the physical and psychological mechanisms which form the inert basis of personality. This could be called denial of praxis, the result being that undesirable behaviour which is systematically ignored and kept 'out of mind' will become impossible for the agent to sustain; but by actively misrepresenting the behaviour as 'illness', it achieves more than outright denial ever could. The psychiatrist never says 'You do not hate': instead, he says 'Your aggression is a symptom'. This response offers the patient a kind of recognition of which he is probably in great need: by appearing to account for his behaviour and experience, it holds out for him a kind of identity. Thus eagerly accepted, this identity soon reveals itself as non-identity; the patient finds himself with a self-concept in which his deviance is portrayed as non-human, malignant process, so that unless he abandons his former self – literally, loses his mind – he will be assigned (in Goffman's word) to perpetual mortification. It is wrong to imagine that the doctor or psychiatric institution initiates this process, for psychiatry is properly seen as a straightforward extension of the reifying procedures already laid down deeply in our consciousness: indeed, the tendency to alienate unwanted praxis, to dissociate it from one's 'self' or cease to identify with it, is embedded in everyday language itself (witness the fact that we describe the praxis of ourselves and others as objects which are owned, e.g. a violent temper, a dirty mind or a loving nature). Moreover, the strategy of denial by reification is not only used by psychiatrists: to dismiss the other person's unwelcome praxis by ascribing it to a 'cause' is a familiar interpersonal ploy. The doctor, however, is a figure whose responses are already vested with a near-magical authority, and his perception of the patient's deviant praxis as 'illness' imposes almost inescapably a reifying self-concept on the latter; Foucault (1967) captures this process in a single phrase, when he speaks of the patient as 'alienated *in* the doctor'.

In medical psychiatry, treatment is conducted within the same ironical 'service relationship' (cf. garages and repair shops, Goffman, 1962) as physical medicine (see Robert Silman's essay, p. 264); it would be unfair to claim that the malignant process being put right is always represented as a physical one however, for (to do it justice) psychiatry recognizes the category of 'functional' illnesses as well as 'organic' ones. Just as bodies may fall ill, so minds can become diseased: minds, in this system, have a predetermined healthy form. The fact that culture as well as genotype is taken into account in defining the well-adjusted, efficiently functioning mind makes the definition no less magical than any of the other normative reifications we described above. It is in the psychiatrist's concept of a 'healthy mind' that we may recognize his ideology.

Thus, there is less difference than is usually assumed between medical psychiatry and psychoanalysis: this must be recognized as inevitable once we see that it is in the language and philosophy from which Freud started that this characteristic ethical confusion and mechanistic dualism is embedded. The peculiar ambivalence of psychoanalysis – for far from reifying everything it encounters, the Freudian touch also delivers large areas of praxis from mystification and repression – suggests that we should see it as a project perpetually trying to break loose from the language it is written in (e.g. drives which flow, are dammed up or diverted in quasi-hydraulic fashion). To concentrate on its reifying aspects would be to miss much of the ideological significance of psychoanalysis: for often its social values are expressed by the reduction of one form of praxis to another, as in the characterization of the rebel as 'father-fixated', or its indifference to the social context of family behaviour. However, this theme is outside the scope of this paper: what is central to our present theme is the use of psychoanalysis to alienate the patient from his deviant behaviour, and to impose a system of values and concepts in which political realities are obscured.

The third main branch of psychiatry, therapies based on learning theory, is easy to relate to our theme as most of its political content has already been analysed in the theoretical context. To apply the methodology of psychology to psychological problems, in place of that of physical medicine, would be an ideal worthy of the revolutionary fervour with which it is pursued, but for the fact that psychology has for political convenience already lost sight of man: all it therefore achieves is the replacement of a blunt instrument for correcting deviance by a sharper one. The technique of 'amputation by reification' is still central in behaviour therapy. Firstly, any meaning in the 'symptoms' is ignored, as before, by the methodological denial of their social or personal context: the patient is then encouraged to look upon them as products of a disordered mechanism, and invited to participate in an experiment which will set the mechanism to rights. Thus, with luck, the patient ends up with a piece of apparatus that works – which may be better than one which doesn't, but is still nevertheless to him a piece of apparatus, not a part of the person he lives. (This is the real reason why the conditioning or deconditioning of penile erections is obscene.) The ethical theory which behaviour therapy embodies is likewise equivalent to that of psychiatry – that is, there is no ethical theory, since human action is reduced to the level of process, where only the spurious norms of 'correctness' or 'normality' apply.

It is important to point out at this stage that, contrary to the belief of most attackers and defenders of psychiatry, a critique such as this does not need to depend on any assumptions about the true nature of 'psychiatric disorders', or to make any value judgements about their desirability. I do not imagine that all, or even most, such conditions are totally a matter of individual praxis, free from any physical causes, or that they are pleasant for those who live with them and for the rest of society. What is being claimed is firstly, that psychiatry forces a reifying interpretation on all behaviour, since its methodology dispenses with the concepts and the information (viz. the knowledge of personal and social goals and contexts) which would enable it to recognize praxis when it saw it; and secondly, that the implicit justification for the actions taken about such conditions is ethically quite spurious.

In addition, of course, I am claiming that both these phenomena are intelligible if we regard psychiatry as a mystified technique for regulating behaviour which challenges the existing social structure and ideology: such a judgement can of course only be reached from an understanding of the historical context of psychiatry and the value system to which it belongs. In this connection, Foucault's *Madness and Civilization* (1967) stands out as a unique analysis. By focusing only on the antecedents of the nineteenth-century medical approach, Foucault dismantles the myth whose moral force provides the main source of resistance to any critique of psychiatry, that of a 'humane revolution' occurring in the nineteenth century in which psychiatry 'comes to the rescue' of the insane.

Foucault postulates, via the art of the middle ages, a pre-classical consciousness of madness similar to that which anthropologists report in some 'primitive' societies: madness seen as a region on the continuum of existence, a comment on the rest of life from which certain lessons may be read. Gradually, however, European society develops an allergy to the 'immorality of the unreasonable', and strives to put it first out of sight, then out of mind. In this era, the vices of the insane are closely linked to those of the unemployed – 'wantonness, sloth, profanity and debauchery': so that in the great confinements of the seventeenth century, the two are imprisoned together.

Until the Renaissance, the sensibility to madness was linked to the presence of imaginary transcendences. In the classical age, for the first time, madness was perceived through a condemnation of idleness and in a social immanence guaranteed by the community of labour. This community acquired an ethical power of segregation, which permitted it to eject, as into another world, all forms of social uselessness (Foucault, 1967, p. 58).

In the classical age, then, madness is seen primarily as an affront to the three pillars of authority – the family, the Church and the established powers: its control is therefore a police matter, 'police', Foucault adds, 'in the precise sense that the classical epoch gave to it – that is, the totality of measures which make work possible and necessary for all those who could not live without it'. That men's minds should be policed in this way Foucault regards as one aspect of 'the great bourgeois, and soon republican, idea that virtue too, is an affair of state, that decrees can be published to make it flourish, that an authority can be established to make sure it is respected'. Thus, 'an astonishing synthesis of moral obligation and civil law is effected. The law of nations will no longer countenance the disorder of hearts.' Perhaps Foucault should have drawn more attention to the converse of this assimilation: especially today, the important thing is not that deviance in personal matters is regarded as an offence against the state (though this is still as true as ever), but that a challenge to the political system is 'defused' by being reduced to 'weakness of character'. Thus, in the conceptual universe we inhabit today – in which the bourgeois synthesis of virtue and loyalty has been fully perfected – the only stereotypes available for those who rebel against the family order, the work ethic, the class system, or any other social institutions are the deformed character-types of schizophrenic, mixed-up adolescent, drop-out, layabout, misfit, vandal, thug, delinquent, criminal, militant, anarchist, and so on – all of them (poor things) 'immature', 'unbalanced', 'disturbed', people, i.e. defective as *individuals*. Hence, the much-vaunted philanthropy of psychiatry, which treats all transgressions against society as products of 'sick minds', is on a par with psychological approaches to delinquency and crime: though it appears to be on the side of the deviant, it adopts this pose chiefly in order to eliminate the social significance of his actions.

The next stage in the exposition of Foucault's historical interpretation of psychiatry is the demonstration that if, and only if, we return the work of Pinel and Tuke to the context of their age's experience of madness, it becomes not the opening of a new humanitarian era but the logical working-out of the classical perspective. Having recognized that madness required different forms of correction from idleness, the age now 'saw' (in Tuke and Pinel) that the madman had to be treated as a kind of infant, since his folly proceeded from weakness of character. Thus, Tuke founded The Retreat on the model of the family: a family in which psychological coercion replaced physical restraint, whose children were constantly watched over, reprimanded and blackmailed into submission by the threat of withdrawing love.

There were social occasions in the English manner, where everyone was obliged to imitate all the formal requirements of social existence; nothing else circulated except the observation that would spy out any incongruity, any disorder, any awkwardness where madness might betray itself. The directors and staff of The Retreat thus regularly invited several patients to 'tea-parties'; the guests 'dress in their best clothes, and vie with each other in politeness and propriety. The best fare is provided, and the visitors are treated *with all the attention of strangers*. [My italics] The evening generally passes with the greatest harmony and enjoyment. It rarely happens that any unpleasant circumstance occurs; the patients control, to a wonderful degree, their different propensities; and the scene is at once curious and affectingly gratifying' (Foucault, 1967, p. 249).

Although the madman is thus given an identity and a part to play, we recognize in this part the archetype of psychiatry's concept of the patient – the identity of a non-person: 'The city of reason welcomes him only with this qualification, and at the price of this surrender to anonymity' (Foucault, 1967, p. 250).

Foucault evidently regards this account of the work of Tuke and Pinel as so paradigmatic for the next century-and-a-half of psychiatry that he is content to end his history there. 'What we call psychiatric practice,' he writes, 'is a certain moral tactic contemporary with the end of the eighteenth century, preserved in the rites of asylum life, and overlaid by the myths of positivism.'

The 'rites of asylum life' to which Foucault here refers have been nowhere more amply documented, for our own age, than by Goffman (1962). The process of 'mortification', i.e. reducing the inmate to the status of non-person, is seen by Goffman as a common property of many total institutions (concentration camps, prisons, nunneries, workhouses): it involves reflecting back to the individual a view in which he has no status or autonomy and in which his actions do not make sense – unless, that is, he accepts the forms of status and significance the institution has reserved for him. Scheff (1963) was essentially documenting the ways in which the same process occurs outside the psychiatric hospital – indeed, in the social consciousness of the individual himself: he points out that children acquire a remarkably complete concept of what it is to be mad, crazy, nuts, etc., in the first few years of life.

'The myths of positivism' also referred to are the subject of this paper. They involve, firstly, the methodologically reinforced conviction that whatever the patient does is a reflection of malignant process, and secondly, the normative component of this reification, the corollary that what is 'diseased' must be 'cured'. Szasz (1961) was among the first to point out the questions begged by descriptions in terms of 'symptoms': the moment a piece of behaviour or experience is described as a symptom it becomes by definition process and not praxis. This is because a symptom is fixed, and not permitted to vary according to the context in the way required of purposive or communicative behaviour: to the extent that it is correlated with an internal, antecedent 'illness', it cannot have 'directive correlation' (Sommerhof, 1951) with an external, subsequent 'end'. (The possibility has seldom been explored that it might be partly correlated with both.) Furthermore, as we have noted, psychiatry becomes methodologically blind to praxis by dispensing with the concepts and the information necessary to identify the meaning in its context (Laing, 1960). Laing and Esterson (1964) set out to show how 'psychotic' behaviour could be regarded as intelligible once these were restored: the paradigm of observational and descriptive techniques they set out is perhaps a more fundamental challenge to psychiatric orthodoxy than the particular interpretations they suggest, for though the interpretations may be overtaken, the data remain.

The other positivist myth, in which social ideals are metamorphosed into biological concepts of 'health', 'balance', etc., does rather more than 'overlay' the moral tactic Foucault speaks of: with its introduction, the moral or political dimension in psychiatry goes underground, and is not seen again for a hundred and fifty years. Thus, there is a qualitative difference between Tuke's interpretation of madness as individual perversity, and its reification into malignant process, symbolized in the fact that Tuke's goal was overtly religious – the restoration of virtue – whereas that of modern psychiatry is overtly medical – the restoration of health. Both goals are, on the present view, political ones, but the medical disguise is even more invulnerable than the religious one – for who can condone the perpetuation of illness?

One might expect that the discipline called 'social psychiatry' might concern itself with some of the phenomena Foucault speaks of: instead, by failing to stand back from its parent culture, it simply becomes another of these phenomena. This is because (to borrow again from Goldmann) it achieves not a *synthesis* of sociology and psychiatry, but merely a *sum* – a result of the fragmented, hierarchical view of the sciences according to which statements about individual behaviour are logically independent of, and therefore academically isolated from, statements about its social context.

In this section we attempted to describe the ways in which psychiatry itself, from the moment that 'illnesses' are defined, can be seen as a sociological phenomenon: any research which tries to discover the sociology of 'mental illness' by starting from data collected and described according to psychiatric methodology can never in all eternity discover the sort of realities Foucault and Laing describe. Likewise the modern psychiatrist's willingness to accept 'multiple causation' (Hays, 1964) is empty talk as long as it fails to comprehend that the sociological interpretation calls into question the very nature of what is being 'caused'. Most attempts at 'social psychiatry', in fact, take the psychiatric data for granted, and merely correlate them with environmental variables like social class, 'stress' or family processes defined in the most simplistic terms. Brown (Brown and Rutter, 1966) seems to consider the differing perceptions of family situations by differing members of the family at different times merely as a kind of 'noise', or experimental error introduced between him and 'what is really going on': committed, for 'scientific' reasons, to a methodology belonging to the study of inert, physico-chemical realities, he is unable to see that these modulations of perspective *are* what is really going on in the family. By this criterion of 'reliability', the patient's own perspective of his family is totally useless, hence not even worth collecting: after all, it is a psychiatric datum that he has 'lost contact with reality'.

We might turn to the social psychologist for an analysis of abnormal behaviour which could reveal any praxis within it: but turning to Argyle, we find that, since the psychiatric data are accepted at their face value, the only problem for the social psychologist is to find a cure.

In appearance schizophrenics look odd and untidy, and they do not wear their clothes well. Their mood is flat and apathetic, their speech rambling and incoherent, while some are mute. Their movements are jerky and uncoordinated, and include gestures and postures which may symbolise various private fantasies. ... They simply cannot communicate properly, or take part in *ordinary social encounters* (1967, p. 134) [My italics.]

Schizophrenics 'fail to communicate' in much the same sense, for Argyle, as unruly children 'fail to behave' – that is, they fail to communicate *the right things*. (Alternatively, this failure is like 'loss of contact with reality' – 'reality' always being as defined by the psychiatrist.) One also wonders what 'ordinary social encounters' Argyle imagines to be open to a diagnosed schizophrenic. Thus, Argyle will come to the aid of the schizophrenic and teach him to 'communicate' but his price is the same one Tuke demanded – the patient has to accept that, as a madman, he must remain 'the perfect stranger'.

The simple fault in all such work is the failure to recognize that psychiatric diagnoses embody value-judgements, and psychiatric classification is an act of social praxis: this failure ensures a complicity between the social psychiatrist and the agents of this praxis, so that the former never disentangles himself from his own ideological framework. The titles alone of much contemporary work (*The Burden on the Community,*

Hill, 1962, *Prevention of Disordered Behaviour,* Weinberg, 1968) betray this complicity.

If we are going to try and interpret the whole edifice of modern psychiatry, with al l these attendant myths and rituals, in political terms, it is quite clear that a very sophisticated concept of 'politics' is required. Specifically, phrases l ike 'the politics of psychiatry' wil l only become fully credible when we understand the subtle complicity that obtains between concepts of personal integrity and political stability. Such phrases do not refer to the certification of individuals for their 'political views'; Tarsis (1966) is right to say that this is not the way Western psychiatry works, but quite misses the point that the very issues of personal stability, adjustment, maturity, balance, integration, etc., which do concern Western psychiatry are themselves subtly metamorphosed political issues.

Scheff (1966) presents a subtle variation on this theme, in introducing the idea that once a person becomes labelled as 'mentally ill', he is typecast in a role which gradually becomes indisinguishable from his 'real' self. Scheff describes the type of transgression that invokes this categorization as 'residual deviance', i.e. violation of unwritten and personal norms by behaviour which is bafflingly odd, eccentric, peculiar or irrational. However, this terminology (borrowed from Lemert, 1951) may be obscuring rather than clarifying the social meaning of madness: it begs the question of whether 'residual deviance' really is made up of personal foibles, or whether it is social praxis artfully misrepresented by psychiatry as personal foibles, or social praxis on to which personal foibles have been grafted through the rebel's acceptance of a stereotyped role in which they are integral parts of the 'rebellious' character. (To the bourgeois mentality, the rebel is in every sense an 'impossible person'.) Scheff's analysis, which does not itself penetrate very far along the political dimension, is valuable because it makes available this last interpretation of deviance: it suggests that a person who sets out simply to challenge social or familial norms may himself fall into accepting a stereotype in which such rebellion is inextricably allied with personal degeneracy – thus unwittingly providing another confirmation of the stereotype. Thus, the rebellious student today is regarded as a bourgeois who has not grown up, not as a person with different ideals; for this reason public attention focuses on his violation of the sacred bourgeois canons of personal maturity – regular washing, neat appearance, civil deportment and methodical organization of work, entertainment, sex and sleep: and those who cannot resist the stereotype offered do indeed begin to act and think in terms of these issues alone. In this context, perhaps the most instructive example of residual deviance is bad spelling: the conventional response (cf. Ricks, 1969) is to interpret misspelling in student writing as proof that either the students have never read the words in print, or that they lack the mental capacity to remember how they are spelt – whereas for the most part this indifference reflects an attitude (originally spread by the underground press) that spelling too well is as suspicious as washing too often.

This example shows that in some types of residual deviance, a subtle dialectic may arise between praxis and process, making it exceedingly difficult to reach a true interpretation: thus, the 'sick mind' role which Scheff postulates may be a form of praxis which actually disguises itself, ironically, as process – rather as bad spelling does in our example. This possibility is important because it cannot be guaranteed in advance that all psychotic behaviour will turn out to be meaningful, if we only apply Laing's approach sufficiently thoroughly: and one may not wish to ascribe the residue of apparently impenetrable obscurity to 'scrambling' in the input-output mechanisms. The problem of formulating a criterion for 'meaningfulness' is a very vexed one; this becomes obvious in the context of art, for whether a person regards Joyce, Jackson Pollock or Cage as nonsense seems to reduce ultimately to the question of whether he accepts or rejects the realm of experience being offered – which is a kind of political choice. Thus, it may be impossible ever to prove or disprove objectively that madness does or does not 'make sense'. It is seldom appreciated how little the question of causation has to do with this issue: though we might understand Mozart's productivity by examining his frontal lobes, we would get no nearer to his music in this way; and the answer to whether *Finnegan's Wake* is meaningful or not certainly does not lie in James Joyce's urine.

But if any meaninglessness remains in madness, we must consider not just the hypothesis that it is due to faulty mechanisms, or that it is part of a role (Scheff), but the possibility that it is that phenomenon whose spectacle, Foucault claims, our civilization cannot tolerate: namely a realm of praxis that defies rationality and completely cuts off its agent from the human world of mutuality and communication. To Foucault, the madness of Nietzsche, Van Gogh and Artaud is the point at which their art finally breaks down, for 'where there is a work of art, there is no madness': there is a fundamental incompatibility between this remark and the view that tries to find *intelligible* praxis in all psychosis. Perhaps all that has been discovered in the last ten years is how inaccessible anything like the realities of 'mental illness' must remain from inside our present conceptual universe.

### The uses of an ideological critique

The whole of this paper has been an exercise in setting scientific thought in its social–historical–political context; it has attempted to return particular thoughts to the minds in which they occurred, for the purpose of showing how beliefs and values common to the civilization to which the scientist belongs have shaped (and necessarily distorted) his science. One may reasonably ask, however, what difference such a 'meta-scientific' analysis makes at the level of science itself.

In the English intellectual tradition, as we have already noted, the motivation or the context of thoughts is considered an irrelevant issue, since the intention behind a statement does not affect its truth or falsity: one cannot reject a proposition just because one disagrees with the speaker's values (the *ad hominem* argument). This principle is fundamental to academic life, indeed to rationality itself, since to accept propositions solely on the grounds of their congruence with one's own political beliefs is to eschew reality altogether. Therefore, this approach concludes, to take an interest in the mind in which a proposition occurred is to replace logic by psychology, and to founder in a mire of relativity: so the only true questions the psychologists should ask are, Is the law of effect true? How much of intelligence is innate? Are psychoses endogenously determined? and so on.

Although the premises in this argument are undoubtedly correct, the conclusion drawn from them is demonstrably false. These are not the only questions the psychologist should ask: there are also questions that should be asked *about* these questions, to seek out the assumptions and biases embodied in the underlying concepts and techniques: and this methodological study, as I have tried to show, must be informed by an understanding of the scientist's framework of beliefs and values, which at this level is synonymous with his ideology. In other words, a genuinely objective science of man must always become aware of its own ideology if it is to take any action against the biases that ideology imposes.

Nothing like objectivity will ever be reached without a recognition of one's own subjectivity. In saying this, however, I am not taking sides with those who claim that such a science must be, or can ever be, apolitical. What I am saying is that it must be apolitical in so far as it is ever possible to eradicate one's own biases: but in at least two senses, not usually recognized by those who cultivate the ideal of an academic world divorced from politics, it will remain quite inescapably a political activity.

In the first place, all societies require their members to live in a state of at least partial unconsciousness. As long as it is true that social systems are kept in existence by the suppression or mystification of some aspects of themselves – which, for the logistic reasons we have mentioned, means effectively for ever – the exposure of those aspects will be a political activity. Therefore, that brand of academic reactionaries who would cut back the social sciences because of their 'subversive effects' may not be so mistaken after all: there must come, at a very early stage in the human sciences, an abrupt confrontation between the interests of political stability and those of truth. Consequently, those who have avoided this confrontation can usually be assumed to have done so at the expense of the latter.

Secondly, there is a certain type of political relativity which the human scientist can never escape: even for the purpose of criticizing ideological assumptions, one is forced to adopt (as I have conspicuously done) certain working assumptions about the nature of man – and definitions of human nature are precisely what ideologies are made of. Hence, my own political commitment resides in the belief that human beings *might*, to an important extent, display the properties of minds – have experiences, intentions, thoughts, imagination, creativity, autonomy and so on: and someone with different politics might feel perfectly justified in abandoning this kind of talk altogether. What makes the issue uncontestable is the self-fulfilling nature of human self-concepts: just as the Freudian analysis creates a Freudian patient, so the mechanistic psychologist can not only live his own theories, but also devise a system in which others live them too. Therein lie the positive dangers of allowing him too much of a hand in society's construction.

## References

ANDERSON, P. (1969), 'Components of the national outlook', in A. Cockburn, and R. Blackburn (eds.), *Student Power*, Penguin.

ARGYLE, M. (1967), *The Psychology of Interpersonal Behaviour*, Penguin.

BLACKBURN, R. (1969), 'A brief guide to bourgeois ideology', in A. Cockburn and R. Blackburn (eds.), *Student Power*, Penguin.

BROADBENT, D. E. (1958), *Perception and Communication*, Pergamon.

BROADBENT, D. E. (1961), 'Human perception and animal learning', in W. H. Thorpe and O. L. Zangwill (eds.), *Current Problems in Animal Behaviour*, Cambridge University Press.

BROWN, G. W., and RUTTER, M. (1966), 'The measurement of family activities and relationships; a methodological study', *Human Relations*, vol. 19, p. 241.

CHOMSKY, N. (1957), *Syntactic Structures*, Mouton.

CHOMSKY, N. (1959), 'Review of Skinner's *Verbal Behaviour*', *Language*, vol. 35, pp. 26–58.

CHOMSKY, N. (1968), *Language and Mind*, Harcourt, Brace & World.

COOPER, D. (1967), *Psychiatry and Anti-Psychiatry*, Tavistock.

DEUTSCH, J. A. (1956), 'The inadequacy of the Hullian derivations of reasoning and latent learning', *Psychological Review*, vol. 63, pp. 389–99.

FOOT, P. (1968), *The Politics of Harold Wilson*, Penguin.

FOUCAULT, M. (1967), *Madness and Civilization*, trans. R. Howard, Tavistock.

GALANTER, E., and MILLER, G. A. (1960), 'Some comments on stochiastic models and psychological theories', in K. J. Arrow, S. Kovin and P. Suppes (eds.), *Proceedings of the First Stanford Symposium on Mathematical Methods in Social Sciences*, Stanford University Press.

GOFFMAN, E. (1959), *The Presentation of Self in Everyday Life*, Penguin.

GOFFMAN, E. (1962), *Asylums*, Penguin.

GOLDMANN, L. (1969), *The Human Sciences and Philosophy*, trans. H. V. White and R. Anchor, Cape.

GURWITSCH, A. (1966), *Studies in Phenomenology and Psychology*, Northwestern University Press.

HAYS, P. (1964), *New Horizons in Psychiatry*, Penguin.

HEBB, D. O. (1949), *The Organization of Behaviour*, Wiley.

HENRY, J. (1966), *Culture Against Man*, Tavistock.

HINDE, R. A. (1966), *Animal Behaviour*, McGraw-Hill.

HILL, D. (1962), *The Burden on the Community*, Oxford University Press.

HULL, C. L. (1935), 'The mechanism of the assembly of behaviour segments in novel combinations suitable for problem solutions', *Psychological Review*, vol. 42, pp. 219–45.

HULL, C. L. (1952), *A Behaviour System*, Yale University Press.

KUHN, T. (1962), *The Structure of Scientific Revolution*, Chicago University Press.

LAING, R. D. (1960), *The Divided Self*, Tavistock; Penguin.

LAING, R. D., and COOPER, D (1964), *Reason and Violence: A Decade of Sartre's Philosophy 1950–1960*, Tavistock.

LAING, R. D., and ESTERSON, A. (1964), *Families of Schizophrenics*, Tavistock.

LEMERT, E. M. (1951), *Social Pathology*, McGraw-Hill.

MERLEAU-PONTY, M. (1962), *The Phenomenology of Perception*, trans. Colin Smith, Routledge & Kegan Paul.

MERLEAU-PONTY, M. (1965), *The Structure of Behaviour*, trans. A. L. Fisher, Methuen.

MILLER, G. A., GALANTER, E., and PRIBRAM, K. (1960), *Plans and the Structure of Behaviour*, Holt, Rinehart & Winston.

MOORE, G. E. (1903), *Principa Ethica*, Cambridge University Press.

RICKS, C. (1969), 'Student thought', *Listener*, no. 81, p. 2085.

ROSENTHAL, R., and JACOBSON, L. (1968)., *Pygmalion in the Classroom*, Holt, Rinehart & Winston.

RYLE, G. (1949), *The Concept of Mind*, Hutchinson; Penguin.

SARTRE, J. P. (1967), Preface to F. Fanon, *The Wretched of the Earth*, Penguin.

SCHEFF, T. (1963), 'The role of the mentally ill and the dynamics of mental disorder: a research framework', *Sociometry*, vol. 26, pp. 436–53.

SCHEFF, T. (1966), *Being Mentally Ill*, Weidenfeld & Nicolson.

SKINNER, B. F. (1938), *The Behaviour of Organisms*, Appleton-Century-Crofts.

SKINNER, B. F. (1959), *Cumulative Record*, Methuen.

SOMMERHOF, G. (1951), *Analytical Biology*, Oxford University Press.

SUTHERLAND, N. S. (1964), 'Visual discrimination in animals', *British Medical Bulletin*, vol. 20, no. 1, pp. 54–9.

SZASZ, T. S. (1961), *The Myth of Mental Illness*, Harper & Row.

TARSIS, V. (1966), *Ward 7*, Collins.

TREISMAN, M. (1960), 'Stimulus-response theory and expectancy', *British J. of Psychol.*, vol. 51, p. 49.

WATSON, A. J. (1961), 'The place of reinforcement in the explanation of behaviour' in W. H. Thorpe and O. L. Zangwill (eds.), *Current Problems in Animal Behaviour*, Cambridge University Press.

WEINBERG, S. K. (1968), *The Sociology of Mental Disorders*, Pt VIII, Staples Press.

# Sociological Theory:
# The Production of a Bourgeois Ideology
## Mark Harvey

## Introduction

This chapter will deal with three interconnected problems:
What is ideological about bourgeois sociological theory? Why is bourgeois sociological theory ideological? What is the basis for an adequate critique of bourgeois sociological theory?

In answer to these questions, four main theses:

1. Bourgeois sociological theorists (and even some Marxists) have worried themselves silly over the subjectivity or objectivity of their knowledge. In the formation of knowledge, however, what counts is not the relation between subject and object, not even dialectic between them. What counts is the relation between theory, practice and the product of practice.[1]

2. Bourgeois sociological theorists will necessarily continue to be both worried and silly in so far as they do not and *cannot* realize that an object of theory is the product of practice. 'Society' is only an object, knowledge is only of the subject, in so far as these theorists hang a notice on their object saying: 'Keep off'; 'Do not touch'. Whereas the natural scientist constantly, relentlessly and progressively, transforms nature, the sociologist obstinately abstains from transforming society, in the name of value-free (read action-free), neutral, and even empirical, science.[2] The relation between subject and object only becomes a problematic when the subject must 'keep off' the object. It only becomes a problematic when *the object is not a product of a practice* of which a theory is the theory.[3] In other words, the bourgeois obsession with subjectivity and objectivity is *the effect of a particular relation between theory and practice.*

1. Marx has sketched out the basis of this thesis in his Theses on Feuerbach.
2. Cf. F. Engels, 'Feuerbach and the end of classical German philosophy', in Marx and Engels (1968 edn).
3. I should like to mark the difference between these theses and anything emanating from the idealist pen of one L. Althusser. In talking of the object of a science as a product of practice, I am referring to real transformations of the real world, and not to a re-working of *concepts* (considered as raw material) into a theory (considered as the product of the transformations of this raw material). In talking of practice, I am *not* talking of a specifically theoretical practice, but of a social and, at times, even political practice of the transformation of society.

3. This particular relation between theory and practice in which knowledge is unrelated to any systematic transformation of its object, is the origin of both the ideological *function* and the ideological *nature* of bourgeois sociological theory. Action-free knowledge serves the maintenance and conservation of the capitalist system by representing this society as it directly and immediately appears or manifests itself.[4] And bourgeois methodological practice is arbitrarily restricted to registering only the way that society appears and manifests itself immediately, e.g. questionnaires, participant (i.e. passive) observation, surveys, analyses of value systems. *This is the ideological function of bourgeois sociology.* Society is known only as it is, and then only as it appears. A knowledge of what society could be, or even of what lies behind the appearances, is systematically excluded. Compare the knowledge gained of the power structure of a university by an occupation with that to be gained by a questionnaire, when some potential respondees – the police, perhaps – would not be on the scene at all.

4. At the same time, in bourgeois sociological theory, there are fundamental contradictions between theory and methodology, which result from this arbitrary restriction of methodological practice to the registering of appearances. This is the origin of the *ideological nature* of bourgeois theory. For, the effect in knowledge of his relation between theory and practice is to make *knowledge abstract*. By this I mean that the knowledge based on an abstention from any transformation of its object cannot, by that fact, be anything other than a representation of a reality, a detached understanding, explanation, or description, – the product of a process of knowing contained entirely within itself.[5] If the production of concepts is dissociated from the production of the objects of those concepts, then those concepts will always be abstract in relation to their objects, and will always bear an *unreal, uncertain, relation to them.*[6] A knowledge which refuses to be based on any practice, is a knowledge which can never be a theory of practice, can never lead to theorized practice. The function of bourgeois sociological theory is to give a representa-

4. The critique of knowledge based on taking appearances as reality is to be found extensively in Marx's *Capital*, and in his *Theories of Surplus Value*. See in particular the section on 'the fetishism of commodities' in *Capital*, vol. 1.

5. The Althusserian concept of knowledge as a process taking place entirely within itself is here squarely marked as a *radically* ideological concept.

6. Marx's characterization of ideology as abstract knowledge can be found above all in his critique of abstract concepts in bourgeois economic theory. See the Introduction to the *Contribution to the Critique of Political Economy*.

tion of a politician's political practice. It cannot, and must not, give a theory *of* political practice.

*Corollary*. Whenever sociological theory is used, put into practice, it is abused. The theory of complex organizations or systems theory can indeed be used for personnel management. But such theory is strictly subordinate to the use to which it is put, and is never a theory of that use. Thus, it is a representation of complex organizations, not a theory of organizing. The theory is subordinate to a practice that is external to it, an untheorized practice that essentially 'must not be touched' – the running of the business enterprise. The theory *serves* the existing practice, makes the business enterprise, or whatever organization, run better. The use of psychoanalysis for advertising is another clear example of this subordinate relation of a theory to an external practice.

These four theses – the obsession with subjectivity and objectivity, the particular relation between theory and practice that produces the 'gap' between subject and object, the conservative function of bourgeois sociology, the ideological nature of its knowledge – are intended to be statements which describe general, structural features of bourgeois sociological theory. The rest of the chapter will be devoted to demonstrating how these general features are reflected in the variations between four major bourgeois sociological theories – Durkheim, Weber, Parsons and phenomenology. This variation between different theoretical standpoints will show a covariation between (a) the relation between theory and practice or methodology in each theorist and (b) the contradictions in that relation. The account will be necessarily schematic. But there is a principle which guides the schematism. A basic contradiction runs through bourgeois sociological theory. It is a contradiction which emerges when the sociologist's theory of knowledge is applied to the sociologist's own theory or knowledge. Or, put another way, it is *a contradiction between theory* (the sociology) *and methodology* (statements about the principles or foundations of the sociologist's own knowledge). So the account will have the following structure. Each sociologist will be examined first in terms of his implicit or explicit sociology of knowledge, second in terms of the stated foundations of his own knowledge, and finally in terms of the contradictions between the two.

### Durkheim
*Theory*

Durkheim's sociology, when applied to the explanation of social forms of knowledge, is the most elaborated and comprehensive of all the bourgeois sociologists to be dealt with here. He explicitly sees his work as a theory of knowledge (Durkheim, 1964b).[7] Consequently he does make a serious attempt to account for the form of thought – its logical structure; the coherence of thought – its principles of validity; the ideality of thought, e.g. the absence of any physical conditions to the validity of the equation $2+2 = 4$; and the differentiation of knowledge into logic, geometry, physics, religion. Moreover, Durkheim's theory of knowledge has, to put it politely, a dual aspect: he attempts to account both for *the social existence* of knowledge – the frames of knowledge into which people are ineluctably socialized – and for *the origin* of the structure, coherence, ideality and differentiation of knowledge. To put it more bluntly, his theory of knowledge conflates these two aspects, so confusing respectively the *reproduction* and the *production* of knowledge.[8] But then his theory, more than most contemporary ideologies, does at least cover both aspects even while covering up their differences.

Durkheim's theory of knowledge, in its most coherently argued form is built up in the following way. Beginning with the particular example of religious knowledge, he posited, or rather abstracted, a property which was common to all religions. The differences between the gods, rites, symbols, etc. of different religions are abstracted to find a common property, a generic 'religiousness' about all religions. Pursuing the abstraction, this character of religiousness is seen to lie in the fact that all religions make a fundamental distinction between the sacred and the profane. This distinction is the universal underlying structure of all religious thought. (It's not important for present purposes whether or not one accepts the empirical validity of this abstraction, or the nature of Durkheim's evidence for it.) This distinction is an absolute one. There is complete discontinuity between the sacred and the profane. You can't become less and less profane until you are sacred, or *vice versa*. The two are *logically* distinct classes. What is the origin of this distinction? How did it come to be thought? There are a number of characteristics about it which have to be accounted for, and it is in his account of these characteristics that Durkheim is led to make general statements about all forms of knowledge, not only religious 'knowledge'. One such characteristic, the *logicality* of the distinction, the separation of beings, things, ideas, or whatever, into

7. The account in this section is largely based on this work and on Durkheim and Mauss (1963).

8. A contemporary sociologist, B. Bernstein, makes an exactly parallel error in his revamping of Durkheim (1972).

The language used here to describe Durkheim is given a Bernsteinian gloss in order to bring out this parallel.

two separate classes has already been mentioned. Other characteristics would include the *causal* nature of the sacred – God the creator, – and its *non-physical* character. So Durkheim sets about accounting for the origin and nature of these characteristics.

To begin with, and this is typical of him, he uses a method of elimination, and in so doing excludes two principal possible, origins of religion. (Disregard the plausibility of the argument.) He excludes a psychological or subjective origin of the distinction between the sacred and the profane. In particular he rejects theories suggesting an origin in dreams – an obvious candidate in so far as dreams contain images of people and things for which there is not necessarily any physical correlate in reality. Psychological origins of such a distinction, however, are inadequate because, amongst other things, they fail to account for the following properties of religious knowledge.

1. A religion is a code held in common by a society as a whole, and is, as such, distinct from such dreams, ideas, fantasies, whims, which are had only by individuals. Some dreams are only significant for the individuals that have them. Therefore what is individual about individual dreams or fantasies, can never be the origin of what is common about common knowledge. Yet being common to all the members of a society, is one of the essential characters of religious knowledge.

2. If the sacred-profane distinction of a given society objectively constrains individuals to accept it, sacredness must have a more solid basis than do the fleeting fantasies which characterize dreams. Even if religion is a mystificatory form of thought, full of illusions, its existence is far from illusory, and so requires an explanation as objective as its objective existence.

These two arguments can readily be seen to apply to knowledge in general, and not only to the distinction between the sacred and the profane. Knowledge, as a commonly accepted code through which individual experience is mediated, cannot have an origin in the fluctuations or variations of the thoughts, experiences, or fantasies of individuals. Knowledge, e.g. maths, as a code which *constrains* an individual's thought along certain lines, cannot be as subjectively variable as, characteristically, is individual thought: it must have an objective basis, a basis outside the individual.

The second major possible origin of the distinction between the sacred and the profane, nature, or the *object* of human experience, is also eliminated. All kinds of wondrous things happen in nature, lightning, rain, night and day. These things when described in language by man, take on the property or benevolent or malevolent agents. In 'The lightning struck Ted Heath on his way to the seashore', the lightning appears just as much a benevolent agent as is Ted Heath a malevolent one, and far more remarkable. So, natural agents come to be seen as spirits which have their own causality, as a result of the experience of nature. Durkheim rejects this argument on three principal grounds:

1. The distinction *in knowledge* between the sacred and the profane is both an absolute and a logical one. Nature is remarkable, less remarkable, and even at times pretty mundane. It certainly does not fall neatly into two distinct categories of the wondrous and the ordinary.

2. Through sense experience, nature produces impressions which are very fluctuating from individual to individual. Sense experience of the object could never be the origin of the stable, absolute, categories which all individuals in a society accept.

3. As with the argument against a psychological origin, this explanation via nature rests on the invention of illusory causes to natural phenomena, which would be eliminated simply with the growth of knowledge. Zeus goes out as the scientific explanation of lightning comes on. But something as constraining as religion, or as a logical distinction, cannot be accounted for on the basis of inventions due to ignorance.

Again these arguments have some generality. The formal structure of knowledge cannot be derived from an object which is not itself endowed with such structure. Sense experience is too unstable a source of information to be an adequate source for those stable categories of knowledge through which sense experience is interpreted. The hypostasization of inventions of the human mind accounts neither for the origin of such inventions, nor for the power that the hypostasizations exercise over the human mind.

Having dismissed these two possible origins of religion – the psychological subject and the natural object – Durkheim has cleared the ground (at least to his satisfaction) for discovering an origin of knowledge which objectively constrains the psychological subject; (b) which intrinsically has the kind of structure which could account for the structure of knowledge; and (c) which is distinct from any natural or physical objectivity. For Durkheim, society satisfies all these conditions. Society has a structure. For the primitive societies with which Durkheim was concerned, the clan structure marked people off into absolutely distinct groups. People are born into a clan without choice and so are objectively constrained to belong to it. Durkheim presents evidence to show that different clans distinguish between the sacred and profane in their totems in such a way that religious distinctions reflect the social distinctions of the society.

In short, the classification of men into groups is at the origin of the classification of things into different, logically distinct, classes. Finally, society is an objective but non-natural, non-physical force.

Moreover, if logical distinctions originate in social distinctions, spatial coordinates originate in the social space of a society: the spatial arrangement of the clans in a tribal camp, say an arrangement in a circle, is such that members of each clan grows up in a specific place in a *common* spatial framework. The seasonal rituals of society are at the origin of a common, societal framework of time. Logic, space and time, these are the categories of knowledge – the framework of knowledge without which all coherent thought would be impossible. They provide the necessary constraints on thought without which all individual, subjective, thought would be impossible. And the source of this necessary constraint is the social framework which, preexisting the individual, is his objective environment.

So forms of knowledge are imposed by social forms. Such forms are essential to all knowledge of natural reality. But they do not bear any necessary relation to that reality, stil less derive from it. Society is both objective and non-material, non-physical. Its forms express themselves more or less directly in forms of knowledge. This leads Durkheim to make an important step in his argument. Having these properties, society is seen as 'the subject which contains all subjects within it'[9] (1964a, p. 441). Society becomes the objective subject. Instead of categories of knowledge belonging to the individual subject, they simply belong to society. They are only objective and constraining with respect to the individual subject, member of the social subject. With respect to the objects of knowledge, they remain founded in a source quite distinct from those objects, namely, society. Psychological subjectivity of thought is simply replaced by social subjectivity of thought.

*Methodology*

In his methodology writings (see Durkheim, 1964c), Durkheim is concerned to establish sociology as an objective science. By this he means several things.

1. His own knowledge must be objective. Sociology must only take into account those facts which the sociologist could not avoid observing what-

9. This step is often missed in accounts of Durkheim which make him a simple positivist, all knowledge coming from the object of knowledge as such. He says: 'Since the universe does not exist except in so far as it is thought of, and since it is not completely thought of except in society, it takes place in this latter; it becomes part of society's interior (sic) life' (1964b, p. 442).

ever the values or interpretations he may have. So, all preconceptions must be abolished to attain sociological objectivity. Facts must be defined with reference only to the inherent properties of the observable data.

2. The reality which is the object of sociological analysis must be the one objective reality. The object of sociology has nothing to do with the way that individuals in society subjectively experience or interpret social reality – take such experience seriously and you would have as many social realities as you have individuals. On the contrary, the object of sociology is the one unique social reality which no individual can avoid being constrained by, e.g. the currency, the law, the division of labour or the language you grow up in or with.

In fact, Durkheim makes a confusion, which leads to many theoretical contradictions, between what is social and what is objective about social objectivity. Thus to be objective, society must contrain and coerce individuals from 'above'. He says we are victims of an illusion if we think that man makes social reality, since in fact it 'forced itself on us from without' (1964c, p. 5). Punishment for deviance is evidence of this constraint, of this external reality forcing us into a social mould. Here objectivity is linked to social coercion.[10]

To be social, on the other hand, social reality must be recognized as a new level of reality, distinct from all individual, psychological, reality. This reality is the reality required to account for the distinctively social phenomena – the social suicide rate, as opposed to the individual suicide. There must be a distinct social reality to explain those facts which are not properties of individuals as such but rather are common to all individuals of a society. But Durkheim conflates what is distinctively social about social reality with what is objectively constraining. The confusion is as evident as it is ideologically significant. Social causality is confused with social coercion. Explanation is confused with explanandum. Durkheim abstracts what is social from what is individual, and gives the social an independent reality. But this social reality is at the same time the objective reality which coerces the individual to be social. Society is seen as objective because coercive, and coercive because objective. This is, however, only an internal, theoretical confusion; far more important are the contradictions between his theory and his methodology.

*Contradictions between theory and methodology*

The problem of subjectivity and objectivity deeply penetrates the tissue

10. 'A social fact is to be recognized by the power of external coercion which it exercises or is capable of exercising over individuals' (1964c, p. 10).

of Durkheim's theory of knowledge. Rejecting the origin of the categories of knowledge in both the individual subject and the natural object, he posits their origin in society. Society is both objective, in the sense of external to the subject, and subjective, in the sense of being an origin of knowledge independent of the objects of which we have knowledge. What is the source of this problem of subjectivity and objectivity? How does it reflect in knowledge an effect of a particular and contradictory relation between theory and methodology?

*First contradiction.* If Durkheim's theory of knowledge were applied to his own sociology, then his own claims about the methodological basis of his own knowledge are invalid. If society imposes the categories of knowledge through which we look at the world, then society as subject also imposes on the sociologist the way in which society is looked at – a kind of mediated introspection. If his theory of knowledge about what causes us to have knowledge is correct, then he is simply caused by society to have that theory. Far from having the objective knowledge that he claims, the knowledge of an external reality whose existence is independent of our means of knowing it, society causes its members to know society in a particular way.

*Second contradiction.* If society is objective because it *coerces* individuals into its norms and forms, and not only because it *causes* effects on individuals then the sociologist's knowledge of that society also is the normative, non-deviant, knowledge of society; again not objective knowledge.

So, if Durkheim's theory of knowledge is applied to himself, then his own sociology is neither objective nor neutral, but subjective and normative. This is quite contrary to his own methodological and epistemological claims.

Durkheim himself partially gives away the origin of these contradictions. His sociology, he says, implies the recognition that the sociologist cannot know society by acting on or within it. Society is an external reality which imposes itself on us; it is a 'system of realized facts' (1964a, pp. 34–5), given as such to the sociologist's impotent gaze. Therefore in lieu of an active transforming experimental method, the sociologist is forced into the next best thing, the comparative method. This comparative method enables the sociologist to *abstract* what is common to all variants of social forms. This, we saw, is what Durkheim did when abstracting what is common to all religion: the distinction between the sacred and the profane. In other words, common or general concepts are produced by a purely theoretical practice *essentially* detached from any action on the object of knowledge, a pure practice of abstraction. The distinction between social reality and individual psychological reality, is similarly produced solely by Durkheim's powers of abstract thought. The result of such a purely theoretical practice of abstraction is a product, a concept, which has no reality outside the head of one Emile Durkheim. By indulging in the empirical collection of (untransformed) data and the theoretical practice of abstracting common or general concepts about them, the actual, historical, practice of producing empirical social reality is necessarily disconnected from the theoretical practice of producing concepts about it. Thus his social reality *is* a reality external to the production of theory about it, a reality which therefore *does* impose itself on Durkheim as a 'system of realized facts'. At the same time, his theoretical concepts *are* produced by a practice dissociated from the production of that social reality, so yielding a purely abstract knowledge. This *real dissociation* between theory and practice which leaves the object, 'society', out there, and the theoretical practice of Durkheim in Durkheim, has the effect in the production of knowledge of dissociating the object of knowledge from the subject of knowledge. This dissociation finds its index in the two contradictions between theory and methodology, where society is both the external object and the original source of knowledge.

Finally, the ideological function of this relation between theory and practice is directly manifest in Durkheim. He says that, as a result of the knowledge that society is an external, alien, objectivity, all revolutionaries will know that nothing can really be changed by action. Instead, the 'system of realized facts' is 'entitled to our respect'.[11] At the same time, this insight into social reality is a gift for the ruling class, since the job of maintaining the *status quo*, or the job of coercion, is nothing but the job of expressing the objectivity of social lreality:

The duty of the statesman is no longer to push a society towards an ideal that seems attractive to him, but his role is that of a physician: he prevents outbreaks of illness by good hygiene, and he seeks to cure them when they have occurred (1964c, p. 75).

11. 'There has been good reason to upbraid certain theories which are thought to be scientific for being destructive and revolutionary. They construct, but they do not observe. (Exactly.) They see in ethics, not a collection of facts to study, but a sort of revocable law-making. . . . Ethics for us is a system of realized facts. . . . Such vital facts are entitled to our respect' (1964a, p. 35). See the whole of this passage, which is explicitly designed to impart 'a conservative attitude'.

## Weber
### *Theory*[12]

Rationality rides high in the West, and alone in the West, at least in Weber's scenario. This for him is the *significance* of Western culture. Experimentation and rational science, systematic music and architecture, rational bureaucratic nation states and parliamentary systems, formal legal systems, and not far behind, the business enterprise, ride with rationality, alone in the West.[13] This loneliness of rationality in the West is what grips Weber's imagination and sociology. A major focus of his sociology is on giving an account of rationality in relation to human action. The following section will deal with the way he treats this relation, to the exclusion of other, less central if interconnected, elements in his work. A further limitation of this section will be to treat the relation between rationality and human economic action, and in particular capitalism. This relation will, however, be taken as an instance of a more general Weberian obsession, the relation between values and empirical factual events.

Weber defines capitalism by its rationality, by the rationality of its organization (1964, pp. 184–212, esp. p. 211). This should provoke incredulity, rather than a critique of Weberian rationality as a bourgeois rationality.[14] For the question is not so much one of why a definition of capitalism in terms of rationality serves the ideological functions of misrepresenting capitalism as a system as coherent and beautiful as the rationality of mathematics, although of course it does serve this function (1970, p. 24). The question is more fundamentally one of why Weber chose to define capitalism in such spiritual terms, in terms of rationality, rather than in terms of, say, the economic form of exchange of commodities in the market. The short answer is that Weber's sociology delimits its field of study to action endowed with meaning for the person who acts – what Weber calls the 'subjective meaning complex of action'. What counts, therefore, is that action is defined in terms of the meaning principle action has; and, in the case of capitalism, that meaning principle is one of rationality. The very title of one of his principal works on the

12. The principal works of Max Weber referred to here are: *The Protestant Ethic and The Spirit of Capitalism* (1970); *The Theory of Economic and Social Organization* (1964); *The Sociology of Religion* (1966).

13. Weber makes this point emphatically in the Introduction to *The Protestant Ethic* (1970), e.g. pp. 13, 26.

14. Marcuse gives a good example of this kind of critique of Weberian ideology. His is a less radical critique than that developed here, since it concentrates on the content of the knowledge, and not on the conditions of production of ideological knowledge (see Marcuse 1965).

subject, *The Protestant Ethic and the Spirit of Capitalism*, is illuminating in this respect.

What then is meant by the rationality of capitalism? Why is it necessary to explain the origin of capitalism in terms of the origins of rationality? What is an ethos of rationality?

To see how Weber defines capitalism essentially by its spirit, and that there are theoretically systematic reasons why he did so, it is worth looking more closely at the spirit. He says, 'The impulse to acquisition, pursuit of gain, of money, of the greatest possible amount of money has in itself nothing to do with capitalism' (1970, p. 17). This is principally because such avarice has stormed all over the world, at all historical epochs, and is not specific to the West.

Capitalism may even be identical with the restraint, or at least the rational tempering of the irrational impulse. But capitalism is identical with the pursuit of profit, and forever renewed profit, by means of continuous rational capitalist enterprise (1970, p. 17).

His notion of rationality is further specified when he refers to the necessity for an enterprise to rationally calculate each of its economic actions 'So far as the transactions are rational, calculation underlies every single action of the partners' (1970, p. 19). Further Weber makes clear that for him the 'central problem' (1970, p. 24) is rational organization of labour; this, he recognizes, presupposes formally free labour (i.e. that the labourer is without ownership of the means of production, and is forced to sell his labour-power, is seen as less significant than the formal spiritual freedom of not being tied by legal or traditional obligations to work for a particular employer – e.g. a feudal lord). Hence, he says, although economically an enterprise may even have the characteristics of other capitalistic firms, *if* it relies on traditional ties to customers for its output, traditional ties to workers for labour, or traditional sources of raw material, rather than at each stage rationally calculating its action to maximize profit, *then* this enterprise is not truly, i.e. *spiritually*, capitalistic. Hence also, for Weber, one of the principle obstacles to capitalism is the refusal of workers to cooperate, and this refusal to cooperate is seen in the similar terms of what Weber amusingly calls 'an inner (i.e. spiritual) obstacle':

Wherever capitalism has begun its work of increasing the productivity of human labour by increasing its intensity (i.e. increasing exploitation), it has encountered the immensely stubborn resistance of this leading trait of pre-capitalist labour, its traditionalism and dependence on custom (1970, pp. 26–7).

Having thus defined capitalism by its rationality, by its meaning-principle, it is clear that the Weberian explanation of capitalism is essentially an explanation of the spirit of capitalism. Thus he looks for a source of rationality, the source of a spirit. And in true idealist fashion, the source of a spirit can only be another spirit, or in this case a truly religious spirit, Protestantism. In Protestantism and in particular in Calvinism, there is on the one hand ascetism, a principle fortuitously appropriate for capital accumulation; and on the other hand, the notion of a calling, of being one of the elect, which is miraculously suited to the rational control of each step one makes in life. In short the origin of the spirit of capitalism is to be seen in *systems of values*, the ethos of Protestantism. And Weber analyses this system of values to see how its inner articulations lead to those anti-traditionalist, rationalistic spirits which so gloriously surround the tables of so many boards of directors.

The general character of this sociological analysis can be summarized.

1. He makes a distinction between the actuality and the spirituality of human action, and interprets the former in terms of its approximation to the latter. Where the spirit is willing, the flesh will more or less follow.

2. He makes a distinction between that action which is significant for the actor, and that action which is not, the latter being thereby excluded from the domain of sociology.

3. The spirit is analysed for its inner connections, and these are in turn related to a general value system – rationality is related to the ethos of rationality.

*Methodology*[15]

In dealing with Weber's methodology, I shall be concerned briefly with four major interlocking principles – (1) the distinction between value and fact, (2) the *verstehen* method (3) the ideal type (4) and value relevance of sociological theory.

1. First of all, then, Weber made an absolutely primary distinction between normative statements and statements of fact, and affirmed that the former could not be derived from the latter. Normative statements would concern the criteria of validity internal to a conceptual system, e.g. mathematics. However much you study the way people do multiplication tables, only the rules of mathematics would say what was an error. Similarly, a factual, empirical study of Chinese astronomy could never determine whether Chinese astronomy was correct – that would entail an evaluation of it – but could only entail statements concerning what

15. For this section see Weber, *Methodology of the Social Sciences* (1949) and Weber (1964, pp. 87–115).

Chinese astronomers said were correct statements in their astronomy, according to their value system. In short, it is impossible to deduce from statements about how people think in fact, statements about how they should think. On the other hand, there are 'practical evaluations' or direct value judgements. Whether one should join a trade union cannot be decided on statements of fact about the work situation. Statements of fact, like 'the law of the land is upheld', are quite distinct from value judgement, like 'the law should be upheld'. So, the worker, if he did but know it, joins unions on 'very definite metaphysical principles which are never demonstrable by science' (1949, p. 24). The point is that Weber, in arguing that statements of value cannot *logically* be derived from statements of fact, seems at the same time to be deluding himself into thinking that people's value judgements are not actually derived, or emerge, from factual situations. He certainly makes it an argument for a sociology in which values are empirically analysed without judging whether they are right, wrong, or mystificatory. Instead they are analysed as value systems with their own internal norms.

2. The *verstehen* method, or understanding method (1949, pp. 40–41; 1964, pp. 93–8), is essentially a method for understanding value systems. The sociologist is asked to show a preparedness to suspend his own value systems, and analyse other value systems in terms of their basic axioms, in terms of *their* normativity, and to see the rationale of a value system – e.g. Protestantism – in terms of its own rationality. It is a combination of analysis – seeing the way the propositions of a value-system hang together; and empathy – getting on the inside of a value system other than one's own.

3. Granted that norms cannot be derived from facts, a person's value system is seen by Weber as that which endows his actions with meaning, with significance. Sociology is defined by Weber as those actions for which the actor has some meaning. Now if action has some meaning for the actor, is oriented towards a value end, it corresponds to the ideal only when the means empirically appropriate to that end are in fact used, and the empirical consequences of those means taken into account. Thus, if the actor has rationality as a value system, then his actions approximate more or less to that ideal rationality. But, for the sociologist, what is interesting is above all the case of complete correspondence, for then the action is fully interpretable in terms of its significance for the actor. This constitutes what Weber calls the ideal type. An ideal type is the principle of significance by which actions have meaning for actors – thus the ethic of rationality is an ideal type, an analytic construct that the sociologist makes of the significance that action has for actors.

4. If actors are oriented by the significance they attach to their actions – by the goals they pursue – and if the sociologist makes a construct of what the principle of that significance is, then the sociologist in making this construct is also guided by what he himself finds significant in data, according to *his* value system (1949, pp. 67–73). As Weber says, there is a distinction between making value judgements – condemning capitalism as irrational for example – and selection of facts about capitalism which seem relevant to the sociologist's value-system, e.g. defining the capitalism in terms of the spirit of rationality. Selection of facts on subjective grounds of significance for the sociologist's own values, is inevitable. The 'value relevance' to the sociologist is the basis for the selection of facts. An ideal type is therefore a construct based on the significance for the sociologist of what is significant for the actors of an historical epoch. Weber's concern for rationality led him to select facts (to put it mildly) which, significant for him, defined the spirit of capitalism as rationalistic.

## The contradictions between methodology and theory

On the surface, all seems quiet and consistent in the relation between theory and methodology in Weber. Methodological distinctions between fact and value, between ideal type constructs and *verstehen* analysis, appear plainly in his theoretical work on capitalism and Protestantism. There, he clearly establishes what he considers to be the 'universal significance' (1970, p. 31) of Western society, its rationality. He refuses to account for value systems – the spirit of capitalism, or Protestantism – in terms of factual social situations, and indeed does not employ any methodology designed to do so. He establishes an ideal type of capitalist action, which is not supported by a vast weight of references to the empirical reality of nascent capitalism, but is more designed to present an interpretative schema by which empirical facts are rendered intelligible. The absence of surface contradictions, however is singularly misleading. Again, I'm arguing that the essential contradictions are *between* methodology and theory, and so don't appear on the surface. I will point out only two of the more fundamental contradictions.

1. Empirical analysis of value systems: *the ideology of pluralism.* An empirical sociology of value systems must not make value judgements of those value systems. Chinese astronomy or Protestantism must not be judged. Instead they must be analysed on their own terms. Accepting their internal rationale, the sociologist must, by empathy and analysis, illuminate the significance that value systems give to human action. There is a major contradiction here. All value systems are represented as correct

on their own terms. Value judgements or normative systems, are all treated as valid in terms of their own definitions of validity. This, however, is nothing else but an implicit theory about the nature of validity, and a disputable one at that. To refuse to make value judgements about other value systems itself entails a value judgement that the validity of a value system is only relative to that value system. This may be a tenable position. But if it is, then it would be a value judgement, which at the very least condemns those theories which *do* judge other value systems by describing them as false consciousness, for example. The contradiction is that Weber does *condemn* making value judgements – and so makes one. In the theory, he presents an empathetic, neutral, analysis of Protestantism. In the methodology, he condemns making value judgements. But in presenting the Protestant ethic on its own terms, he is making a value judgement – that Protestantism *is* valid on its own terms, and is *not* a bourgeois *mystification* of work.

This contradiction is however a direct product of the dissociation between theory and practice. For the *verstehen* method is a method, a practice, which perfectly illustrates the sociologist refusal of any practice which transforms its object, in this case people's consciousness or values. Instead it accepts all value systems as they are, in their own internal subjectivity, and communicates with those internal subjectivities by means of empathy. The practice of empathy is in principle a practice which aims to transform the values of others *as little as possible*. Hence it can understand those value systems *only* from the point of view of *their* inner rationale, never from the point of view of what transforms people's consciousness, never from the point of view of the production of value systems. It can at most analyse the product, the value-system, and at worst only the package, the way the value-system *presents* itself. One value system is therefore as valid as *any* other. Hence the pluralism, and hence the contradiction.

2. A further contradiction can also be seen in the relation between the theory of significant action and the methodology of the ideal type. Weber himself argues that the ideal type is a kind of Utopia, the ideal case when the actor's action is in complete correspondence with the sociologist's interpretative scheme of the significance of that action for the actor. The level of consistency is that, if the actor's action should be interpreted according to its significance for him, then so should the sociologist's own interpretation, his theory-making, be done according to its significance for the sociologist. The level of inconsistency, the contradiction, is that this makes strictly impossible an epistemological distinction between

one person's value system, say the sociologist's, and another's, say the actor's. He cannot make a distinction between a science or theory of value systems on the one hand, and value systems as objects of that science on the other. Is Weber the ideologist of rationalism or the sociological theorist of rationality as a value system? Since the ideal type is explicitly constructed for its value relevance to Weber, Weber himself would seem to have made himself unable to answer this question. Indeed, he himself implicitly admits this when he talks of the difficulty of distinguishing between the sociologist's ideal type and the dominant idea of an epoch (1949, p. 94).

This second contradiction marks a second mode of dissociation between theory of an object and practice on that object. Facts are looked at in terms of their relevance to values, to a subjectivity. So the facts which enter into a theory do so on account of a *selection* based on significance for the subject, Weber. The facts are there, not as a product of practice on empirical reality, but as an abstraction from reality as it phenomenally appears. Wanting any other mode of production of facts, subjective selection of facts from an infinity of facts is the only alternative.[16] Hence the mind-twisting problem of whether the product of such a selection, the ideal type, is a subjective artefact or corresponds to empirical reality. Yet the problem of subjectively selecting facts only poses itself when the theorist confronts the whole array of phenomena. It does not occur for the scientist who confronts himself only with the products of his experimental practice.

## Parsons
### Theory[17]

There are many similarities between Parsons and Weber. If Parsons is much less consistent, more formal and abstract, and often completely lost in a labyrinthine systematicity of his own construction, it is probably because of, rather than in spite of, these features that Parsons has had a far more penetrating ideological effect.

Parsons puts forward what he calls an action frame of reference. By this he means, with Weber, that a sociologist makes a necessary demarcation of his field to include only those actions and objects that have significance for the actor, the ego. Parsons is insistent that, although there are a number of innate needs in man's nature (need dispositions) these needs

16. For Weber's own presentation of his problem see Weber (1949, pp. 72–84).

17. The principal works of Parsons referred to in this section are *The Structure of Social Action* (1949); *Toward a General Theory of Action* (1962); *Sociological Theory and Modern Society* (1967).

are not satisfied only by a specific, determinate, set of objects. So there is a necessary selection of the objects towards which an actor acts, a selection which is governed by the actor's *orientation* to those objects. Further, the actor is not determined unilaterally by the environment as to what objects or aspects of them, he acts towards. Hence it is the orientation – the significance for the subject – that is determinative, and so forms the basis of Parsons's 'voluntaristic theory of action'. Parsons makes a further distinction between culture and the action system. Culture for Parsons is essentially unattached to any actor, hence unmotivated by any need dispositions, and as such inactive (1962, p. 76). Culture applies various value *standards*, common to members of a group, which essentially affect the *orientations* of actors (by being 'internalized' by personalities or 'institutionalized' by collective codes of behaviour). For example, it sets down common values for what is a correct knowledge (a cognitive mode of orienting to objects), for styles of gratification whether in sex, art or cooking (a cathectic or aesthetic mode of orienting to objects) or finally for deciding between alternative orientations on the grounds of their respective values, as with moral codes, legal codes (an evaluative mode of orienting). Culture, in general, is a system of values that regulates the orientation of actors, whether actors are individuals or collectivities. The idealist character of this theory is evident, first in the centrality of subjective orientations, and then in the cultural regulations of them. In passing, quite a lot of Parsons's time is spent in making formal distinctions such as that between the cognitive, the cathectic and the evaluative. But none deserve so much awe as the central artefact of his abstract intellectual production, the pattern variables (PVs).

Each actor, individual or collective, is faced with a horrible choice when orienting toward objects and immediately prior to committing a 'sociological' action. *How* am I going to act significantly towards it? *What* is going to be significant? Well, according to Parsons, there is no angst-provoking infinite choice of significances. In fact, I face not an infinite choice of possible significances, but a series of dilemmas, and a happily brief series at that. More, any sociological action I may commit entails a resolution of these dilemmas, and there are in all only four (at least in the latest Parsonian version) (1967, ch. 7). On the one hand, each actor has just two dilemmas as to *how* he can orient to objects. First he can orient to an object *either* as a source of immediate gratification, *or* without seeking gratification from the object at all. Acute distinction, Parsons. Having overcome this dilemma, the second one is to orient *either* to only a *specific* aspect of the object, *or* to *diffuse*, multiple aspects of the object. A formal distinction of profundity and antiquity which has racked mankind from the start, this is the difficult distinction between the One and the Many. Having sorted out how to orient to objects, the actor then has to turn to the nature of the significance which is attributed to the objects themselves; and here again two dilemmas. Am I interested in what the object is (quality), *or* in what it does (performance)? And then, is the object of *universal* significance to anyone in society, or of significance only to a *particular* actor? These are the dilemmas which confront all actors at all times. Nobody can dispute that such formal distinctions can be made. Only Parsons affirms that they must be made and spends thousands of pages making them. As dilemmas, they pattern our orientations and the significances of objects at all times, so constituting an essential framework of sociological action.

However, before closing this section on the basic elements of Parsons's theory, I cannot leave it without pointing out a difficulty. Parsons gives his pattern variables (PVs) at least three different statuses within his theory. This theoretical inconsistency is present even at the surface of his writings. At one time, he says that the PVs are a part of culture, a component of culture, actually operating to regulate the actor's orientations.[18] Secondly, he says that PVs are the sociologist's way of describing the cultural regulation of actor's orientations, and as such form part of an empirical and testable theory of social action.[19] But thirdly, in his recent and 'headier' moments, he describes PVs as categories of social science,[20] that is, as the necessary structure for all social scientific theory, just as space, time, velocity, etc. are categories for all physical sciences. As such, they are beyond empirical tests or demonstration, and are purely analytical distinctions.

## Methodology

Parsons puts forward two basic methodological points. The first (he says) he takes from Weber and Kant: this is 'the empirical scheme of proof' (ESP). The second is more specifically his own: the position of 'analytical realism'.

18. 'They (the pattern variables) are inherently patterns of cultural orientation, but they become integrated both in personalities and in social systems' (1962, p. 76).

19. 'The pattern variables apply (*sic*) to the *normative* or ideal aspect of the structure of systems of action; they apply to one part of its culture. They are equally useful in the empirical description . . . of concrete action. . . . When they are used to characterize differences of empirical structure of personalities or social structures . . .' etc. etc. (1962, p. 76 again!).

20. 'The pattern variables . . . are . . . sets of categories, for classifying the components of action. They provide a frame of reference within which such a classification can be made. . . . These categories may be used analytically; they imply *theorems* – propositions that admit of logical, not empirical, proof' (1967, p. 194).

To deal with the ESP briefly (1957, pp. 148–9; 1949, pp. 610–24, 728–31), it contains three propositions.

1. A theory must be coherent, and its coherence has a formal proof, logical or mathematical. Coherence is not an empirical matter.

2. Empirical data must be defined in terms of basic, operationalizable, empirical observations – data must be defined with the means by which they can be observed.

3. There must be a logical relation between the theoretical terms and the statements concerning actual observations, such that the theory can be empirically validated.

Provided that such relations between theory and fact hold, then a theory is a scientific theory. Parsons does accept that there is a selection of facts in all social sciences, and that this selection is affected by the 'value relevance' of those facts to the sociologist. But, he says, there is a selection of facts based on the standpoint of the scientist and his interests in *all* sciences. (Again, it's interesting that Parsons sees the problem as one of selection and not production of facts.) Selection as such does not therefore mean unscientific selection. So, in principle, there is no epistemological difference between the selection of facts by the sociologist and by the natural scientist (1957, pp. 150–51).

*Analytical realism* (1962, pp. 50–51; esp. 1949, pp. 728–31). The position of analytical realism is that the analytical or logical distinctions (of the kind seen in the PVs) made by the theorist actually do exist in reality. They are not immediately apparent in the concrete phenomena. But analytical distinctions can be made which abstract certain elements as the theoretically important ones. There is therefore a relation between the analytical distinctions and *some* elements of the concrete phenomena. So this abstract or analytical reality does in fact exist, and is not a theoretical fiction. For Parsons, an analytical distinction is not an intellectual artefact which serves only as an heuristic device, like Weber's ideal type. But there is a systematic ambiguity here, which corresponds to Parsons's inconsistency over the PVs. Is the analytical distinction *made in* reality, in the phenomena, or only in Parsons's head? Does the abstraction as such exist in reality? Or does the analytical construct have correspondences with only certain elements in reality, elements which concretely are not separate or distinct from others? Or again, do the PVs exist *in* culture, or only in Parsons's head?[21]

21. This confusion is quite manifest in the following quotation; 'As opposed to the fiction view (Weber's ideal type) it is maintained here that at least some of the general concepts of science are not fictional but 'grasp' aspects of the objective

### Contradictions between methodology and theory, with a subscript on Parsons's sociology of knowledge

Being a sociologist whose relative inferiority to Weber and Durkheim seems inversely proportional to his influence, Parsons already partially manifests in his writings those contradictions which become fully clear when applying Parsons's own sociological theory to his methodological principles.

1. First contradiction. The vacillation with which he treats the status of his PVs is indicative of a central problem. Is he to treat his own mode of classifying orientations and significances, his PVs, as part of a culture system, say twentieth-century American culture, which hence regulates *his own* orientations as a sociologist? At a superficial glance, it might seem that he could do so, and that his sociological theory could be described as affectively neutral, and (not to be modest) as of universal significance to mankind, and so on. But this does not avoid the contradiction. The classification scheme, which claims to classify all cultural systems, cannot itself be only part of one particular cultural system. If he claims that his distinctions, being formal, are of universal validity, then they cannot be part of one particular cultural way of looking at human action. So, his own sociological classification scheme *must* lie *outside* culture. A classification scheme cannot be at the same time a universal classification scheme and one of the cultural systems defined by that classification scheme. The contradiction is therefore between the sociological theory (which would necessarily include the sociologist's theory in the cultural system) and the claims made for his own knowledge (which would seem necessarily to exclude his theory from the cultural system). One clear instance of this contradiction which is quite patent runs as follows. Parsons accepts that some moral or scientific concepts are classed as universalistic. But he says they are universalistic only within a given culture. The sociologist however must adopt a relativist position, seeing such universalism as belonging only to a particular culture (1962, p. 74). Apply this to Parsons. Are Parsons's PVs universalistic, or must one be relativistic and say that they belong to a particular culture? Or is relativism itself a cultural orientation which is universalistic only within a particular culture? He cannot escape *his own* contradiction.

external world. This is true of the concepts here called analytical elements. . . . The position here taken is, in an epistemological sense, realistic. . . . Concepts correspond not to concrete phenomena, but to elements in them that are analytically separable from other elements. . . . Hence it is necessary to qualify the term realism with 'analytical'. It is the possibility of making this qualification that renders the resort to fictionalism unnecessary' (1949, p. 730).

2. Second contradiction. Essentially the same contradiction applies to the ESP. Here Parsons explicitly states that he is giving universal rules for what is a valid empirical scientific theory (1967, p. 149). So again, the rules themselves, if they define the universal formal validity of all social science, cannot themselves be part of a specific cultural system. But then that means that the sociologist who applies these rules must have his 'action' regulated by rules lying outside culture. So where is the sociologist, inside or outside a cultural system?

*Subscript on Parsons's sociology of knowledge* (1967, ch. 5). In answer to this question, and as if to make open confession to being a bourgeois ideologist, Parsons quite explicitly defends the rupture between the production of theory and any form of practice. He does so by defending a particular place for the scientist in (or, more precisely, outside) society. As seen above, he says that the selection of facts on the basis of value relevance is inevitable. The result of this selection he calls a value science integrate (a complex which includes both values as selecting content, and science as the abstract rules which govern the form into which the content is put). The value science integrate is not ideology. Ideology comes in when the values in question are not universalistic to a society, but derive from a particular group's interests. This he calls secondary selection, and the result is ideology. Unfortunately (for Parsons) sociologists are not a self-supporting autonomous bunch of individuals. They have to have relations with other particular groups within society – via purse and other strings. This is so particularly when social scientists become involved with the practical activities of other particular groups – action which is significant for *the values* of those groups, of course. If the social scientist relates his theory too much to the practical needs of other groups, he comes under tremendous pressure for secondary selection. Political science (the theory) is in danger when it becomes connected with politicians' practice. Economics as theory is in danger when becoming too closely related to businessmen's practice. So, what's the solution? The sociologist – presumably in danger when becoming too closely related to *any* group in society – must keep away from practice of any kind. And this means keeping within the university. Fortunately (for Parsons) there are now institutions which specialize in the practical applications of theory. Such technological institutions act as 'buffer institutions', 'mitigating the pressures which impinge on the cultural community and which would otherwise constitute more seriously disturbing sources of strain (1967, p. 159). It is an arrant defence of the purest ivory-tower university. As such it points to a source of the contradictions described above. For it shows that the rupture between theory and practice is itself *an effect of a real division of labour* and not the effect of some theoretical or conceptual fault in the social scientist's mind. It is the effect of the rupture between those institutions which specialize in the production of knowledge about society and any practice in society, a rupture between university and society. The university must be as outside society as possible. The confusions over whether the products of Parsons's intellect lie inside culture or outside it, are the effect of a *real* divorce between the production of a theory of the object (society) and the production of the object of the theory.

## Phenomenology
### Theory[22]

Phenomenology is a typical example of a distinctively bourgeois radicalism that seems to have succeeded in luring many people on the left into a bourgeois position. This confusion of the left has been made worse and less excusable by the fact that, in its sociological applications, phenomenology has lost all that made it radical. The following account will deal first with the theoretical foundations of phenomenology, second with some of its direct applications to the social field, and third with bastardized, 'sociological', phenomenology. What makes phenomenology radical is that it gives principled grounds (a) for treating people's consciousness of (social or other) reality seriously; (b) for saying that it is man's consciousness that makes social reality and not social reality that makes man's consciousness; and therefore (c) for recuperating an alien social reality dominating man by affirming that social reality is a humanly experienced reality. The radical appeal is perhaps clear. These principled grounds have been developed most rigorously by Husserl and Merleau-Ponty. Their arguments differ markedly and I shall put forward only the bare skeleton of their respective positions.

Phenomenologists ask not the question of how the subject knows the object (an exclusively epistemological problematic); instead they ask how consciousness and the objects of consciousness coexist in such a way that makes the knowledge of objects possible (an ontological–epistemological problematic). This is already a radical approach, since,

22. For this section see principally the following: E. Husserl, *Ideas* (1967); E. Husserl, *Cartesian Meditations* (1960); E. Husserl, *Phenomenology and the Crisis of Philosophy* (1965); M. Merleau-Ponty, *The Phenomenology of Perception* (1965); A. Schutz, *Collected Papers* (1962); A Schutz, 'Phenomenology and the Social Sciences', in M. Farber (ed.), *Philosophical Essays in Memory of E. Husserl* (1968); P. L. Berger and T. Luckmann, *The Social Construction of Reality* (1967).

for example, if Parsons's ESP is a universal formal methodological rule, then there is a problem (posed directly by phenomenologists but, as we have seen, untheorized by Parsons himself) as to how and where this universal norm for knowledge *exists* – in culture, out of culture, or in an ivory tower university. In answering this problem phenomenologists put forward a variety of arguments to show that consciousness could not exist in the same manner as do the objects in the world, at least not as they appear to naïve consciousness or natural science. Look at a series of objects on a table. Now it seems as if those objects exist before I am conscious of them, and irrespective of whether I am conscious of them or not. If objects exist as they appear to exist irrespective and prior to our consciousness of them, then it would seem that they would have to be considered as a condition of our consciousness of them. But, the phenomenologists argue, things are not what they appear. In fact the mistake is to make those objects which are *only* objects as they appear to consciousness, the condition rather than the *product* of consciousness. We must be wrong in our natural or naïve attitude that experiences objects as pre-existing our consciousness of them. So, Husserl says, we must invert the relation between objects and consciousness as it appears to us in our naïve or 'natural attitude', and try to grasp the consciousness of objects as constitutive of the way objects appear to us. Suspending our natural attitude (what is called the phenomenological reduction) allows us to examine this 'consciousness of objects', while making absolutely no judgements as to whether those objects exist or not. You don't say that objects don't exist. You simply suspend your judgement, so that you can see how those 'objects of consciousness' are constituted through consciousness of them. You deal with your experience of yourself and objects to see how your reality is constituted through experience. This is what was meant by putting forward principled grounds for treating consciousness seriously, for saying that man's consciousness is not conditioned by an external and pre-existing social reality but constitutes it. All objects are nothing but objects of experience. The crucial point is that consciousness or experience is seen as absolutely originary – creating the world in which it lives. Radical phenomenology could not accept that there is a social reality which conditions the way in which we are conscious of it, a reality prior to, external to, and surrounding consciousness. Instead, the self, social reality, natural objects, are nothing but objects of experience, objects that are synthesized in and through the flow of consciousness. To treat consciousness as theoretically fundamental, consciousness must be seen as the creator of the world in which it lives.

Applying these principles to the social field, Husserl and Merleau-

Ponty are quite insistent that it is each living experience that constitutes his or her social reality. Husserl (1960, 5th meditation) suggests that other people are only syntheses of the ego's own consciousness. Interacting with what are only products of your own consciousness is only possible because you synthesize other people in the manner that you experience yourself. You posit other consciousnesses as consciousnesses like yourself. This is why Husserl calls his phenomenology of the social world an 'intersubjective monadology' – a social world of others each of which is experienced as absolute constitutive of his own social reality. Merleau-Ponty also sees the social world as a product of each person's experience. But unlike Husserl, he does not see the ego as the source of consciousness which creates a world of other egos in its own image. Instead he says that the ego is *also* the product of synthesis which occurs through the flow of experience. The experience of a self can be of a self as a part of a crowd, in which the self is not distinguished from any other self. The subject, or self is only a continually fluctuating entity ever being synthesized out of the flow of experience.[23] This flow of experience is absolutely consitutive of social reality. There are as many social realities as there are 'flows of experience'.

If phenomenology is radical, therefore, it would seem that there could be no sociology in any normal sense of the word, principally because one can no longer speak of any social reality. At most what is left to do is an examination of the modes of experience through which our consciousness of social reality is achieved. This approach does have a radical appeal however, precisely because it does reject 'normal' sociology, by rejecting any scientific approach to society. Normal sociology which *is* bourgeois claims to be scientific. Reject scientific sociology and you reject bourgeois sociology. But nothing could be more mistaken. As I shall hope to show, this line of 'reasoning' is profoundly regressive rather than revolutionary.

Turning now to the bastardized versions of phenomenology, these can scarcely be treated seriously as theory, since they so lack any principled position. Schutz, Berger and Luckmann present not only a theoretically inconsistent form of phenomenology, but one which has lost all its radical foundations, even though Berger and Luckmann use shockingly radical language – e.g. the word dialectic. At the same time they synthesize, or rather agglutinate the influences of such unfamiliar friends as Marx, Lukács,

23. 'I am given already situated and involved in a physical and soeial world – I am given to myself, which means that the situation is never hidden from me, it is never around me as an alien object, and I am never in fact enclosed in it. . . . My freedom (*sic*), the fundamental power (*sic*) which I enjoy of being the subject of my own experience, is not distinct from my insertion in the world' (Merleau-Ponty, 1965, p. 360).

Weber, Durkheim, Husserl, Schutz, Mannheim – which, naturally, is not to accuse them of being eclectic. These terrible triplets, Schutz, Berger and Luckmann, want basically to preserve the importance of consciousness while depriving themselves of all principled reasons for doing so. For, what they do is to say, with phenomenology, that all social reality is only experienced social reality. Then, they take these 'experiences of social reality' as the objects of their 'new' discipline. Finally, and this is the radical departure from all radical phenomenology, they re-insert 'experiences of social reality' back into a surrounding external environment of social reality (Schutz, 1962, vol. 3, p. 87) – to see 'experiences of social reality' in a social context. In so doing, they deprive 'experiences of social reality' of their radically originary or creative character, and so deprive themselves of all principled grounds for treating consciousness as fundamental. Their examination of 'experiences of social reality' in a context of social reality leads them to treat these experiences as things, as objects within that social reality, thus denying the very crux of the whole phenomenological position. The result is that in place of so many social realities as there are experiences of social reality there is now a social reality of so many experiences of social reality.

## Methodology

The phenomenological reduction suspends the natural attitude, suspends normal judgement in the existence or non-existence of the objects of consciousness, and only looks at 'consciousness of objects'. The phenomenologist then reflects on the modes in which consciousness synthesizes its objects through the flow of experience. What does this reflection entail? Basically, philosophical reflection as practised by genuine phenomenologists is an attempt to grasp the necessary, the *essential* modes of experiencing. The phenomenological reduction is in fact a systematic and explicit foundation for a pure method of reflection. As a result of suspending existential judgements about a reality beyond our consciousness of it, phenomenology excludes *all* methods of knowing consciousness *other* than that of consciousness reflecting on itself. Hence, its validity is that of the absolute self-evidence of its statements as founded in a rational discourse.

## Contradictions between theory and methodology

In phenomenological theory, consciousness is constitutive of the reality in which it lives. In its methodology, the phenomenologist founds a method of pure reflection, which does two things. First, for the theorist, it excludes all methods of knowing consciousness other than by reflection.

Hence it precludes itself from any transformation both of consciousness and of the objects of consciousness. The contradiction is patent. The theory claims that consciousness is in general constitutive of the reality in which it lives. So reflection upon or contemplation of consciousness can thus only lead to *an abstract knowledge* of that consciousness, a knowledge detached from any practice of producing or transforming, consciousness or experience. But consciousness is constitutive of the objects of consciousness *only when* all means of producing objects of consciousness other than purely experiencing them have been excluded. The contradiction is then between a theory which states that consciousness is alone constitutive of the objects of consciousness and a methodology which makes sure that consciousness can be known only as it is when all means of producing 'consciousness of objects' other than just being conscious of them have been excluded.

The regressive and ideological character of a knowledge produced by a knowledge disassociated in principle from any means of transforming its object, should also be clear. As a result of the phenomenological reduction, instead of seeing alien social objectivity as the cause of my subsequent consciousness of it, I now know that that social reality is only my false experience of an alien social objectivity. So, instead of seeing social reality as a world out there, I can now see it as a product of my own experience. I have reappropriated social reality for myself, certainly – in my consciousness. Alien social objectivity is looked at by phenomenologists *only* as a false consciousness.[24] This is the real significance of those phenomenological shrinks like R. D. Laing who take it upon themselves to change only false consciousnesses. Meanwhile, consciousness is wilfully disassociated from any means of transforming that reality *in* reality. Consciousness may change. Reality does not.

The ideological function of this 'radical' theory is equally founded on the same disassociation of a consciousness purified from any means of transforming consciousness or objects of consciousness. If phenomenology leaves experienced reality as it is, at the same time it leaves the experience of it in the same absolute position as before. The way we actually experience reality phenomenally excludes any practices of transforming that experience other than a kind of glorified consciousness reform.

As such, phenomenology only reproduces the central contradiction in bourgeois theory, present in Durkheim, Weber and Parsons, in which the subjectivity of experience is counterposed to an objective social world. Here too, the particular variant of this contradiction, in which the

24. See in particular Berger and Pullberg's article (1966), where they end up by seeing the whole problem of false consciousness almost as one of a loss of memory.

objective social world appears as some kind of an illusion is the product of a particular relation between theory and practice. For the method of producing a theory of consciousness is nothing but a method of reflection disconnected from any means of transforming consciousness or the objects of consciousness.

## The structure of the contradictions in bourgeois sociological theory

By way of summary, I think it would be worth just turning back to the original four theses and rereading them in the light of the accounts given of Durkheim, Weber, Parsons and phenomenology. But apart from that, I shall set out the structure of the variations in the contradictions of bourgeois social theory. Structure is in fact much too strong a word to describe these variations; the demonstration lacks the rigour which could permit me to talk of structure in any strict sense. None the less, it does seem to an extent that a change in the nature of the theory and methodology does seem to produce a *connected* change in the nature of the contradictions between the two.

Durkheim puts forward an almost positivist theory of knowledge. Social reality consists of facts like things imposing themselves on him. Social objectivity also causes individuals to experience the world in a certain and necessary way. Therefore we have an objective subjectivity, with society as the subject. If this theory applies to Durkeim himself, then his knowledge is not an objective knowledge of an external reality, but simply society causing itself to be experienced in a certain way, via Durkheim the sociologist. Weber puts forward a theory of understanding the significances of social action, and of making constructs, ideal types, of significant action: his own knowledge is equally subjective as the subjectivities he is examining; his sociology cannot claim to be a theory of value systems, therefore, without turning itself into just another value system. Parsons puts forward analytical categories for analysing cultures, as absolute logical framework; but if his categories are not considered only for their logical formality but are treated also as existing, they must exist somewhere, even if for Parsons that somewhere is as nowhere as possible: therefore his knowledge cannot be the universal form for sociological knowledge which he claims, but must be a particular cultural code. Finally phenomenology has a theory in which subjective experience is constitutive of its experienced reality. But the subjectivity of this experience is only ensured by a method which detaches experiencing the world from any other form of contact with it.

The abstract character of the knowledge similarly varies, while remaining equally abstract. Durkheim abstracts common features from objective facts. The result is the supposed universality of a lowest common denominator, the distinction between the sacred and the profane, which has no real existence outside Durkheim's head. Weber constructs ideal types which bear no stricter relation to reality than any utopia, as he virtually admits himself. Parsons sits in an ivory tower as remote as possible from anywhere, showing infinite skill and patience in making banal logical distinctions about whose relation to reality he can never quite make up his mind. Phenomenologists get lost (*sic*) in contemplation, producing endlessly recurring rational discourses on consciousness meditating about consciousness. The *ideological nature* of the knowledge is thus clear. *None of the above practices of producing knowledge bears any relation to any practice of producing the object of that knowledge*, that is, in the case of social science, *any relation to any practice of transforming and producing social reality*.

The *ideological function* of the knowledge is evident in that, in all cases, the reality is represented *either* as it directly appears, as with the *verstehen* method or the phenomenologists' reflection on phenomenal experience; *or* in terms of formal categories existing only in the sociologist's mind for interpreting, classifying or selecting facts from reality as it appears. It *cannot* be a theory of the production of that reality when the production of the theory is dissociated from the production of reality.

As such bourgeois sociological theory is an ideology. But as was seen explicitly with Parsons this ideology *is not just a false consciousness*. It is the effect of a *real* disassociation between theory and practice, a disassociation which has the following two critical aspects.

1. There is *a division of labour* between intellectual and all other forms of practice – the phenomenological philosopher in a state of pure contemplation, Parsons in his ivory tower. In the social sciences there is therefore an institutional dissociation between theory and practice which is the basis in reality for the production of ideology.

2. Then there is the actual *repression* of any link between the practice of theorizing and the practice of transforming the object of the theory, society. In particular the repression of the student movement in England is quite largely a repression of social science students, since by virtue of the real relation between their theory and practice, they are at the centre of the production of ideology. They are repressed precisely at the point where they attempt to establish a real relation between theory and a practice of transforming an aspect of the object of their theory, the university in society.

This critique has not been a critique of the ideological content of the bourgeois sociological theory. It has been a critique of the *conditions of production* of that ideology. So, to combat ideology is not just a question of changing people's consciousness or stripping them of their illusions. To combat ideology is to fight a political struggle both against this division of labour, and against this class repression, and so to attack the very conditions of production of ideology. Critiques of course content on their own are nothing. It is the relation of a university to society under capitalism that must be destroyed. To criticize ideologies once they have been produced would be an endlessly recurring task. To revolutionize the conditions of production of knowledge is alone the definitive struggle against bourgeois ideology.

## References

BERGER, P. L., and LUCKMANN, T. (1967), *The Social Construction of Reality*, Penguin.

BERGER, P. L., and PULLBERG (1966), 'Reification and the sociological critique of consciousness', *New Left Review*, no. 36.

BERNSTEIN, B. (1972), in M. Young (ed.) *Knowledge and Control*, Collier-Macmillan.

DURKHEIM, E. (1964a), *The Division of Labour in Society*, Free Press.

DURKHEIM, E. (1964b), *The Elementary Forms of Religious Life*, Allen & Unwin.

DURKHEIM, E. (1964c), *The Rules of Sociological Method*, Free Press.

DURKHEIM, E., and MAUSS, M. (1963), *Primitive Classification*, Cohen & West.

HUSSERL, E. (1960), *Cartesian Meditations*, Nijhoff.

HUSSERL E. (1965), *Phenomenology and the Crisis of Philosophy*, Harper & Row.

HUSSERL, E. (1967), *Ideas*, Allen & Unwin.

MARCUSE, H. (1965), 'Industrialization and capitalism', *New Left Review*, no. 30, pp. 3–17.

MARX, K. (1965), *Capital*, Moscow.

MARX, K., and ENGELS, F. (1968), *Selected Works*, Lawrence & Wishart.

MERLEAU-PONTY, M. (1965), *The Phenomenology of Perception*, Routledge & Kegan Paul.

PARSONS, T. (1949), *The Structure of Social Action*, Free Press.

PARSONS, T. (1962), *Toward a General Theory of Action*, Harper & Row.

PARSONS, T. (1967), *Sociological Theory and Modern Society*, Free Press.

SCHUTZ, A. (1962), *Collected Papers*, 3 vols. Nijhoff.

SCHUTZ, A. (1968), 'Phenomenology and the social sciences', in M. Farber (ed.), *Philosophical Essays in Memory of E. Husserl*, Greenwood.

WEBER, M. (1949), *Methodology of the Social Sciences*, Free Press.

WEBER, M. (1964), *The Theory of Economics and Social Organization*, Free Press.

WEBER, M. (1966), *The Sociology of Religion*, Methuen.

WEBER, M. (1970), *The Protestant Ethic and the Spirit of Capitalism*, Unwin University Books.

Part Three
## Critiques of Ideologies

# 'The Philosophy of Education'
# or The Wisdom and Wit of R. S. Peters[1]
## David Adelstein

Richard Stanley Peters is the founding father of a new discipline called 'the philosophy of education' (Peters and Hirst, 1970, p. 14). His writings, and those of his followers too, appear centrally upon the syllabus of virtually every education course for teachers in England. It is therefore necessary to confront this new discipline seriously.

At the outset, we are indebted to Ernest Gellner's study, *Words and Things*, which examines the underlying presuppositions of what Gellner calls 'linguistic analysis', a philosophical method of which Peters is a typical representative. The definitive characteristic of the method, despite many other differences amongst its practitioners, is that it engages in what it calls 'conceptual analysis'. It is because the new 'philosophy of education' takes this procedure as its starting point that it is subject to Gellner's critique. *Words and Things* consist of a rigorous demolition of this brand of philosophy. Gellner sums up his attack in the thesis that:

There is a set of philosophers who positively glory in proving by arguments (whose logic is not in general so superior to that employed earlier for the opposite purpose) that philosophy has no guidance whatsoever to offer (although inconsistently they also show, or think they do, that there can be no philosophic reasons for revising our concepts and hence, incidently, our values). A future social historian may well speculate whether we have here a class of people already convinced of the unimportance of their thought and endeavour, embracing a philosophy which provides them with a seeming justification of their feeling. Their hostility to ideas – which presumes new and general ideas to be 'paradoxes' and all 'paradoxes' to be confusions – is perhaps intelligible on similar lines, and also in terms of the particular educational institutions in which linguistic philosophy flourishes (Gellner, 1968, p. 276).

The linguistic philosophers have offered no rebuttal or response to the charge in *Words and Things*. It seems that their very premises preclude the possibility of any reply – if the charge that paradox is to be explained away is a correct characterization of the school then no major dispute such as this can arise within their terms of reference. All that could happen is that the apparent disagreements be shown not to really exist. The power

1. First published May 1971 by the Students Union of the London University Institute of Education, with whose permission it is now republished.

of Gellner's assault, however, is so great that this too has proved impossible.

Paraphrasing, and extending Gellner's critique, the following criticisms of Peters's work will be made:

1. That he uses 'philosophy' both to attack 'value systems' and at the same time to support present, socially dominant, values.
2. That he is immune to new ideas and social theory.
3. That his system of thought provides a justification for this immunity.
4. That his philosophy acts to conceal all real contradictions in a verbal whitewash.
5. That this function of 'philosophy' is only understandable in the context of the educational system in which it operates. It provides a technique for confirming the traditional role of teachers in the face of criticism and conflict, that is to say, it gives ideological reassurance.

It is, of course, not the explicit intention of the 'philosophy of education' to defend the position attacked above. Its exponents do not see it in that way at all. What the present criticisms do, is to assert that the stated positions of the school are in contradiction with its actual effects. More precisely, it will be argued that the Peters brand of philosophy protects itself from criticism by not making its premises explicit. The reader of Peters undergoes a strange experience in the course of his study – he is never quite sure what is going on. He is told that philosophy is a 'second-order activity' for the purpose of 'conceptual clarification', but what exactly this means is never stated but is left to the experience of the reading. For this reason, it is necessary for us, at the start, to examine his actual methodology. It will be seen that in the very procedures of 'conceptual clarification' lies the mystificatory power of this new philosophy.

## Methodology

Philosophy, according to Peters, has undergone a revolution in the twentieth century. No longer do philosophers consider grand problems of knowledge and being, but they are likely to be 'embarrassed' by them. In fact 'one of their main occupations has been to lay bare such aristocratic pronouncements' (Peters, 1966, p. 15). We are told that this is not, however, a newly acquired role, 'Socrates, Kant and Aristotle did much the same.' Modestly Peters says, 'what is new is an increased awareness of the nature of the enterprise'.

That Socrates, Kant and Aristotle, and all other significant philosophers in history, did, in fact, tackle the larger questions which today appear to 'embarrass' philosophy, is not accounted for; how these figures could lay bare 'aristocratic pronouncements' and at the same time formulate them, is not explained. It is being said that the new philosophy consists both of a return to the tasks of the great philosophers and of a revolution in these tasks. *The Revolution in Philosophy* edited by Gilbert Ryle is frequently cited to support the contention. It is never made clear though, how philosophy can be simultaneously a revolution in, and a continuation of, a tradition. Let us stick with the new tasks, however, and see the means by which 'aristocratic pronouncements' are to be 'laid bare'.

The new philosophy aspires to be only a 'second-order' discipline. This means that it does not confront substantive disciplines on their own ground, but rather it accepts them (science, art, etc.) as going concerns and seeks to merely 'analyse their concepts'. Philosophy is now a passive discipline in relation to knowledge; it would not wish to intervene, to synthesize, but only to analyse concepts, to philosophize about concepts.

How then, in the Peters scheme, is a concept to be analysed? First, a concept is analysed by looking at the way it is used in language, by trying to suggest, what Gellner calls, its 'paradigmatic usage'. Secondly, the 'paradigmatic usage' is highlighted by contrasting the use of the concept with the way in which other concepts are used. What the concept is, is worked out by consideration of what it might normally be thought to be, which, in turn, is elucidated in the light of what it is not. The latent assumption behind the procedure is that the more one says what a concept is *not* the more one knows what it *is*. The vital question of whose 'normal' usage of a concept is being suggested, and of whether this usage corresponds to reality, is never posed. That people, dare we say, social classes, might have different, unshared usages and meanings, seems never to have occurred to our analysts. The blithe assumption that all concepts are shared and are correct, that we all basically agree, enables the imposition of unshared and incorrect concepts upon any opponent. Later we will show that this assumption, never validated, of shared usage and experience, of basic consensus, constitutes the core of the ideology of the new philosophy and generates its basic power to confuse, its 'usage' in blurring real conflicts.

What, are we told, is the point of conceptual analysis? 'Our understanding of what it is to have a concept covers both the experience of grasping a principle *and* the ability to discriminate and use words correctly' (Peters and Hirst, 1970, p. 4). It is important to note here that it is not suggested that the principle behind the concept is to be articulated. On the contrary, it is to be 'experienced' alongside the 'ability to discriminate and use words correctly'. The new philosophy puts much emphasis upon philosophy as an 'activity' which must be learnt and understood as such; it is not considered as the explication of the principles through language, but rather the experiencing of them in action *in* language. For this reason philosophy does not generate any clear propositions; it consists, instead, of verbal activity on the assumption that this of itself, and only this, can reveal the principles behind concepts. These principles are not to be clearly stated but are to be suggested or insinuated through examples of their usage.

Underlying this methodology is the belief that the principles are already present in 'ordinary' language, and that through the analysis of ordinary language these principles can be understood. It takes certain words and assumes that, in their everyday usage, exist all the relevant concepts. It therefore excludes the possibility of new concepts being born which are not already inscribed in ordinary language. It believes 'we already know too much about human behaviour, albeit in a rather uncoordinated manner. Common sense, which is incorporated in the concepts of ordinary language, has creamed off most of the vital distinctions' (Peters, 1958, p. 155). It is this aspect of the philosophy which allows it, as will be shown at a later point, to reduce and 'analyse' out of existence any new theories which provide concepts that are critical of 'ordinary' concepts.

Now linguistic philosophy takes its starting point from the *Philosophical Investigations* of Wittgenstein, but it does not necessarily accept any of Wittgenstein's conclusions. The school institutionalizes the methodology of conceptual analysis without accepting its tenets in any particular case. In common with many other linguistic analysts, Peters is, therefore, an eternal eclectic, which is another way of saying that the possibility, in fact frequency, of self-contradiction does not dismay him. To be able to detect contradiction is to extract clear principles, to generalize, to say that the principle behind one statement contradicts the principle behind another. But this is a procedure to which Peters has strong resistance. His approach consists not in the *formulation* of principles, but rather in *evoking* them; he does not spell them out but insinuates them, usually in the form of a truism. When he remarks that 'one thing we know about machines is that mentality is not one of their attributes', the triumph behind the statement *implies* that something more is being said.

A sense of depth in platitude pervades Peters's literary style. We can compare it with the style of the long tradition of writers analysed by Raymond Williams in *Culture and Society*. These writers and thinkers, unable to propose explicitly their new ideas and criticisms, developed their literary powers to suggest and evoke them. They were, as Williams shows, actually trying to say something concrete, to generalize and relate ideas about society. The work of Peters, on the other hand, is merely the pretence of saying something positive, a charade masked in the recitation of truism; it is a feeble caricature of the lineage he quotes in his defence.

The unwillingness to generalize explicitly and to specify contradictions between concepts contains an in-built resistance against criticism. Because very little is said, because most is insinuated, it becomes necessary to read between the lines in order to point out the contradictions, as this discussion is attempting to do. It is necessary to say what has not been said, and thereby to open the critic to the charge that what is being criticized is not the actual position of the philosopher, that he never said what the charges suggest. No student can have entered a criticism in a philosophy of education seminar without being told this. In this way, within its own terms, Peters's philosophy is allowed unlimited scope for eclecticism. It does not recognize its eclectism because it does not specify its premises and thus does not perceive its inconsistency. This enables him to embrace any idea, any fact, any thinker, without fear of self-contradiction – and he does. At one point, in the space of four pages, Peters cites no fewer than Locke, Berkeley, Hume, Plato, Aristotle, Socrates, Descartes, St Augustine, Kant, Piaget, Hegel, Marx and Liebniez in discussing the platitudinous proposition that people do not 'develop as deposits out of an atomic individual experience' (Peters, 1966, pp. 47–50).

If Peters's contentions are not to be made explicit how are they to be conveyed? 'One of the cardinal points in philosophic method is to show points by means of example' (Hirst and Peters, 1970, p. 2). Let us examine an example of a Peters example. In analysing the concept of society why not begin by distinguishing men from birds? The unstated assumption here is that there must be something obvious in the way in which birds live, which, when contrasted against the way humans live, will yield insight into the latter. Now, there are many ways in which man distinguishes himself from bird, most notably that man lives in society and bird does not. We can thus reach the disturbing reminder that 'the way in which a man lives in a society is quite different from the way in which a woodpecker lives in a tree' (Peters and Benn, 1959, p. 13).

The belief that, by making a contrast between the concept under discussion and another, chosen, it appears, at random, for no principle is given by which 'bird' is selected to contrast with 'man', is a central implicit methodological tenet of Peters's philosophy. That he never validates the choice of contrast does not prevent his work consisting of its dogged application; that it results in incredible banality seems neither here nor there.

The aversion to explicit generalization is itself a particular generalization – it is a generalization that generalizations cannot be made. And, because generalizations cannot be made, any point of view can be held alongside any other. This then is the ideological advantage contained in his reliance on examples – all points of view can be embraced at one time.

When contradiction is pointed out, it is very easy for our philosopher to say that different concepts are being used and that the contradiction is merely due to conceptual confusion. He can do this by refusing to generalize from *his* use of a concept to any other, by refusing to relate one concept to another. By citing a contextual usage, 'conceptual analysis' appears to oppose the abstracting and isolating of concepts, whilst, in fact, its particularizing of each usage constitutes an effective atomization of each concept. Under the guise of generalizing, seeing each concept in its context generalization is actually being exorcized, for each context is shown to be different. By differentiating between each and every context, our analyst refuses to relate concepts to each other, and at the same time he manages to embrace them all. In this way, the language used to describe any real situation of conflict can be manipulated in order to make it seem as though the conflict were imaginary, whilst what is truly imaginary are the 'concepts' which our philosopher is wielding.

Going beyond Gellner, we can situate this mode of philosophy in its exact ideological context by examining its avoidance of the idea of contradiction. That the real social world is one in which classes and segments of classes, that is real social generalities, engage in contradictory, and therefore often conflicting, activity, is ignored by our philosophers. Instead of seeking solutions to conflict in the critical activity of ending the conditions which give rise to the conflict, a task which requires new knowledge and action, the philosophers would insist that the conflict was due to conceptual confusions and that, if only those involved would apply a bit of conceptual analysis, they would realize that there was no contradiction after all.

In this way the philosophy would deny reality. It thus constitutes an ideological technique for the removal of the real world, a specialism for mystification. The man well trained in 'conceptual analysis' has at his disposal a ready method for hair-splitting, side-tracking and confusing. As soon as the victim says anything, under the pretext of 'clarification', he is led down an endless tunnel of instances in which the philosopher would use different words in different circumstances. And should our victim be trying to say something new, something which the philosopher might not already understand, should the victim offer concepts which are not to be found in 'ordinary' usage, they will immediately be reduced to the philosopher's already given concepts. The technique automatically preempts any new knowledge and theories about society and thus excludes the need for critical action.

The belief that something really is what 'normal' usage holds it to be. is the unstated, unsupported assumption behind 'conceptual analysis'. The implication that there is something valid in enunciating conventional usage, that insight is gained by so doing, is the foundation of the 'new' philosophy. To clarify the use of a word or concept when it may be misunderstood, is, of course, an important task. But the unsolicited clarification of the use of words when there is no suggestion of their being misunderstood, the derivation of what is obvious and understood from the outset, announces the staggering boredom of the 'philosophy of education'.

## Epistemology

What justification are we given for this extraordinary drudgery? 'Conceptual analysis', it is claimed, is a necessary preliminary to the asking of further questions. In this case 'conceptual analysis' and 'further questions' appear as two complementary, but discrete, areas of inquiry. But what is the relationship between the two and how do they affect each other? When do we know that we have undergone enough 'conceptual analysis' and that, say, scientific analysis is ready to begin? Does not 'conceptual analysis' limit the possibilities of scientific analysis, and upon what grounds does it do this? It seems implied that conceptual analysis provides the *form* and scientific analysis, in this case, the *content*. But even the most cursory knowledge of the history of science indicates immediately that scientific knowledge always proceeds simultaneously in form and content, that the categories of thought and the objects to which they apply are always totally connected, that each new theory inevitably asserts its own right to exist against what was previously thought.

Here again, we face a problem which is never answered because it is never posed directly: what is the relationship between knowledge and the categories within which knowledge is cognized? What is the relationship between what is known and the means by which it is known? Previously this had always been a seminal problem for philosophy. Would we not expect the new philosophy to indicate under which criteria of knowledge and relation to reality it is working? But no. Now such problems are considered to be 'metaphysical' traps. The most to be specified is that philosophy is a 'second-order' discipline, the meaning of which will only be explained through example. Instead of confronting these problems critically, linguistic philosophy assumes from the start that they cannot possibly exist. Should anyone raise them the question will be depicted as a 'metaphysical' pitfall and conceptual analysis will come forth to demonstrate that there is not really a problem after all (Hirst, 1965). Without any further guidance on these questions it becomes necessary for us to analyse the 'analysis' of 'concepts' to see what is implicit in the relation between 'first-order' and 'second-order' procedures and to see what view of reality and the world lies beneath these procedures.

More precisely, we must ask whether it is assumed that reality conforms to the concepts which are being analysed. When it is said (which it is) that education involves voluntary participation by those being educated is it supposed that this is actually the case in our institutions of education? If the answer is 'yes' the entire question is presumed answered without any grounds whatsoever being given. 'Yes' implies that an extremely contentious theory, that reality conforms to the usage of everyday speech, is proposed and accepted without a shred of evidence. If the answer is 'no' then the crucial question of what the reality is, of whether education really is voluntary, is ignored. There might, of course, be an intermediate position of weak relationship, yet still, without its specification, nothing can possibly be understood. In practice, because this question is not put, both alternatives are used without regard to their total opposition. Where it is noticed that the analysis of a concept has patently little to do with reality it can be said that no claim was made that the real situation should be designated by the concept. Alternatively, so long as the discrepancy between reality and the concept is not immediately noticeable, it can be pretended that the usage is the reality. The pretence is inscribed in the whole discussion: without making clear whether 'education', for example, is the concept or the actuality all options are left open.

This ambiguity is built into the whole framework of the philosophy. It is said that conceptual analysis is only useful if further questions are to be asked. It is, though, a necessary preliminary to the asking of further questions. What then is the relationship between conceptual analysis and the asking of further questions? Are they as distinct as they seem? Not entirely, because 'in the process of trying to make explicit the principles which underlie our use of words we should have become clearer both about how things are and about the sort of decisions that have to be faced in dealing with them' (Peters and Hirst, 1970, p. 10). So, the way things are, given reality, does in fact outline itself in 'conceptual analysis'. 'By determining which cases are central (to the use of a word) we come to learn a lot more, not just about words, but about the structure of our social life and the assumptions that underlie it' (Peters and Hirst, 1970, p. 11). Thus, in the guise of a necessary preliminary clarification of concepts, we are in fact about to perceive the real nature of social life; in the course of a supposedly neutral demarcation of categories we are in fact presented with a wholly unneutral picture of the world.

There is here another indication of the vacuous formality of this mode of philosophy. The interesting and significant problems of the relationship between categories of thought, the 'concepts', and the real situation, of whether our ideas fit reality, are avoided. The discussion of the concepts takes place without any attempt to relate them to existing conditions.

Nothing new, exciting, substantive or interesting is achieved or even attempted – a commitment to triviality dominates the work.

Peters considers himself to be a Kantian in epistemological matters, though he has never explained what he understands this to be. His methodology, in epistemological terms, consists of a crude and contradictory coexistence of empiricism (the view that knowledge through sense data is a reflection of material reality) and idealism (the view that knowledge is a product of ideal, non-material reality). Now, linguistic philosophers claim to have overcome this problem and all such epistemological problems which have troubled philosophers in the past. They avoid all these problems by assuming them not to exist, by regarding them as false problems, as traps to be avoided. But to solve a problem by ignoring it, is the most uncritical, retreatist way imaginable, a way which in fact plunges head-over-heels into the very trap supposedly avoided. Linguistic philosophers claim to have abolished metaphysics (false problems) from philosophy; in fact they have reintroduced the crudest form of metaphysical contradiction, a metaphysic of no metaphysics. By ignoring the 'metaphysical' problems of empiricism and idealism and the contradictions between the two, they attempt to gain the best of both worlds at the cost of any consistency. The procedure of analysing language can assume either that language reflects reality or that reality is a reflection of language. Its methodology is therefore both empirical in its collection and assessment of relevant data, yet idealist in its ready acceptance of the categories in which data is received. Thoroughgoing empiricism has the contradiction that its theory of knowledge (that all knowledge is a sensory reflection of material reality) cannot itself be validated under its own criteria. And idealism bears the contradiction that within its theory of knowledge (that all reality is a reflection of idea) any theory can be embraced and no criteria for the resolution of differing theories can be posed. In this way, because no 'metaphysical' guidelines are acknowledged, because any 'knowledge' is accepted as legitimate, Peters's empirical propositions are not subject to empirical refutation, and his idealist propositions are unapproachable, uncriticizable. The work is empiricist because it rejects *a priori* reasoning; it is idealist because it accepts, *a priori*, any, empirical or non-empirical, category.

This hidden epistemological eclecticism is blatantly ideological. It does not stipulate its premises and its grounds for knowledge and therefore for action, and can thus rationalize any of its own actions and combat any opposing action without fear of self-negation in either case. It is magnificently pliable and pragmatic; it can deal with any situation. It defends only the *status quo* because it takes the *status quo* as its starting point, as its terms of reference.

## Distortion of social theory

We will now see how the fundamental epistemological eclecticism allows Peters to criticize any social theory without taking the theory's own propositions about itself seriously. It enables him to discuss a theory as though from the same premises, but in fact from different ones. He is able both to accept any theory *in toto* on one level and to reject it *in toto* on another level. In other words, any theory is correct, but where it appears to conflict with another the conflict is sidestepped by saying that the two theories are dealing with different questions. No two theories can contradict each other, it is said, because no two apparently contradictory theories deal with the same question.

His thesis is that 'different and logically appropriate theories should be developed to answer different sorts of questions rather than all-inclusive theories to answer all of them' (Peters ,1958, p. 154). From this position any explanation becomes permissible because it can be said to be answering only its own question. It turns out, when we analyse the way in which people speak and give explanations of behaviour, that there are four 'logically distinct' types of explanation. For the ignoramus who was under the impression that there were thirty-seven different types of explanation, the first chapter of Peters's *The Concept of Motivation* shows, by analysing language usage, that there are really only four. So it becomes a job of deciding which types of explanation are appropriate, and in which cases, a job of putting each theorist in his place as defined by Peters.

We find, for instance, that the unconscious in Freud is only applicable in cases which are 'deviations from prescribed patterns and goal seeking' (Peters, 1958, p. 149). Now, Freud certainly did not intend the unconscious to explain all behaviour, but this does not mean that it applied only to cases which deviate from the norm. Peters twists Freud's distinction between conscious and unconscious mental activity so that it is identical with the distinction between normal and abnormal activity. According to Peters, we can then see which actions are explicable in terms of unconscious mentality and which are not: 'some actions have such obvious and acceptable reasons that reference to unconscious wishes seems grotesquely out of place' (Peters, 1958, p. 61). In other words, only when an action is not obvious or acceptable will unconscious explanations be sought, when, for example, 'we ask what *made* Jones eat his hat'. No rule is given for knowing when to ask the purposive question and when to ask the non-purposive question. The question never answered is *who* decides whether the action is obvious and acceptable and *how* it is decided.

Freud himself, did not make the equation of consciousness with 'normality' and unconsciousness with 'abnormality'. He explicitly ascribed unconscious mentality to every person including the most 'normal'. But Peters is 'not here concerned with the truth of Freud's speculations – only with the sort of speculations they are' (Peters, 1958, p. 83). He therefore attempts to put Freud's categories into his, Peters's, categories. He refutes the pleasure principle with a couple of 'obvious' examples, assuming that he has actually understood the meaning and relations of Freud's concepts. If he had understood them, though, he would not employ 'common sense' against the new concepts because 'common sense' embodies the old concepts. By separating the form from the content, the 'truth' from the 'type of truth', he is able to distort the implications of the theory. Instead of confronting the theory directly, instead of agreeing or disagreeing, the issue is evaded by relegating the theory to a place of peripheral importance, to the 'deviant' case; it is encased in a box made by Peters. That this is inconsistent with the theory itself is overlooked; that it involves accepting the theory in terms of which it does not seek acceptance, is ignored.

Marx is discussed a little more openly, much more misleadingly. He is commended for his awareness of 'the social dimension of the development of mind' (Peters, 1966, p. 49), though, on the other hand, he did go a bit too far in 'ignoring the importance of individual centres of experience'. The consistency of Marx's view is not examined; what we want is just the right mix of the two extremes arrived at through philosophical arbitration. We are told: 'The vision of a classless society, in which true fraternity will be possible, is the fabricated hope which provides the dynamic of Marxism' (Peters, 1966, p. 219). We are not told why this is so. Perhaps it is because: 'Marxists are committed to the doctrine that major social changes are brought about by changes in technology and that ideas are comparatively impotent save in so far as they are reflections of the underlying reality of economic change' (Peters, 1966, p. 219). As nowhere can Marx possibly be interpreted as having derived social change from technology we can only surmise that Peters's stunning refutation rests upon his never having read Marx.

The rejection of both Marx and Freud relies upon Peters's interpretation of *their* terms in *his* way. On one occasion he tells us that Marx was a determinist with classical seventeenth-century ideas of causality. Marx, however, coming from an entirely different philosophical background, specifically distinguished himself from classical determinism: 'The materialist doctrine that men are products of circumstances and upbringing, and that, therefore, changed men are the products of other circumstances and changed upbringing, forgets that it is men themselves who change circumstances' (*Theses on Feuerbach*). In a typically philistine fashion Peters attempts to negate Marx by arrogantly assuming that his concepts and relations are the same as those of Marx. Not only are Marx and Freud so distorted; they are even blamed for encouraging social disquiet because their theories 'justify or excuse, their (people's) failure to take responsibility for their own lives by an appeal to causes' (Peters, 1963, p. 55). If not for Marx the working class would not tend to mistake its station in life, to discard its 'responsibility' to labour for others; if not for Freud people 'would responsibly' repress their sexuality in order to preserve the bourgeois family. There is a truth in these fears expressed by Peters, but in an inverted form. Both Marx and Freud have assisted revolutionary activity with their theoretical writings but, unless magical powers are being seen in them, they could hardly have caused the real conditions which give rise to revolutionary activity.

Behind Peters's insistently polymorphic, anything-goes, philosophy, beneath his treatment of Freud and Marx, is a particular notion about the nature of social existence. It is that human action is basically 'purposive' and that these purposes are 'irreducible' (Peters, 1958, p. 150). Society consists of people pursuing certain goals within a framework of rules. According to Peters, explanations of human behaviour, except in very special circumstances, must be given in terms of the purpose of the behaviour – the conscious reason the actor provides for what he does. At a later stage we will be told the exact opposite: that we cannot really say what are the purposes of doing things. For the time being though, this notion of explanation assumes that the reason a person says he doing something, the actor's own consciousness, is in fact, the true consciousness. Peters fails, as usual, to provide criteria for deciding whether a given rationality is correct and assumes that any 'obvious' rationale is 'acceptable'. His view implies, for example, that when the US government states that it is fighting in Vietnam to defend freedom and democracy, that this is so. The example shows that his type of explanation fails where it is most needed: when those in conflict provide contrary reasons for their behaviour.

In the guise of rationality, here is a view which is profoundly anti-rational. The supposed rationality of the actor obscures the irrationality of the criteria with which the actor's rationality might be assessed. It is implied that it is obvious when we can and when we cannot accept the actor's rationality. But it is precisely because the grounds upon which to base this 'obvious' are never stated, that the outlook is fundamentally non-rational.

We can begin to discern in this non-rationality a particular stance, a blockage, against social theory. The conviction that adequate explanation lies essentially in understanding purposes behind behaviour, the actor's own meaning, is, in fact, another way of saying that behaviour requires no explanation, that it is fundamentally self-explanatory. To state the purposes of an action is usually unnecessary because the actions speak their purposes in themselves. The 'theory' therefore implies that no theory is necessary. It says that human behaviour is obvious in itself and that we must accept actions at face value. It promotes the 'obviousness' of everything, the common-sense world that requires no further illumination than what it itself thinks about itself. Marx's maxim of theoretical understanding that, just as a man is not judged by what he himself thinks of himself, so no period of history nor any social behaviour is to be judged by what it thinks of itself, by its own consciousness, finds its opposite in Peters: he would judge social behaviour only in terms of its own consciousness. He would therefore wish to preempt any recognition of social theory by refusing to contemplate anything deeper than the surface reality. The task of anthropology and sociology becomes merely to fill in the content (Peters, 1958, p. 156).

It is precisely in this respect that the revolutionary sciences of Marx and Freud are relevant. Marx's analysis of the mode of production shows how the consciousness of the actual agents in that process is not usually the correct consciousness of what is going on. *New knowledge* is therefore necessary in order to understand, and, by changing the conditions of the conflict, end it. This is what Marx's science begins to do. Similarly, in understanding psychological conflict, Freud's specification of unconscious mental activity, by making the unconscious conscious, begins the task of abolishing the conditions of this conflict. Peters presents the world as uncomplicated and rosy, with only the deviant in need of correction. That the whole social structure is weird, mad, exploitative and begging for understanding and change is beyond his philosophy. 'Psychology', he says, and presumably he means sociology too, 'has not soared into its Galilean period . . . because the highly general theories, which, it was hoped, would emerge, are *logically* impossible' (Peters, 1958, p. 156). This view places Peters on a par with the ecclesiastics who resisted Galileo's theory on the grounds of 'logical' impossibility.

By challenging even the feasibility of social theory, the 'new' role which philosophy has chosen for itself becomes discernible. The 'old' philosophy, as total visions of being and knowledge, has, in the course of history, peeled off into particular layers of scientific thought. Natural science was the first to go; political economy and Marxism brought the beginnings of social science, which was followed by psychology, especially Freud, so that there is now no area which is not subject to the potential of scientific inquiry. Meanwhile, back in English universities, professional philosophers, hitherto oblivious towards social thought, are suddenly faced with the problem of their own self-justification. As they already occupy posts in philosophy departments, what grounds can they give to convince us that theirs is a necessary and independent discipline? With all of philosophy's traditional concerns becoming subjects of scientific inquiry, what can philosophy now claim to be its subject? The answer to these questions is posed in them: deny the possibility of social science, or, at any rate, deny its ability to create its own concepts; relegate social science to the surrogate status of concern with only exceptional, deviant cases. Philosophy is what it has always been – different from everything else, only now, since the 'revolution', it is more different from everything else and therefore more what it has always been. In this way, philosophy, as a 'second-order' discipline, is defined as different from any other discipline and thus no other discipline or method of inquiry can challenge its status. Once it is so conceived, as unchallengeable, it is indeed impregnable within its own terms.

We must remember the history of the various disciplines which are taught under the broad subject of education. In England the syllabuses consisted initially of crude, usually associationist, psychology which itself was traditionally a branch of the 'old' philosophy. Then, with continental influences, the scope of this psychology gradually widened. After the Second World War, sociology departments arose in most of the universities and the sociology of education became an important subject. At the same time many historians, with more sociological outlooks, began to study the history of education.

These developments contained contradictory implications: on the one hand they aroused suspicions that official pictures of the nature of education were not exactly the reality – Freudian psychology and progressive education suggested hitherto unfamiliar areas of oppression of children and pupils; sociological studies showed the functions of the education system in maintaining class relationships; historical studies showed how unidealistic and reactionary were many of the intentions behind the inception of different aspects of the educational system (Simon, 1963). On the other hand, because their studies do not take place within a political context, they tend to leave those to whom they are addressed somewhat in the air. It is very difficult for a teacher to know how to respond actively to the results of such studies.

This is another indication of the way in which the education system is laden with contradictions, which any authentically scientific study threatens to reveal. So here we have a social activity, education, crying out for objective analysis yet resisting it because of the potentially explosive consequences. What nicer coincidence than to fill this hollow with another, already hollow, self-styled 'philosophy of education'? There is an overriding sense in the writing of Peters, of an elaborate academic defence of the *status quo*; it is not surprising, therefore, that the ideology of the 'new' philosophy comes in very useful in the sphere of education.

## The ideology of education

Built into the philosophy that has been described above is a particular view about the nature of society and the meaning of education. The suppositions about philosophy itself can be transposed to yield suppositions about social reality, in this case about education. This is what Peters does. From his view of the purposefulness of social being he derives a concept of the purposefulness of education, its essential 'worthwhileness', which in turn derives from its encapsulating the social traditions of 'public modes of experience'. The pupil in this schema is someone who is 'initiated' into the 'public mode of experience'; the teacher is the initiator, from which accrues his 'necessary authority'. Language and forms of knowledge are the carriers of the public mode of experience.

The first thing to note about this structure of concepts is that it is sociologistic; it locates social reality outside the individuals who make up the society. The social resides in 'impersonal content and procedures which are enshrined in public traditions' (Peters, 1964, p. 35). It foists social reality above and beyond its members, in other words, it reifies the social. The social becomes something which individuals are not born into, but into which they must gain entry. The structure of social relations is not seen as being produced in each individual through the relations of production and the means of production, but is determined from somewhere outside. The crucial question then becomes: who mans the gates to the kingdom of public traditions? Never clearly stated, the answer that can be inferred is, we intend to show: the self-appointed guardians, the spokesmen of the traditional ruling institutions.

Supporting the sanctity of public traditions is a particular view of history – a monolithic march of civilization which finds its highest form in the ruling institutions of today (Hirst, 1965, Peters, 1964). The test of time has given us the solid institutions we know and these should not be tampered with. (Even if crumbling around us?) This view of history again places the 'social' outside its members; it reifies 'tradition' into something autonomous, forgetting that each member of each generation of each class has to *actively* reproduce the conditions of a tradition if it is to survive. The reification of tradition s blank idealism, it is blind to the real nature of history, its contradictory and revolutionizing paths; it refuses to see that the reputedly highest forms of public tradition, of culture and civilization, can contain within them the highest forms of barbarism, a most stark example of which would be Nazi Germany.

Peters's sociologism resembles two different traditions: on the one hand, the anti-individualistic current in nineteenth and twentieth-century social and educational thinkers such as Burke, Coleridge, Arnold and Newman, and on the other hand, European sociology, especially that of Weber and Durkheim. It constitutes, however, not a synthesis, but a syncretism, a formal and feeble imitation of both traditions. We do not find the stylistic brilliance and vigour of his English ancestors, nor their suggestiveness, nor imagination, but merely the incantation of platitudes containing supposed depth. In common with Weber, Peters uses the concept of authority and the notion of purposeful behaviour, of *verstehen* (understanding the actor's own ends) for the explanation of behaviour. But nowhere do we find the vast sociological material which Weber employed to substantiate his ideas. In common with Durkheim is the notion of the social as 'external and coercive' upon the individual, but, once more, we are not given the finely conceived relations between the social and the empirical with which Durkheim supported his ideas. Search as we may through volumes of Peters to find what exactly the 'public mode of experience' is made of, we get no nearer than remarks like: 'It is largely a matter of the company which people keep, from which they pick up their mode of experience' (Peters and Hirst, 1970, p. 31). His philosophy is a shrunken imitation of classical sociology, formal and contentless.

Not only does Peters lack the potency of his predecessors, he also inherits their weaknesses. Both Weber and Durkheim struggled with the epistemological contradiction between idealism and empiricism. Weber opted for a dualist, but essentially idealist, position. Durkheim believed he had solved the conflict which lay between *a priori* and empirical reasoning by situating the categories of reason in what he saw to be an autonomous social setting, but he wavered in his conception of the 'social' never sure whether its essence was in ideal or material conditions. The impalpability of the autonomous 'social' made him uncertain what exactly it was. Peters, as we have seen, falls into the same contradiction. He is never sure whether language, which he is analysing, is a reflection of reality, or reality a reflection of language, though his treatment of the 'obvious', the world as it seems through ordinary language, implies the latter. To view social behaviour as essentially purposive is to deal only with the surface, with things as they seem, to deny a reality other than a given *idea* of it.

The view of philosophy – the analysis of language usage – arises because language usage is itself seen as a 'public mode of experience', if not the essential 'public mode of experience'. But how is this concept of the 'public mode of experience' derived? It is derived from the analysis of language, it is apparently one of the many truths implicit in language. The concepts of language and the world are therefore tautologous: Language usage and the public mode of experience are the same thing, though each is used to justify the other. We will now see the basis upon which the use of words and concepts is constructed, and the way in which examples are chosen. It so happens that the 'public' is the 'public' deemed by our philosopher to be correct, the usage he chooses is the usage which fits in with his viewpoint.

As well as language, the 'public mode of experience' resides in the 'forms of knowledge'. According to P. H. Hirst, a collaborator of Peters, these forms of knowledge are 'the basic articulations whereby the whole of experience has become intelligible to man, they are the fundamental achievement of mind' (Hirst, 1965, p. 124). Hirst shows through 'conceptual analysis' that there are seven different forms of knowledge which are 'logically' distinct (except for geography, which is a 'hybrid') because the usage of words around these different disciplines have different connotations. By coincidence, these seven different forms of knowledge constitute more or less, a typical grammar-school curriculum. No doubt, the grammar-school curriculum embodies most of the public traditions.

Now these forms of knowledge cannot, in the long run, be justified because 'justification is only possible if what is being justified is both intelligible under publically rooted concepts and assessable according to accepted criteria. . . . But [these] principles themselves have no such assessable status, for justification outside the use of principles is not possible' (Hirst, 1965, p. 126). So, to question whether 'ordinary language' and publicly institutionalized knowledge is in fact the site of reality is impossible because reality is only known through them. Hence also the epistemological problem of what reality *is*, disappears and nothing new can ever be said.

Not satisfied with limiting the explanation of human behaviour to the statement of purposes, we are now told that the purposes cannot really be known. This crude contradiction amounts to saying that human purposes already exist in society and we must not challenge them. For the same reason, nothing new can ever be said because it must always be said in the old language. We cannot justify the present forms of knowledge for the same reason that we cannot create new concepts. To 'question the pursuit of any kind of rational knowledge is in the end self-defeating, for questioning itself depends on accepting the very principles whose usage is finally being called into question' (Hirst, 1965, p. 127).

Because all questions of life cannot be answered at once it is concluded that a given state of institutionalized knowledge cannot be questioned, because the justification of knowledge is its inscription in a public tradition, knowledge cannot be questioned. We see here how Peters's reification of the social and its history precludes the possibility of critical revision. Under the umbrella truism that all questions of life, meaning and purpose cannot be answered at once, it appears that any questioning of the *status quo* is being prevented. Necessary ignorance is being used to perpetuate unnecessary ignorance, in the cause of the existing system. Rather than using doubt and uncertainty in the exploration of new ideas and social relations it is being twisted into a fear of anything new and a blanket defence of the existing authority. Thus doubt, instead of questioning authority, is being used to bolster it.

The 'case' for authority is demonstrated as follows: it is argued that it is socially necessary because it is an 'empirical fact' that without authority the strong will dominate the weak (Peters and Hirst, 1970, p. 114). Here we have a perfect example of an argument from the 'obvious' back to the 'obvious', an idealist-empiricism. This crude Hobbesian argument depends upon bestowing the power instinct, which capitalism so bountifully fosters, upon man in general; it deduces eternal individual nature from the nature of man in a given form of society; its category of 'empirical' fails to see that this 'empirical' is relative to the observer. Peters and Hirst have the temerity to inflict their self-image of power-lustful man, upon man in general, regardless of class and society.

At this point it becomes possible to deduce the other components of the Peters's notion of education. We have been presented with the social and its history as an unquestionable edifice of 'public modes of experience and tradition'. The point of education therefore is to inculcate these modes of experience. Why? Because they are inherently 'worthwhile' (see Peters, 1966). 'Education' necessarily involves the 'worthwhile' as, because there is a special word for it, it must have purposes distinct from any other social practice. Because 'education' is itself and nothing else it must be inherently 'worthwhile'. Through a similar process of 'conceptual analysis' it is concluded that the concept of 'education' contains 'principles of learning' and is undergone 'voluntarily' by its pupils, who, in turn, are to be 'respected as persons'. Furthermore, 'education' cannot be used in the same way as 'indoctrination', nor 'instrumentality', but can only be used as 'education', which is 'worthwhile'. Now, any birk assumes that in discussing education he must be discussing what is worthwhile. No one would advocate a position without believing it to be worthwhile. The real question we face is how to determine what is worthwhile, how to know the actual meaning of education in practice, whose 'worthwhile' to accept. Can Peters seriously believe that anyone would favour 'indoctrination' rather than 'education'? Not even the most indoctrinating of educators would call their methods 'indoctrination'. The real question is not whether a person advocates 'indoctrination' or 'education' in abstract, but of what he supports in practice, not the connotation of the words but the denotation of the practice.

Now, why does Peters spend so many pages telling us that education involves the 'worthwhile'? The reason is that the teacher may not have a very good idea of what he is doing and why he is doing it. So, along comes Peters to explain that what the teacher is inculcating is the 'worthwhile'. 'A teacher has got to know what he is doing. Philosophy is absolutely necessary to get them to be able to manage on their own. We start with educational problems and use philosophy to clarify them' (*Times Educational Supplement*, 1971). Just in case the teacher is not aware of what he is doing and cannot manage on his own, the philosophy of education will come to his assistance. That there is a good reason for the teacher doing what he is doing, regardless of whether the teacher is aware of it or not, is never doubted – it is automatically assumed that there is a good reason and that philosophy will reveal what it is.

How do we decide what is worthwhile? 'What then should we introduce children to? Poetry or push pin? This is a problem at the core of his work,' according to *The Times Educational Supplement*. 'Conceptual analysis' again comes to our aid. It begins by asking why some subjects are taught on the curriculum and others are not. The existing system is taken, therefore, as already containing the reasons; it is merely a matter of elucidating them. Why, 'for example', teach science, history and literary criticism, rather than games? Well, the former, Peters shows us, have a whole range of words associated with them, 'far ranging cognitive content', 'progressive development', 'excellence', etc., which games do not have. We always suspected there was a reason for studying science rather than cricket, and this is it. 'If the participants in games came to look upon games as exercises in morality, aesthetic grace, or in understanding others, they cease to be merely games' (Peters, 1966, p. 159). Science has words associated with it which imply that it is more worthwhile than cricket, because, if 'cricket' had those words associated with it, it would no longer be 'cricket'. In other words, 'everything is what it is and not another thing' (see Gellner, 1968), and everything that is taught is 'worthwhile' because it is taught, and if it were not 'worthwhile' it would not be taught. In this way Peters deftly rebuts those who criticize what is taught; with breathtaking intellect he escorts us from starting point back to starting point, highlighting, *en route*, that everything we already do is worthwhile and that there is no cause for doubt.

Let us follow the argument a little further. If 'education' is the transmission of the 'worthwhile', the 'worthwhile' consists of the fruits of civilization and, therefore, not every Tom, Dick and Harry can have access to it. It is a slow process of 'initiation'. 'It is of course important that people should be initiated gradually into the procedures defining a discipline', as it 'takes time and determination to master' (Peters, 1964, p. 36). The child or the student is in 'the position of the barbarian outside the gates'. Who will let him in? 'The procedures of a discipline can only be mastered by an exploration of its established content under the guidance of one who has already been initiated.' Peters employs this image of initiation very deliberately and it forms a central part of his system. It cannot, therefore, be regarded as fortuitous that the image originates in the practice of the craft-guilds in medieval times in which they preserved their monopolies and power by restricting entry into their trades and professions. Not only did the ritual of initiation restrict entry into the ranks, but it also ensured that those admitted were not at odds with the system, that they were not likely to be critical because they had spent such a long time and made such great sacrifices under such constant surveillance, in order to gain admission.

Just as the old craft-guilds were often called 'mysteries' because they kept their techniques a secret in order to preserve their power, so our schools, in Peters's scheme of things, ought more aptly to be called 'mystifactories':

Now the teacher, having himself been initiated, is on the inside of these activities and modes of thought and conduct. He understands vividly, perhaps, that some created objects are beautiful and others are not; he can recognize the elegance of a proof or a paragraph, the cogency of an argument, the clarity of an exposition, the wit of a remark, the neatness of a plot and the justice and wisdom of a decision. He has perhaps (*sic*) a love of truth, a passion for justice and a hatred of what is tasteless. To ask him what the aim or point of life is, into which he himself has been initiated, seems an otiose question (Peters, 1964, p. 42).

Hands up all those who can remember the sort of teacher from their school days, or, alternatively, hands up all those who recall the teacher living the fantasy of being such a creature. It is an illusion, a masquerade of certainty and authority, a crass picture of mystification. Just like the concept of philosophy, so the entire view of education, is a pretence that something significant is taking place. He who questions this performance is said to be 'uninitiated' into its inner secrets and rites.

As only the 'initiated' are prepared so properly, they must be given authority over the 'uninitiated'. Earlier authority was justified in order to protect the weak from the strong; now it is to protect the 'initiated' from the 'uninitiated'.

Civilized men do not grow up overnight like mushrooms; they become civilized by being brought up by others who are civilized . . . whether they like it or not the experienced must function for a time as authorities and this type of authority must be institutionalized if it is to be effective (Peters and Hirst, 1970, p. 115).

Why the 'uncivilized' cannot appreciate their backwardness and take on trust the advice of the 'civilized' rather than being forced to accept it by institutionalized authority, is never explained. Authority, we are informed, requires 'discipline' and 'punishment' in order to maintain itself. Now, the contradiction in the principle of authority is the principal site of educational conflict, and its function, in relation to the class structure of society, is not well understood. This means that the teacher cannot be sure of the efficacy of his practice in the classroom. Peters's philosophy, by its justification of authority and punishment comforts the teacher, who relies upon authority: 'the value of direction and command is underestimated by modern educational theory, at least perhaps with the less intelligent children' (Peters, 1964, p. 41).

In one of his franker moments, Peters stipulates that teachers have taken over the role of priests, they are secular ideologists:

when there is no unified ideal that can be handed on by the priests, who else is there to stand between the generations and to initiate others into the various aspects of a culture within which the individual has eventually to determine where he stands? If teachers are not thought of as, to varying degrees, authorities on this culture how effective are they likely to be in a society in which most of the pressures on young people are not in the direction of education? (Peters, 1969, p. 17).

Whether the teacher is an authority or not is beside the point that he should be *thought of* as such.

Peters's outspokenness on issues such as authority is part of his general attitude to individualistic and progressive theories. Seeing their tendencies to overlook the full radical and political implications of their theories, he counterposes a return to the womb of unabashed conservatism. Hence, theorists who stress individual self-development, are criticized for their bias against the social, for their lack of emphasis upon 'public modes of experience'.

We are warned of the many dangers that will arise if too much scope is given to individual self-development. Children may behave irresponsibly by choosing, for example, not to study technology in a 'technological society' (Peters, 1969, p. 10). That this choice might in fact be a criticism by children of adult 'technological society' does not occur to Peters, for whom the 'civilized' are always right and the 'uncivilized' always wrong. Moreover, progressive education methods 'may lead to a certain type of promiscuity amongst children', they may begin to mistake their place and speak when not spoken to (Peters, 1969, p. 13).

As far as suggestions for integrated curricula are concerned, Peters remarks that: 'Surely one of the great achievements of our civilization is to have gradually separated out and got clearer about the types of concepts and truth-criteria involved in different forms of thought' (Peters, 1969, p. 14). Only a 'philosopher' oblivious of the many sectarian debates in the epistemology of science, mathematics, history, psychology and sociology could say something as dumb as this. If Peters had spelled out his own epistemology his criticism would have more force, but, as we have seen, this is one of his many areas of evasion. He merely assumes these principles to be clear in our 'civilization' as revealed in 'ordinary language'. He thus has the temerity to criticize refined and sophisticated epistemological theorists without ever venturing onto the same ground himself, but taking refuge in the sponge of 'civilization'.

We also find that it is somewhat easier for the teacher to be authoritarian than liberal. Informal teaching methods present 'unpredictable demands on the teacher's knowledge in such unstructured situations' (Peters, 1969, p. 18). The more structured the situation therefore, the more the teacher will be in control, the less his knowledge and authority will be under question. No doubt it is a soft option for a teacher to resort to autocratic methods, especially when the class is very large. This situation, however, should not result in a defence of authoritarianism, but in an active critique of the relation of teacher to taught and of the authority principle itself.

The presentation of 'public modes of experience' and 'initiation' into them, embodies a direct threat to any independent thinking. He who thinks for himself, especially if this is in a manner critical of the present structures, is liable to be put down for not being 'initiated' into the 'public mode of experience'. At the same time, for those in authority, this picture of reality provides confirmation. The incredible concepts which Peters himself generates could only have been invented by an ideologist who covers up real problems: if we are worried about not really understanding what we are doing to the kids in the process of 'teaching', let us show why what we are already teaching is 'worthwhile'; if we feel we may be curtailing the freedom of the pupils and the students, let us remember the 'paradox of freedom' which tells us why one can only be free so long as he is not free; if we are not quite sure why the children must obey us, let us study 'the justification of authority'; if they do not obey us, let us resort to 'the justification of punishment'. The chapter headings of *Ethics and Education*, the main text for students, read like a catalogue of easily-assembled kits of ideological self-justification. A common Peters aside is: 'It may be middle-class but all I can say is, thank God somebody has got it right' (*The Times Educational Supplement*, 1971).

## Conclusion

Throughout the discussion of Peters it has been suggested that the institutional practice of education contains social contradictions. The problem of 'educating people', a phrase which he uses frequently, reveals the essential elitism in his attitudes, and forgets that the educator must himself be educated. It therefore divides the process into two parts: those who do the thing and those to whom it is done. This inherent division gives rise to the teacher as authority and ultimately to the whole class division of society which is mediated in the educational system. It is sufficient to note, for the moment, a number of immediate indicators of the contradictions. We might notice that what is supposedly the most liberating of activities, the search for knowledge and truth, is, in educational institutions, actually motivated by the lowest instinct of self-advancement as written into the examination system. We can see that the very imposition of an organization to 'educate' automatically creates the needs for discipline and order – every teacher, before anything else, is faced with the initial requirement of establishing his authority. Moreover, the decision as to what to teach involves a view of the world and embodies all the contradictions contained in that view. It is these contradictions which, we have seen, furnish the subject matter for the 'philosophy of education' to resolve ideologically.

This ideology rests on its attempt to persuade the teacher that the doubts he may have about his role, and the criticisms the students may make, are inevitably misguided. It would have the teacher believe himself to be party to the secrets of civilization even if he cannot explain why. It shows why the system cannot be criticized by those who are not part of it, the 'uninitiated', the students, the uneducated. Until you are in you cannot criticize, and you will only be allowed in when you have lost the urge to criticize – Peters is the inadvertent Joseph Heller of education. His writing rationalizes the socializing, adaptive functions of education, justifying the authoritarian *status quo*.

It should now be clear that by 'ideology' is meant the technique for manipulating concepts so that they appear to explain social contradictions, but, by merely repeating tautological assumptions, in fact excuse them. Ideology reflects in 'concepts' the way individuals, groups and classes behave in practice and seemingly provides a justification for this practice. Instead of making a scientific inquiry into the nature of the contradictions, ideology only depicts the social world as though the contradictions do not exist, it excludes or distorts the concept of contradiction. It therefore precludes new knowledge and new consciousness of reality.

In keeping with this function of ideology, most academic discussions and criticisms merely consist of obscurantism. Peters's philosophy is an ideal example. He is able to produce a 'criticism' of any theory – he likes to think of himself as a practical philosopher (*The Times Educational Supplement*, 1971) – at a moment's notice, because his technique consists only of referring back to the 'obvious'. Without ever really saying anything concrete or significant himself he is apparently able to negate all other ideas. Academic discussion thus becomes a game of 'criticism', but not a genuine searching after truth. Academics wield ideas in order to play with them, to maintain their authority and to put others in their place. It is only able to get away with this because it protects itself in an elaborate mystique of authority. But, one day, students may suspect that their kings are wearing no clothes. . . .

Finally, we must note the relationship of Peters's type of thought to the English social structure. As the English ruling class is not the product of a thoroughgoing bourgeois revolution, it has never been called upon to articulate its bourgeois principles clearly (see Anderson 1965). Its intelligentsia never developed any refined social theory. Instead, it has relied in practice upon a pragmatic conservatism, never venturing to generalize, always yielding at weak moments and repressing severely when strong. Its mode of arguing is traditionally eclectic – no trade unionist or student negotiator can have avoided the problem of the filibuster of examples when bargaining with the bosses or authorities. Peters's style of thought is an exact replica of the customary mode of response of the English ruling class to a challenge from below. It is a tortuous, apparently blundering, in fact very subtle and resilient, defence mechanism. It uses boredom, false bonhomie, procrastination, insinuation through example and failure to spell out its premises, in order to fob off its opponents. Authority comes naturally to it but thinking does not. When asked for justifications it responds reflexively by assuming the justifications to exist already in 'civilization', 'common sense' and 'ordinary language'. It therefore repels new ideas and theory because it assumes no need for them, believing 'we already know too much about human behaviour' (Peters, 1958, p. 155).

Just as an oppressing ruling class will never admit its oppressiveness, so an ideology, which plays the role of confirming the oppression, will not (and cannot) openly admit that this is what it is doing. Forces of reaction never conceive of themselves as such and will go to great lengths to present themselves as other than they are and to protect themselves against criticism. The basis of this article has been that the philosophy of Peters fulfils just such a function without ever recognizing that this is what it is doing. It was, therefore, necessary for this discussion to concentrate upon what the philosophy actually *does* rather upon what it *says it does*, the way in which it arrives at conclusions rather than any specific conclusions. For this reason, we have made an analysis of his method of thinking and working and subjected this to criticism, rather than attacking his stated position. The stated position is unattackable because it consists of innumerable shades of opinion with countless contradictions and it can always be said that the words were being used in however many different ways are necessary to defend the position. For every view expressed in his work there can be found, somewhere else, the opposite view. This article has, therefore, tried to show Peters's ideology by examining the contradictions contained in the unsupported premises upon which his methodology, not his stated position, rests.

## References

ANDERSON, P. (1965), 'The origins of the present crisis', in *Towards Socialism*, Fontana.

FREUD, S. (1962), *The Ego and the Id*, Hogarth Press.

GELLNER, E. (1968), *Words and Things*, Penguin.

HIRST, P. H. (1965), 'Liberal education and the forms of knowledge', in R. D. Archambault (ed.), *Philosophical Analysis and Education*, Routledge & Kegan Paul.

PETERS, R. S. (1958), *The Concept of Motivation*, Routledge & Kegan Paul.

PETERS, R. S. (1963), *Authority, Responsibility and Education*, Routledge & Kegan Paul.

PETERS, R. S. (1964), *Education as Initiation*, University of London Institute of Education.

PETERS, R. S. (1966), *Ethics and Education*, Allen & Unwin.

PETERS, R. S. (ed.) (1969), 'Perspectives on Plowden', *A Recognizable Philosophy of Education*, Routledge & Kegan Paul.

PETERS, R. S., and BENN, S. I. (1959), *Social Principles and the Democratic State*, Allen & Unwin.

PETERS, R. S., and HIRST, P. H. (1970), *The Logics of Education*, Routledge & Kegan Paul.

SIMON, B. (1963), *Studies in the History of Education*, Lawrence & Wishart.

*The Times Educational Supplement* (1971), 'Profile of R. S. Peters', 5 March.

# An Analysis of the Military
# in Underdeveloped Countries:
# A Case Study in Ruling-Class Sociology
Susan Vickery

In this chapter, I look at a concrete instance of the class bias of sociology, namely the prevailing explanations of the role of the military in underdeveloped countries.

The literature on standard student reading lists displays some of the methods and assumptions of modern sociology. These sources embody an implicit model of underdevelopment and development, and this model is politically partisan; it implies a distorted account of the whole historical relationship between advanced industrial and underdeveloped countries. This account is wholly in the interests of the ruling classes of the former, the international bourgeoisie. In short, *the concept, and thence the study, of imperialism is strictly ruled out*.

This piece is not so much a methodological innovation as a prosecution of the official sociology for its blatant *trahison des clercs*, for its crass political blinkering to enormous facts of social reality. As Conor Cruise O'Brien (1967) puts it, the present danger to scholarship is not from revolutionary ideas, but from subordination to the counter-revolution. Many studies of countries in the underdeveloped world are 'subtractions from the sum of knowledge', which give anyone who knows about these countries 'a shock of unrecognition'.

## Survey of the standard literature

Over the past twenty years there have been successful military *coups d'état*, a host of failed coups, as well as series of coups and counter-coups, in a number of countries in Africa and the Middle East, in Pakistan, Indonesia and endemically in Latin America (First, 1970). Sociologists are interested in these military interventions in government because they appear to represent the political instability of underdeveloped countries.

Their explanation of the frequency and success of coups in underdeveloped countries typically orients around two questions:

1. What makes the takeover of governments by the army *possible*, strategically and politically?

2. What are the motives and social composition of the armed forces that explain *why* they should *want* to intervene directly in government?

I shall describe the literature under these two headings. The names that appear here are to be found on standard student reading lists.

### The possibility of military coups

Shils (1962), writing in a collection of readings produced for Rand Corporation,[1] explains the success of coups as due to the nature of the military as a particular kind of institution in the context of an underdeveloped political and social system. Although the colonial army was peripheral, it was often the only national organization that existed after colonial withdrawal. Particularly in sub-Saharan Africa, most newly independent states had no other bureaucratic national institution with the requisite degree of discipline, hierarchy, mobility, personnel and private communications network. Governments of the new states also consciously developed the military in preference to other institutions because the army was a prestige symbol and an image of national independence. The President of Mali said to the army: 'Vous êtes le signe visible de notre indépendence'. If the army is to be a realistic as well as a symbolic force, it obviously must reach comparable levels of competence to its enemies; so although other institutions of the state could lag behind 'modern' standards, it was (literally) self-defeating for an army to do so. This, in conjunction with the highly centralized nature of government in the underdeveloped countries, and the absence of intermediate institutions and associations, Shils's argument goes, makes it strategically and politically very easy for the army to take over state power. Strategically, because a disciplined, cohesive and small group of officers can take control of the institutions of government simply by making a well-planned attack on the presidential palace, the airport and the radio station. Politically, because the civil governments of underdeveloped countries are often unpopular owing to their failure to develop the country economically as they promised at national independence; they are remote from the people owing to an elite education and western orientation; they are separated from the people by the 'underdeveloped' polity, which makes it

1. As another instance of Rand Corporation's work: 'As early as 1965, the American Embassy in Saigon distributed to correspondents a Rand Corporation study on the air and artillery bombardments. The study concluded that the peasants blamed the Viet Cong when their hamlets were blasted and their relatives killed; in effect, that shrapnel, white phosphorous and napalm were good political medicine. The study was dismissed by reporters as macabre proof that the government could always find a think tank to tell it what it wanted to think' – *Sunday Telegraph*, 4 April 1971.

impossible for people to participate in politics. This, according to Shils, means that there is usually no legitimate channel for opposition to the government elite, so oppositional groups with the monopoly of force will win.

Finer (1962), in a pretentious work in the field, *The Man on Horseback: The Role of the Military in Politics*, also concentrates his explanation on the political structure of these societies. The concept 'level of political culture' supplies a broad analytical framework to explain both the dominance of the military in underdeveloped countries and its formal subordination in advanced countries: the overtness of military control is said to be in inverse proportion to the level of political culture. A high level of political culture exists where the government is legitimated by the population. Where these conditions do not hold there is widespread corruption, coercion and intervention by groupings such as the military. Finer's definition of a high level of political culture is a political system where:

1. The 'political formula', i.e. the belief or emotion by virtue of which the rulers claim the moral right to govern and be obeyed, is generally accepted. Or, to say this in another way

2. The complex of civil procedures and organs which jointly constitute the political system are recognized as authoritative, i.e. as duty-worthy, by a wide consensus.

The criteria by which he says we can assess public attachment to and involvement in the institutions of regime are:

1. Does there exist a wide public approval of the procedures for transferring power, and a corresponding belief that no exercise of power in breach of these procedures is legitimate?

2. Does there exist a wide public recognition as to who or what constitutes the sovereign authority, and a corresponding belief that no other persons or centre of power is legitimate or duty-worthy?

3. Is the public proportionately large and well mobilized into private associations? i.e. do we find cohesive churches, industrial associations and firms, labour unions and political parties?

Like most of these writers, Finer's idea of what constitutes the highest stage of social and political development is the splitting image of his (equally erroneous) idea of the political system of western capitalist 'democracies'. Like many of the others, too, his concepts are ultimately derived from a Parsonian (Parsons, 1964) account of the evolution of societies. Much of Parsons's work has become sociological common sense. The chief elements of his account of development are as follows. As societies develop through time, social tasks become *differentiated*, that is, roles and institutions become more *specialized* and more numerous. Greater differentiation provides a society with the means of handling more various and complex practical tasks, and of *adapting* to a greater variety of unpredictable problems and circumstances. So a higher degree of differentiation is regarded by Parsons as a higher stage of *evolution* of a society. Differentiation and specialization, however, mean that a society has the new problem of *integrating* the new separated and specializing sectors. Otherwise social conflict would be rampant. A vital element in 'successful' development, therefore, is a political system with which all sectors can identify, to which they all guarantee legitimacy, and in which they have a system of participation conceived very much on the lines of Finer's concept of 'political culture'. Finer's concept is a special case of Parsons's notion of the degree of differentiation and integration.

Another sociologist of development, Eisenstadt (1967), also derives his analysis of the Third World military governments from this model of development. In his essay on authoritarian regimes, he says that political instability, defined as military takeover or dictatorship, is not correlated in underdeveloped countries with the normal indices of economic development. He locates the key variables at the *political* level. Military governments tend to appear when a society which is beginning to *differentiate* fails to develop *integrative* mechanisms, that is, the political institutions and associations capable of providing some kind of consensus for the conflicting social forces now that the traditional symbols (feudal, tribal) which integrated the primitive society have been lost. This development of differentiation is assumed by Eisenstadt to be evolutionary. He gives no account of the historical process of interaction with advanced countries whereby the changes in social structures might have been induced. Hence his unquestioned notion of 'traditional' society, which is supposed to have persisted until very recently in the underdeveloped world.

I want to emphasize that according to this model of development originating with Parsons, the difference between advanced and underdeveloped countries is a difference along a continuum of development, a linear scale of evolution, where the advanced countries are simply a few stages further on than the underdeveloped countries. The process of development is regarded as *sui generis* to a society, and the problem of development today becomes a question of 'catching up'. 'Rapid development', a concept used by development agencies, becomes, in United Nations terminology, a question of telescoping so-called evolutionary processes of growth that spanned three centuries or more in the western world.

Within a model with these assumptions, the relationship between 'development' and 'underdevelopment' is purely formal, analytic in Parsons's sense (1945). The two societies are merely compared for their relative progress along a supposed linear scale, i.e. measured for relative values of the same variables. But this masks the true historical relationship, whereby the process of development in the west *produced and continues to reproduce* the underdevelopment of the colonies and ex-colonies. Frank (1967; 1969), shows that Chile and Brazil lost their feudal features centuries ago when the European colonials first arrived. Their economy and social structure were, from the start, entirely subordinated to the demands of the imperialist country. Potentially rich countries have been *made* poor; underdevelopment is not an original state, as the linear model suggests, but an *active process*, perpetrated by some countries on others.

The linear model makes the quite false assumption that the underdeveloped world today is basically like precapitalist Europe. The only concession made to there being a *qualitative* difference, is to note that contemporary underdeveloped countries have before them the *image* of industrial society, the access to advanced technological knowledge, and their elites have experienced the western way of life. This means that the contemporary underdeveloped countries have the ability to plan their industrialization in a more deliberate and directed way than did precapitalist Europe. But sociologists do not, on the other hand, recognize the *structural* effects on underdeveloped societies that European and American exploitation have had over the centuries, which have altered any traditional social structure, which the societies may at one time have had, out of all recognition,[2] so that the usual 'traditional'–'modern' dichotomy becomes meaningless. Nor is enough recognition given to the fact that the existence of an already developed capitalist world market makes economic development much harder for countries industrializing today than it was for precapitalist Europe; at the very least it makes the process a qualitatively different one.

The sociological conceptualization of development presented here leads to reactionary policies of all kinds, ranging from, at the most liberal, the idea that the 'haves' should give to the 'have nots' to help them 'catch up', through to Powell's moralism which implies that the Third-World races are inferior because they have not developed like Europe, and must be left to 'save, even one grain of rice per peasant per day' in order to deserve development (Powell, 1970). This racism itself is a function of imperialist history.

2. Polly Hill (1963; 1970) has shown that the agrarian sector in Ghana is by no means organized in a traditional or feudal manner, but is highly capitalistic.

## The 'motives' for military coups

Within the above problematic of the *possibility* of coups, some writers ask the complementary question of the *motives* of the military.

Eisenstadt takes the crucial determinant of the successful integration and stabilizing of a developing society to be the emergence of an elite with the appropriate 'modernizing vision', an elite oriented towards western methods and political forms. This makes successful development depend on the will, intentions and foresight of a national elite. Eisenstadt has little to say about the conditions for the emergence of such an elite, nor does he elaborate what social forces these elites (including the army, though he does not think the army is such an elite) might conceivably represent.

Shils, Johnson (1962) and Lissak (1967) do regard the military as a modernizing force, due to the high level of technological skill required and the officers' contact with the west. Sometimes this modernizing drive of the armed forces is expressed in terms of the class origins of the military or of particular sections of it, particularly in Halpern's work on the Middle East and in works on Latin America by the aforementioned authors.

Until the first quarter of the century the officers in Latin American armies were drawn from the landed oligarchy. The younger officers now represent the growing number of professional urban social groups, who want a modern industrial society, and who recognize that popular mobilization is required; their coups therefore appear less as 'palace revolts', and more as articulations of the needs of wider sections of the population (Alba, 1962). Halpern (1962) describes the same social transformation of the armed forces in Egypt and Syria. After the Second World War, the traditional elite of landowners and small-property bourgeois failed to expand the civilian economy, and to give more responsibility and status to the civilian bureaucracy. The army appeared to be the only route to upward mobility, and high-school teachers and lawyers began to leave their professions for the army. This new army of the middle class was the instrument that carried out the coup that brought Nasser to power.

Finer disputes the idea that the interventions of the military in government can be explained in class terms:

The most facile of all the theories of military intervention seeks to explain everything in terms of class interest. According to this theory, the military support the civil power when it is drawn from a similar social class and overthrow it when it is drawn from a different and hostile class.

Since, in many countries, the military has intervened successively on the side of radical and conservative regimes, Finer finds this an impossibly oversimplified explanation. And, of course, he is right to reject this *vulgar* class analysis, that only looks at social groupings *within* the underdeveloped society in question. As we shall see in the ensuing account of coups in African and Latin American countries, the class which illuminates the role of the military is the international bourgeoisie. However accurate Halpern's description of the social composition of the Egyptian army, this in itself does not constitute an explanation of the coup without an analysis of the way in which foreign interests in Egypt, which were supported by the existing government, represented a positive obstacle to the purposes of the classes represented in the army.

Some writers, for example Gutteridge (1969), are uncritically attached to the military's own justifications. The army classically claims to represent the 'national interest', so that when the civilians seem to be botching the job of government, the officers feel honour-bound to step in 'as saviours of their country' in the words of the Chief of Staff after the 1948 army coup in Venezuela. Gutteridge accepts the Ghana Generals' claim that they had overthrown Nkrumah in order to do away with the corruption, totalitarian rule and economic mismanagement which was 'destroying' the nation (Afrifa, 1966).[3] Although Finer warns that 'sectional bodies all plead the national interest when making claims for their own benefit', neither he nor the other writers offer an explanation much deeper than the self-professed motives of the officers themselves. The notion of the army as a 'modernizing force', while not relying on the statements made by the officers, does not depart from an acceptance of the army's *actions* as serving the national interest. No serious attempt is made to examine or contrast either the policies undertaken by civil and military governments, or the genuine obstacles to development that existed, in order to gain a concrete understanding of the actual behaviour of the armed forces in power.

In the next section, I recount some exemplary military coups and briefly describe the history and social structure of African and Latin American countries.

### Case histories

A major task of underdeveloped countries is to generate surplus required for economic development, which needs the creation of national industries. In Europe, this process was achieved largely by the efforts of an energetic

---

3. Afrifa was one of the officers who took part in the coup.

national bourgeoisie, who had enormous help in accumulating capital by exploiting the colonies. In African states, there is no such class. Fanon (1961) describes the situation common to the new African states. There is much talk in the standard literature already cited about 'the new middle classes'[4] developing in underdeveloped countries. In fact these new middle strata are not strictly bourgeois owners and accumulators of capital (Ledda, 1966). They are a *comprador* bourgeoisie consisting of lawyers, white-collar workers and liberal professions. They fill the intermediary roles in the economy, such as traders, commercial travellers, business officers, commercial houses, general and transport agents. They run the channels through which the big foreign companies have to pass. They are middle-men between the domestic market and the foreign import–export firms, they do not themselves own the major sources of capital, the banks, industries, etc. The small section of the native entrepreneurs that *does* exist is either associated with foreign capital or is engaged in secondary industries (Baran, 1957; Magdoff, 1969). Fanon explains that as individuals, the members of this *comprador* bourgeoisie benefit from their dependence on foreign capital, receiving status and financial rewards, and yet they are in no position to initiate industrial development since industry, banking and commerce, the decisive levers of the economy, remain in the hands of foreign capital.

Foreign ownership and investment exercises a powerful hindrance to development. Large monopoly firms have sole rights over the pricing and marketing of what is usually the single crop of the country. Being monoculture economies, this makes the developing country highly dependent on the fluctuations of demand for their crop in the world market, and on obtaining guaranteed prices from the monopolists. Many countries are also highly indebted to a former Mother Country, or to certain of its corporations, for goods acquired on credit – and so are vulnerable to sudden demands for repayment of the debt (see Hayter, 1971, p. 10). The constant struggle to repay the debt also makes it difficult to carry out radical reforms in the economy. Foreign countries are thus able to exert considerable pressure on underdeveloped countries' governments to allow tax preferences to foreign companies wishing to start industries, in preference to industries started by indigenous capital. The surplus thus accumulated is shipped back to the Mother Country along with raw materials extracted from foreign-owned mines and farming lands. It is not in the interests of the capitalist economies of developing societies to permit genuine industrialization of underdeveloped countries, using

4. The ambiguities in the concept of 'middle class' as used by sociologists is discussed by Stavenhagen (1967).

*native* capital, because these countries constitute a massive consumption market for the products of the developed countries. These developed countries insist upon free trade between themselves and the underdeveloped countries, which can only be to the disadvantage of the latter.

This provides the background necessary for understanding the Ghana military coup. When Nkrumah came to power in 1957, the economy was based on cocoa, the marketing of which had been entirely in British hands since the setting up in 1945 of the Cocoa Marketing Board. The ostensible purpose of this Board was to protect the Ghanaian farmer from the uncertainties of the world market. But by setting a domestic price lower than the world price, the Cocoa Marketing Board made a profit, which accumulated, and could be used by the cocoa farmer when world prices collapsed. In fact, however, this reserve fund was channelled to London after the war to support the pound. Thus the profits from cocoa production were *not* accumulated in Ghana, and the growth of a Ghanaian capitalist class was stunted (Fitch and Oppenheimer, 1966). Instead, what did develop was a stratum of small businessmen, contractors, wholesalers, etc., and a class of elementary-school graduates who filled the political power vacuum in the absence of a true African capitalist class. These were the leaders of Nkrumah's Convention People's Party. When Nkrumah came to power after independence he did not immediately try to break the power of the Cocoa Marketing Board. Industrialization was virtually impossible because foreign merchant capital controlled the channels of exchange in Ghana, keeping imports from Britain as a major priority. Unlike the United States in Latin America, Britain had not used capital to set up profitable industries inside Ghana, but instead used the country purely as an outlet for her own manufactured products. By 1961, Ghana had an enormous balance of payments deficit, yet Nkrumah could not impose import and exchange controls because of the opposition of the two largest blocs of capital in the country, the foreign banks and commercial firms. His attempts to impose import controls led to a further withdrawal of foreign investments, and the economic situation worsened: 'The task of defending the economy against the unregulated power of foreign business units in Ghana had to be undertaken or economic collapse would result.' The seven-year 'socialist' plan[5] was launched in 1961. It was seen as a set of institutional means for dealing with colonialism; it aimed at state ownership of key sectors, starting with trade and marketing, but at first it hardly touched manufacturing, agriculture and

5. The complex reasons why a specifically *socialist* planning strategy was adopted in 1961 cannot be discussed here, but the elements of an explanation are outlined by Murray (1967).

mining, still tried to attract foreign capital, and continued to depend on credit for durable purchases. The plan was a relative failure because the CCP did not take control of enough sectors of the economy, did not loosen dependence on foreign capital from the west, and by its half measures, antagonized numerous social groups. By 1965, the country had an increasing balance of payments deficit and a decreasing inflow of foreign investment. The United States government of President Johnson was withholding investment and credit guarantees from potential investors in Ghana. British creditors were demanding their money back. The price of cocoa on the world market had plummeted.[6]

This situation was the congenial context for the military coup which occurred in 1966 (Murray, 1966). The army claimed to be responding to the totalitarian one-party system and to the economic decline which they attributed to Nkrumah's prestige spending, 'corruption' and 'mismanagement', rather than by looking at the structural obstacles to development posed by the foreign stranglehold on the Ghana economy. The officers said that they had no particular social or economic policy except 'efficiency'. But in fact the military junta immediately undertook a policy designed to favour British and other foreign interests, and to reverse Nkrumah's anti-colonial plan. The programme of state-ownership was abandoned, and General Ankrah announced that the private sectors of the economy would predominate. Friendly relations were reopened with Britain and foreign aid requested. Investments began to flow in, under preferential conditions. British creditors and the International Monetary Fund became suddenly more lenient in their urgent requests for debt repayments (Hayter, 1971, pp. 33–40).

A similar pattern can be observed in Sierra Leone, where a military coup occurred in 1967 (Pomeroy, 1970). There was an extreme indebtedness to United States, British and West German bankers, the repayment of which absorbed 22 per cent of the country's revenue for the year. In March 1967, the neo-colonial regime of Sir Albert Margai lost an election to Stevens, who had a programme for expropriating foreign-owned mining companies that dominate Sierra Leone's economy. The army immediately staged a coup and returned to the neo-colonial policies of preference for foreign capital whose profits were always removed from the country rather than reinvested to develop a national industrial system.

There are two respects in which the picture in Latin America differs somewhat from the account of Africa. First, the United States has invested

6. The price of cocoa on the world market had fallen from £352 per ton in 1957 to £100 per ton in 1965.

in industry within Latin American countries to a greater extent than Britain, say, has in Ghana. This means that although the surplus has not accumulated in Latin America, and is not reinvested there, to create the possibility of indigenous industrial growth (Black, 1968), nevertheless a large section of the population now works in urban industrial areas. Secondly, during periods of recession for the world capitalist system (Frank, 1967), some indigenous industry was able to develop owing to the temporary loosening of contact with the metropolitan countries, which were preoccupied with their own internal stability. This allowed the growth of a small national bourgeoisie. These two facts present the possibility of an alliance between the growing labour unions and the national bourgeoisie against United States' interests, and so the appearance of what I shall call 'national reformist' as well as 'conservative' military interventions. A conservative intervention is one in which the military intervenes to permit industrial development to be hampered by giving preferential terms to foreign countries. A national reformist intervention is one where the military intervenes to attempt to create *national* industry owned by a national bourgeoisie.

The military coup in Brazil occurred in 1964 and was a 'conservative' coup. After the recovery of the western countries, after 1934, the ruling alliance of the national bourgeoisie and the agricultural landed and commercial interests, began to crack. With the renewed activity of US corporations in Brazil, a succession of coups and changes of government represented at some times the social forces which benefited from and depended on the United States (the agricultural interests, whose products were marketed and priced by the US monopolies), and at other times, those social forces whose existence was eroded by the US (the national bourgeoisie) in alliance with the mass of the people, whose per capita income was declining. In 1961 a popular uprising brought to power President Goulart, a representative of the national bourgeoisie, and associated with the labour unions. He was faced with an acute economic crisis: an enormous foreign debt, falling production, rising prices, falling exchange rate, and was confronted with what is now becoming the classical dilemma of reformist governments of developing countries – either he could give in further to foreign interests, which would help bail Brazil out, but which would also further increase the US stranglehold on the economy and continue the decline in the profits of the national bourgeoisie; or else he could make a more radical move, expropriate the foreigners and develop an internal industrialization programme.

He vacillated, and in 1964 Carlos Lacerda took over in a military coup. The President, Castello Branco, now 'handed the Brazilian economy over to the Americans lock, stock and barrel' (Frank, 1967). Foreign capital got special privileges; legal restrictions on the removal of capital abroad were lifted; the US corporations were compensated for companies which earlier anti-colonial governments, such as Goulart's, had expropriated for Brazil; the US Hanna mining company was granted authorization to build a private port that 'transformed the Hanna Company into the absolute master of the internal mineral market of the country' (Petras and Rimensnyder, 1970).

A military coup in Peru occurred in 1968, and was a national reformist coup. Like Brazil, Peru had a recent history of frequent coups and counter-coups alternating between reformist anti-colonial and conservative pro-American regimes. In 1968 a military coup was led by Velasco, with the idea of a bourgeois revolution from above. This military government planned rapid industrial development; expropriation of landed estates, especially foreign-owned; a reduction of imports; a reduction of foreign industrial ownership. However, once the plan was put into operation, with the expropriation of International Petroleum Company, the United States threatened to cut off government aid to Peru, and to cut the sugar quota. Velasco was also faced with an enormous foreign debt; and US industry would not cooperate in helping to develop Peruvian industry with investments. So Velasco's dilemma was like Goulart's in Brazil. Whether or not Velasco will sacrifice national development to meet the demands of foreign investors, or whether he will locate alternative sources of capital through internal savings and closer relations with Communist countries, is not yet certain. The former seems likely, since in December 1968, Southern Peru Copper, a US corporation, got a contract to invest 355 million dollars (Frank, 1967).

A programme of nationalization and expropriation comparable to Velasco's was undertaken after a coup in Bolivia in 1969, led by reformist army officers.[7] Another national reformist coup in the Dominican Republic in 1965, was led by a section of the army which supported the reformist ex-President Juan Bosch. The coup developed into a popular uprising that could have led to another Cuba, and the United States invaded the island to reinstate the army's right wing and the landed ruling classes (Huberman and Sweezy, 1965; Petras, 1966).

These case studies cannot, as they stand, point to a new theory of the role of the military, but they do show what some of the elements of a theory would be. Such would have to challenge the whole problematic of the two major questions under which I have characterized the bourgeois

7. Further details in contemporary issues of *International: A Survey of British and World Affairs*.

approach. My project here is purely a critical one, designed to convict the academics of craven subordination to American ideology. Nevertheless, it is, to say the least, a *prima facie* likelihood from what I have said that in any genuine theory of the role of the military, a key category would have to be the international bourgeoisie, as in Lenin's *Imperialism, the Highest Stage of Capitalism*.

American and British sociologists typically seek to explain the military coups in terms of functional relationships holding *within* the underdeveloped societies. The military is regarded as *an endogenous variable in a national model*. The major *exogenous* variable that is concealed is the international bourgeoisie, operating through monopolies and investment in the underdeveloped countries. Interventions by the army are precipitated either to maintain the interests of this class, or to force the country from its shackles. Which direction the intervention takes depends on the possibilities for the growth of a national bourgeoisie in the underdeveloped country.[8]

Military interventions play a crucial role in the international structure of dependence relations holding between developed and underdeveloped countries.[9] The coups cannot be understood without grasping the historical relations of structural interdependence which Frank calls *the development of underdevelopment*. But the key variables (degree of differentiation, existence of democratic institutions, etc.) by which the sociologists define development and underdevelopment on the linear model, prevent this understanding.

8. The calculations of the imperialist countries include the value to themselves of having capitalist, even *relatively* independent, states existing in the underdeveloped parts of the world as military buffer regions protecting the metropoles from the Communist States; it is therefore not entirely ruled out that certain strategic underdeveloped countries may be permitted or encouraged to develop national capitalism of a relatively independent kind.

9. The character of neo-colonialism was defined in the Resolution on Colonialism and Neo-Colonialism adopted at the First Afro–Asian–Latin American People's Solidarity Conference (Havana, 1966): 'To guarantee its domination, imperialism tries to destroy the national, cultural and spiritual values of each country, and forms an apparatus of domination which includes national armed forces docile to their policy, the establishment of military bases, the creation of organs of repression, with technical advisers from imperialist countries, the signing of secret military pacts, the formation of regional and international war-mongering alliances. It encourages and carries out *coups d'état* and political assassinations to ensure puppet governments; at the same time, in the economic field it resorts to deceptive formulas, such as the so-called Alliance for Progress, Food for Peace and other similar forms, while using international institutions such as the International Monetary Fund and the International Bank for Reconstruction and Development to reinforce its economic domination' (Woddis, 1967, p. 62).

## Political conclusions

It has been the thesis of this paper that underdeveloped countries are controlled by the exploitative relationships of imperialism (as exemplified by the military system). In particular, limits (defined by imperialist interests) are set on the development of national bourgeoisies – that is, on indigenous capital formation. These countries are thereby prevented from developing along the lines of the industrialized countries: the fact that some have developed on these lines depends on and actively sustains the fact that others cannot follow them.

Given these structures, it is therefore utopian to look to a putative genuine independent bourgeoisie, not flunkey to imperial interests, to lead their countries along the capitalist road to development. Any talk of a 'genuine' national bourgeoisie in an underdeveloped country – i.e. an anti-imperialist bourgeoisie on the European nationalist model – is dealing in a strictly artificial postulate, which can be hypothesized only to contrast and clarify a social reality which (it is the thesis of this paper) necessarily excludes such a bourgeoisie. In political terms, then, the future lies in a non-capitalist road to development. The condition *sina qua non* is the political–military overthrow of imperialist domination. This will not be done by the dependent pseudo-national bourgeoisies; nor, necessarily, by the doubly dependent proletariats of the colonial cities;[10] and when it is done it will not be for the purpose of merely setting up 'genuine' bourgeoisies.

In the national liberation struggles, there is the chance of circumventing the 'law' that 'the bourgeois period of history has to create the material basis of the new world' (Marx, 1969 edn, p. 119). The theory of Permanent Revolution was developed to explain how the tiny Russian proletariat could lead the masses in revolution that would both carry out industrialization in place of a bourgeoisie too weak for the task, and combine this development with the building of socialism. The experience of peasant revolutions in China, Vietnam, Algeria and Cuba now permits us to extend this theory, so that it is no longer doctrinally dependent on the concept of the proletariat, however small, as the only class on which a modern revolution can be based. For 'the revolutionary character of a social

10. Frantz Fanon's *The Wretched of the Earth* (1961) argues that the *only* revolutionary hope lies in the peasantry and the marginal class. James Petras, however, shows from voting statistics that the main social base for Allende's ruling Marxist party in Chile consists of the proletariat of the urban–industrial centres, the mining sector and urban working-class women. He levels this evidence against the view that urbanization, and especially higher pay for some workers, gives rise to 'integrated', 'bourgeoisified' or 'aristocrat' working classes in the underdeveloped worlds (1971). There is a thriving left-wing debate on these issues, which I merely touch on here.

class is historical, i.e. temporary, relative and changing. One cannot therefore trace 'everlasting, sole and natural revolutionary classes', although of course, some classes 'are more promising in this sense than others' (Shannin, 1971, pp. 42, 45).

At the political leve1 of students and their studies, the fallacies and mystifications in the sociology of development must be exposed. This is a two-pronged attack. First, it attacks the imperialist universities, by showing the ideological and bankrupt nature of their social science. Secondly, it attacks the government agencies and development organizations whose policies thrive on the ideology churned out by the universities.

Students can reconstruct their studies for themselves, by self-education and in groups organized outside the regular classes, using sources of theories and data which will not on the whole appear on their reading lists, like those referred to in the section of this paper which discusses the case studies. The useful material can be found in a whole range of socialist journals and pamphlets, as well as in publications by a few radical publishing houses. Self-education of this kind will inevitably involve students in a choice whether or not to pursue exam criteria. They will be told, as I and others have been told, that we are not using 'sociological concepts' at all. Part of sociology's falsification of society lies in its abstraction of a 'social' level of phenomena, which it claims to analyse as though it were autonomous of 'economic', 'political', 'historical', 'psychological' and other phenomena (which are falsified in their *own* university departments). This fragmentation of reality – which renders it strictly incomprehensible – reproduces the general fragmentation of the bourgeois world view, based on its social division of labour. It also reproduces the specific fragmentation of academic labour into professional specialities. Any student's attempt to re-totalize social concepts, so as to explain the political and economic framework of the 'social' is therefore resisted both by the teacher's general world outlook and by his specific professional interests.

In constructing a total theory, of which only the foundations so far exist in the Marxist tradition, we have to be careful not to treat a specific study such as Frank's as though it were just another abstract functionalist model which can be applied to any society that comes along. Frank's account of the development of underdevelopment is the result of a concrete historical study of a specific pair of countries, Chile and Brazil, and should not be dogmatically extended to African and Asian countries without equally concrete analysis.[11]

11. (a) Nor, it goes without saying, is Frank's model the last word or, in fact, anything more than a staging post in the theoretical exposure of imperialism. It has already

Our re-education would make best sense in the context of ongoing political work inside and outside the university. The universities are themselves a part of what they study: they train professional and national elites, they carry out research for the big corporations which perpetuate underdevelopment; they provide information and analysis for governments and international agencies. (Analogue: napalm was produced by Harvard to the specifications of the War Department.) A particular case relevant to the subject matter of this paper is an institution like the School of Oriental and African Studies, which trains personnel for the governments of underdeveloped countries, personnel which will be giving preferential treatment to the metropolitan countries. Students here already provide examples for future action: the Socialist Society at the School regard SOAS as a plant for the training of national elites and for counter-insurgency technique and ideology. Their strategy is that (a) the resources of SOAS (libraries, access to special information, etc.) should be used to produce radical counter-theory, and (b) the institution should be disrupted, in view of its own purposes (in so far as (a) and (b) are compatible). Such a strategy opens an English institution to political action by English students: there is also the complementary action of, for example, the Tricontinental Movement (Oxford). It consists of a group of students, themselves from underdeveloped countries, and studying at British universities, who are preparing to go home and join the liberation struggles of their peoples. These students approach the study of development by posing the questions of revolution, by asking the question how is imperialism to be destroyed?

Marx wrote that the general relationship between the intellectuals of a class and the class they represent is 'that in their minds they do not get beyond the limits which the latter do not get beyond in life, that they are

---

been criticized by the left, especially in a paper which came out after my piece was written. Laclau (1971) argues that Frank's analysis takes too much notice of the process of exchange and not enough of the underlying mode of production, and that the latter can often be shown to be precapitalist up to recent times.

(b) On the method of 'concrete analysis':

'The categorical demand of Marxist theory in examining any social question is that the question be formulated within *definite* historical limits, and if it refers to a particular country (e.g. the national programme for a given country), that the specific features that distinguish that country from others within the same historical epoch be taken into account' (Lenin, *The Right of Nations to Self-Determination*, section II).

'Thus the different laws for directing different wars are determined by the different circumstances of those wars – differences in their time, place and nature . . . and those applying to one cannot be mechanically transferred to the other' (Mao, *Problems of Strategy in China's Revolutionary War*, ch. 1, *How to Study War*).

consequently driven, theoretically, to the same problems and solutions to which material interests and social position drive the latter practically' (1852). In the training of the national elites of imperialism, the falsification of social reality is seen as not merely an intellectual lie, but as preparation for reactionary social practice: these personnel have to be made to see the world through the eyes of the ruling class they serve. The variables and processes which the sociologist's model conceals in theory, define policies which the power structure cannot undertake in practice. Compare the blindness of military sociology with the constraints on organizations like the Overseas Development Institute. As Hayter writes:

Research at the ODI was based on the assumption that 'aid' was good and that the major objective of 'aid' could reasonably be expected to be 'development' in, and for, the Third World. Aid could be criticized for falling short of this objective, and proposals could be made for improving its contribution to development. But the central assumption was that the imperialist countries were 'helping' the Third World to develop. The possibility that they were, on the contrary, stunting and distorting development in the Third World through exploitation, and that the Third World could not develop until imperialism was destroyed, was not considered. Nor could it be, since ODI, like aid, is merely the smooth face of imperialism (1971).

It is a sign of how servile the intellectuals have been in the past that the World Bank thought it could suppress by threats the book in which this paragraph was written. It is a sign of the changing political climate that this author nevertheless published the truth.[12]

There is no specifically academic level of operation which can disjoin theory and practice, fact and value. This implies that we must support all racial and national liberation struggles and the collapse of the metropolitan imperialist regimes. We must differentiate ourselves from the liberal academics who think they are 'helping' underdeveloped countries by producing abstract analysis and policies *which fail to seriously consider which social forces are capable of making genuine social change in the underdeveloped world*. While they are sometimes honestly concerned for the 'starving millions', these liberal academics are fastidious and fearful about populist movements and revolution. The social position of these academics themselves is so excessively secure and privileged that they seem to find it impossible to take seriously as a possible or probable means of liberation, revolution in the Third World. One very often hears them say in seminars that a student who simply wishes to *discuss* the peasant revolution is being 'utopian' and is posing an unrealistic alterna-

12. See Greene (1970, ch. 3, section 3, 'The great "foreign-aid" fraud'). This is a good explanation of why Aid does not aid.

tive. The social position and limited experience of academics make it hard for them to think of social change in terms other than *reformist* and carried out *from above by an elite*. They cannot answer the question we have about development, because they have set up the problem in a reactionary and imperialist way from the start.

Revolutionary students will not help the Third-World revolution by writing abstract development programmes for the consumption of other academics, which do not pose the question of revolution. The Italian C. P. asked Ho Chi Minh how they could help the Vietnamese people: he answered that they should go and make the revolution at home. We live in the imperialist metropolis: we must do as Bobby Seale said, and attack the 'head of the octopus'.

## References

ALBA, V. (1962), 'The stages of militarism in Latin America', in J. J. Johnson (ed.), *The Role of the Military in Underdeveloped Countries*, Princeton University Press.

AFRIFA, A. A. (1966), *The Ghana Coup*, Cass.

BARAN, P. (1957), *The Political Economy of Growth*, Monthly Review Press.

BLACK, E. (1968), *The New Strategy of US Investment in Latin America*, *Viet-Report*, April–May, New England Free Press.

EISENSTADT, S. (1967) 'Breakdowns of modernization', *Economic Development and Cultivated Change*, vol. 12, no. 4.

FANON, F. (1961), *The Wretched of the Earth*, Penguin.

FINER, S. E. (1962), *The Man on Horseback*, Pall Mall Press.

FIRST, R. (1970), *The Barrel of a Gun: Political Power in Africa and the Coup d'Etat*, Allen Lane The Penguin Press.

FITCH, B., and OPPENHEIMER, M. (1966), *Ghana: The End of an Illusion*, Monthly Review Booklet.

FRANK, A. G. (1967), *Capitalism and Underdevelopment in Latin America*, Monthly Review Press.

FRANK, A. G. (1969), 'The development of underdevelopment', *Latin America: Underdevelopment or Revolution*, Monthly Review Press.

GREENE, F. (1970), *The Enemy: Notes on Imperialism and Revolution*, Cape.

GUTTERIDGE, W. (1969), *The Military in African Politics*, Methuen.

HALPERN, M. (1962), 'Middle Eastern armies and the new middle class', in J. J. Johnson (ed.), *The Role of the Military in Underdeveloped Countries*, Princeton University Press.

HAYTER, T. (1971), *Aid as Imperialism*, Penguin.

HILL, P. (1963), *The Migrant Cocoa Farmers of Southern Ghana: A Study in Rural Capitalism*, Cambridge University Press.

HILL, P. (1970), *Studies in Rural Capitalism in West Africa*, Cambridge University Press.

HUBERMAN, L., and SWEEZY, P. (1965), 'Revolution and counterrevolution in the Dominican Republic: why the US invaded', *Monthly Review*.

JOHNSON, J. J. (1962), 'The Latin American military as a politically competing group in a transitional society', in J. J. Johnson (ed.), *The Role of the Military in Underdeveloped Countries*, Princeton University Press.

LACLAU, E. (1971), 'Imperialism in Latin America', *New Left Review*, no. 67.

LEDDA, R. (1967), *Social Class and Political Struggle in Africa*, New England Press pamphlet, reprinted from April 1967 issue of *International Socialist Journal*.

LISSAK, K. (1967), 'Modernization and role expansion of the military in Developing countries', *Comparative Studies in Society and History*, April 1967.

MAGDOFF, H. (1969), *The Age of Imperialism*, Monthly Review Press.

MARX, K. (1852), *The Eighteenth Brumaire of Louis Bonaparte*, p. 51 in Moscow pamphlet.

MARX, K. (1969), in H. C. d'Encausse and S. R. Schram (eds.), *Marxism and Asia*, Allen Lane The Penguin Press.

MURRAY, R. (1966), 'Militarism in Africa', *New Left Review*, no. 38.

MURRAY, R. (1967), 'Second thoughts on Ghana', *New Left Review*, no. 42.

O'BRIEN, C. C. (1967), in *The Morality of Scholarship* by Northrop Foye *et al.*, ed. Max Black, Cornell University Press.

PARSONS, T. (1945), 'Systematic theory in sociology', in G. D. Gurvich and W. E. Moore (eds.), *Twentieth-Century Sociology*, Philosophy Library.

PARSONS, T. (1964), 'Evolutionary universals in society', in *Amer. Soc. Rev.*, vol. 29.

PETRAS, J. (1966), 'Dominican Republic: revolution and restoration', *New Left Review*, no. 40.

PETRAS, J. (1971), 'Two views of Allende's victory', *New Politics*, no. 1.

PETRAS, J., and RIMENSNYDER, N. (1970), 'What is happening in Peru?', *Monthly Review*, February.

POMEROY, W. (1970), 'The army and coups in developing countries', *Labour Monthly*, March.

POWELL, E. (1970), 'It's Your Line', BBC Radio 4, 1 December.

SHANNIN, T. (1971), 'Workers and peasants in revolution', *Spokesman*, vol. 10, March, p. 42.

SHILS, E. (1962), in J. J. Johnson (ed.), *The Role of the Military in Underdeveloped Countries*, Oxford University Press.

STAVENHAGEN, R., (1966), *Seven Erroneous Theses about Latin America*, University Free Press pamphlet, reprinted from *New University Thought*, vol. 4, no. 4.

WODDIS, J. (1967), *Introduction to Neo-Colonialism*, Lawrence & Wishart.

# Economic Theory in Class Society
## Rose Dugdale

### Rejection of the logic of reformism

The last decade has seen a most striking polarization between left and right throughout developed and underdeveloped parts of the capitalist world. One reflection of this development has been the growth of student movements.

The battles can be traced around the world, from Berkeley, to Latin America, where students have made universities into red bases in active support of guerrilla struggles (Brazil, Venezuela, Peru, Bolivia, Mexico, Guatemala) to the Middle East, with violent clashes between students and state (Turkey, Iran, Jordan) to revolutionary movements in Pakistan, India, Ceylon, Afghanistan. In the developed countries, the student movement has spread throughout Germany, Japan, France with the General Strike of May 1968, to Spain, to Italy, where student and faculty strikes have paralysed academic life, to Canada, where one morning the people of a rich, quiet 'democratic' country woke up to martial law on the streets, and back to America, where numerous universities have called off academic life and directed resources to bringing down those structures which perpetrated the Vietnam war.[1] Students have openly declared war on American capitalism and its tentacles of power across the continents. Increasingly students are leaving the campus for the movement of organized opposition to the ruling class; for work in trade unions, in political parties, community action groups. This is the context of course critique: students are now fighting out their economics in the streets.

These steps towards direct action reflect a rejection of course reform and associated demands for participation in college government: a rejection, in fact, of the logic of reformism.

The reformist tradition, that of J. S. Mill, sees nothing inescapable in the present – except the irrational. It holds that the ills of society can one and all be overcome by democratic decision in the light of reasoned argument. Decisions are neutral choices between rational alternatives and change in society will follow on a more enlightened theory. On such

1. See for example resolutions passed at Berkeley, New York, Columbia, etc. at the time of the Cambodia invasion.

a view the improvement of our society rests crucially on more and better education. It is this problematic given by the logic of reformism which has been rejected by the actions as much as the theory of the student movement. Change in a society does not occur through intellectual developments in universities. The war in Vietnam will not cease because a brand new Russell or Chomsky publishes wiser insights which finally offer the rational proof we were waiting for – that, after all, slaughter, destruction, torture, wage-slavery, are morally wrong. (Analytic philosophy has long since protected us from such a 'proof' – 'ought' will not be derived from 'is' – though philosophy does not mind if you care to keep on trying.) Whether philosophy realizes it or not, students have begun to see the hypocrisy of 'Yes, indeed society must change – we will bring about change through educational enlightenment and the victory of mature philosophical reason.'

More fundamentally the nature of this hypocrisy is explained by a quite distinct view of the relation between education, ideas, theory and society, change-reality. No longer are the ultimate causes of social change to be sought in the undetermined neutral progression of ideas, from the false into insight into eternal truth and justice. Ideas are themselves dependent upon, and developed for and within, a particular society ruled by a particular class. Ideas are not autonomous, self-determined, self-propagated with a history which is over and above the history of their authors. 'The ruling ideas are the ideas of the ruling class' (Marx and Engels, *German Ideology*). For it is the ruling class which is conscious – a point Mill is keen to insist on – and in so far as they rule, they rule also as thinkers. Students have begun to see that the history of man is not given by the autonomous development of ideas. There is an inextricable link between the content of a particular theory, and the method by which that theory will admit of disproof. When the ideas of liberalism are opposed within its own problematic, the logic of reformism, then under this challenge the *status quo* can remain just as it is.

The recognition of the dependence of ideas upon social conditions places course reform in a quite different perspective. Reform of courses cannot be seen as a way of changing society through the educational system. A change in socio-economic conditions will no doubt generate changes in ideas, but the relationship is not simply reversible.

Economics deals explicitly with these socio-economic conditions. In the words of textbooks, economics is about what is produced, how, for whom and by whom. It provides therefore the most interesting example of the interdependence of theory and social conditions. Now it has often been suggested that economics is an aplogetic for the political-economic system (see Robinson, 1962; Baran, 1957; Baran and Sweezy, 1968). But this thesis may be argued at different levels.[2] It may be argued at the level of the assumptions of economic theory,[3] or in terms of the questions economics defines as relevant.[4] Alternatively, economics courses can be attacked for the way economic theory is taught, and the purpose of such training. Instead I want to show *why* economic theory falls under all these attacks: how it be *must* apologetics because of its methodology.

The purpose of taking such an abstract approach to the ills of economic theory is to refute the hypothesis that although economic theory is bad, it could be better if we simply pursue it further. Generally speaking, the methods of economics combine the worst kind of *a priori* reasoning with the worship of what are consequently uninterpretable raw empirical data.[5] I want to show that this methodology results, principally, from a static world view which is premised on a denial of class conflict. Hence within the methodology itself there is an apologetic for the *status quo*. This methodology constrains the argument, for or against an economic theory, to an abstract debate between equally unreal, trivial and irrelevant alternatives. This non-choice within economic theory, which is guaranteed by the methodological weaknesses of the theory, exactly parallels the non-choice, within a class society, between 'democratic' parties. It is no more possible to oppose economic theory within its problematic than it is possible to find a real method of changing the socio-economic system within that system. The reason is the same: both theoretical and political systems mystify, deny and thus perpetuate the essential dynamic force of capitalist society, namely class conflict.

2. See for example Marx's characterization of the different schools of criticism among the bourgeois economists, who tend to fall out with their own theory as the contradictory character of capitalism increases: the Fatalist economists (the Classicists of Smith and Ricardo), the romanticists (the blasé fatalists), the humanitarian school ('which takes to heart the bad side of existing productive relationships . . . sincerely deplores the distress of the proletariat . . . and counsels the workers to be sober, to work hard, and to have few children . . . and advises the bourgeoisie to put a deliberate zeal into production'), and finally the Philanthropic school which 'denies the necessity of antagonism; it would make all men bourgeois; it wants to realize theory in so far as it is distinguished from practice and contains no antagonisms . . . an antagonism which constitutes those relations (of the bourgeois relations of production) and is inseparable from them' (see *Poverty of Philosophy* (Seventh and Last Observation)).

3. For example, economic theory assumes the essence of rationality to be responsiveness to the profit motive.

4. For example, how we can increase growth. See J. K. Galbraith's criticism of this aspect of economics.

5. As Kalecki has said, 'Economics consists of theoretical laws which nobody has verified and of empirical laws which nobody can explain.' Rationalism and empiricism are two sides of the same bourgeois coin.

**Economics as ideology**

*Its irrelevance*

The most striking feature of economic theory for the first-year university student is its blatant irrelevance to the problems which most students would suppose economics to be about. Economic theory courses plunge into the general equilibrium model, where, with the help of the invisible hand of perfect competition, and some ridiculous assumptions, we are supposed to come out with the answers to all questions about who gets paid what, what gets produced, and what price it will be sold for, whilst everyone maximizes satisfaction, profits, efficiency and use of their time. Whilst economic theory bestirs itself to take on the beautiful intrigue of the cardinal measurability of utility, several hundred thousand Indians are starved out of the population statistics. Meanwhile the US Government hands over a lump sum incentive to farmers to maintain productive land fallow. Whilst economic theory bows before the secret mysteries of the constancy of the shares of profits and wages in the national income, and proclaims the obsolescence of classes, 5 per cent of the adult population of the UK continues to hold 75 per cent of the total personal wealth, and some 10 per cent of the population lives below an estimated subsistence minimum. While America generously cracks up its aid budget to send the marines into Vietnam to maintain (euphemistically) US spheres of influence, economists ponder the wonders of the Taiwan, Hong Kong, Japanese, Thailand growth rates: searching for the determining factors of 'Take-Off'. Whilst economists debate among themselves the curious paradox of comparative advantage (that all will gain from free trade, and end up specializing in the product they produce most efficiently), the underdeveloped countries end up monoculturing a commodity which nobody wants, least of all themselves.[6] Whilst economists can't quite make up their minds as to whether it is $2\frac{1}{2}$ per cent or 5 per cent unemployment which is needed to keep down the rate of inflation, unemployment moves towards the million mark. As economic theory leaps into the pleasures of distinguishing econometrically between cost-push and demand-pull theories of inflation, the UK, with the benefit of successive stop-gos, has achieved nineteenth in the OECD Growth League of twenty. As economists contort themselves into position over whether there is after all any difference between the new monetarism and the Keynesian approach, the shortfall in UK investment and the consequent technological backwardness guarantee failure to compete with our political partner, the US,

6. For example, sugar, coffee, jute, sisal, rubber, cotton: for all of these there are now substitute products available in the developed countries.

driving us into the EEC, and so necessitating a 'shake out' of labour, and trade-union legislation which will ensure that when prices increase wages will not.

## Its relevance

It would of course be absurd to hold that economic theory is ideological simply in virtue of its failure to treat of supposedly economic problems. Paradoxically one way in which economic theory is relevant (politically) lies precisely in this apparent irrelevance. If economic theory fails to deal with those social political questions which fall within its sphere of interest, then in so far as the questions are ignored, the *status quo* remains unaffected: silence is complicity. The relevance or the irrelevance of economic theory is a way of pointing to the impossibility of political neutrality.

But there is another sense in which economics is far from irrelevant to the problems of the times. Historical examples show the nature of the relationship between economic theory and socio-economic conditions. From its origin theory has reflected contemporary conditions. For example, Quesnay, who devised the Tableau Economique (a prototype of Leontieff input–output analysis) held the view that only one factor of production, land, could produce a surplus (more comes out than is put in). This theory was used to 'justify' a single tax – a land-value tax. Since merchant capitalists, financiers and industrial tradesmen merely lived off this surplus, the guilds, subsidies and privileges to industry should be abolished. Now this theory appears less ridiculous when it is seen in its historical context of mid-eighteenth-century France. The court was grossly in debt, the clerical and lay nobility lived at court exempt from tax, and agriculture was inefficiently organized into small units. Thus the proposal of a single tax was undoubtedly progressive. The court needed money, agriculture needed rationalization, industry needed the impetus of more competition, less protection, a lower tax burden, and an influx of destitute labour from the rural sector to put pressure on wage levels. Quesnay's theory, however mysterious a construction, 'justified' just what was needed.[7]

Quesnay's theory is a good example of what Schumpeter has chosen to call the Ricardian vice: 'the habit of applying results of a theory, which is

7. The example is especially interesting because the reform advocated depended upon a strong monarchy (reflecting the contemporary ideology of monarchical absolutism). It served to strengthen the monarchy, and at the same time hastened its overthrow through the encouragement given to the growing manufacturing sector – the bourgeoisie. In the long run, because the policy was successful in its object of strengthening the monarchy, it served also to hasten the opposite effect – the overthrow of the monarchy.

excellent, can never be refuted, and lacks nothing but sense, to the solution of practical problems'. Solutions which, as Schumpeter goes on to say, are solutions precisely by virtue of their socio-political acceptability (1954).

The vice was well named. On the basis of his well-known theory that profits depend upon the price of wage goods (which, as he had set up his theory, was analytically true) Ricardo lent 'scientific' authority to the demand for repeal of the corn laws. The repeal is usually recognized as a crucial step in setting the conditions for England's future economic growth. But the theory also lent a domestic stimulus to growth. Cheap food from abroad put pressure on the agricultural sector, and a larger army of unemployed drifted to the towns in search of work, putting further pressure on wages and rasing the rate of profit. Ricardo's theory was indeed the theory of the industrial revolution.

What is interesting about these two examples is that, contrary to our well-trained expectations, economists did not hit upon the correct theoretical model which then determined the correct policy. On the contrary, these theories were in themselves absurd, or trivial, or both, but social and political conditions made them useful and acceptable.

Perhaps the best example of the interconnection of economic theory and economic conditions is the debate between mercantilism and free trade (Robinson, 1966). Joan Robinson's essay shows how the adoption of one or other theory was independent of the inherent correctness of either, but was determined by economic conditions. England held rigidly to mercantilism in both theory and practice during the period when she held no strong advantage over her competitors. But under reverse conditions, when England assumed the dominant place in an expanding capitalist world, she stood only to gain from the unrestricted play of market forces. Theory then turned to an admirable *a priori* justification of free trade: the theory of comparative advantage. Free trade in fact worked to England's advantage precisely because the assumptions of the model were not fulfilled.[8]

After the slump economic theory has begun to have second thoughts on the superiority of free trade. Now the gnomes preach of the virtues of credit-worthiness, insisting on major cutbacks in response to minor balance of payments deficits to the detriment of UK competitiveness with the US, whose interest these gnomes predominantly represent. The theory now lends 'scientific' respectability to the vain pursuit of the 'true' exchange rate. Devaluations are enforced or encouraged, through the international agencies and teams of visiting economists to the under-

8. Assumptions of no migration of labour, no international investment, and full employment, and perfect mobility and adaptability of factors within countries.

developed world, as the cure for balance-of-payments problems. Most less developed countries have complied with this proposal at some time over the past twenty years.[9] The role of economic theory here is to lend justification to the view that the best way for the LDCs to settle their immediate balance of payments, or debt-financing problems, is to deliver a net real resource transfer to the developed countries.

These examples of the relationship between economic theory and social reality, far from standing in contradiction to the original argument that economics is ideology because it is irrelevant to the crucial economic questions, in fact reinforce the argument. To generalize the Ricardian vice: the applicability of economic theory appears, in these examples, to consist in the triviality or analytic character of the theory. Criteria of acceptability for economic theories do not seem to rest with falsification or verification of the theory, but in its political uses. Economic policy is not derived from economic theory. Rather, the dictates of economic need and political-economic policies, determine acceptability of the theory – acceptability *by* the ruling classes, *for* the ruling class.

Now the relevance or irrelevance of the theory to economic conditions is not the result of a conspiracy by a few wise men determined to guarantee economic theory the vacuousness which would allow such flexibility to the users of the theory. Economics is not apologetics because of a conspiracy to ignore questions which might lead to the questioning of our political system. Economics is apologetics in virtue of its methodology. I want to show that the limitations of economic theory as suggested in these examples are in fact logically explicable in terms of the basic methodological approach towards the relationship between theory and reality.

### Methodological inadequacy
*The demand for a positive theory*

'As a science, economics can concern itself only with the best means of attaining given ends; it cannot prescribe the ends themselves' (Samuelson, 1967). Most economic textbooks will take up the first few pages in exhorting the student to beware of the value judgement. Trained as we are in the empiricist tradition, we all of course recognize the standard of

9. The net effect is a transfer of real resources from underdeveloping to developed countries. Import prices will rise by the full amount of the devaluation, yet imports are already restricted to the barest minimum, and therefore cannot be cut back through the supposed free-market mechanism of supply and demand. Export prices, higher in domestic currency terms, provide further incentive to increase supply and therefore in the long run fall, precisely because of the competitiveness in the supply of primary products to over-flowing markets in the developed economies.

reputable scientific work in the paradigm of the natural sciences. There are difficulties in following this paradigm: we are warned that although we may believe we can simulate conditions, controlled experiment is impossible, and there may be differences between the inorganic world and the organic, animal kingdom of economic theory.[10] Nevertheless we must make a continuing watchful effort to maintain these standards. Then, with the support of philosophy, and the impossibility of deriving 'ought' from 'is', we can leave the 'ought' statements alone to the province of personal choice, and the democratic vote, where they of right belong.

Economists have continued to repeat this methodological precept in blissful ignorance of some recent perceptive remarks in the field of philosophy and science (Kuhn, 1962; Feyerabend, 1970). Kuhn has cast serious doubts upon this paragon of the virtues of objectivity – the natural sciences. After all, it is not at all clear that science advances as Popper would have us believe, from hypothesis to falsifying evidence and so the replacement of the hypothesis by a better theory. Science, it has been argued, at any one time works within a paradigm, a collection of accepted theories; the paradigm not only determines which are the relevant questions, what should qualify as an answer, but it also defines the terminology in which the questions may be asked, and the methods and tools by which the theory may be tested. The history of science appears to show that many theories, long since falsified, continue as an accepted part of the paradigm. Thus even in the natural sciences, it is not clear that relativism can be avoided, or that the scientific observer can maintain the god-like status of neutrality.[11] These steps appear to make of natural science a

10. It is of central importance to any theory whether it assumes an irreducible division between organic and inorganic matter. A. I. Oparin (1959) shows how both organic and inorganic substance has developed (historically) out of one and the same substance. This model of the world eliminates, from the outset, the inbuilt dualism of pre-Marxist theory, between spirit (God) and bare matter, between mind and body, between the rational and the empirical, between fact and value, between subject and object. Both inorganic and organic matter develop dialectically – from the force of contradictions between the opposites which define their essence (see Engels – *Dialectics of Nature*, pp. 8–24 especially); *Anti-Dühring*, part 1 on Philosophy; or see a very useful collection, Selsam (1963).

11. Furthermore from the Heisenberg uncertainty principle it is not even clear, *a priori*, that the nature of objects in the world is such that objectivity could be a possible condition for the scientist. See for example Mao '*On Practice*': 'If you want knowledge you must take part in the practice of changing reality. If you want to know the taste of a pear, you must change the pear by eating it yourself. If you want to know the structure and properties of the atom, you must make physical and chemical experiments to change the state of the atom. If you want to know the theory and method of revolution, you must take part in revolution' (1966).

false god, which not only must the social sciences fail, but equally the natural sciences as well.[12]

What Kuhn may throw at theories in the natural sciences would seem indubitably to hold in the special case of economics. For example, once we have, by assumption, opted for the paradigm of maximizing models, we have at the same time delineated the relevant questions, the definition of terms (which terms are to have sense) the methods of testing (the analytic tool box) and the sort of answers we are looking for. The optimizing paradigm imports the assumption of the rational man, maximizing profit and satisfaction; the assumption that the concepts of an optimum, or maximization, can be filled out uniquely, and the tool box containing methods of playing with first and second differentials. The questions that can be asked sensibly within this paradigm are interestingly limited. Once given the paradigm, certain questions are already ruled out as having no sense. This dominance of the paradigm prevents our moving outside it, to give these notions sense. For example, the problem of maximizing satisfaction within a given distribution of income will make us want to ask questions about where the optimum income distribution lies. Yet, in accepting to talk in terms of utility at all, with the built-in impossibility of interpersonal utility comparisons, we have already made it impossible to give sense to the notion of the optimum distribution of income.

These examples suggest certain conclusions. Firstly, economic theory cannot be lent a positive character through adoption of a paradigm which rules out some evaluative notions as lacking sense. Moreover, a theory is not neutral in virtue of the fact that it tells us nothing of the real world. Any theory directs interest towards one problem rather than another. To say nothing about the *status quo* implies as much about the *status quo* as does a theory which founds directives for change. The difference between the theory which pretends neutrality, and the theory which claims to have implications for economic policy, is that one theory implies, if only tacitly, that things should remain as they are, the other that things should change. And lastly, even techniques cannot be seen as neutral, because one set of techniques will exclude others. A theory in defining reputable concepts delimits possible answers. When one set of techniques is defined

12. The incommensurability between paradigms, for example Einsteinian and Newtonian physics, suggests that we have no absolute, objective criterion which can establish the truth of one, and the falsity of the other. Where the language of one theory, and its techniques, cannot be mapped into another theory, Popper's falsificationism falls down. If we accept Quine's approach in *Word and Object* (1960) towards untranslatability, Kuhn's thesis is reinforced at the level of language itself. This relativism brings with it a serious attack on the notions of synonymity, meaning and identity.

as having meaning, we say something about how things are, and how things are is just what is supposed to remain an open question. Keynes's National Income matrix, Quesnay's Tableau Economique, Marx's reproduction scheme are all different ways of dividing up the economic universe, tautological within the paradigm which each defines. Because none is subject to proof within its own theory, we cannot conclude that this is grounds for the neutrality of the system. Nothing follows from the tautology, A = A except, of course, that we are talking in terms of 'A', that 'A' is defined within the system – that it is a reputable concept.[13]

In general the problem in achieving positive economic theory is the problem of how to simplify the real world in a model. Something must be excluded from the complexities of how things are: and this must involve hypotheses which embody prejudgements about the world. These assumptions cannot themselves be justified. Hence the demand for a positive economic theory is logically unsatisfiable – a point which is independent of our individual prejudices or political preferences. For obvious reasons the economist will begin from the *status quo*, which, likely as not, he will simplify out of all existence, but in taking the *status quo* he has already committed *petitio principii*. In oversimplification he redoubles this error; however much he worries the subtle niceties of his model, his conclusions can have no relevance to real conditions. There are two faults here. The first is to pretend a virtue, which the theory cannot have, of pure objectivity. The second is to attempt through successive abstraction to strip away its remote grounding in the *status quo*, which is to strip the theory bare of any and all empirical content.[14]

13. By techniques we mean terminology and concepts acceptable within the theory. For example models which purport to deal with 'optimum' solutions, in marginalist terms, where 'maximization of satisfaction' is defined as acceptable in the theory but is indefinable operationally, lend the theory inbuilt untestability and lack of empirical content at its very core. Given this paradigm, no questions are then in order as to how satisfaction could be increased. The lack of neutrality of the 'pure analytic tool box' is considered below, p. 177. There is another obvious sense in which the demand for a positive theory which shuns the evaluative poses difficulties. Much of economic language is value loaded, for example 'normal profit' (the only profit to exist in the long run under conditions of perfect competition) or, even the term 'demand' which means 'effective demand' (demand backed by money). But it is also doubtful semantically whether there is a clear distinction between statements such as 'profits are the reward for entrepreneurial risk and abstinence', and statements like 'Entrepreneurial skill and abstinence should be rewarded'.

14. How, it may be asked, could a theory be otherwise: all theories must abstract, and in doing so commit *petitio principii*. Correct. Philosophy–economics–sociology, in so far as it is the result of the division of labour, involves the divorce of theory and practice. Theory becomes in essence abstract (see Mao, footnote 10) and at the same time ideological in justifying and perpetuating the accompanying division of classes.

## The abstractness of theory

The positive–normative dispute is only the beginning of the methodologically false pretensions of economic theory: the inbuilt inability of economic theory to relate its models to the world in a logically satisfactory way. The abstractness of economic theory, which we have seen by no means secures neutrality for its models, perhaps is the most striking feature of the body of microeconomic theory. The feature of abstractness is intimately connected with the *a priori* character of this part of theory. As the so-called accidents are stripped away from the 'substance' of the economic problem, theory gets left with a residue of logical categories.[15] Economics then becomes the business of the armchair philosopher evolving hypotheses *in abstractum* to 'test' them within the confines of logic guided by political–philosophical preferences.[16]

Economic theory is littered with 'discoveries' of natural laws, which ascribe eternity to the *status quo*. For example, marginal-revenue-product theory purports to explain through allocation of resources[17] the distribution between wages and, euphemistically, rent (which in a two-factor model of capital and labour is profit). Here the relative growth of profits oddly becomes a function of two factors, growth of population and technological change. Man can expect to have little control over these factors.

---

What is fundamentally wrong with bourgeois theory is not that its models commit *petitio principii*, but that the principle selected is the wrong one (this is the point which the section on p. 174 takes up), namely the assumption of a static world where relations of production are immutable and eternal, as opposed to an assumption that the essence, and therefore direction, of the socio-economic system is given by the dynamic force of the two poles of a contradiction – capitalist class and the proletariat.

15. See *'The Holy Family'*, where Marx discusses speculative philosophy's treatment of reality by abstraction from particular fruits to the pure substance 'The Fruit'.

16. Marx's attack on classical economics, in *The Poverty of Philosophy*, argues that economic theory attempts to discover in empirical relationships, immutable, eternal laws of nature, which 'slumber in the impersonal reason of humanity'. The discovery of these laws shows the capitalist order to be the natural order.

17. Yet this model is *still* current orthodoxy for the basic economic theory course, despite Joan Robinson's demonstration of the impossibility of measuring capital independently of its valuation. Recently the theory of 'double-switching' has again dared to suggest that the problems of distribution and allocation cannot be identified. This time it has been shown that as the price ratio of capital to labour rises it is not true that the profit maximizer will employ more labour and less capital. Fundamentally the attacks are the same. Capital cannot be considered independently of time. For capital is embodied labour (over time). But bourgeois economic theory wants two factors of production, labour and capital, so that both can earn a 'justified' reward. So despite theoretical overthrow, neo-classical theory proceeds apace, and rejections follow, with ever-increasing complexity, in its train.

They are determined within the natural order of things – and so, by implication, the share of profits in income is fixed in heaven.

Another example is the oft-quoted constancy of the share of wages and profits in the total product. This 'inexplicable' fact has been considered as partial evidence for a further remarkable abstraction, the Cobb–Douglas production function. This function enjoys the most ridiculous properties which add up to assumptions of constant returns to scale and constant elasticity of substitution of factors. These properties are as mystical and mathematically elegant as the constancy of shares in the abstract world of classical economics. The relationship between those who earn profits and those who produce them is ignored.[18]

Perhaps the best example within economic theory of an immutable law is the law of supply and demand, with the associated derivation of the equilibrium 'just' price. This equilibrium model suffers all the characteristics of abstractness in its assumptions, which bear little relationship to the nature of markets, and fails of all but intuitive 'proof', despite fifty years of effort in this direction. As Blaug says:

The concept of a demand curve has, after all, only limited practical applicability. A demand curve, like a supply curve, is an aid to straight thinking. It is nothing but a device for organizing forces that influence price into one or another category. The Marshallian 'cross' of demand and supply helps us to understand why a free market [it doesn't exist] tends to clear itself [markets don't except in the sense that what is bought is always sold], why an equilibrium price once reached may be stable [which is true by definition] and how prices act as signals transmitting relevant information to buyers and sellers [ideological nonsense]. They permit us to indicate without quantitative precision what would happen to price and quantity if income or technology underwent specified changes [intuitions tell us as much without quantitative precision].[19] It is not too much to say that almost everything we know about the behaviour of the economic system can be illuminated by way of reference to the fundamental cross of supply and demand [which well illustrates the advances of economic theory] (1964).

Yet these natural laws have been 'applied'. The natural eternal laws of supply and demand continue to lend a 'scientific' justification for the doctrines of *laissez-faire* and free competition. So long as the government

18. It has recently been shown by Fisher that so-called econometric 'proofs' of the validity of the Cobb–Douglas function, and hence of the marginalist theory expressed in it, are due simply to the mathematical structure of the function in relation to the method of proof, and not to the accuracy of its representation of reality (1971).

19. Not to mention informed 'intuitions' about externalities on the demand side (bandwagon, snob, Veblen effects), externalities on the supply side, economies of scale, lagged relations, and the interdependence of demand and supply through advertising.

does not interfere with the free play of market forces, God's invisible hand will look after the interests of all. Specifically, the theory justified Trevelyan's conviction at the time of the Irish Famine that it would be economically disastrous to allow the import, still less encourage the gift, of wheat to relieve the famine-stricken peasants. It is estimated that nearly two million starved in the process of protecting the free play of the laws of supply and demand (Woodham-Smith, 1962). Equally the 'cross' explained the functions of the labour market, determining wage rates and employment levels. This application of the theory has the ridiculous corollary that unemployment only occurs where workers refuse to work for the equilibrium 'just' wage. During the slump of the 1930s this theory 'justified' demands, reinforced by American pressure, for cuts in wages and the dole to end the economic disaster.

But perhaps the most fundamental way in which the abstractness of theory reflects its ideological character is shown through the model of perfect competition. A perfectly competitive market, because of its absurd assumptions, could not exist, yet as a theory it is used to justify *laissez-faire* policies. Because, under these ridiculous assumptions, it can be shown that government intervention in markets will distort the system away from its natural equilibrium of maximum profit and efficiency, the model is used to support calls for less government interference. However, although economists may have seen through this case of the Ricardian vice, they have not, it seems, seen the methodological ineptitude of starting with a model whose assumptions disclaim any relation to existing conditions, and then attempting to apply the model by building into its abstract structure a selection of practical 'accidents' or exceptions (for example, the models of pure monopoly and monopolistic competition). If a model starts from an *a priori*, abstract (quite unreal) set of assumptions, then it cannot (logically) explain the world with the addition of selected 'accidents' which lend the model reality. The relationship between theory and reality cannot be 'begin from the ideal, abstractum, and then work down to the practical detail', because until you have built in all the empirical content of the individual case, you cannot have sufficient reason, within the model itself, for supposing your selection of accidents to be the correct one.

## Individualistic methodology: the non-structural character of theory

The development of the theory of the firm, from the original model of perfect competition, epitomizes the inherent weakness of abstract, 'ideal' models. But it also points to another weakness of the theory, its non-structural character. The guiding principle of the many successive approximations of the theory of the firm towards reality was the principle which lends the model determinacy – the principle of maximization of profit. But the trouble is that although certainly firms do aim to maximize profits (despite reticence of theory on this matter now it has adapted to the separation of ownership and management), economic theory has no way of making sense of this notion in applying its original ideal model to the world of oligopoly. Pre-Keynesian economic theory is closely allied with the philosophy of possessive individualism. Each man acting in his own interests acts for the benefit of all, or, logically, the behaviour of the totality, or group, is a simple aggregation of the behaviour of the parts. Now the theory of oligopolistic markets is an interesting case where this individualistic methodology cannot accommodate real conditions. In oligopoly, given the principle of maximization of profit, one firm's estimate of its own best practice depends upon the firm's expectations of how its competitors will respond to its own decisions, and the same point applies to each firm within the market. Here then the market cannot be explained via explanation of each individual firm's behaviour, in isolation from other firms; rather each part of the market can only be explained when the individual firm is considered, and defined, as a firm within a particular group, or structure. At the present, the best that economic theory has been able to offer in pursuit of its individualistic methodology is an application of the theory of games which, with the help of many years' computer time, can work out one best strategy for one firm.[20] But clearly this can provide no understanding of how in fact the firm within an oligopolistic structure does behave.

The same methodological failure occurs in demand theory through the embarrassment of certain externalities. For example, the Veblen effects, or the bandwagon and snob effects, indicate that consumers' preferences are not mutually independent. Economic theory cannot simply aggregate the behaviour pattern of individuals to derive the behaviour of the group. Despite these developments, and their strong challenge to welfare economics, economists still attempt resistance to this methodological flaw. For example, Samuelson writes:

We economists are twitted that our books always harp on Robinson Crusoe. True enough: we do find that the economic decisions of a single man furnish a dramatic way of simplifying our basic principles. But these days we have an even more dramatic device for illustrating the fundamental facts of economic

20. To work out the most efficient way to assemble a product with one hundred parts gives $110! = 9 \cdot 3 \times 10^{157}$ possible alternatives, which with a high speed computer, inspecting $10^6$ orderings per second, would take $3 \times 10^{114}$ years to cover all possibilities (see Clarkson, 1968).

life: we use the example of a fully collectivized society ... the contrast between such a model and our realistic everyday world is, of course, enormous. And therein lies its value (1967).

For the unreality of the present theory we are intended to substitute the artificial triviality of another logical abstraction – what Samuelson calls the communist utopia of 'Marxist Stalinist Russia'.

In fact economic theory has not been short of proofs of the underivability of the whole from the sum of the parts. Most notably, Arrow's proof that a social welfare function cannot be derived from individual preferences, still remains largely ignored in the literature; textbooks of welfare economics, the supreme glorification of perfect competition, still run off the press.[21]

It is a fundamental tenet of Marxist thought that the individual cannot be defined or understood in isolation. Not only is the built-in individualism of economic theory itself a reflection of our ideology, but it founds abstract and structurally incorrect theory, which through its inapplicability, or triviality, becomes justification for political views such as the doctrine of *laissez-faire*. This doctrine is itself interestingly deceptive since it promotes, under conditions of developing capitalism, the very conditions it seeks to eliminate. The more intense the competition between firms, the faster the weaker brothers will fall out, providing stimulus to further monopolization and concentration of industry.[22]

Economic theory thus works at the level of appearances – the level of the words of politicians. It should work at the level of understanding the dynamics of the system, which here consist in the principle of self-interest, maximization of profits, which work unilaterally in the direction of larger conglomerate industrial structures. The ideological attachments of the *laissez-faire* doctrines which profess aversion to such development at the same time can only act to further it.

### A-historicism of economic theory

A cause, or further reflection, of this methodological failure to deal with the structural relationships of economic units is the a-historical character of theory. The most obvious example, and well explained in its methodologi-

21. Another example of a totality which cannot be treated as the simple sum of the parts is Keynes's savings paradox: whereas each individual saves more to make himself richer, everyone (the aggregate) gets poorer *ceteris paribus*. Another example comes from Foreign Trade Theory: though it is in the advantage of each country individually to pursue protectionist policy, it is not in the advantage of all.

22. It is for instance by no means inconsistent that Enoch Powell should support free competition: the small manufacturer will gain a certain warmth of heart, but the economic conditions necessitating increasing concentration will thereby be intensified.

cal implications by Frank (1967), is the economic theory of underdeveloped countries. A whole branch of economic theory, from Rostow to Lewis, poses the question of the vicious circle of underdevelopment. Answers to the basic problem of how to get into the growth league traverse the full gamut of ideology from arguments for more missionaries introducing the Christian virtues of abstinence (to raise the savings ratio and lower the birth rate) to more tax-holidays for foreign 'enterprise'. Rostow's famous theory of 'take-off' posits countries as being at various levels of development (pre-take-off, take-off and self-sustaining rates of growth) but no explanation is offered about movement from one stage to another, or why some countries have made the grade, and others haven't. It has now been pointed out by several economists that a static dualistic approach to the problem cannot provide a solution, since it refuses to contemplate the historical development of underdevelopment where the cause must lie. The economists' approach to the problem of underdevelopment is comparable to the doctor faced with a sick child, who argues from a theoretically abstract model of his own conditions of perfect health to the weaknesses of the child's basic organisms, forgetting to inquire what filth the child ate for supper the previous night. Several historical examples (India, the Philippines, Peru, for example) suggest that countries have gone 'backwards' relatively to the developing capitalist countries. This suggests strong evidence for the view that the answer to the problem of underdevelopment will not be found outside the context of the historical conditions which have generated these conditions. Development (statistically and practically) does not occur in isolation, but in changing relationships between countries.[23]

Thus the theory of underdevelopment in its methodological inadequacy fails from the outset because it considers each country in isolation from the group of which it is a part, which determines the characteristics of the individual. The a-historical character of the theory is part of a wider structural weakness of methodology, the undynamic character of the theory.

### Economic theory as undynamic

In most economic theory, time is the sum of comparative static positions (as the totality is the sum of the parts). Where the absence of time is felt,

23. Frank shows – through analysis of the metropolis–satellite relationship – how development of capitalist countries has been at the expense of an increasing gap between developed and underdeveloping countries, and that far from the LDC remaining in a 'feudal' state as compared with the DCs, capitalism by replicating its own economic relationships within these LDCs has made them as much a part of capitalism as is the proletariat a part of industrial capitalism in the DCs.

the method is simply to move these points closer together. Most obviously, in Keynes, the theory allows for jumps from one equilibrium position to another; but, since Zeno, it has been clear that a line is not the sum of points, and thus a set of comparative static points cannot found a dynamic theory. Time is not neutral, nor is it redundant, as the neo-classicist, with his reversible marginal curves, would have us believe.

It is precisely this failure to 'add in' the time factor which dogs the Keynesian income determination model, through the unresolved controversy of how the short-run consumption function can jump on to the path of the long-run function. Shifts from short to long run remain indeterminate. This failure to introduce the dynamic element of changes in demand and income leads to the serious indeterminacy between employment and income levels. Herein lies one aspect of the irrelevance of the Keynesian model to economic conditions today, for in this model inflation and unemployment are at opposite poles, and inconsistent with each other. On the other hand, in cases where it can be argued that economic theory does contain a dynamic element (the cobweb theorem or much of trade-cycle theory) this dynamic element derives from an elegant mathematical self-generative function substituting for a theory. For example, the combination of the multiplier and accelerator theories will, with certain parameters, generate self-damping cycles of economic growth. However, the particular values of the parameters are patently absurd in relation to the assumptions and expectations of the model (Samuelson, 1939). Instead, exogenous floors and ceilings are imported, which leave the paths between indeterminate.

Economic theory suffers from an inadequate concept of causation: economic hypotheses and methods of testing are based on a Humean view that the cause must precede the effect and be constantly conjoined with it. Now it is known that the crucial macroeconomic variables are intercorrelated. Neither the nature of the hypothesis, nor the method of its testing, can provide independent corroboration for any particular favourable regression result, which would confirm that the hypothesis is the correct way round. An example is Kaldor's theory of the relationship between growth of output and change in productivity in manufacturing.[24] Now it has been shown that the causal relationship here could as well be the other way round. If all we have as evidence for a causal hypothesis is regression results, indicating constant conjunction, then how could our methodology ever allow more than intuition in support of any particular hypothesis? In addition it is logically possible to have two inconsis-

24. The theoretical 'justification' for the introduction of the Selective Employment Tax, though of course not necessarily the 'justification' for government or Treasury.

tent theories, both equally satisfactory at 'explaining' the data. How can the method in economic theory offer any way of distinguishing between them aside from intuitions?

The assumption behind this view of causation is the crux of methodological inadequacy of empiricism. It lies behind all equilibrium theory. The world is assumed to be such that its dynamic is provided by a tendency to move into equilibrium, disturbed occasionally by aberrations. The assumption is that the world is naturally in harmony. Such an approach, dating at least from Parmenides – that all is at rest – has always presented difficulties for a theory of causation. Where after all can the first push have come from? If, however, we adopt an alternative to this model of the world, where the nature of things is conflict, not equilibrium, then the structure of the world is one of movement; it is rest which has to be explained. Persistently in economics we meet the condition that where A causes B, so B also causes A. For example, an increase in income causes increased investment, but, equally, increased investment causes increased income. Or, the development of England causes the underdevelopment of India, which itself then causes further development of England (Robinson, 1966).

Is economic theory correct in adopting the Humean view of causation as a linear relationship? It is this billiard-ball explanation of the development of the world which provides the prime methodological inadequacy, and fundamentally explains the ideological, apologetic content of economic theory. For it is this seemingly innocuous tenet of faith in a stable world which provides the basis for erecting present economic relations into eternal immutable laws made in the heaven of mystical speculative construction. It is this conception of the world which underlies the false polarity offered within this methodology between vacuous *a priori* reasoning of speculative construction versus the uninterpreted mass of raw data of empiricism.

If however socio-economic relations are seen as essentially explicable in terms of the contradiction between classes, the world is seen as essentially dynamic, the individual elements as structurally interrelated and co-determining. In recognizing the conflict between these two world views, we also can see explicitly the class bias of present economic theory. The alternative world view does not propose a better way of doing bourgeois economics. The alternative world view poses an economics which is not ideology, but is a part of changing the world, because economic relations can only be understood in the experience of changing them (see footnote 11). In explicitly taking the part of the proletariat in the conflict between classes, economic theory ceases to be abstract, it unites theory and practice. With the victory of the proletariat, the division of labour itself ends, and with it the need for theory which is necessarily abstract and therefore ideological.

In summary economic theory performs the ideological function of apologetics for the capitalist system not merely through providing propaganda in textbooks, or failing to raise relevant political-economic questions. It is ideology because its methodology is inadequate. It assumes a relationship between theory and reality which insists on the autonomous movement of ideas. Economic theory reflects philosophical individualism, the supremacy of rationality in *a priori* abstract thought, and a view of the world as naturally tending towards rest, harmony. Hence economic theory can develop and puzzle at length upon theories which are vacuous. It is in virtue of their emptiness, that such theories can be used to lend 'scientific' justification to political-economic policy. It is then economic developments themselves which determine how the theory will be used, and thus its acceptability. Because of the persistence of the Ricardian vice, economics can justify anything, for anything follows from a tautology. Economic theory does not even have the honour of setting the problematic of the tautology. The problematic is set by economic needs. But the form of the tautology sets the definition of relevant questions and methods of approach. Hence within ideology, ideology cannot be rejected.

## Course reform: proposals

Roughly there are two kinds of proposal for course reform in economics. The first is derived from Professor Joan Robinson who suggests that economic theory courses should henceforth be divided threefold, into the history of economic theory, economic history of the developed and colonial–neo-colonial world, and statistical methods and techniques. What is important in this suggestion is the apparent faith in the possibility of neutral techniques: the pure analytical tool box. This supposition is one which is common amongst 'left-wing' economists. They tend to believe that the economics student is lucky, for the future communist world will need its planners, and the good revolutionary can catch up on these techniques under capitalism.

There are important respects in which techniques are not neutral. Some techniques are obviously tied to particular economic or philosophical approaches like optimizing models. For example, linear programming which works within the assumption of linearities and independence of consumer and producer units, or game theory, which presupposes assumptions of an individualistic, non-structural, Benthamite, world. The regression techniques of econometrics stipulate as an essential condition the absence of auto-correlation. Yet a dialectic view of the world starts from the assumption that events are to be explained through their auto-development, the conflict between the two poles of a contradiction which are the essence of the object.

But the most interesting candidate for neutrality is input–output techniques. The theory is that if the politicians will give us the objectives (outputs) the technicians will tell us the most efficient means (inputs). But this broad confidence in the powers of techniques raises fundamental questions, not only at the level of economics, but equally for revolutionary theory. The solution to the input–output matrix requires the assumption that techniques and coefficients are merely a matter of engineering. Whether or not these coefficients are adjusted for social benefit, they can only be determined by present allocations of factors. Any particular decision will predetermine future choices, in that it will guide what is 'learnt by being done' and what paths research and development should follow. Worship of the planner overlooks the inherent circularity in the planning exercise.

At the more political level, the difference between the capitalist and the communist economy is not the difference between anarchy of the market, and planned production and allocation by the technocrat. Planning cannot be instituted from the top. It is something which grows out of the socio-economic practice of workers' control and the integration of means and ends at the factory level. The choice of what should be produced is not independent of the choice of how it can be produced. Nor is the choice to be made on a utopian *tabula rasa*, but through adjustment of present techniques, product mix and final products. What is fundamentally at fault with the capitalist economic system is not only that it wastes human and natural resources in producing a Baran and Sweezy type surplus of soap powders and nuclear bombs, goods which people do not 'really' want. What is fundamentally at fault is that under capitalism there is no integration between ends and means of relations of production, between political choices, and the practice of production on the shop floor. The worship of the planner, and his techniques, is merely a replication of the division of labour, the divorce of politics from economics, of theory from practice.[25]

25. An important parallel can be drawn here with Lenin in 'What is to be Done?' where he approvingly quotes Kaustky on the need, in the emergence of socialist consciousness, for profound scientific knowledge of modern economic science, which is the preserve of the bourgeois intelligentsia (see Magri, 1970, for some implications of this Leninist view of the nature of a Revolutionary Party). In Hegelian terminology the problem for the planner is the unification of the general (social need) with

Although of course there may be uses for such techniques, it would be quite wrong to regard them as neutral *vis-à-vis* the theories of economics. But a further reason must warn us against the suggestion that course reform should provide for the study of such techniques, for it is a demand precisely consistent both with the development of economic theory as ideology, and the development of job markets for economists. Questions of economic theory have tended to be replaced by questions about terms and techniques: the reasons for this development are clear from the methodology of the theory and its ideological role. For one way to keep a trivial, ideological theory in play is precisely to keep on generating unanswerable questions upon which the proof of the theory can at least be made to look as if it depends. Partly in virtue of the methodological inadequacies of the theory, especially its abstractness, the triviality of the theory tends to generate a succession of developments in elegant mathematics, concerned with proving the theory. Its own triviality breeds, and feeds on, the development of mathematical extensions and formulations. This increasing mathematization, which pervades economic theory via mathematical reformulation and econometric methods of testing, has had two important effects on the form of economics courses, which bear some relation to the issue of course reform.

The first is that the increasing emphasis on mathematical techniques has tended to reinforce an attitude of passive reception of economics by students. It is not up to the student to question his mentors, still less the theory, until he has grasped all the tools. The student who wishes to approach economics in the spirit of political economy will not only be discouraged, but will find the form of an economics course hard to suffer. This tends to generate a pervasive boredom, which ultimately the student will be persuaded to put down to his own personal incompetence and inadequacy.

But the increasing mathematization also reflects and causes a similar approach amongst those who wish to question the theory. The argument is always posed that no one is in a position to question a theory within terms of an altogether different theory until the current theory can be proved wrong. But just as it is part of the nature of economic theory as ideology that it generates its own impossibility of proof, so also it contains impossibility of disproof. But to see this feature of economic theory re-

---

the particular (economic productive units). It is a fundamental part of Marxism that this unification (in the Party or in economic relations of production) is not attained by an ideal blueprint produced by the most modern scientific method and superimposed upon the 'practice' of the proletariat.

quires a historical approach, and mathematization and increasing technical difficulty discourage the interdisciplinary approach. Economic theory
thus incorporates defences at many levels against criticisim; and this
must in part explain how such a curious assortment of trivial, vacuous
theory is still taken seriously. If course reform is to have any practical
relevance to economics as ideology, or to organization of student protest,
it must at least overcome the obsession which the theory itself generates
with mathematical techniques. Learning the techniques is a barrier to
criticism of the theory, as well as a sure pathway, at present, into lucrative
employment.

The second kind of proposal for course reform is that based on a demand
for counter-culture. Economic theory must be applied to the needs of the
working class, to service the workers' revolutionary struggles. The working
class should be brought into the universities to understand the nature
of its enemy, capitalism. This understanding can be given through the
study of *Capital*, or at least in a thorough training of how to fight productivity deals. The proposal is misguided in several respects. Firstly, the
working class for obvious reasons has neither desire nor time nor means
to come into the haven of the university to learn revolution in a weekly
tutorial. The organization and political development which would make
this demand anything but utopian presuppose a very different level of
political consciousness and organization than at present exist. Secondly,
the proposal reflects precisely the attitudes current among the 'left'
today, that people can be taught how to fight capitalism through leaflets,
papers, meetings and lectures. It is not that the students have nothing
to say to the working class (as the C.P. suggested to the French students
in May 1968), nor that the correct place for the petit-bourgeois student is
to tail behind in worship of the class with the mission of revolution.
What is wrong is the conception that theory, as embodied in the party,
can be brought to the workers – the practice, or brawn of revolution –
through the bare spoken or written word. Revolutionary theory is not
qualitatively on a level with bourgeois theory. It is methodologically
distinct, because it can only be learnt, or taught, in the practice of organization. What is needed is to see a way to fight, and this cannot be taught
in theory; it must be found and shown through practice.

What is wrong with economic theory is not just that it reifies the consumer society, or treats man as a statistical average. In the same way,
what is 'wrong' with capitalism is not only that it is immoral, unfair,
inequitable or unjust. What is wrong with the theory is that it is structurally,
or methodologically, inadequate, such that it cannot be corrected within
its own methodology. Attempt at 'disproof' of theory is as incorrect as

attempt at its 'proof'. For proof-disproof must accept the problematic given by this inadequate methodology. These weaknesses in the theory reflect the nature of social conditions which have generated and dictated acceptability to the theory. Capitalism is a structure where to oppose it, from within, is as incorrect as to support it. For capitalism is not a conspiracy, by the rich, which can be altered on substitution of better-intentioned men. Capitalism like its own theory can only be opposed from outside its own system by organizations which are qualitatively distinct, based not on silent majority support for a correct (abstract) theory but on active participation in a struggle to change social-economic relations, to end the division of labour and hence the division of theory and practice.

## References

BARAN, P. (1957), *The Political Economy of Growth*, Monthly Review Press.

BARAN, P., and SWEEZY, P. (1968), *Monopoly Capital*, Penguin.

BLAUG, M. (1964), *Economic Theory in Retrospect*, Heinemann.

CLARKSON, G. P. E. (ed.) (1968), *Managerial Economics*, Penguin.

FEYERABEND, P. (1970), in I. Lakatos and P. Musgrave (eds.), *Criterion and the Growth of Knowledge*, Cambridge University Press.

FISHER, F. (1971), 'Aggregate production functions and the explanation of wages: a simulation experiment', *Review of Economics and Statistics*.

FRANK, A. G. (1967), *Capitalism and Underdevelopment in Latin America*, Monthly Review Press.

GLYN, A., and SUTCLIFFE, B. (1971), 'The critical condition of British capital', *New Left Review*, no. 66.

KALDOR, N. (1965), *Productivity and Growth in the UK*, Cambridge University Press.

KUHN, T. S. (1962), *The Structure of Scientific Revolutions*, Chicago University Press.

MAGRI, L. (1970), *New Left Review*, no. 60.

MAO TSE TUNG (1966), *Four Essays on Philosophy*, Foreign Languages Press, Peking.

OPARIN, A. I. (1959), *The Origins of Life*, Pergamon.

QUINE, W. V. O. (1960), *Word and Object*, MIT Press.

ROBINSON, J. (1962), *Economic Philosophy*, Penguin.

ROBINSON, J. (1966), *The New Mercantilism*, Cambridge University Press.

SAMUELSON, P. (1967), *Economics*, McGraw-Hill.

SAMUELSON, P. (1939), 'Interaction of the multiplier and the principle of the accelerator', *Review of Economics and Statistics*.

SCHUMPETER, J. (1954), *A History of Economic Analysis*, Oxford University Press.

SELSAM, H. (ed.) (1963), *Reader in Marxist Philosophy*, New World Paperbacks.

WOODHAM-SMITH, C. (1962), *The Great Hunger*, Hamish Hamilton.

# The 'Economics of Education'
Adam Westoby

With the very rapid expansion of secondary and higher education in the developed capitalist countries since the Second World War there has occurred, in parallel, a boom in research and teaching of 'the economics of education'. Similar developments have taken place in, for example, 'health economics' and, more generally, the miscellany of subjects in what has come to be known as 'the economics of human resources', including studies of the 'economics' of the plastic and performing arts.

In providing a simplified guide to 'the economics of education' (as opposed to the essentially non-economic techniques of 'manpower planning') I have in mind to do two things. Firstly to show, in a field which exhibits in microcosm the application of the basic methods of neoclassical economics, what these methods are and what they presuppose; and secondly to illustrate – as 'the economics of education' so sharply does – the way in which the thinking of a declining and corrupt capitalist class, whatever lip-service it may pay to its own past achievements, tends to reduce all human activity, all culture, and human beings themselves, to the barren test of cash values in the market-place.

The expansion of post-primary education has not been the result of a deliberate policy for economic growth agreed by the dominant groups of employers – such as gave rise to the post-war arrangements for international monetary cooperation, the flow of American capital into Europe, and the domestic investment and industrial policies of the individual capitalist states themselves. Rather it has come about as the result of pressure from the working and middle classes for enlarged educational opportunities; a pressure which many employers have been willing to accede to because they recognize that better educated workers – like healthier workers – are more productive, and that a modern industrial economy requires a considerable section of the working population to possess forms of skill and training which can only be efficiently provided within the formal educational system.

This recognition is, of course, nothing new. The Mechanics Institutes of the last century were set up by enlightened industrialists precisely to provide the skilled workers and technicians required in the new industries. What is new is the attempt to calculate the gains to the economy as a whole flowing from educated labour. For the first time the state has sought economic criteria to plan the types and scale of courses offered under its education budget. And where was the conceptual framework within which this task was to be undertaken? Why, it was already to hand in the well-tested and all-embracing theories of neoclassical economics.[1]

During the 1950s some economists began to remark that the average earnings of workers with more years of schooling are higher than those with fewer years. In part, of course, this was to be explained by the greater ability, the different racial and geographical composition and the supposedly sharper motivations of these who travelled further through the educational system. But having made, in various studies, statistical corrections for the influence of such factors, they concluded that a part, at least, of the extra earnings were attributable to higher education. Now, as any well-behaved student of economics knows, all income must have a source-cum-recipient (or, as scholastic philosophy more precisely had it, an efficient cause), and the primary sources of income in the modern economy are two in number, namely labour and capital. How, then, are the higher earnings of educated labour to be explained? Naturally by the supposition that these workers carry 'embodied' in them various quantities of 'capital'. Not ordinary capital, you understand, but 'human capital'. And how is this capital created? Well, it is the economic end product of the educational system, its 'output'.

The groundwork having been thus briskly laid the scene was set for a veritable flowering of theories on the 'human capital market'. An excellent summary view of these will be found in Mark Blaug's *An Introduction to the Economics of Education* (1970).[2] In essence the prospective student (or his family) is regarded as a 'profit maximizer'. Considering a given course of education he will compare the extra earnings (after tax) which he expects it to produce and compare these with the private costs (basically the direct cost in fees plus the earnings he will forgo while studying). He will combine – according to one of several mutually contradictory

1. Modern bourgeois economics, of which the basic framework is that the prices of goods, and the quantities produced, are determined by 'supply' and 'demand'.

2. One self-evident difference between 'human' and ordinary capital is that 'human capital' is subject to market imperfections through being inextricably connected to individual human beings, and in civilized societies human beings are not, you understand, bought and sold. Thus it is that Blaug (undoubtedly one of the most clear-sighted advocates of 'human capital' theories) introduces the methods in his volume by way of an eight-page discussion of 'The Economics of Slavery'.

formulae[3] – these sums to estimate a private 'rate of return' or 'present value' for comparison with other available investments, educational or otherwise. As Blaug has it 'Rigorously expressed, we are postulating the existence of a rational educational calculus according to which students or their parents act *as if* they were equalizing rates of return on all possible investment options available to them' (Blaug, 1970, p. 171).[4] Blaug does not explain, we should notice, how a 'rational educational calculus' is provided by the assumption that students or their parents act *as if* they were equalizing rates of return. If they merely act 'as if', it is possible that their reasoning involves quite other factors, or none, and that their behaviour is not based on the reasoning at all. Blaug here swallows *en passant*, and with a casualness only to be marvelled at, the 'pudding is in the eating' theory of psychology according to which motives are those which agents – i.e. anyone apart from 'deviants' – would have had if they were behaving rationally. It is one of the chief glories (and conveniences) of neoclassical economics that it is consistent with virtually all theories of psychology, and with none.

It is hard to disagree with Blaug when he adds, in the very next sentence, 'Put like that it sounds absurd.' Yet what he means by 'absurd' is something relatively superficial – that the stylized picture he is putting forward is patently at odds with reality. Considered seriously, there is a deeper absurdity to the theory. For what is striking about it is its attempt to reduce every element in the economy to a version of the rational, anonymous profit-maximizer who forms the basic animal and essential building block of the neo-classical economic universe. In similar vein the individual 'in general' is traditionally treated in the elementary textbooks as a 'utility-maximizer' and the formal (i.e. algebraic) treatment of his behaviour is identical with that used in the theory of the firm (Henderson and Quandt, 1958). Ideology has here reached the point where the capitalist class, try as it may to study social reality, can perceive nothing but its own image, wherever it may look. Built into the intellectual framework of the central social 'science' is the assumption that, if the hallmarks of the propertied class are eliminated, nothing will remain.

In justice to these dealers in false consciousness it should be said that efforts have not been spared to escape from the absurdities inherent in

3. For a discusssion of the forms and convolutions of these see Massé (1962).

4. Truly, much is required of the modern student. Not only must he diligently perform the role allocated him by the Sunday press as a peddler of pernicious and inflammatory doctrines to an otherwise contented proletariat, but he must be a good businessman to boot. Little wonder if students are sometimes perplexed by their own image.

the theories. The fact that 'utility', if it is to provide a theory with the requisite generality, must be defined so as to be *in principle* impossible to measure (i.e. so that the question 'What is utility?' can *only* have the answer 'What the individual maximizes') has led to the somewhat more sophisticated theory of 'revealed preference'. And, to return to the economics of education and our stockbroker-scholar, there have been no lack of attempts to make the basic picture more 'realistic'. Education, it is admitted, is not only an 'investment good' (like steel mills) but also a 'consumption good' (like toffee). The problem, however, of deciding what proportion of it is 'investment' and what 'consumption' has proved insuperable. This turns out, fortunately, to be a secondary consideration. For the modern educational planner is primarily interested in the *social* rate of return (as opposed to the private). His calculations are thus based on the social costs (subsidies and grants to students, the capital and labour costs of educational institutions, the foregone earnings of students) and the social product of the educated labour produced – usually taken to be accurately measured by its pre-tax earnings. A great deal of ink has been consumed in debates on what elements (increased civic responsibility in the population, and hence a reduced 'law and order' budget; the release of married women into the labour force due to the child-minding functions of nurseries, and so on)[5] should be counted among the social costs and yields, all of it turning on the question of how much a (marginal) increase in the scale of this or that type of education may be expected to add to present and future gross national product.

A great volume of applied literature estimating and comparing the rates of return to various types and levels of education, in developed and underdeveloped countries, exists and grows day by day. This effusion has in no degree been inhibited by the discovery, by a number of more serious theoretical economists, that the foundations of neo-classical theory are themselves logically incoherent. (For a critique of neo-classical theory, see Rose Dugdale's essay in this book, pp. 159–81 and Vaisey, 1969.) The way in which the demise of neo-classical theory has been ignored in the 'economics' of education, as in most other areas of applied economics based on the theory of marginal revenue product (the theory that the 'price' of a factor of production is determined by its marginal contribution to total output) is an object lesson in the fundamentally abstract character of economics teaching and research. While one may make one's assumptions as improbable and speculative as one pleases, the unforgivable sin is to be at fault in one's logic. And when a logical flaw is discovered in the very foundations of the econometric studies to which regiments

5. For an entertaining assortment see Weisbrod (1962).

of highly-paid social scientists and millions of dollars worth of data gathering and computer time have been devoted in the last fifteen years, the only dignified response is – silence.[6]

This is not to say there is *no* residual caution about the realism of the particular assumptions. The 'economics of education' scarcely appears in most undergraduate economics syllabuses in England. As a discipline it rides on the premise that the theories of 'rational resource allocation' through the imputing of prices, may be applied virtually wherever one pleases. For the initiated the existence of such studies seems to confirm the 'generality' of neo-classical theory. There is the risk, however, that the naive might discover in them evidence of its vacuousness. Thus only those who have satisfactorily served their time at the altar are permitted to roam the Elysian fields.

6. This sensitivity on matters of logic, and the cavalier attitude with regard to reality, are the vestigial traces of the gentleman-scholar in the modern economist. After all, it is self-evident that *facts* are ordinary, rather vulgar things, easily accessible to the mob in the course of their everday business (an observation which, in British empiricism has achieved the dignity of a full-blown philosophical method). The proper manipulation of logic on the other hand, requires a well-trained mind and plenty of leisure. Hence economic theory has become, in practice, the Political Economy of 'As If', for whom reality is essentially subjunctive.

## References

BLAUG, M. (1970), *An Introduction to the Economics of Education*, Allen Lane The Penguin Press; Penguin, 1972.

HENDERSON, J. M., and QUANDT, R. E. (1958), *Microeconomic Theory*, McGraw-Hill.

MASSE, P. (1962), *Optimal Investment Decisions*, Prentice-Hall.

VAISEY, J. *et al.* (1969), *The Economics of Educational Costing*, Part IIIa, Gulbenkian Institute, Lisbon.

WEISBROD, B. A. (1962), 'Education and investment in human capital', *Journal of Political Economy*.

# The Faith of the Mathematician
## Martin Thomas

'*Allez en avant et la foi vous viendra*' – *Jean le Rond d'Alembert*, eighteenth-century mathematician, faced with an inconsistency in the infinitesimal calculus.

No one needs a sophisticated command of the methodology of political theory to point out that a question such as 'Plato: totalitarian or democrat?' is tendentious. But in the field of the sciences there is no elucidated tradition of criticism to which one can refer oneself. So this article is concerned with tentative remarks about some particular aspects of one particular field in one particular science.[1]

### The infinitesimal calculus

The field chosen is the *differential and integral calculus*. That is, the study of the processes of differentiation ($dy/dx$) and integration $\left( \int_b^a f(x) \, dx \right)$. This field is equally of central importance in the practice of modern mathematics and a focal area in the history of mathematics (Boyer, 1959; Baron, 1969; Bourbaki, 1960, pp. 178–221).

The prehistory of the calculus certainly extends back to the Greeks. However, 'Newton was the first man to give a generally applicable method for determining an instantaneous rate of change (*i.e. differentiation*) and to invert this in the case of problems involving summation (*i.e. integration*)' (Boyer, 1959, ch. 5). The problem had thus been posed of making mathematical sense of these processes of differentiation and integration. In retrospect, the chief difficulties were those of adopting an arithmetic point of view – essential for the rigorous formulation of the calculus – rather than the geometric point of view current previously; and of elucidating the concept of a mathematical *function* – this idea had to be made basic, rather than that of *variable*, before clarity was achieved. The new concept of *variable* itself had been an integral part of the initial founding of the calculus by Newton, Leibniz, etc. Partial attempts, trying to elucidate the concept of limit (what does it mean to say that one

1. We refer only to mathematics education in universities.

quantity approaches another indefinitely nearly?), of 'ultima ratio' (limiting ratio of small increments), of instantaneous speed, of infinitesimal (infinitely small quantity), proliferated until the 1870s, when Moray and Weierstrass produced a stable formulation. These attempts developed in relation with the many paradoxes and impasses thrown up by the practical development of the calculus.

Calculus is normally taught on two levels. The first level, appropriate for elementary mathematical physics, proceeds in a manner quite similar to that of the early nineteenth century. Though infinitely small quantities are officially abjured, variables dominate rather than functions, and the concept of limit is left intuitive. The second level is indispensable for any sort of moderately advanced pure mathematics. Here we proceed in a modern and more or less axiomatic fashion, starting (usually) from some explicitly stated postulates about the real-number system, and building up the theory by rigorous deduction. This normally comes into a first-year university course. Now the phenomenon of the two levels is not in itself necessarily noxious; arguably it is a technical inevitability.[2] But, as we've seen, the two levels are linked by a complex history marked by subtle conceptual innovations. It seems to me that the logical relations between the two levels reflect the richness of the historical relations.

How, then, is the relation between the two levels handled in practice? I shall argue that no concepts adequate to comprehend the relation are present in university mathematical education. Mathematics is not simply a matter of deductive structures of formal logic, not simply a matter of formal derivations of indisputable conclusions from indisputable axioms or arbitrary postulates.[3] But the only method mathematical education has for dealing with the failure of mathematics to be encompassed by deductive models is a few catch-all phrases. Thus one level is 'unrigorous' (but, apparently, good enough for elementary students or physical scientists) and the other 'rigorous' (for the crude, absolutely rigorous; for the more sophisticated, relatively rigorous). Mathematical concepts cannot be rationally criticized, either because they are considered arbitrary or because they are considered to directly reflect reality. Thus the concept is there because it's there because it's there. All there is in the history is successive elimination of deviations from today's rigour. Mathematics

2. It is worth emphasizing that recent developments in mathematical logic have shown that the approach using 'infinitesimals' is not necessarily logically unsound (see Robinson, 1967).

3. This point has been elaborated by Georg Kreisel (see, for example, Kreisel and Krivine, 1967).

is something inert, a brute fact, not something created by human reason.[4] For the student, mathematical work becomes often enough an imposition which is just the price he pays for being at university, or, at best, a pursuit offering intellectual interest on the same level as crossword puzzles.

## The ideology of mathematical education

'At the time of the *noblesse de robe* and of mercantile capitalism, a bourgeoisie of lawyers, merchants and bankers gained a certain self-awareness through Cartesianism' (J. P. Sartre, 1964). The mathematicians of that age subscribed to Descartes' 'third precept' – 'to put my thoughts in order, starting with the objects most simple and most easy to know, to climb bit by bit . . . to the knowledge of the most complex' (*Discours de la méthode*, Part II). Euclidean geometry was regarded as an archetype for mathematics. Axioms were self-evident truths. Truth was propagated through mathematical theories by deduction starting from the axioms and ending with theorems. Any mathematical exposition not conforming to the Euclidean deductive model was not respectable, and, in fact, was outside the bounds of rationality. Thus certain important parts of mathematics – definitions, conjectures – were consigned to the realm of arbitrariness.[5] Thus mathematics not conforming to the criteria of respectability (e.g. calculus, which could be founded deductively only on a basis of arithmetic, not of geometry) caused enormous confusion and pragmatism.

The situation today is similar in some respects. I shall try to trace the broad outlines of the developments of today's 'ideology of mathematical education' from the 'Cartesian' starting point. The downfall of the conception of truth coming from axioms which represent elementary features of reality is often held to date from the founding of non-Euclidean geometry (1829). 'Non-Euclidean geometry and abstract algebra were to change the whole outlook on deductive reasoning, and not merely enlarge or modify particular divisions of science and mathematics' (Bell, 1945, p. 330). In the first place, however, it did *not* follow from the existence of

4. It has been argued that this appearance of mathematics (or any science) as a brute fact is something inseparable from the nature of science. For science to be sociologically possible, there must at any given time be a basic framework of theory accepted by all scientists. Science students just have to learn this basic framework, whether they like it or not. It is not necessarily the case that any rational account can be given for one particular framework being chosen rather than another (see, e.g. Kuhn 1962 – especially ch. 12). There is not space to discuss this argument here – I will just state that I don't accept that the history of science (of mathematics, at least) is as unintelligible as Kuhn makes out.

5. This account is drawn largely from Lakatos (1961).

non-Euclidean geometrics that mathematicians regarded Euclidean geometry as just one geometry among a variety of arbitrary systems. Consider, for example, the mathematician Cayley, speaking fifty-four years later, in 1883: 'Non-Euclidean *spaces*, he declared, seemed to him mistaken a priori; but non-Euclidean geometries ... were accepted as flowing from a change in the definition of distance' (Russell, 1956, pp. 41–2). Moreover, we should have to ask what the conditions were for non-Euclidean geometry to 'change the whole outlook', rather than being ignored or condemned as light-minded nonsense or becoming an *accepted* anomaly.

Before the seventeenth century a narrow mathematical basis sufficed for all science. The infinitesimal calculus – developed from the needs of physical science, on the whole against the mathematical scruples of those who developed it – widened that basis sufficiently to create an anomaly in the 'Cartesian' model. That is, calculus could not be made rigorous when Euclidean geometry was the basis and standard of rigour. With the increasingly various demands of science since then, there has been an accelerating proliferation of new branches of mathematics. If mathematics still adhered to the 'Cartesian' conception, then it would find itself, at best, in a permanent state of pragmatic muddle. The development, in particular, of mathematical logic, a branch of mathematics which takes mathematical systems as its object, renders the idea of a single deductive system of mathematics untenable.

Two developments in the practice of mathematics helped to form a new conception. First: the study of the 'foundations of mathematics'. Weierstrass, in the 1870s, had produced a satisfactory formulation of the differential calculus on the basis of the theory of real numbers. Later in the nineteenth century Dedekind reduced the theory of real numbers to the theory of the natural numbers $0, 1, 2, \ldots$ Peano produced a set of axioms apparently adequate to the theory of the natural numbers. Frege, and later Russell and Whitehead, with the aid of the theory of sets newly developed by Cantor, attempted what seemed to be the last stage in the definitive establishment of the foundations of mathematics. Their programme was the reduction of the whole of mathematics to logic, by the definition of numbers in logical terms. Russell and Whitehead in their monumental *Principia Mathematica* (1910–13) carried out a derivation of large parts of mathematics from elementary axioms. However, one of their axioms (the 'axiom of reducibility') was less than logically self-evident, and the envisaged reduction of mathematics to logic has never been technically plausible.

Second: the axiomatic method. Much of modern mathematics has been put into the form of formal systems – deductive systems, with specified axioms and rules of inference, using a formalized language. i.e. the axioms are assumptions, not self-evident truths, and the mathematics is not directly related to reality (contrast Euclidean geometry, where diagrams play an important role). A classical example is the axiomatization of group theory (1854). But it was not until the foundational research just described that the 'axiomatic method' achieved maturity. The precision which the axiomatic method afforded was an essential for the delicate task of determining just what concepts and postulates were necessary. Since then, and particularly in the last twenty years, there has been an explosive proliferation of new branches of mathematics, formulated on the axiomatic method.

The axiomatic method has been the main prop for a formalist ideology. Questions of mathematical truth as such, it is declared, are meaningless – one can only ask whether such and such a statement is or is not proved in such and such a formal system. One must of course inquire as to whether the formal system is logically consistent – but, apart from the criterion of consistency, mathematics can have nothing to say about the choice between different formal systems. This view enjoyed a brief philosophical vogue in the early twentieth century; for when the 'Cartesians' came to analyse mathematics down to its logical base, they exposed the fact that that base did not exist. Russell was forced to write, in *Principia*, 'The reason for accepting an axiom . . . is . . . that many propositions which are nearly indubitable can be derived from it. . . .'

Formalism appeared as a necessary synthesis of pragmatism and infallibility. The whole apparatus of truth through deduction was maintained: but the choice of the basis of the analysis was consigned to external determination.

The plausibility of formalism as a philosophy was more or less killed by certain mathematical discoveries of the late 1920s and early 1930s, notably Godel's theorems (1931). Godel showed that the mathematical systems used to formalize elementary number theory were not capable of proving all the truths of elementary number theory and that the consistency of those systems could not even be proved inside the systems themselves, let alone on weaker assumptions.[6]

### 'Cartesian–formalism'

Formalism persists as an element of an ideology, which we call, for the sake of having a label, 'Cartesian–formalist', moulding the conceptions

6. There have been attempts to salvage a new formalist philosophy of mathematics (Curry, 1951).

and methods of modern mathematical culture. The monolithic model of 'Cartesianism' has been discarded for a pluralist mathematics. Axioms, rather than being self-evident truths, are now just assumptions, the postulates of a formal system. It is clear that some formal systems are preferred to others, though it is not clear why. Definitions and conjectures are as much as ever beyond the scope of rationality.

At first sight the sheer *inefficiency* of the system of mathematical education is inexplicable. Even in terms of being able to answer university examination papers or the problems which are set as 'exercises' in mathematics courses, the results are poor – though these exams, etc. require only a moderate level of fairly stereotyped technical competence. Surely this situation serves the interests of *no one*; we should expect, at the very least, to see 'Cartesian–formalist' ideology mercilessly criticized and to see continual attempts to make the teaching of mathematics less arbitrary? We don't see such criticism or attempts; it follows that the determinant of the formation of the culture of mathematics (what is respectable, what is rational, how mathematics should be explained, etc.) is not the full development of the creative powers of mathematicians (or mathematics teachers).

In the seventeenth century mathematics was, more or less, part of the culture of the ruling class, and teaching mathematics amounted to passing on that culture. Today most students are taught mathematics in order that they may do certain skilled jobs where they will be paid wages and will give a service to their employers rather than to themselves or the community as a whole. They will engage in alienated labour, not free creation, and that is what they are trained for. The employing class as a whole has an interest in maintaining a certain amount of (certain sorts of) research in mathematics, and accordingly a proportion of mathematicians are engaged in independent research. As far as the rank-and-file mathematician is concerned, however, the object of his training is to make him able and willing to do a job which is more or less routine. On the other hand, it is impossible to say in advance what that job will require, and certain that no mathematician will be able to make do with a fixed set of techniques throughout his working life. Thus what is required of the mathematician is not so much command of the various techniques taught in his university course, but the quality, much celebrated in the ideology of mathematical education, of 'mathematical maturity'. This comprises facility in the basic techniques, an ability to learn further special techniques, and a degree of work discipline. In principle, one could proceed by teaching the basic material together with a critical discussion of methods, concept formation, the ways in which theories are applied, etc. Actual practice proceeds more by a lengthy unfolding of numerous segments of mathematics, in the course of which the basic material and the way it is used is drummed in by sheer repetition. (It doesn't matter much, then, that the students' understanding of the more advanced sections is small.) How could it be otherwise when there are no concepts for the critical discussion? The critical onslaught of formalism did not go so far as to create such concepts. It had no compulsion to: its mandate was only to transform mathematics from hereditary culture of the ruling class to tool for alienated labour.

'Cartesian–formalist' ideology is dominated by certain concepts which serve to obscure the questions it leaves unanswered. Thus 'mathematical maturity' – 'mathematical maturity, by which we mean the patience to follow mathematical thought (*i.e. the textbook*) whither it may lead, and a willingness to postpone concrete applications until enough mathematics has been done to treat them properly (*i.e. to regard mathematics as a brute fact, an end in itself*)' (Preface to Kreider, Kuller, Ostberg and Perkins, 1966). 'Rigour' is a criterion given great stress in the teaching of pure mathematics – and very properly, too, one would suppose. What masquerades as 'rigour', however, is concern with the formal details of deductions. Of course, formal correctness *is* extremely important in mathematics – but if modern mathematical philosophy has established anything, it is that formal logic is inadequate by itself as a basis for mathematical truth. Some thinkers 'having formulated (quite correctly) a criterion for formal precision ... conclude (wrongly) that this criterion defines the limits of mathematical thought. However, experience in foundations as well as in informal mathematics shows the contrary to be the case' (Kreisel and Krivine, 1967, p. 263). The justification of 'Cartesian–formalists' for dealing with one mathematical problem rather than another is often that the problem is 'interesting'. This concept serves only to block further questioning.

## Motivation and heuristic

However, it is not *simply* a 'Cartesian–formalist' ideology, not simply a deductive presentation, that we find in modern mathematical education. There exist certain partial attempts to resolve the contradictions in that standpoint. The first is that of 'motivation'. Definitions, axioms, and so on are 'motivated'. Since the definitions, axioms, etc. are never actually put into question, the justification is rather empty. A typical technique is: 'to prove this theorem, we need a stricter condition: it turns out that the necessary condition is ...' There does not occur any real relating of the different levels of mathematical abstraction and rigour. The way a new approach is introduced is often thus: 'you will have approached this problem in such and such a way before. That isn't sufficiently rigorous for our purposes; we'll do it differently, like this. . . .' This 'motivation' has a historical consciousness, unlike the primitive 'Cartesian–formalist' standpoint. But this amounts at best to a *narrative* of the genesis of some concept; never a theoretical, critical account. Old concept and new concept may be *put side by side*.

The second, more far-reaching, attempt to go beyond 'Cartesian-formalism' is that of 'heuristic'. Mathematical heuristic was brought into the teaching of mathematics by George Polya (1954; 1957; 1962).[7] Polya's concern is with secondary-school mathematics; his arguments are therefore not directly relevant to the university situation. However, they do to some extent represent a theoretical response to 'Cartesian-formalism'. It's a response with firm links to 'Cartesian–formalism' (see his remarks on definition and proof (1957, pp. 85, 215). ) He represents his area of concern as 'the study of means and methods of problem solving'. The problems are given in advance and 'clearly conceived'. He sums up his view with this injunction to high school teachers:

Let your students ask the questions: or ask such questions as they may ask by themselves. Let your students give the answers: or give such answers as they may give by themselves. At any rate avoid answering questions that nobody has asked, not even yourself (1962, vol. 2, p. 120).

Mathematical heuristic has been taken to a more radical level by Imre Lakatos (1961, 1963–4).[8] Lakatos starts from Polya, Popper and (in 1961, at least) Hegel.[9] His concern is with the 'logic of mathematical discovery'. Instead of the orthodox view, seeing infallible deductions as the medium of truth, he offers a structure of 'proofs and refutations'. Primitive conjectures lead to attempted proofs. Counter-examples to the conjecture

7. Polya is a former professor of mathematics (professional field: classical analysis) at Stanford University.

8. Lakatos's reactionary politics (he has contributed to the 'Black Papers') should not obscure recognition of the great value of those works. Lakatos does, however, appear to believe that exposition should be modelled on a rational reconstruction of the historical process of discovery, a view which completely writes off the internal structure of mathematics in favour of its historical dialectic. Nor is there any basis for finding where the original conjecture comes from. Nor any basis for studying the 'scientific revolutions' of mathematics as distinct from its bread-and-butter work. Or studying mathematical *methods* (e.g. the axiomatic method) as distinct from theorems.

9. Lakatos's approach is not at all orthodoxly Popperian, even though Lakatos currently Professor of Logic at LSE, is a noted partisan of Popper. Lakatos's very object of study is one eschewed by Popper: 'the act of conceiving or inventing a theory seems to me neither to call for logical analysis nor to be susceptible of it' (Popper 1968, p. 31).

lead, through examination of the proof, to deduction of guilty 'hidden lemmas'. The 'hidden lemma' is then made explicit in the statement of the conjecture, thus arriving at a *proof-generated* condition. New counter-example . . . and so on.

Motivation and heuristic (in Polya's form, at least) imply no decisive break from 'Cartesian–formalism'. Instead they supplement it. Instead of criticizing and going beyond the 'Cartesian–formalist' idea of rigour, they say 'rigour is not everything'. All they provide is a *commentary* on each episode in mathematics; they are incorrigibly piecemeal in their approach. At best, they are an attempt to make explicit the practical wisdom the student develops to deal with 'Cartesian–formalist' mathematics – at worst, verbiage to pad out the sparseness of a formal presentation.

### The textbooks

To be more specific, let us see how six standard university textbooks (those of Apostol, 1963; Burkill, 1962; Courant and John, 1965; Lang, 1964; Scott and Tims, 1966; Spivak, 1965) treat two important topics in the calculus. Since lectures, the other major means of mathematical instruction, are usually (in my experience) compiled by the lecturer piecing together what he considers to be the best from each of the textbooks covering his subject, an approach via textbooks will not distort our picture of mathematical education.

First, the concept of *variable*. In elementary mathematical physics and in the traditional exposition of the calculus (first-level teaching), variables are mathematical objects. As well as ordinary constant real numbers like $0$, $1$, $\sqrt{2}$, $3 \cdot 141\,59 \ldots$, etc, there are variable real numbers $x$, $y$, $z$, etc. They do things like representing physical quantities, like 'becoming very large and positive' or 'taking the value zero' or depending on each other. A function is a relation between two variables, a dependent variable being a function of an independent variable. Thus in the usual way of speaking one says: if $s$ represents the distance traversed by a body falling under gravity, and $t$ the time for which it has been falling, then $t$ is an independent variable, $s$ is a dependent variable, and they are connected by the function $s = \frac{1}{2} g\, t^2$ (where $g$ is a constant, the gravitational acceleration – about $9 \cdot 81$ if we're working in m.k.s. units). Under certain conditions variables may lose their identity. If we write

$$ ' \sum_{n=1}^{N} 2^n ', \text{ or } ' \int_{a}^{y} f(x)\, dx ', $$

then '$n$' or '$x$' are *bound variables* and no longer represent anything definite. We cannot speak of $n$ or $x$ being a function of (say) $z$, though we might say that $N$ or $y$ were functions of $z$. In fact, we might write

$$\text{`}\int_a^y f \text{'} \quad \text{instead of} \quad \text{`}\int_a^y f(x)\, dx\text{'}$$

so we see that '$x$' has a purely auxiliary function.

Since the latter half of the nineteenth century it has been – for various (practical) reasons – necessary to work with another conception of 'variable' and 'function'. Now functions are mathematical objects, but variables are not. One speaks of a function as being a *set*, a collection – namely the set of points making up its graph. Thus 'the function $s = \frac{1}{2}gt'^2$ becomes the set of points $(0,0)$, $(\frac{1}{2}\times 9\cdot 81 \times 1, 1)$, $(\frac{1}{2}\times 9\cdot 81 \times 2, \sqrt{2})$, $(\frac{1}{2}\times 9\cdot 81 \times (3\cdot 141\,59\ldots)^2, 3\cdot 141\,59\ldots)$, etc. We still talk of 'variables' – but in a different sense. They are now just formal devices of terminology. They don't name anything, they don't refer to anything. Indeed, it is only to statements containing only bound variables that a definite interpretation is assigned. (We consider the phrases 'for all ...' or 'there exists ...' to bind a variable; so that, for example,

$$\text{`for all } N, \quad \sum_{n=1}^{N} 2^n = 2^{N+1} - 1\text{'}$$

has a definite interpretation – in a given domain of interpretation: natural numbers, some non-standard domain of numbers, etc. – while

$$\text{`}\sum_{n=1}^{N} 2^n = 2^{N+1^{-1}}\text{'}$$

has not.) Statements containing non-bound variables may occur in the course of chains of deduction in such ways as: 'suppose there exists a greatest prime number'. Then let $p$ be that number. Then $p!+1$ is a prime number. But we know 'for all numbers $n$, $n!+1$ is greater than $n$'. Therefore $p!+1$ is greater than $p$. So we have a contradiction. But '$p!+1$ is greater than $p$', for example, has meaning only as a part of the chain of deduction. On the previous conception, to say 'as $x$ approaches 0, $f(x)$ approaches 1' is to record an elementary mathematical fact; on the 'new' conception it can at most be a fanciful paraphrase of a statement about ordinary, 'constant' real numbers, like 'for all $e$ greater than 0, there is a $d$ such that for all $t$, if the magnitude of $t$ is less than $e$, then the magnitude of $f(t)-1$ is less than $d$'.

A good account of variables and functions would certainly be genuinely difficult – some sort of familiarity with formal logic, with the concepts of syntax and semantics, is probably required to give a satisfactory account of the 'new' conception of variable. However, the textbooks seem to work on the principle: if you can't answer a question, then pretend it doesn't exist.

Courant and John use the old conception consistently: page 17: 'Whenever the values of certain quantities $a$, $b$, $c$, ... are determined by those of certain others $x$, $y$, $z$, ... we say that $a$, $b$, $c$, ... *depend* on $x$, $y$, $z$, ... or are *functions* of $x$, $y$, $z$, ... The mathematical law assigning unique values of the dependent variables to given values of the independent variables is called a function.' Apostol, on the other hand, uses only the new conception. He makes no attempt to 'demystify' the concept of variable – we find this coy remark: 'We shall introduce a very general definition of function in which the 'variables' need not be numbers but may be objects of any kind' (p. 27). Why, the reader might well ask, the inverted commas round 'variable'? Lang states the new conception (p. 8): 'A *function* is a rule which to any given number associates another number'; but then uses the old conception without explanation. Page 20: 'As $x$ becomes very large positive. ... As $x$ approaches 0 ...' etc. What is this thing '$x$'? And, p. 63: 'the distance $s$ is a function of $t$'. Spivak gives a quite extensive discussion, but doesn't really confront the difficult problem; starting from a 'provisional definition' as follows: 'A function is a rule which assigns to each of certain real numbers some other real number', he defines terminology such as 'the function $f(x) = \sin(x)$', gives considerable discussion of points which don't concern us here, and finally, asking such questions as 'what happens if we break the rule?' proceeds to the definition of a function as a set.

All the above are more or less 'Cartesian–formalist'. Burkill attempts motivation, but succeeds only in confusing the two conceptions (pp. 47 *et seq.*). 'You are familiar with the dependence of one real number $y$ on another $x$ which is commonly determined by formulae such as

$$y = \frac{1}{x^2+1} \quad \text{or} \quad y = \sqrt{\{(2-x)(x-1)\}}.$$

... These two examples are ... illustrations of functions.' 'Strictly speaking, the function $f$ is the set of all pairs of numbers $(x, y)$ which are related by the rules defining the correspondence.' (What sort of numbers are 'related' – constant numbers 0, 1, etc. or variable numbers $x$, $y$, etc.)? Scott and Tims make a more persistent attempt at motivation and thus the more fully expose the poverty of this approach. They give (pp. 28 *et seq.*) the usual account on the old conception of '$y$ is a function of

$x$' – i.e. there is a formula connecting the two variables. Then they say: we need not have a 'formula', any 'rule' which 'when $x$ is decided, fixes corresponding $y$s' will give a function. They argue that the 'rule' conception is equivalent to a conception of a function as a set of pairs of numbers – i.e. the new conception. But then we're brought back to square one with the remark 'We commonly call $x$ and $y$ *variables* since they stand for any number in their respective classes.'

My experience and observation is that lack of conceptual analysis here causes quite deep confusion at many points. Many students will write nonsense such as

'$\sum_{n=1}^{\infty} a_n$ converges for all $n$'.

The equation

'$\int_a^b f(x) \, dx = \int_a^b f(y) \, dy$'

will cause real difficulties of comprehension. If $f$ is a 'function of $x$', what is it that makes this function a function 'of $x$' rather than of $y$, $z$, etc.? Are '$y = x^2$' and '$z = y^2$' two different functions or two ways of representing the same function? Not to mention the difficulties found in the theory of differentiation, especially with the chain rule and partial differentiation, most of which can be traced back to confusions in the concept of variable.[10]

A second example: uniform convergence. At the beginning of the nineteenth century it became apparent that an infinite series of continuous functions could sum to a function which was not continuous: i.e. one could have

$$f(x) = \sum_{n=1}^{\infty} f_n(x)$$

for all $x$ and all the $f_n$s continuous, but $f$ not continuous. This caused something of a crisis, since it was taken as axiomatic that 'what is true up to the limit is true at the limit'. After many years of confusion, a concept of 'uniform convergence' of a series was formulated by Seidel – not just through good luck, but specifically through an analysis of a

10. These difficulties are *not* the same as those arising in the historical development of the concept of function. A main difficulty there, for example, was whether the new definition, which accepts many things as functions which don't come under the old definition, was not too broad.

'proof' by Cauchy that the sum of series of continuous functions must be continuous. (This is a good example of a 'proof' which 'proves' a false conclusion advancing mathematics.) (This account is taken from Lakatos, 1961.)

Burkill, Lang, and Scott and Tims do not cover this topic. Courant and John produce the crudest form of 'Cartesian–formalism'. 'The distinction between the concept of the convergence of functions and that of the convergence of curves is a phenomenon which the student should clearly grasp. ... It is natural to require somewhat more than the mere local convergence of our approximations' – and Courant and John state the condition for uniform convergence with no more ado. The great nineteenth-century mathematicians, Cauchy and Abel, who struggled unsuccessfully for years with the problem, must indeed have been stupid to miss this 'natural' requirement, which every student 'should clearly grasp'! A number of examples of non-uniform convergence follow, to show what oddities can arise, and finally the main theorems about uniform convergence are proved. Apostol's is a fairly orthodox motivated exposition (pp. 390 *et seq.*).

Our chief interest in this chapter will be the following kind of problem: Given that each term of the sequence $(f_n)$ has a certain property (for example, continuity, differentiability, integrability), to what extent does the limit function $f$ also possess this property? ... We shall find that pointwise convergence is usually not strong enough ... we are led to a study of 'stronger' methods of convergence that *do* preserve these properties. The most important of these is the notion of *uniform* convergence.

There follows a reference to the problem of iterated limits (i.e. when do we have

$$\lim_{n \to \infty}\left[\lim_{x \to a} f_n(x)\right] = \lim_{x \to a}\left[\lim_{n \to \infty} f_n(x)\right] ?),$$

to which uniform convergence is also relevant. Then some examples of non-uniform convergence. Then the statement of the definition of uniform convergence. Spivak's treatment is an interesting example of motivation. He begins (p. 412) with: 'The first of these (*counter-examples*) shows that even if each $f_n$ is continuous, the (*limit*) function $f$ may not be.' He then gives several counter-examples. So far, so good; the orthodox sequel would be of the form: 'We see some stronger condition is required: it turns out that the appropriate condition is. ...' But Spivak writes: 'This particular sequence of functions (*from one of the counter-examples*) behaves in a way that we never really imagined when we first considered functions defined by limits ... if ... we draw a strip around $f$ of total width $2\varepsilon$... then the graphs of $f_n$ do not lie completely within this strip, no matter how large an $n$ we choose'; and devotes some discussion to this before arriving at 'This condition (*of uniform convergence*) turns out to be just the one that makes the study of limit functions feasible.'

Clearly Spivak is uneasy about the baldness of the usual exposition. But his remark: 'This particular sequence ... behaves ...' is no less 'out of the blue' than would be the definition itself. What is lacking is a theory of conceptual innovation, a non-metaphysical epistemology of mathematics.

## A way out?

In general, students accept the current system of mathematical education, though often resentfully. And so they must, as a mass, for lack of an alternative. At present we have no theory of mathematical concepts on which to construct such an alternative. At best, students can press collectively for the adoption of a 'heuristic' approach – this could well bring a few advantages, but, if my analysis is correct, cannot overthrow the basic orientation. Without a revolutionary theory, there can be no revolutionary movement.

## *References*

APOSTOL, T. M. (1963), *Mathematical Analysis*, Addison-Wesley.

BARON, M. E. (1969), *The Origins of the Infinitesmal Calculus*, Pergamon.

BELL, E. T. (1945), *Development of Mathematics*, McGraw-Hill.

BOURBAKI, N. (1960), *Elements d'histoire de mathematiques*, Hermann.

BOYER, C. B. (1959), *A History of the Calculus*, Dover.

BURKILL, J. C. (1962), *A First Course in Mathematical Analysis*, Cambridge University Press.

COURANT, R., and JOHN, F. (1965), *Introduction to Calculus and Analysis*, Interscience.

CURRY, H. B. (1951), *Outlines of a Formalist Philosophy of Mathematics*, North Holland.

KREIDER, D. L., KULLER, R. G., OSTBERG, D. R., and PERKINS, F. W. (1966), *An Introduction to Linear Analysis*, Addison-Wesley.

KREISEL, G., and KRIVINE, J. L. (1967), *Elements of Mathematical Logic*, North Holland.

KUHN, T. S. (1962), *The Structure of Scientific Revolutions*, University of Chicago Press.

LAKATOS, I. (1961), 'Essays in the logic of mathematical discovery', Ph.D. thesis, University of Cambridge.

LAKATOS, I. (1963–4), 'Proofs and refutations', *British Journal for the Philosophy of Science*, vol. 14, nos. 53, 54, 55, 56.

LANG, S. (1964), *A First Course in Calculus*, Addison-Wesley.

POLYA, G. (1954), *Mathematics and Plausible Reasoning*, Wiley.

POLYA, G. (1957), *How to Solve It*, Anchor.

POLYA, G. (1962), *Mathematical Discovery*, 2 vols., Wiley.

POPPER, K. (1968), *The Logic of Scientific Discovery*, Hutchinson.

ROBINSON, A. (1967), 'The metaphysics of the calculus', in I. Lakatos (ed.), *Problems in the Philosophy of Mathematics*, North Holland.

RUSSELL, B. (1956), *Foundations of Geometry*, Dover.

SARTRE, J. P. (1964), *The Problem of Method*, trans. H. Barnes, Methuen.

SCOTT, D. B., and TIMS, S. B. (1966), *Mathematical Analysis: An Introduction*, Cambridge.

SPIVAK, M. (1965), *Calculus*, Benjamin.

# Class Struggle among the Molecules
Jonathan Slack

## Introduction
### Three definitions of organic chemistry

It is most important for a work of criticism to make it clear what is under attack. This essay mainly refers to the discipline of organic chemistry,[1] but it should be evident from some of my remarks that I feel this type of criticism to have more general significance.

What, then, is organic chemistry? Elementary textbooks tell us that it is 'The science of carbon compounds'. In other words, there are carbon compounds in the world and the science that studies them is organic chemistry. We will see why, strictly speaking, no discipline could ever really do this, but we shall retain this definition as a conceptual tool and later refer to 'chemistry-as-a-science'. In order to find out what a discipline contains, it is necessary to go to lectures or to read textbooks. I shall refer to the content of instruction as 'chemistry-as-taught'. The last definition is provided by the fact that organic chemistry is its practice. It is the totality of research activity by chemists in institutes of higher education and in industry. We will call this 'chemistry-as-done'.

This essay will ignore issues such as the incorrectness of some material which is taught, the way in which it is taught, and selectively which results in the teaching of one topic rather than another. Such questions lie well within the framework of existing controversy among academics. Rather more important, in my view, is that there are profound differences between the three definitions above. The later sections will examine in detail what these differences are and why they have arisen. But first we shall set the scene in a more general way.

### 'Technoscience'

We can probably regard most human activities as being a mixture of science and technology. Everybody is familiar with the notion of a 'pure' science even though it is doubtful that any such activity actually exists.

---

1. For brevity I have frequently referred to 'chemistry', but I usually mean organic chemistry.

The nearest thing to a 'pure' technology might be a craft skill which cannot be explained but only learned alongside the master. Even then, however, we see that it must have a small scientific component since there are always some generalizations that can be made about the activity which might be regarded as a rudimentary body of theory.

If scientific endeavour organizes its object by the generation of theory,[2] then the technological component continuously *reorganizes* it. Reorganization alters the 'shape' of an area of the discipline because the technology will drive towards certain goals; it recasts the existing structures and sets up new ones. Later we shall come across cases in which there are no new structures or if there are then they are vague in the extreme. I then take the liberty of referring to disorganization or *deformation*.

It is common to draw a distinction between 'pure' and 'applied' science. Everyone agrees that no hard and fast distinction can be drawn, but the idea is that applied science produces results which are immediately useful while pure science produces theory. But what is useful? It is impossible to give an answer to this outside of the social context. One might for example argue that *all* scientific work is useful because at least a few people will be interested in and will read every article on a particular topic. They will have a *need* for the articles, and they will *consume* them by reading them. Of course we have an intuitive feeling that this is not what the word 'useful' really means. In fact it is pretty obvious that in capitalist society a thing is regarded as useful when it leads directly to the formation of capital: i.e. when some company can make a profit out of it.

So reorganization of theory does not proceed along *any* channels but along particular ones. If certain values are current among those who rule society then certain goals are sought and disciplines are mobilized to achieve them. This is what I will mean when I say that a science is valuc-laden.

It has recently become fashionable to announce that science is being misused and that individual scientists should take responsibility for the results of their research activities. This line of argument usually revolves around the concept of a neutrality of science that is being violated. What I have argued in this section and will, I hope, substantiate by reference to organic chemistry below, is that we have no sciences; we have only technosciences, which are not, and never can be, neutral.

2. The idea that facts are contingent on, or exist within the framework of, pre-existing theory is now fairly generally accepted among philosophers of science (see for instance, chs. 2, 3 and 4 of Harré, 1970). Scientists themselves are, however, more likely to put down examples of this to 'human weakness'.

*Reorganization*

In my view, the reorganization of organic chemistry takes the following form: that major theoretical problems of the organization of knowledge are evaded and attention is concentrated on a technique oriented activity, the synthesis and analysis of 'useful' substances, which none the less retains the neutral flag of chemical theory. This is a deformation of chemistry-as-taught with respect to the aspirations of chemistry-as-a-science. Moreover I hope to show in the third section that the causes can mostly be traced back to the activities of the chemical industry.

## The structure of chemical knowledge as taught
*The different theoretical approaches*

The basis on which modern chemistry[3] rests is the concept of a pure substance; a sample of which is composed of molecules, all having the same arrangement of atoms and being represented by the same chemical formula.

Since the methods of structure determination and identification are very largely agreed by all chemists, the molecular structures of compounds are items of everyday experience to them. Compounds, or their reactions are *facts* to the chemist. We may see that this is true by looking at textbooks. We may be told that A is converted to B under certain conditions but we are not given evidence that, when this was first observed, 'A' did indeed have the structure A and 'B' was indeed B.[4] By 'theoretical approach' I mean the method of exposition, or theory, by which the facts of a discipline, in this case the compounds, can be rendered intelligible.

The first point, which should be firmly established, is that there are *too many* compounds. Estimates of the number described are of the order of a few million but the number which we have good reason to believe could be prepared is so close to infinite as to make no difference. This is sufficiently important to require illustration. It is possible using recursion formulae (Herze and Blair, 1931) to calculate the possible number of

3. The concept of 'substance' as we have it today totally depends on the atomic theory and associated techniques of weighing and assay. For a discussion of previous concepts of substance see Woodger (1929).

4. To take a completely random example:

'Aldehydes and ketones form *oximes* when treated with hydroxylamine

$$R_2CO + NH_2OH \rightarrow \left[ R_2C \begin{smallmatrix} .OH \\ .NHOH \end{smallmatrix} \right] \rightarrow R_2C = NOH \text{ (vg)}'$$

(Finar, 1967, p. 177). The statement is an entity to be learned, recited, used in evidence for or against a theory, but not to be questioned in itself.

saturated hydrocarbons or other compounds built up according to well-known rules.

*Methane Series*

| Number of carbon atoms | Number of compounds |
|---|---|
| 1 | 1 |
| 5 | 3 |
| 10 | 75 |
| 15 | 4347 |
| 20 | 366,319 |
| 30 | 4,111,846,763 |

The number of possible compounds rises very rapidly with chain length, and this is even more pronounced for monosubstituted compounds:

| R–X Primary, Number of carbon atoms | Secondary and Tertiary Number of compounds |
|---|---|
| 1 | 1 |
| 5 | 8 |
| 10 | 507 |
| 15 | 48,865 |
| 20 | 5,622,109 |

The implication is clear. There are too many carbon compounds for us ever to enumerate the properties of more than a tiny fraction of them. The science must find some way of organizing the knowledge into a theoretical structure.

In chemistry-as-taught there are two ways in which this is done, although it is not clear that the nature of the difference between these two approaches is generally appreciated. One, which we shall call the classificational view, is that presented in numerous school and university textbooks.[5] It is basically a way of classifying molecular structures. Compounds are divided into *homologous series*, the members of which differ only in the length or branching of a hydrocarbon chain. Each series exists for one functional group (hydroxyl, amino, carboxyl, etc.) and it is assumed that because the hydrocarbon chain is relatively unreactive the properties

5. These are legion but probably the most commonly used are Finar (1967); Fieser and Fieser (1968); Roberts and Caserio (1964).

of all members of the series are determined mainly by the functional group. So, for example, instead of studying $n$ million alcohols we study just ethanol, isopropanol and $t$-butanol as representatives of the primary, secondary and tertiary series.

The second view is one of reaction types.[6] There may be $n$ million compounds but they only undergo a few types of interaction. With a sufficiently perfect theory, we could, if presented with two hitherto unknown compounds, predict whether they would react, how fast they would do so and what products would result. The basic categories here are things like acids, nucleophiles or free radicals. This is a more abstract view although at present it is probably a less coherent one.

The trouble with both these approaches is that they are very limited. The difficulty of the classificational approach becomes obvious when it is recognized that if there are $n$ monofunctional series then there will be $n^2$ bifunctional ones, of which $n(n-1)$ will contain two *different* functional groups. It is possible to accommodate bifunctional and simple aromatic compounds into homologous series but this fails as soon as the structures become a little bit complicated. The mechanistic approach simply has not got enough predictive power to carry us anywhere much at the present time. There have been some successes, notably the Woodward–Hofmann selection rules, but much of the explanation provided is still *post hoc*.

However, anyone familiar with organic chemistry will be well aware that the subject does not stop dead at the limits of these two approaches. Slowly and almost imperceptibly the classificational view merges with a 'synthetic' one. When compounds of the next order of complexity are reached, like for instance phenanthrene (1) or quinoline (2), virtually nothing is said about what they do, but a great deal is said about how to make them.

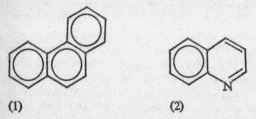

(1)                          (2)

Leaving aside until the next section the process by which these compounds are selected for consideration, we have here the first mode of deformation

6. In the last few years very many of these have been published. They all take their arrangement and scope from Ingold (1953). A much used university text is Sykes (1970).

of organic chemistry. The classificational and mechanistic approaches are the kinds of things one would look for to constitute chemistry-as-a-science. But as soon as a rather low threshold of complexity is passed these theoretical approaches are abandoned in chemistry-as-taught, which then becomes a set of recipes for making particular substances.

*Importance*

A study of the question of importance will reveal why the two approaches do not overlap to more than a small extent, and will reveal the second mode of deformation.

It is fundamental to the integrity of any scientific paradigm[7] that one fact is counted more important than another. This is stoutly denied by some academic scientists, fearful that once judgement is let loose, *their* work might be considered trivial. But it is not difficult to justify. In the chemical sciences, because of the basic nature of the concept of substance, the principle can be reworded as: 'One substance is more important than another.' If there are $n$ million substances and we study only a few, are those few selected at random? Of course not, the ones selected depend on the theoretical approach adopted. We might view a theory (among other things) as a grid which sweeps up through the infinite field of compounds and elevates certain of them into a prominent position.

If this is accepted then it becomes easy to show why there is little overlap between a classificational and a mechanistic textbook.[8] In the classificational view the important compounds are those which have typical structures, in the mechanistic view they are those which undergo typical reactions. So for instance very elementary mechanistic textbooks abound with structures such as (3), because they illustrate steric restraints on substitution and elimination reactions, whereas such compounds, the bicyclic halides, might not even be mentioned in quite an extensive classificational text.

(3)

7. To find out all about 'paradigms' see Kuhn (1970).
8. Some books try to combine the views, e.g. Ellis (1966), but I think that this creates more confusion than it resolves.

Now in fact the compounds which are mentioned in textbooks are not just those that are important from some theoretical standpoint. Whether simple or complex there are a large number of compounds which are important and are included for some exogenous reason. This is the second mode of deformation. The compounds concerned may be there because they are useful (i.e. profitable) in their own right, or because they are used for making things which are in their turn useful (i.e. profitable). Diethyl malonate (4) is a very important synthetic reagent, but is hardly of great

(4)

classificational prominence as the diester of the second dicarboxylic acid, nor of great mechanistic prominence since its most important reactions (carbanion formation and nucleophilic substitution) are always studied by reference to other examples.

Anyone who has studied chemistry will recognize (5), (6) and (7) for three quite different sorts of reason.

$CH_3 \cdot CH_2 \cdot NH_2$     $CH_3 \cdot CHOH \cdot CHOH \cdot CH_3$

(5)                                (6)

(7)

Ethylamine (5) is recognized because it is obviously the second member of the series of amines. Pinacol (6) is recognized as the example for a type of rearrangement reactions. Trinitrotoluene (7) is recognized because it is an important explosive.

Because in chemistry substances have the status of facts, important substances are those studied, and we now see the way in which they are selected, it should by now be clear that in a very rea¡sense the facts in organic chemistry are not only contingent on the theoretical standpoint, but also on exogenous values confused and conflated with these theories.

*Simple reactions*

The third deformation arises because of the type of reaction that is considered worthy of presentation. It should be evident that if the subject matter is bent towards the synthesis and analysis of useful (i.e. profitable) substances the reactions by which these substances are made should give *one product*, in *high yield*, under *easily attainable conditions* and in a *short time*. It is overwhelmingly this kind of reaction that is to be found described in textbooks. The only exception is in mechanistic chemistry where the distribution of products is sometimes used to deduce information about the relative lability of sites on a molecule, or the preponderance of different mechanisms.

To the extent that this is true it seriously limits organic chemistry as an attempt to understand carbon-compounds-in-the-world. The inadequacy of the subject has been a serious difficulty facing investigators of the origin of life (Bernal, 1967, ch. 4). One of the problems here is to explain how complex biochemical substances came into existence in the first place. Formalisms based on the well-known, fast, high-yield reactions were inadequate, and it came as something of a surprise when it was first shown in 1953 that many organic compounds characteristic of living organisms were formed in small amount by passing an electric discharge through a simulated primeval atmosphere (Miller, 1953). Subsequent research of this sort has revealed reactions which could never have been discovered by organic chemistry as such but which have contributed to the origin of life (Calvin, 1969, ch. 6).

A further point which should be made about the concentration on such reactions is that they actually make it harder for people to learn organic chemistry. 'Messy' reactions giving a mixture of products may be omitted altogether. For instance many schoolboys may not know that amines can be oxidized at all even when aniline turns a dirty brown colour in the bottle! Probably more important, it is sometimes claimed that to learn lists of syntheses and properties for compounds is good for you because you learn each reaction twice.

e.g.   $R \cdot COOAg + Br_2 \rightarrow R \cdot Br + AgBr + CO_2$.

The Hunsdiecker reaction is both a property of silver salts of carboxylic acids and a method of synthesis of alkyl halides. However in practice, medium-yield reactions tend to be listed as properties and not syntheses and the more elegant syntheses tend to be too obscure as reactions to be listed as properties. The result is more confusion.

## Natural-product chemistry

This is a subdiscipline which does actually come under semihumorous criticism from many chemists themselves on account of its apparent futility. While it may be fairly futile from a scientific point of view, the reasons for its existence are not difficult to trace.

Natural-product chemistry is said to be taking place when some plant material, say a sample of Amazonian bark or Arctic lichen, is extracted or steam distilled to yield a substance. The structure of the substance is determined, a paper published, and then the investigator moves on to the next sample. This may be accompanied by a certain amount of biosynthetic speculation.

It should perhaps be pointed out that the number of plant species is very large and that very many plants contain very many substances. It is therefore impossible to arrive at any definitive end to this business. The best way to regard it might be as structure determination for the sake of it.

Arguments issued in the defence of natural-product chemistry are as follows:

1. That all this is to do with 'life', which we all agree is important and worth studying.

2. That although it is of no scientific importance, it can be good training for research students.

3. That it has resulted in the discovery of a number of important medicinal products.

The first point is certainly wrong. Those compounds which are regarded as 'natural products' are mainly members of one of the four classes of alkaloids, isoprenoids, polyketides and shikimic metabolites. These are all 'secondary metabolites'; that is they are not central to the life processes of the plant, and in fact their function is usually obscure or non-existent.

The names of natural products which enliven chemical indices from abietic acid to zierone and zingiberene do not adorn *J. Biol. Chem.*; conversely few natural product chemists could distinguish between UDPG and dApT. The truth is that in 'natural product chemistry' and in biochemistry we usually deal with two quite different selections of biological molecules (Bu'Lock, 1965, ch. 1).

It is true that before biochemistry became a science[9] it was legitimate to grub around collecting any information that might conceivably have anything to do with the composition and function of living organisms. Now, however, we know that the key regulatory enzymes and other important molecules are present in very small amounts compared with excretory products, structural materials, reserve foodstuffs and the functionless secondary metabolites.

The second point is a significant one. Structure determination for the sake of it is quite a reasonable activity for a research student according to those industrialists who define the Ph.D. as a 'training in practical techniques' rather than the hitherto accepted 'significant contribution to knowledge'.

As for the last point, it is of course very true. But this only reinforces the concept of natural-product chemistry as an adventitious, technique-oriented addition to the rest of organic chemistry. The random screening of bizarre molecular structures for biological activity is carried out by many drug companies who do not claim to be advancing science but are turning out useful (i.e. profitable) substances.

To summarize this section: the reorganization of such theory as organic chemistry may possess is aptly described as deformation. The three modes of deformation are those discussed under the subheadings above:

1. When all but very simple compounds are considered synthetic recipes are substituted for theory.

2. The compounds described are selected by a variety of unstated criteria.

3. Only fast, high-yield reactions are considered.

It is not difficult to encapsulate all these points, and also the character of natural-product chemistry, in the notion that organic chemistry as a science of carbon compounds is deformed towards making useful (i.e. profitable) substances and finding their structures.

9. The history of biochemistry is scarcely documented. I get the impression that the best periodization would be very roughly:
(i) 1840–1920: Application of modern chemical analysis to living organisms and their products.
(ii) 1920–50: Appreciation of universality at the chemical level: composition and metabolism.
(iii) 1950 onwards: Discovery and investigation of informational and self-replicating macromolecules.
The dawn of biochemistry as a *separate* science would be the point at which it acquired a distinct field of investigation from physiology and medicine.

**Mechanisms of deformation**

*The chemical industry*

The case that the reorganization I have discussed actually exists can be made stronger by showing in what way it has come about. Its ultimate origin lies in the fact that in our society chemistry is done on a large scale for profit. The chemical industry employs relatively few people (411,000 in 1968) but is highly capital intensive and of considerable economic importance. What it does is perhaps best illustrated by a table such as the following:

| Sector | Sales £m (1968) |
| --- | --- |
| 'General' | 1101 |
| Resins, plastics, synthetic rubber | 449 |
| Pharmaceutical | 344 |
| Soap, detergents | 185 |
| Paint | 176 |
| Fertilizers | 165 |
| Dyestuffs | 128 |
| Toiletries | 122 |
| Photographic | 74 |
| Explosives, matches | 67 |
| Glue | 47 |
| Pesticides and disinfectant | 35 |
| Total | 2893 |

(*Chemical Age*, 9 January 1970)

It will be noticed that the large bulk of these products are organic chemicals.

The energies of the employees of a chemical company are directed towards making substances that are useful (i.e. profitable) for that company. Employees of a chemical company do of course include research chemists. Nobody pretends that the chemistry they do is value free. A scientist working in the chemical industry may be told that he is doing good by helping to develop new products for the general benefit of society. In fact under capitalism much of the research he is instructed to do will be concerned with such problems as: updating old products to give them a new image, evading a competitor's patent, 'proofing' the company's own patents, varying a competitor's product to enter a profitable niche and so on. The reason for this is that *knowledge* has the unfortunate characteristic that you can give it away but still have it. Capitalism makes knowledge into a *commodity*; its circulation must be restricted by secrecy and its use by the patent laws so that it can be bought and sold for profit.

So the character of industrial research is that the scientists are told what to do, are mainly concerned with short-term problem solving, and much of their work must be kept secret. Finally, here is a memorable quotation from a scientist working for a medium size US chemical company:

I've come to see economics as another variable to be dealt with in studying a reaction – there's pressure, there's temperature and there's the dollar (Klaw, 1968).

### Direct overlay

This is how it is in industry. But I am claiming that the values which pervade industrial research thoroughly permeate the entire discipline. How does it come to influence the thinking of teachers, research workers in institutes and universities, or authors of textbooks, all of whom might consider themselves to be 'pure' scientists?

The first way in which I think this occurs is through 'direct overlay' of values, that is through direct ideological pressure on individual scientists. A message which enters all our heads is that of the *virtue* of useful (i.e. profitable) substances. We hear of *wonder* drugs, of *miracle* washing powders, *new*, *exciting* fabrics, and so on. Some of this message is delivered through pop journalism, some the capitalists pay to have delivered through advertisements.

It is also possible that the virtue of such substances is promulgated through chemical folklore. Every chemist knows how Perkin made his fortune out of the dye mauveine, the dye he first synthesized by accident after an attempt to prepare quinine by the oxidation of allyl toluidine. The activities of the alchemists, the western ones at least, were also pointed very clearly in one direction. We might not be so interested in gold today but a modern pharmaceutical company might well make a bomb with the elixir of life.

### The manpower question

This is becoming a well-worked theme, but it should none the less be mentioned here. Another important way in which the deformation is brought about is the continuous demand by industry and its government that the universities should turn out people who are useful (i.e. profitable). The Swann Report spells this out succinctly:

119. In the recent Memorandum of Guidance, the University Grants Committee recognized 'a gap between what post-graduate studies have traditionally provided and what industry would like to receive', and stated that 'it would be valuable if the universities collectively made a further deliberate and determined effort to gear a larger part of their "output" to the economic and industrial needs of the nation'. The Committee advised . . .

1. A shift of post-graduate effort from the more traditional type of course to something which is avowedly more 'vocational' and often shorter in duration.

2. Training methods designed to ease the transition from the academic to the industrial world, along the lines of 'Bosworth matching courses' or any other deliberately designed approach.

3. A greater emphasis on applied research than has been customary.

4. The provision of more short post-experience courses.

It should by now be clear that 'useful' chemical manpower is that which can make things, determine molecular structures, do what it is told and keep its mouth shut. Many students are actually well aware of this, and their fears are unlikely to be assuaged by some of the lyrical waxings which come from big business:

There is even an artistic beauty about a chemical plant at night bathed in an orange fluorescent glow and the quiet movement of the night-shift operators as they go about their preordained tasks (Collinson, 1969).

While we are seeking the mechanisms of deformation we should at all times remember that only a slight pressure and a subtle injection of values is necessary since the majority of chemists have no consciousness of any method or theoretical structure to their subject. They have been brought up to believe that

1. They practise something called 'scientific method' which always produces the right answers in the end.

2. That what they study consists of homogeneous and neutral 'fact'.

3. That 'arty' generalizations are to be mistrusted.

### The consequences of deformation

It is a little difficult to discuss this since I know of no occasion on which some of the questions I have raised have previously come to light. However the course that such a discussion might take could probably be predicted from a consideration of what I call *overt intrusions*; that is the actual description of the activities of the chemical industry in the midst of a chemical text. This is found more in school textbooks than in university ones.

There are three types of overt intrusion. An industrial process may be described as a 'fact', to be learned and examined like any other fact; a section on a particular compound may be followed by a catalogue of its uses; and certain substances may be included for consideration solely because of some industrial importance. This last is an extreme form of the important compounds deformation mentioned earlier (in the deformation proper the exogenous substances are those concerned at every stage of the technology of analysis and synthesis, not just the end products).

Now some point proudly to these overt intrusions as examples of 'making education relevant', 'relating the course to society', etc. But if this sort of thing is to be considered a virtue then certain questions necessarily arise. Why is it, for example, that the overt intrusions are juxtaposed with 'facts' about chemistry? Might it be a desire to see one gain the epistemological status of the other? For instance statements such as the following are clearly of different type but might appear side by side.

1. Benzene *is* nitrated by $NO_2^+$.

2. TNT *is* manufactured on a large scale.

The first organic chemistry book I ever used told me that:

[Perspex's] outstanding property is its clarity, which gives objects made from it a brilliant and beautiful appearance. It is used for making the hoods and gun turrets of military aircraft (Heys, 1956, p. 147).

These days a certain amount of educational material is put out by the chemical industry, and here the overt intrusions are quite blatantly ideological:

The oil industry consists of many companies, or groups of companies in competition with each other. Their main concern is to make sure that the products of the oil industry are available when and where they are needed and in the quantity and quality required.

Intense competition keeps quality high and prices low and encourages the development of new and better products (Shell International Petroleum Co. Ltd, 1968).

If it is good to teach students about the chemical industry then why is it not good to assign ethical qualities to substances along with their physical and chemical ones? We might for instance say that CS is a *bad* chemical because it can only ever be used by a few people with something to protect against many people with nothing to lose. Terylene or indigotin are *neutral* chemicals. Under capitalism their production is an exploitative process, under socialism they are used for the common good. Penicillin is a *good* chemical. And so on; this is not meant as serious advice, but simply to point out to educators that the overt intrusions are not just a few more interesting and apolitical facts but are really of considerable ideological significance.

Our conclusion from this should be that overt intrusions as such are not necessarily bad. They are bad when they are introduced uncritically. I am inclined to think that this is also the case for the general reorganization of organic chemistry, the description of which has been the main subject of this chapter. I hope I have justified my definition of 'techno-science' in the introduction, shown why reorganization must be inevitable in a given society and why the resulting technoscience cannot be 'neutral'. The practical consequence of a lack of awareness of reorganization are

1. That any theoretical structure the science may have is rendered more obscure, and education therefore made more difficult.

2. That carefully chosen items of information about the *status quo* are elevated to the position of scientific 'facts'.

3. That social and political issues which are raised are not discussed.

In conclusion I want to deal with four points which may have arisen in the reader's mind. First I hope I have nowhere given the impression that pure university science is good and applied industrial science is wicked. I consider that there is not and there cannot be any such thing as pure organic chemistry, and so there is little point in ascribing virtues to it.

Secondly, I do not think it can be denied that organic chemistry to some extent distorts itself. So many of the compounds known are man's own creations and do not exist in nature, therefore the very existence of the subject presupposes a certain technology of synthesis. However, I think that this is a minor source of deformation compared to the socially determined reorganization.

Thirdly, if sciences have some ideological character because of their situation in society then does this mean that they will change if there is a major upheaval in society, specifically a socialist revolution? In few if any cases is there a *complete alternative structure* for a discipline waiting in the wings except in those cases in which the object of study is itself altered (the theory of the firm might not withstand the abolition of the profit motive and the institution of workers' control). However, in all cases we might expect a change in the general view of the field and an aware-ness of its articulation with society. This would be accompanied by a greater or lesser degree of intra-theoretical change.

Lastly, if the reorganization is inevitable can anything constructive be done by socialist scientists in their specific capacity as scientists?

I think there is. It is important that questions of method as well as those of technique be aired in scientific courses. It is also important that the overt intrusions be replaced by a full discussion of the social and political ideas which they embody.

To a limited extent it might be said that the latter is already being attempted. The new Nuffield A-level course does indeed discuss the pros and cons of the use of pesticides (under DDT) and the nature of bio-degradable detergents (under fatty acids). But then the environment game is pretty soft stuff. Maybe it is felt that such a discussion is safer than one dealing with (say) weaponry or (say) the cost of pharmaceutical products; topics which lie a little closer to the cog wheels of the capitalist economy.

## References

BERNAL, J. D. (1967), *The Origin of Life*, Weidenfeld & Nicolson.
BU'LOCK, J. D. (1965), *The Biosynthesis of Natural Products*, McGraw-Hill.
CALVIN, M. (1969), *Chemical Evolution*, Clarendon Press.
COLLINSON, H. A. (1969), 'Graduate scientists in industry', Chemical Industries Association.
ELLIS, G. P. (1966), *A Modern Textbook of Organic Chemistry*, Butterworth.
FIESER, L. F., and FIESER, M. (1968), *Organic Chemistry*, Reinhold.
FINAR, I. L. (1967), *Organic Chemistry*, Longman, 5th edn.
HARRE, R. (1970), *The Principles of Scientific Thinking*, Macmillan.
HENZE, H. R., and BLAIR, C. R. (1931), *Journal American Chemical Society*, vol. 53, pp. 3042, 3077.
HEYS, H. L. (1956), *A New Organic Chemistry*, Harrap.
INGOLD, C. K. (1953), *Structure and Mechanism in Organic Chemistry*, Bell.
KLAW, S. (1968), *The New Brahmins*, Morrow.
KUHN, T. S. (1970), *The Structure of Scientific Revolutions*, Chicago University Press, 2nd edn.
MILLER, S. L. (1953), *Science*, vol. 117, p. 528.
ROBERTS, J. D., and CASERIO, M. C. (1964), *Basic Principles of Organic Chemistry*, Benjamin.
Shell International Petroleum Co. Ltd (1968), *Oil for Everybody*.
SWANN Report (1968), 'The flow into employment of scientists, engineers and technologists', Cmnd 3760, HMSO.
SYKES, P. (1970), *A Guidebook to Mechanism in Organic Chemistry*, Longman, 3rd edn.
WOODGER, J. H. (1929), *Biological Principles*, Routledge & Kegan Paul.

Part Four
## Critiques of the Career of the Student

# Doing Eng. Lit.
Joe Spriggs

Undergraduate Eng. Lit., as defined by its exams, sees itself in the continuum of the *written* English word, and so eliminates the cultures of most exploited classes and peoples since man began. This must be a world record.

Let's be clear, then, what we're talking about:

1. Lit. Crit. – old craft industry undergoing teething pains of the first few years as a factory system.

2. Eng. Lit. – tiny select little segment of the world's output of 'verbal transformations of reality'.

3. Doing Eng. Lit. – three years spent under marching orders to process 2 by 1.

This article is concerned with the workings of 3.

For a start this means we need to remind ourselves that education is not simply what happens when someone 'qualified' starts making the teachery noises he remembers people making towards him a few years earlier (i.e. the present state of university 'teaching'). How we learn is also *what* we learn. This is sometimes clearer to true reactionaries than our liberal friends.

To allow oneself in a book of course criticism to be restricted to the 'content' of courses would be like discussing capital punishment in terms of guillotines, ropes and electric chairs. And it is precisely in this way that much debate about Eng. Lit. courses goes on. 'I would hate to think of anyone leaving university with a degree in gobbledegook without a thorough grounding in early medieval gooking.' It is the approach that accepts:

1. The concepts of a frozen syllabus – a meal of knowledge goodies dished up by your favourite academic host.

2. The concept that something is *more* or *less* worth studying in itself i.e. that facts or events or even ideas are not seen to exist in moments in time, space or social circumstances ignoring that it is their origins, context and purpose that make them more or less worth studying.

3. The concept of the educated gentleman – the man who attended the meal was fed with 'good' facts and is now ready to do society a good turn.

All three are among the 'unseen' elements of the education process of a university: means by which the mere attendance at a university guarantees certain orientation or alignment for society at large.

*The frozen syllabus* is the way in which most of us have been educated since the age of ten. Though it is considered legitimate for a student to choose *between* courses, it is considered illegitimate for him to evolve one for himself – or, more significantly – collectively. Don't question it. Just do it. It is maintained on irrational non-intellectual grounds, i.e. the compulsion of the exam system. Each frozen syllabus is then guarded from each other frozen syllabus as if somehow it was the mind itself that was divided up in this way. As far as Eng. Lit. is concerned this means learning how to exclude yourself from the debate about society. You may make vast gestures towards this area as 'related subjects' or assume they're all tidied up and comprehended and our job is to get down to text. And so we hedgehop from one sanctioned text to another; literature's main cause, purpose and consequence seems merely to beget itself in genius-shaped parcels for chaps like us to appreciate. On either side of us, huge areas of 'other people's business' flash by as we head hard for a 'pure' literary critical utterance. Of course most of us never reach the heights of tedious irrelevance sustained in most academic journals of literary criticism. At the student level it means masquerades like this: in the *Knight's Tale* (G. Chaucer, 1390) Emelye is supposed to be a 'symbol'. I wrote about this on and off for something like five years and my total ignorance of the psychological process by which a 'symbol' is supposed to work, the origins of virgin cults, the function such a cult might have had for Chaucer or his audience, what remnants of it live in my consciousness as a middle-class male and why, never stopped me from 'doing very well at Chaucer'. I was ignorant. So what?

What is important is that at no stage, even when I began several quite lunatic speculations in these 'side' issues, was it possible to find within the references and academia of lit. crit. any help. I should have been concentrating on the relationship of theme and structure, summarizing analogues, and merely reiterating again and again that the *Knight's Tale* is very stylized and shows great craftsmanship and surely the Knight would have got the free dinner.... But it was no part of my 'academic' work that either started me off or kept me informed on how I might locate myself in this world – to see myself as part of a highly specialized specific social group and that *this fact* might have some bearing on what I liked why I liked it and what nonsense I was writing about it.

## Study good things

Because Doing Eng. Lit. can simply mean remembering books for exams, it seems logical to argue about what books they are you are obliged to remember. Arguments about Eng. Lit. courses easily degenerate into talk about the validity of reading Anglo-Saxon *or* James Joyce *or The Autobiography of the Alexandra Palace Organ* as fixed points of goodness in the frozen fragment. The question that has to be asked is who or what am I doing this for? Who am I justifying this study to? To sort this one out, one needs a theory of society. As we know, most discussion about Doing Eng. Lit. doesn't muck its hands with this kind of stuff. Doing Eng. Lit. is good for *you* so it's good for the frictionless functioning of the body politic to have more 'good'.

*The educated gent* believes he furthers the good of society merely by existing. As far as the Eng. Lit. world is concerned this often means a totally absurd piece of individualism: doing Eng. Lit. and Lit. crit. means 'saving' the civilization of the past. It's this kind of thing that gives masturbation a bad name.

Literature neither makes the world better nor worse. It's like language – necessary. Reading the canon of Eng. Lit. is a totally different matter, because the moment you define literature within any boundaries then you start to present a value-system: a national picture, a class picture, a certain kind of historic convention and so on. The extravagant goatsfart about what love of literature means is particularly pernicious because it is the tiny area Eng. Lit. that is alluded to in the name of the general. As it stands, Eng. Lit. faculties are the institutional forms that propose, maintain and express an ethic that runs throughout our society – art makes the whole beastly materialism of life and society bearable. In actual fact what makes the beastly world so bearable is precisely the chance to belong to the elite that can lecture at an institution that expresses this ideology where it is economically bearable to live in the beastly world . . . i.e. the ethic arises out of and reinforces the social situation.

## Exams

In spite of all the well-meaning words, the sympathies, the I-hate-doing-this – in spite of all the sympathetic liberal bilge that academics inundate students with as they near finals, the overriding influence on what is *not* studied, what *is* studied, how it is studied, or why it is studied, is the exam system.

Many Eng. Lit. academics are constantly pained by the system they put into practice but are without the intellectual means to combat it; as this would involve their own destruction. They talk about 'necessary evils' and 'learning in spite of, if not because of, exams'. Everywhere there is talk of dissertations, oral exams, long-term appraisals, short-term appraisals. Progressives infiltrate exam boards to make life 'easier' for students. But one thing is certain, every year bands of those special humans, those trained in sensibility and judgement, men and women with civilization oozing out of every pore sit round tables hour after hour arguing about half marks here, the vintage year of '66, or whether someone is worth a 2:1 who gets C+ (+ ?) on his Shakespeare paper.

A recent telly programme showed two York Eng. Lit. academics sitting down after a seminar solemnly discussing whether Jim Smith's 'intervention' in the previous discussion on Wilde was worth 64 or 65 per cent. Apart from the near-insanity of their thinking that they were making meaningful 1 per cent 'objective' distinctions here, what the hell kind of atmosphere is that for the great uplifting discussions about all things bright and beautiful?

The anomalies are huge: what is assessable about an Eng.Lit. exam paper? How come ideas and original thought (which academics claim they can recognize in exam scripts) have intrinsic gradeable value? Where is this 'value' situated? In a consensus of liberal intelligence? Is Leavis alpha beta or straight alpha? How would a liberal consensus grade a polemic against the liberal consensus? Who is doing the assessing for whom? And on what qualifications?

Of course it is no joky little coincidence that the foremost qualification to be an examiner is to have been a success at exams. The compulsion of an exam system is the highest level of intellectual justification of the course that many academics can run to. Middle-class academic hacks do not believe in, or dare risk the autonomous generation of theories of study. The concession made in this direction is the great con-job of options. This is market-economy democracy. Rather than set up structures (conferences, democratic faculty boards, seminars) in which students and teachers (or – God forbid – outsiders like scientists or workers) thrash out the first principles of their studies or the philosophy behind the linking of one aspect of reality with another, alternative exam-sized chunks of knowledge are offered as the means by which the individual will 'spontaneously generate his own linkages'. Reading Byron is so much of an ecstatic experience (Dylan gives you such a buzz) that the only way in which I can convince you of it is to set you an exam in it. This will make you read Byron in a certain way, read certain things about Byron and spend many happy hours trying to remember the whole in a manageable form for me to test whether you *did* read Byron . . . or you did read the right criticism . . . or you did spend those happy hours trying to remember it all . . . or that you came to the *right* conclusions about Byron . . . or that you came to the wrong ones in the *right* kind of way . . . not that I want to let *my* value judgements interfere in any way. I just love the way you hate Byron.

The more liberal the regime, the more absurd it becomes. As the exams become less and less 'fact-orientated' and more and more scope is made for dissertations, reference to books, use of essays then the more irrelevant and false becomes this thing: the grade. That is to say as the work becomes more thoughtful and significant so the encapsulation of the grade-system becomes relatively more obscene. It makes personnel grading *more* significant, the area of the examiners' value judgements about your value judgements based on an even broader foundation of sympathy or antipathy and so puts even more power into his hands. As it is, Eng. Lit. exams are still littered with the whole exploded paraphernalia of paraphrasings and gobbets and context questions. Examiners are quite happy to give marks (i.e. 'objective assessment') for 'evidence of work' (i.e. regurgitated quotations, or erudite comparisons) a notion as value-laden as *Mein Kampf*. It's difficult to think of a more hideous sight than clusters of academics poring over piles of exam scripts squeezing the sweat out of the pages into measuring flasks. But then we always have to remember the sad state of the Eng. Lit. academic's nerves. He is never fully and totally confident that either he himself or the vast hordes of students who listen to him, are actually doing something that anyone out there in the big wide world cares very much about. He needs to constantly reassure himself by the criteria of that materialist world he has escaped from, that his pursuits are valid. We shall see later how this is reflected in the kind of critical work that is encouraged. Exams maintain: the fragmentation of knowledge; the concept of knowledge as private property; the rendering of reality into exam-sized units called facts; the authoritarian justification for study; the maintenance of social discipline by competition; the reduction of an individual's totality into a quantifiable fact; and the overall binding cement that it is the very act of obeying the rules and producing evidence of 'hard' – i.e. not enjoyed – work that constitutes the education of the exam-system.

Now, let us say loosely that one of the functions of literature is an invitation to share and widen experience by creating representations of man's social and material relationships.

I don't wish to claim an intrinsically humanizing quality for literature here – Steiner has already drawn the picture of the concentration-camp commandant reading his Goethe and turning on the gas taps. Moreover, simply to share or widen experience does not necessarily in itself mean that the experience concerned is one of 'use' to humanity. Griffith's *Birth of a Nation* shares the glorious aspirations of the Ku Klux Klan with us. However, if my function of literature is correctly defined it can be seen that much of the exam system works in direct contradiction to that function. The fundamental contradiction lies in the fact that the institutions of university, the faculty, the seminar group are means by which large numbers of people are *brought together* and yet the underlying momentum is to *divide* them by institutionalized competition – competition for grades, knowledge-hoards, brain-power, social standing and in the final step – for jobs. This like the other characteristics of exams does not exist by some chance misfortune but as a consequence of and a reinforcer of the same phenomenon in capitalist society. Men are brought together into great enterprises of coordinate production only to find that the majority of men are deprived of the fruits of that enterprise.

### The essay and 'criticism'

In most Eng. Lit. university courses the essay is the major, if not, sole official activity the student performs when faced with lit. In Real Life across the centuries men have done all sorts of things in, around and in response to literature: re-enactment, retelling, re-expressing in different forms; 'using' it as illustration in arguments, discussions or thought concerning why people behave in such and such a way and so on. The Eng. Lit essay does none of these.

At the end of three years at university, two years in the sixth form and two or three years on O-Levels, the average student has probably written about three hundred of the things, and as a body of verbiage they constitute for each individual the Great Achievement that is a liberal education. I would argue they constitute the hard core of intellectual hypocrisy. Of course the obsession with them is part of the exam system – and this explains the formulae of their structure: the proposition, the arguments for and against and the salty conclusion all help the examiner flailing about counting facts, and measuring evidence of work and 'good method'. Again and again one reads in examiners' reports (amongst the sneering list of spoonerisms, howlers and other examples of what tired people do when put upon rather heavily by sneering collectors of spoonerisms and howlers) appeals for 'freshness', and evidence that they were not merely reading coughed-up versions of old essays. Yet *they* are the ones who perpetuate the system which guarantees that just such a cough-up

will occur. It is a formula that demands the broad pontificatory judgement:... 'and so for these reasons I feel that D. H. Lawrence's poetry
does not rank as highly as Hopkins' but is certainly more important than
Hardy's.' You learn to make utterances like these that you either know
mean very little or, tragically, you think are tremendously important fine
discriminations between art as evidenced by the great 'objective' criteria
of lit. crit. (see later). You learn how to lob in a hotch-potch of the big
wigs of lit. crit. as evidence of 'breadth of reading'. These days the job
has been made very easy because all those academics who spend their time
marking these important utterances also maintain their financial status
by churning out 'Casebooks', 'Symposia' and the like.

You write the books about the books so that the students can write
the essays about the books about the books, so that they can pass the exams
you set them. It would be quite joky if it weren't all done in the name of
keeping the nation civilized. When did the nation get a look in?

You learn to avoid putting down your first-hand personal sensations,
doubts and questions (even though this is what an author writes for and
at). *More fundamentally* you avoid engaging in an argument with what is
actually being *said* in the lit. Instead you learn to make the little paeans
and eulogies within the framework and craft-lingo of the 'discipline'.
So Macbeth is a greatplay because of its 'amazing *range* of imagery'
(that's worth five quotes and ten marks at least) but the Mystery plays
are greatplays because of their amazing *stark simple* imagery 'Rich and
sensuous' is good. Chaucer's great because he's so 'realistic' but *Beowulf*'s
great because it's so 'symbolic'. 'Irony' is a very good thing too and there's
'ambiguity' which has reverberations (illustrate with three reverbs).
Simplicity is good but complexity is getting a good price too. Then there's
'themeandstructure' and 'effectiveness' where you 'prove' effectiveness
because themeandstructure are united though quite who it's effective for
or why is not clear. Understatement is 'effective' – though cliches are not.
A really profitable filler is to do a good hack job with analogues whereby
you simply give a series of outlines of a set of 'related works' and claim
one of them has got an influence on one of the others. 'Invoking' and
'conveying' are crucial tools in the enterprise because if something invokes a lot then that's a good thing and if a metaphor conveys 'what it's
like' then you've obviously 'proved' that it's good. The experience generates all kinds of dual standards. Huge enthusiasms are expressed in an
essay for works that will never be returned to again. That is to say it is
quite possible to construct whole examworthy and bookworthy schemes
of analysis, to maybe even force yourself to 'appreciate' the *Dunciads* and
*Sohrab and Rustum* but when it comes to the desert island you'll take

Mickey Mouse and the Doors. And for these you have no scheme of analysis and don't want one. It's nine to five lit. crit. Alternatively – and perhaps this is worse – Mickey Mouse is subjected to the same laboured and tautologous analysis as all the rest. Any reading through one of the heavy pop journals shows it abounds with the old formulae dressed up as the new. It was great because ... it blew my mind (sensation-isms) ... because it said it like it is (credibility-isms) ... because it was beautifully dense, compact, loose, serene, funky, cool, gutsy, clear, (beauty-isms) ... because it sounds like Arbuthnot Crudge Jnr (history-isms).

The defining characteristics of these utterances is that they define nothing and explain nothing. They are essentially print-orientated middle-class man's limp and feeble remains of a once-urgent need to participate in, to re-live and re-enact the spectacles of man. As statements there is nothing intrinsically wrong or right about them (in spite of academics believing that various jugglings of them can be graded like a micro-screw-guage). They are, under normal conditions, liable to lead nowhere and do no one very much harm – unless you're going to become a teacher (an approx one in two chance if you do Eng. Lit.) and insist that it is all terribly valuable and terribly necessary if the world is to survive. They are simply statements that repeat over and over again – 'I liked it'. As examples of communication between people they are essentially non-information. They are addressed to one self as one struggles to re-live the book or film, etc. *on* paper, *in* an essay, *for* an exam. The totality of the operation is grotesque in its uselessness. It is substitute experience, substitute creativity. It belongs to a clerkly class sitting on its arse, alone in studies and libraries removed from any creative transformation of the material world, removed from collective cooperative experience (see Appendix 1). It matches the origins of most of Eng. Lit. 'literature'.

As supposedly *critical* statements they might be possible starting points for some further understanding. For example, to keep a check on one's own second-by-second reactions to a piece of lit. as it is being perceived for the first time could be the *first* step of any analysis. To understand why those reactions changed and altered – were they manipulated by conscious precision by the artist or was it because of certain personal experience of your own?[1] Did some people of one kind of experience (e.g. women, men, orphans, workers) react differently to you and if so why? If we're going to say it's 'effective because it's real', or 'credible' then we can ask why should that make us pleased? A tape recorder might have done better. In other words we might consider the nature of *choices* and *selections* the writer has made in order to present something that is apparently

1. See D. W. Harding on *The Ancient Mariner* in *Experience into Words*.

in seamless continuity with reality: i.e. what were the decisions behind the construction and why were they made? If it 'sounds like Arbuthnot Crudge' then is that simply because they slept together or because of other shared phenomena? At present in rudimentary form many of the statements are simply critics' daily bread; the currency by which a class maintains itself at a reasonable standard of living. They are the noises 'educated' people mutter to each other in a vacuum.

Latham calls his book-works Skoob – 'books' spelt backwards. He is very concerned to see the negative equally with the positive, what is not there equally with what is there. Many of his works are on this theme. It is obviously a theme as much of interest to art as to science, which has been suggesting the existence of 'anti-matter' parallel to matter. The main work in the Lisson exhibition, if I understand its didactic scheme correctly, is about this threshold of something and nothing. Its main feature is two sealed glass globes containing a vacuum inside a vacuum. Although an exhibit of 'nothing', a hole in the atmosphere, the vacuum is labelled dangerous. And it is supported by 'documentary' evidence, laid out on the floor, which includes among other things a 'photograph of an empty space (not available)', and a projector running with a loop of fully exposed film – as if to explore the same threshold in the capacities of modern recording devices (*The Times*).

They are the criteria on which so much of lit. crit. rests – criteria that claim to be *explanations* of goodness and badness; 'objective' measures yet they fail to have any applicability outside of themselves – unlike scientific proofs.

Here is another, this time from that powerhouse of anti-bourgeois culture *New Left Review*:

The central action of the novel is very compact, all taking place within three days: a precisely chosen three days in December 1949 just after the excommunication of Tito, coincidental with the triumphant consummation of the Chinese revolution and on the eve of the campaign against rootless cosmopolitanism. This temporal and technical unity in what might otherwise have been a decentred and episodic work [what's so great about unity and what's the matter with decentred episodes? – I'm rather keen on them myself] corresponds to the underlying unity of the political themes which are being developed. The political and aesthetic dimensions are harmonized with remarkable brilliance [as would a tribute to Adolf Hitler written in the shape of a swastika].

I am not sufficiently well-read to be able to provide a full explanation as to how these tautologous, feebly re-enactive kinds of language have arisen (I was too busy churning it out week by week myself). It is the language of mediation, second-hand experience and armchair thrills.

Actually, it has been argued that the force behind this pseudo-critical junk is a drive to find complexity. What is supposed to distinguish the lit. crittur from a mere reader is that he gets deeper, discovers more meaning, shows that first appearances belie the underlying truth and that what you may have found satisfying and straightforward is in fact very very complex – therefore better. What better justification for his work can a lit. crittur have than to claim insights where the hoy polloy gaze unseeingly. Thus all that stuff about scorning the transient thrill, the stock response and sentimentality. This is why he needs a jargon to isolate himself and a set of pseudo-critical criteria to give his world an 'objective' reality. This is also why Eng. lit. crit. is infused with rabid snobbery and elitism (see Eliot's *Notes Towards the Definition of Culture* and Leavis's *English and the University* where a fine liberal course of study is invented – not for you and me but ideally for the Part 2 Cambridge Honours man. There's universality of art for you).

It is also, for all its imprecision, full of prescriptive – almost moralizing – overtones about what is or is not suitable. Here is Keith Aldritt (1969) on Orwell:

The *undisciplined* preoccupation with horror explains why *1984* leaves such an impression of unpleasantness in *our minds* and why it is *not pleasurable* to contemplate a re-reading of the book. As a work of satiric propaganda *1984* enjoys a reputation which bears little relation to its merit. Private obsessions have impaired Orwell's function in the public role of propagandist [my italics].

Notice the all-embracing 'our minds'. This is the fallacy that the critics' personal response is a universal truth obeying certain laws – in this case: too much of the green and nasties. It is the *post facto* public justification of the private personal sensation and judgement, rendered universal and 'objective' by including all the world and his brother. The only trouble is that he forgot to ask their permission (i.e. provide a *sociology of response*) and in so doing neglected to have a closer look at himself in the act of responding (i.e. *an account of the process of response*). Undaunted by the fact that the book is popular – he makes a final value judgement without engaging himself with the values of the book (i.e. the central confrontation of reader with writer: the *ideology of response*). It goes without saying that he is not concerned with defining the book's position in relation to history. And by history I don't mean the history of lit. but the history of man.

It obviously follows then that Aldritt should write the following:

To the modern student of literature, Orwell's criticism must seem crude and rudimentary. Indeed, Orwell's essays about literature bear very little relationship to literary criticism as that term is now understood. Modern literary criticism, for the most part academic in origin, tends to concentrate upon given texts. Above all it is attentive to the words on the page and to the quality of mind and responsiveness to which the words attest. It is conducted by means of a set of verbal conventions that make for the neutralization, sometimes even for the virtual extinction, of the personality of the critic. It is meticulous in its formulations even at the risk of becoming Alexandrian. With Orwell it is quite otherwise. There is no great reverence for the novel or poem as a thing in itself, nor is there much critical vocabulary. His essays seldom offer a new insight into a work. 'Politics *v.* Literature', for instance, though it is of great interest in terms of Orwell's development and shows among other things the influence of Swift upon the writing of *Nineteen Eighty-Four* has, little to offer the reader who is primarily interested in *Gulliver's Travels*. Compared to the subtleties and complexities of recent published discussion of that book, Orwell's comments strike us as elementary.

The value of Orwell's essay on *Gulliver's Travels* is precisely the way in which it concerns itself with what Swift was concerned with. What *kind* of Utopia did Swift have in mind and what was it that infuriated him about the world as it was? But the object of Orwell's essay isn't merely to explain the jokes to us dumb bleeders, it is a piece of polemic in which Orwell places himself in relation to Swift's ideology as he has defined it. It is valuable precisely because he does *not* neutralize himself (however that's supposed to happen). It is valuable because he has *not* displayed a gawping reverence for the novel as a 'thing in itself' but treated Swift as someone trying to say something that can be argued about. For Aldritt all this can do in his tiny irrelevant little world of 'verbal conventions' and Alexandrian meticulousness is to tell him something about Orwell's own lit. hist. Small wonder he seems so pleased that criticism is located in academe.

It is educative to think back over the experience of looking at lit. in the classroom and university situation, and try to find occasions where the discussion centred in any of the fields I have mentioned: the *sociology of response*, the *process of response*, the *ideological debate* that the work embarks on, or its relation to the history of man.

Consider for example this situation. We, the eager and naïve sixth former, are told: great art justifies its content, which means that the sanctioned authors are intrinsically worth reading until you *learn* to love them. Secondly we learn, e.g. from the Open University selected edition of Hamlet of the 'generalizing tendency of all art in its way of taking us behind and beyond the present towards a universal set of values'. Thirdly, an Ode is dumped on your desk marked: Great. In it there's this bloke who says that 'Beauty is truth, truth beauty' (actually it's not a bloke, but an urn) and it also says 'that is all ye know on earth, and all ye need to know'. Now as it happens this is quite a debatable point but you can be pretty sure of one thing: although this poem will be the source of much talk, thought, comparison, paraphrasing up and down the country – in very few cases will it be the starting point for a discussion as to whether Beauty *is* truth or not and whether any other people in history have had any other ideas about the subject. Because it is Great, it is 'worthy of criticism'. So the philosophy of the poem slides unnoticed into your eager young mind while you spend your time doing all those brilliant things that Keith Aldritt says you can do with literature. This is because you are engaged in the 'discipline of criticism' not 'philosophy'. Of course it is all purely a coincidence that what the urn says about art corresponds to the kind of criticism you are subjecting the poem to, and derives itself from the same philosophy. Keats holds out for us a world into which it would be bliss to escape though it be sadly impossible or impossibly sad. This is necessary because the workaday world has become so repulsive and contorted. A century and a half later classloads of people read this and instead of arguing about whether (say) the world *is* contorted, or whether the escapes suggested would work, they actually carry out a similar escape by means of the feeble re-enactments of modern criticism.

The first step in understanding the literary process is not fully gone into, i.e. the poem is not treated as an idea with which we have engaged as directed by the writer. And this is part of the same philosophy that talks of art, poverty, education, industrial relations and criticism as having nothing to do with politics (or if they do they shouldn't have). In case you're worried about this here's a little gem from an anthology for children called *Fresh Flights* which includes amongst other things the Magnificat:

My gardener sits and
And earns his pay
dreaming the happy
hours away

Till evening comes
When like a shot
He hurries to
his private plot

Where he will work
as one possessed
and never stop
to take a rest

How very splendid
it would be
if he would work
like that for me.

Is this poem 'good' or 'bad'?

If we are going to pretend to being critics i.e. to *explain* something then other factors need to be taken into account. (Of course there is a school of crit. that says that as value judgements are such messy things – throw them out. Confine your talk about literature to its mythic origins, or its literary historical origins or its linguistic origins and so on. This is in one sense final abdication of responsibility.)

We need:

1. To treat literature as an active, value-laden, opinion-full component in the debate about man.
2. To use literature as an opportunity to discover something of the range and kinds of experience available to man.
3. To discover how literature itself functions.
4. To discover how and why literature changes.

This means we need to know more about literature than simply more literature. We need to understand how we relate in the world and why we need to be able to create our own representations of reality as well as simply spectate other people's. We need to make inquiries into *our* private motives and what their social origins are (see Appendices 1 and 2). All this means social commitment and social action. It means becoming aware of the origins of human action and thought. If I write 'Shakespeare was a great judge of nature' then it seems to me that statement needs a hell of a lot more substantiation than can be shown by close 'attention to the text'. If the phrase is simply meant to mean 'O very good, jealous people do seem to do that – my uncle once tried to . . .' then why not say it? Then we can have an argument about jealousy or, if you know my uncle, about my aunt. If the statement has pretensions to really mean what it says then the route is a lot longer, though the starting point may be the same. Somewhere I have to state – or it is explicit by *context*, e.g. in a journal that advocates the extermination of all women and children under five – what my value system, my beliefs about human nature are. If I want to explain something about what Shakespeare was about in Elizabethan times (or in any other continuum he is put) then I had better get clear what Elizabethan man was about and why Shakespeare was so good at 'getting it right'. For that I had better get some idea of the process of what 'getting it right' might mean in the literary process and one way of doing that might be to try a bit of getting it right myself – acting, writing, singing and so on. If I seriously want to maintain that there is something universal about Shakespeare then I better get it clear how he goes down with the Trobriand Islanders. If all I really want to do is write about my experience watching the play then there's not much point in pretending the whole thing is some exact science of judgement that can be used as a means of social training and control for entry into middle management.

## A model of the literary process

At this juncture in the essay it has become necessary on my part to express what I understand to be a model of the literary process. As I see it the response mechanism involves four constitutents in constant fluid inter-relation with each other.

1. The taking up of the invitation: following the conventions of the occasion, i.e. the recognition of the form or genre or pattern to the spectacle.

2. The placing of oneself (or the artists' regulation of the placing – or both) in a certain relation to the spectacle.

3. An ideological interaction – a flow of sympathies and antipathies towards and away from the various conflicting elements within the spectacle.

4. The final evaluation or reckoning process in which the respective feelings concerning the appropriateness of the outcome solidify and become 'experience', 'memory'.

1. The first is a kind of anthropological notion in which the historical and sociological rules are recognized, e.g. you *read* books, *kick* footballs, *watch* plays, etc. – rules that you recognize by virtue of certain social and material relationships you are born into, acquire, shape and are shaped by.

2. The second is a finer version of the first in which the artist(s) regulates the psychological 'distance' between you and the spectacle. It concerns the process(es) by which the spectator is invited to assess the spectacle's correspondence with his own view of reality, e.g. (a) a system that might be sited along a scale that depends more or less on the uniqueness of the event in time and space (see D. W. Harding) i.e. more or less 'symbolic.'
Or e.g. (b) a system that demands you make various *kinds* of 'acts of comparison' (Coleridge) between the spectacle and *your* view of reality, e.g. Brecht's alienation technique.
Or e.g. (c) a system that invites more, or less, as in participation in the spectacle, a Mass or a pantomime.

Each spectator–spectacle situation sets up its own dynamic and this dynamic is both part of the total meaning of the experience and also belongs to specific cultural and social conditions. Needless to say, these conditions are in part a consequence of and in part shape the society's means of survival. This balance between effect or cause of the means of survival is never the same from one spectator–spectacle system to another. In other words the nineteenth-century novel's capacity to change men's minds was infinitely slower and more socially confined than was the radio in Nazi Germany but each required a certain mode of production, a certain development in productive capacity and a certain distribution of power, wealth and leisure for their respective developments.

3. The third is the core of the perceptive process by which protagonists in dramas are seen to be in opposition to each other and whereby the spectator's experience, his 'world-picture', his 'consciousness', his 'ideology' identify the elements of the spectacle – defining their changing characteristics in relation to each other and in relation to him. Warm, cold, hostile, friendly, threatening, feeble, and so on. (It is crucial to remember here that 'consciousness' or individual 'ideology' is derived out of *interactions with other men* (*and with matter*) and that some interactions have more determining power on consciousness than others: e.g. work, family, etc.).

4. The fourth, the evaluating, is the *post-facto* application of the meaning of the first three: Where one's personal world-picture shifts to accommodate or reject the meaning, assessing its worth as a pattern or model of human action. This is obviously a highly complex psychological process involving the whole consciousness as a selective, memorizing, understanding mechanism.

Most criticism is conducted ignoring that the first constituent even exists, e.g. '*Citizen Kane* – great camera work, therefore great film', let alone functions within specific rules in any given society and history, e.g. *Beowulf* and a warrior culture, or that they are defined by the nature of that society's fundamental structures of social organization (or more, accurately, both reflecting and affecting those structures).

As I have shown, much crit. desperately tries to show how evaluation can be made without reference to the interaction process (3); e.g. most of the statements concerning realism and symbolism or image- or symbol-systems.

In fact most criticism I have read either confines itself to one or other of these four constituents or tries to avoid any of them, assuming that the whole process is too mystical to break down. However, as so many critical utterances talk about how 'we' are affected by this or that – and such and such is '*effective*' – the whole process would seem to be self-evident, which it obviously is not.

The process of the *artist*'s means of creating representations of man's social and material relationships, is the other side of the same coin.

Firstly, he is defined by his consciousness, i.e. the unique product of the range of interactions he has carried out and experienced with other men, animals and matter. This consciousness (which is a picture of how he operates in the world and how the world operates in him) constructs 'representations' of these interactions. These interactions are a man's means of survival, the role he plays in his society's mode of production. The 'representations' are man's means by which the interaction systems are established, i.e. his movements, sounds, language and constructions. They both determine and are determined by the interaction systems man sets up with other men (and with matter) in order to survive. The 'representations' are the stuff, the building units of the interaction systems. Games, pictures, dreams, stories, music, rituals, speeches, plays, films, songs, saucepans, adverts, cars, swords, telescopes, grapefruit are all in one sense or another either representations (or at least representative) of the particular interaction systems man has set up in order to survive in a certain kind of way and at a certain level of comfort. Traceable *in* the 'representations' are these interactions – interactions of the man or men who shaped the 'representation' concerned. In actual fact, ultimately there is no other source of value of content but the traces of the relevant interactions.

The act of creation operates as a selecting, expressing, monitoring system – each of which is carried out by the whole consciousness. The basis on which an experience is selected, why it is selected, what modes of expression, what kinds of changes and checks are induced by the monitoring system need social, psychological and linguistic methods of description. I haven't got much further in my understanding of this than to see that it is no use trying to follow the process through along one parameter only, or to switch course from one to another mid-stream. None of this will be absolutely clear until it's known how the mind carries about 'experience' even though it may be possible to assert why it does and with what effects.

As I see it, Marxism provides us with a philosophy with which to approach the subject giving us a certain picture of man, consciousness, and their functioning in society; psychology, e.g. 'personal construct theory', has provided us with a picture of some possible strategies of thought; certain socio-and psycholinguists have suggested relationships between language and society and language and thought and there's some anthropology that has found the structure of the mind mapped out in mythic archetypes and their social functioning.

Meanwhile back at base little old Eng. Lit. bashes on deriving the 'origins' of one work of art purely in another:

The manner of metaphysical poetry *originates* in developments in prose and verse in the 1590s. The greatest glory of that decade is that it saw the flowering of the drama. Metaphysical poetry is the poetry of the great age of our drama. Its master John Donne was, we are told, 'a great frequenter of plays' in his youth. . . . The metaphysical style peters out, to be replaced by the descriptive and reflective poetry of the eighteenth century, a century which sees the rise of the novel and has virtually no drama [my italics].

Bob's your uncle – just like that (compare this with Appendix 1). The notion of a course of study as being in some way complete by establishing these kinds of parallels between 'representations' is the old style lit. course. It is the purest manifestation of the fragmentation of knowledge, the purest manifestation of the aesthetic viewpoint – art enduring time, men and machines like a divinity. It is an ideology compounded by refugees from the grinding mill-wheels of productive labour unable to devise an alternative to the visible. Any given 'representation' exists in various continua – the continuum of its contemporaneous mode of production, e.g. feudalism; the continuum of the alignment of its creators in relation to that mode of production, e.g. a craftsman; the continuum of the relationships it enters at any given time, e.g. Shakespeare's 'Globe' or an Oxford tutorial. To account for these relationships and interrelationships in any given criticism would be actually explaining phenomena.

The normal methods which only pick certain of the continua, may provide limited explanations. When they are honest accounts of the central clash of ideas between spectator and spectacle they will reveal the differing levels and kinds of consciousness concerned. To examine one's own responses and the personal-historic reasons for them, to compare these with other people's must be part of the process that will enable us to set up new modes of production, new interactive systems of survival and may – should we want to spend our lives that way – lead to an explanatory criticism. Of course much modern criticism neglects and misunderstands the relationship of art and society. It is happy to do so. This is because that would be 'sociology' not 'criticism' But it also fails. to come to terms with the ideological crunch point of literature – response – how and why? It is a great gaping hole sitting right in the middle of what is supposed to be a 'critical discipline'.

## Alternative practice

In the 'liberal' 'pluralist' 'post-war' world, English faculties have widened and diversified if not greatly within any given university then from one university to another.

However, in amongst the diversity that is now feasible at British universities there is one factor that remains unchallenged: as a predominantly middle-class elite it has been unable and unwilling to generate any theory, study or practice of popular culture of much significance. The study of folk music is still embedded in whimsy and pastoral, the big ballads are handled as ancient and historic gems, there is no analysis or even collection of oral story-telling or jokes, heaps of broadsides and song collections moulder in library cellars. Whereas the cultural patterns of the middle and upper classes, their literary tastes and output of four hundred years are anthologized, edited, selected, collected, annotated and digested down to O-level size, the culture and accomplishments of the working class over the same period are in a few tatty pieces. The great generalized statements made about individual genius, the 'English' genius, 'civilization', beauty, humour, the meaning of art and the value of 'Good Taste' are all made without reference to what the majority of the people of Britain have been producing and consuming culturally for hundreds of years. Since writing the first draft of this article I watched an Open University programme on rhythm, rhyme and metaphor. A bored and baleful face stared out of the screen reciting chunks of *The Waste Land*. By coincidence I looked at George Thomson's *Marxism and Poetry* on the same day. He locates rhythm and rhyme in their *origins:* the grunting of labour through to the work song, the lullaby, the lament. Thomson was writing a pamphlet for a despised cause, the Open University was invoking great democratic aspirations and using all the vast resources of the mass media. The contrast between the two approaches sums up for me where lit. crit. culture is and where its alternative could be. The one: wittering away to itself in bored, irrelevant little formulae – the other providing a critical basis for an active art. One approach that talks about the great achievements of art belonging to the few and the other that shows those achievements as the possession of illiterate peasants, craftsmen and workers.

This then is not an appeal to absorb this whole section of man's activity into the same passive knowledge machine that grinds through texts of plays rather than act them (Leavis blithely refers to 'pages' of plays); that refuses to see the reading of literature in a continuum with the creating of it (or other art forms). Rather it is to point out the narrow, middle-class irrelevance of creating notions of culture that do not learn from slave, peasant and working-class cultures: cultures brewed in the battle with the material world.

There's some that sing of the hiring fair
and sound out an alarm
But the best old song that was ever sung
It is about the term
The term-time it is near
when we will all win free
And with the hungry farmers
again will never fee

With broad-tail coats and quaker hats
and whips below their arms
They'll hawk and call the country round
a-seeking for their farms
And they'll go on some 20 mile
where people doesn't know'em
And there they'll hire their harvest hands
and bring them far from home

They'll tap you on the shoulder
and ask if you're to fee
They'll tell you a fine story
that's every word a lie
They'll tell you a fine story
and get you to perform
But lads when you are under them
it's like a raging storm

On cabbage cold and taters
they'll feed you like the pigs
While they sit at their tea and toast
and ride about in gigs
The mistress must be ma'am and you
must lift a cap to her
and before you find an entrance
the master get his sir

The harvest time when it comes round
they'll grudge you sabbath rest
They'll let you to the worship
but they like the working best
The dinner hour vexes them
and then to us they'll say:
Come on my lads you'll get your rest
When lying in the clay.

At present the definitions of popular culture are tied up with cock-eyed confusions about mass-culture. People professing to be Marxists tell us that the Rolling Stones uniquely prefigure communist art (*New Left Review*) or that football is either the revolutionary consciousness of the masses (*Black Dwarf*) or a cultural imposition on the masses (*Red Mole*) and so on.

A strategy of alternative practice for students of Eng. Lit. who I assume have become interested in some of the problems raised in this article lies in the area of counter-culture.

1. The debate about books needs to be kept in its natural area – the ideological one i.e. where commitment is – in everybody.

2. Criticism if it is to be conducted – and for most people it is in the final analysis one of the most boring things that can be done with books – needs to find its explanatory feet. This needs history, anthropology, psychology and philosophy more than it needs what has got by as lit. crit. in the past. It needs a model of man – a task that most universities don't regard as a central battleground from which all else stems.

3. One must constantly work towards a notion of places of higher study that are societies of equals within themselves and able to justify their activities to the class that produces wealth. This means the destruction of exam systems and the setting up of open conferences, commissions of research projects with teaching commitments to fulfil, seminars and meetings – all in order to establish schemes of study, philosophies of study and justifications of research projects and a role (if any) for the 'intellectual' in society.

4. In the field of culture and ideology, the principles of Armchair Expertise, brilliance in passivity, fragmentation of expertise, hoarding and competing all need to be broken down. A process that can only be carried out in the final analysis by setting up alternative structures of working, living, playing and studying – ones that derive their values and methods from and direct them towards, the only class that will finally be able to bring such structures about. This is counter-culture and it means the setting up of popular Popular theatre, poetry, song, music, dance, film and television – re-learning re-enactment as a major means of social interaction.

All this means organization, pooling of effort, sharing and generation of ideas, invitation of speakers, singers, painters, film-makers, workers, students from local colleges of further ed., and school kids. It requires the cross-fertilization of ideas across meaningless faculty boundaries, in which people educate each other as they are educated, conducting explanations of their work to those who – in the collective pooling – demand it. It requires 'unexaminable' collective research, collective projects of work, as both the means and ends of discovery and production.

Up and down the country various models for this are beginning to emerge. They need to be strengthened without monolithizing (!) and the lessons learned from their failure or success. Raf Samuel's History Workshops at Ruskin College, Joan Littlewood, the Brighton Combination, CAST, Agit-prop theatre group, the Critics Group (Argo records) and the Festival of Fools, Leeds University arts festival, Ken Campbell's Road Show, Albert Hunt's work at Bradford College of Art (Appendix 2), Cinema-Action, Ewan MacColl and Charles Parker's Radio Ballads (Argo records) are all starting points. Union money could go towards providing bursaries for people with other kinds of experience to come on to the campus – or better – lead students off it. The fact remains that the organs of student self-help in this country are still pitiful compared with those in the States and it gives British students that special air of immaturity and lack of inventiveness in their protest.

I think, in the present university situation to set about constructing alternatives is in the long run more educative, of more use, and more enjoyable than pick-your-issue-and-revolt. When the alternative structures are threatened then there is something to defend. The left has had pitifully little to defend over the last few years apart from isolated individuals victimized while provoking the system into victimizing them.

The alternative to doing the Eng. Lit. creep is the making of popular culture. Its past needs to be celebrated. It needs a theory and practice.

## Appendix 1

### from *Illusion and Reality* by Christopher Caudwell

As primitive accumulation gradually generates a class of differentiated bourgeois producers, the will of the monarch, which in its absoluteness had been a creative force, now becomes anti-bourgeois and feudal. Once primitive accumulation has reached a certain point, what is urgently desired is not capital but a set of conditions in which the bourgeois can realize the development of his capital. This is the era of 'manufacture' – as opposed to factory development.

The absolute monarchy, by its free granting of monopolies and privileges, becomes as irksome as the old network of feudal loyalties. It is, after all, itself feudal. A cleavage appears between the monarchy and the class of artisans, merchants, farmers and shopkeepers.

The court supports the big landowner or noble who is already parasitic. He is allied with the court to exploit the bourgeoisie and the court rewards him with monopolies, privileges or special taxes which hamper the development of the overwhelming majority of the rising bourgeois class. Thus the absolute 'will' of the prince, now that the era of primitive accumulation is over, no longer expresses the life principle of the bourgeois class at this stage.

On the contrary the court appears as the source of evil. Its glittering corrupt life has a smell of decay; foulness and mean deeds are wrapped in silk. Bourgeois poetry changes into its opposite and by a unanimous movement puritanically draws its skirt's hem away from the dirt of the court life. The movement which at first was a reaction of the Reformed Church against the Catholic Church is now a reaction of the puritan against the Reformed Church.

The Church, expressing the absolute will of the monarch and the privileges of the nobility, is met by the individual 'conscience' of the puritan, which knows no law but the Spirit – his own will idealized. His thrift reflects the need, now that primitive accumulation is over, to amass the capital in which freedom and virtue inheres by 'saving' and not by gorgeous and extravagant robbery.

Donne expresses the transition, for he is torn by it. At first captivated by the sensuality and glittering brilliance of the court, the insolent treatment he receives produces a movement away from it, into repentance. The movement is not complete. In Donne's last years, filled as they are with death-thoughts and magniloquent hatred of life, the pride of the flesh still tears at his heart.

Poetry, drawing away from the collective life of the court, can only withdraw into the privacy of the bourgeois study, austerely furnished, shared only with a few chosen friends, surroundings so different from the sleeping and waking publicity of court life that it rapidly revolutionizes poetic technique. Crashaw, Herrick, Herbert, Vaughan – all the poetry of this era seems written by shy, proud men writing alone in their studies – appealing from court life to the country or to heaven. Language reflects the change. Lyrics no longer become something that a gentleman could sing to his lady; conceits are no longer something which could be tossed in courtly conversation. Poetry is no longer something to be roared out to a mixed audience. It smells of the library where it was produced. It is a learned man's poetry: student's poetry. Poetry is read, not declaimed: it is correspondingly subtle and intricate.

**Appendix 2**

from 'Literature in Further Education' by Albert Hunt, *English in Education*

It is a generally agreed educational principle that young children learn through play. It is also generally assumed that at a certain stage young people stop learning through play and have to be taught in a much more formal way.

A little over a year ago I began working with a group of art college students on a play by John Arden and Margaretta D'Arcy, *Ars Longa, Vita Brevis*. It is a play about an art master who tries to impose military discipline on an art class and who is eventually killed in an exercise of the territorial army. The play was based partly on children's games, and when we began working on it, we started by exploring these games.

At first I was a little hesitant in inviting eighteen- and nineteen-year-old students to play games, but the first session removed all my hesitations. We began simply by throwing a ball about. It took about twenty minutes for people to lose their self-consciousness. Suddenly everybody was arguing violently about the rules of games they had played as children. We began to try out variations. It wasn't a bit like the 'games' in youth club socials, where people play at playing. We all became really involved. At the end of about six hours' work, we were exhausted and covered with bruises.

The games in the *Ars Longa* rehearsals were eventually shaped towards the production of a play. But it soon became clear to me that many of them had a validity in their own right and were capable of being developed into complex dramatic experiences.

There is, for example, the game of tig, in which the object is to touch a person who is carrying a piece of chalk. The chalk is passed from one person to another, while one player, who is 'on', tries to catch the one with the chalk.

Played at running speed, this results in the release of a fair amount of physical energy and high spirits. This is in itself valuable in a group, and leads to a rapid breakdown of the kind of inhibitions that stop people from performing in front of other people. But slowed down to a walking pace. the game is capable of endless development.

Thus, the searcher becomes a plain-clothes detective. The piece of chalk becomes an explosive that a group of anarchists is trying to get from one end of the street to the other. The detective doesn't want to create panic in the street. He approaches people quietly and asks them to show their hands. Meanwhile, the players with the chalk adopt certain roles – a newspaper seller, a woman with a pram, courting couples – and pass the chalk round surreptitiously while playing out these roles.

On one occasion we made masks for the players. They were very crude, grotesque masks. Suddenly, the game became very violent – not physically but emotionally. The players with masks turned and jeered at the searcher. They formed a ritual stamp around him. All the violence implicit in the situation of a group against an individual was turned into a precise and concrete image.

Other work has sprung directly out of the study of particular texts.

There was, for example, a piece of work running through several sessions that was based on Sassoon's poem, *The Hero*.

'Jack fell as he'd have wished,' the Mother said,
And folded up the letter that she'd read.
'The Colonel writes so nicely.' Something broke
In the tired voice that quavered to a choke.
She half looked up. 'We mothers are so proud
Of our dead soldiers.' Then her face was bowed.
Quietly the Brother Officer went out.
He'd told the poor old dear some gallant lies
That she would cherish all her days, no doubt.
For while he coughed and mumbled, her weak eyes
Had shone with gentle triumph, brimmed with joy,
Because he'd been so brave, her glorious boy.
He thought how 'Jack', cold-footed, useless swine,
Had panicked down the trench that night the mine
Went up at Wicked Corner; how he'd tried
To get sent home, and how, at last, he died,
Blown to small bits. And no one seemed to care
Except that lonely woman with white hair.

We read the poem, and then I asked the students to try and reduce it to a five word headline in a newspaper. They worked at this for a long time – I've never seen such close attention paid to the text of a poem. Clearly it's impossible to translate a poem into a headline – but their choice of what elements to select told a lot about their response. Thus: OFFICER LIES TO HERO'S MOTHER and MOTHER'S PRIDE AT HERO'S DEATH indicate two different emphases. We spent most of a morning discussing which of the many headlines came closest to the feelings of the poem.

We then went on to discuss the characters in the poem and the attitudes they revealed. Did the woman really feel nothing? Why was she so careful to conceal her feelings? I related her actions – lowering her eyes and folding the letter – to a whole tradition of restraint in British theatre and cinema, and to the attitude that at all costs you must never allow your true feelings to be revealed.

The group then asked if they could act the poem – and at once ran into difficulties. For it was clear that both the mother and the officer were thinking things that couldn't be shown in the actions described in the poem. So far as the officer was concerned, they got round it by inventing another officer who also had letters to deliver, and so putting the information about Jack ('Remember how he panicked the night the mine went up?') into the dialogue.

But the mother defeated them completely. Various girls who tried out the part contorted their faces in an attempt to show that all sorts of things were happening behind those simple words and actions. We even left the poem and tried mimes to see how far precise thoughts could be communicated by facial expression. At last I went for a copy of *The Caucasian Chalk Circle* and we read the scene in which Brecht shows a girl confronting her returned soldier lover across a river. 'Hear now', says the narrator, 'what the girl thought but did not say', and later, 'Hear now what the soldier thought but did not say.' The thoughts are communicated by the narrator through songs. And so we decided to use a narrator. We wrote the letter that the Colonel wrote the mother, and then we wrote her thoughts. A boy brought a guitar and improvised a blues.

This particular project could have gone further – except that when one sees the students for only one morning a week it is difficult to keep up enthusiasm for more than three or four sessions. At first this used to worry me. When I could see possibilities in a situation. I tried to push them. Now it seems to me that this is wrong. What matters is not the finished product, but what is learnt in the process. When the students themselves feel that they have come to the end of something, I find it more useful to try and use what they have learnt by turning to something new.

In this case, we went on to work for a time with *The Caucasian Chalk Circle*. We read the play together, and then took a very short episode to work on – the episode in which Grusha buys milk from a peasant. The text occupies about a page of print, and after reading it we tried it without the script. Two students would act the scene out, and the rest would criticize, pointing out what had been missed, and the points at which the emphasis had been changed. When the actual content of the scene had been mastered – so that in fact the actors were repeating almost word for word the printed text – an argument arose about interpretation. The students playing the old peasant all tended to make him a typical avaricious old skinflint. I remembered Brecht's instructions to his actors – that this man was in fact a completely ordinary farmer who had just been robbed by the soldiers. So without telling the boy playing the farmer what was going on, I told two other boys to go and knock on his door as soldiers.

They pushed him aside, knocked him down, kicked chairs over and left everything in a shambles. He was still picking the chairs up when Grusha arrived, and his response to another knock at the door was no longer one of greed, but of fear and suspicion. Brecht's central point – that people act differently in different situations – was communicated by means of an acting situation.

# Social Workers: Training and Professionalism
Crescy Cannan

This article locates the training and ideology of social workers in the context of their struggle for professional status. Unlike academic courses, social-work training cannot be seen only in theoretical terms; the *practice* of social work is an integral part of the professional training. Therefore this article discusses what social workers do, as well as what they think. I shall discuss the conditions of social work training, the 'welfare state', then casework and professionalism, and lastly, alternative, radical directions.

## Social-work training

Most social-work training takes place in polytechnics, which compared to universities, are poorly financed, with overcrowding, poor union facilities, and very limited library resources. Polytechnics tend to be nine to five institutions, so that students do not have many opportunities to meet students and staff from other disciplines, contacts which in the university situation can be extremely important for a thorough appreciation of what is formally taught (see Robinson, 1968).

Social-work students in particular suffer from this insulation. Their practical work placements mean they are out of college for two or three days each week, and on the days they attend college, timetables tend to be crammed with (usually compulsory) lectures, tutorials and seminars. Apart from lunch-hours there is very little time to discuss courses as a whole, and seminar discussions tend to be too tightly allocated to permit wide discussions of the bases of social-work thinking and practice. Most students are in their late twenties, and for those with children, especially the women, there is very little time for study apart from essential texts.

Students who are interested in the politics of their college find it extremely difficult to attend union meetings and even more so to stand for office. They tend to be cut off from the political affairs of their own colleges, unless they are willing to play truant from course activities.

For the social-work student there is no opportunity to 'stand back' from the world he will enter on qualification, and to re-assess it on the basis of what he reads. Instead he is expected to play the role of social worker right from the start, indeed he has been selected as someone who supposedly has the necessary qualities for that role, as well as academic potential. His practical placements mean he is in constant touch with practising social workers who may be sceptical of the 'theory' he is taught, emphasizing instead experience in the work. Course tutors are unlikely to be very different kinds of people from practising social workers as they will have been in the field themselves, and maintain close contacts with local social workers, especially those who supervise their students in their practical placements (see Edwards, 1966).

While most university students are on grants, many social-work students are seconded from particular authorities to whom they have to return on qualification. Obviously this makes a student think twice about assimilating radical information that could make him want to change his choice of career. On the other hand, it can mean that students become very cynical about the practice of social work, which they find they can only do with their tongue in cheek.

Those social-work students who are not graduates are usually trained on two-year courses which do not generally require any specific educational or professional qualification. So staff are forced to assess candidates on criteria other than academic ones. One of the main barriers to radicalism among social-work students is the belief that social workers are special kinds of people. Selection to a course means you are endowed with mysterious qualities.

This is a basic contradiction in social-work thinking. On the one hand emphasis on professionalism points to a rigorous training in the 'sciences' of psychiatry, psychology and sociology, and on the other to social workers as 'mature' personalities, who have exceptional 'insight' into people's motivation. Maturity and insightfulness are not seen as qualities gained from taking a course, but are seen as characteristics which some people have and others don't. If the social worker has 'insight', plus training, then his judgements have a validity over, for example, political explanations, for the social worker 'knows' that the political militant is in fact 'acting out' his infantile authority problems. While the student's attention is turned towards underlying motives, he ignores the overt content of what is being said and done. In this way the rationality of political arguments is denied.

Neville Jones (1970) found that college tutors use four main procedures when selecting students: documentary evidence, personal statements and essays, interviews and psychological tests. Now while these tests are used to assess the standard of a student's written English, and his IQ, some tutors said they used them to elicit evidence that candidates had 'insight', which was frequently referred to as a quality necessary for selection. 'No tutor attempted to define what was meant by 'insight', nor did they indicate what kind of evidence was needed to substantiate a claim that a particular candidate had this ability'. One important function of selection procedures is to weed out potential deviants; thus tutors select students who they consider will be less likely to radically criticize or defy the *status quo* of the profession.

In spite of the continual emphasis on the individual, the student finds that in some contexts, such as considering forms of community work, that political or socio-economic explanations are offered. Why does it seem to the student that he has to accept psychological *or* socio-political explanations, why does accepting one mean rejecting the other? Social-work thinking is unable to explain the relation of individual to society without subordinating one to the other. The individual is studied in terms of psychology, society in terms of sociology, and the gap cannot be bridged because different conceptual frameworks are used in each discipline. Thought becomes compartmentalized and it is difficult for the student to find a way not only to *link* individual and society, but to *transcend* the separation of the elements, and to conceive of a dialectically inter-related whole (see Goldman, n.d.; Mills, 1959). The absence of any clearly defined philosophy of social work means that the underlying framework which structures the world for the social worker is not made explicit, except in terms of stating values or principles like 'respect for the indi-vidual'.

Seeing phenomena as parts of a whole is further blocked by an insistence on the 'uniqueness' of any problem or individual. Not only this, but causes appear to be so complex, so multiple, that focus on the result is the only realistic course of action (Mills, 1967). The splitting into different disciplines also means that the same problem has different causes depend-ing on the method you use to discuss it. All in all, causes are so mystified, that effects are simpler to deal with.

For example, discussions of the 'problem family' do point out bad housing conditions, low wages, and employment difficulties, but these are seen as precipitating latent emotional crises, and help is discussed in terms of these individual inner problems. Here is an example:

Many problem family parents are still working out in a basic way the very early emotional problems of love and hate, and are still undecided about their own inner goodness and the trustworthy nature of the outside world (Timms, 1962).

Because attention is focused on single deviant individuals or families, it is difficult to see what deviant families have in common with 'normal' families, and thus to see how the family i s a part of a total social structure, which relates the individual to that structure. In this sense the family is an institution mediating between the individual and a repressive society, so family breakdown has a *social* significance, instead of being an instance of individual failure.

Should a student show signs of outrage or criticism, this is managed by promptly 'social working' him. The content of what he says is ignored, and he is defined as 'acting out' some deep-seated problem of the psyche, so that what he is saying is not guided by rational consideration:

It may be that inadvertently or deliberately, the supervisor selects for the student a client whom he finds particular difficulty in helping. Often the reason for this is that there is something about the client or his problem which, as it were, touches an exposed nerve ending in the student because of its similarity to some personal difficulty he has not yet been able to face. When this happens, the supervisor, through her supportive relationship with the student, attempts to help him gain insight into his own behaviour in order that he should become more free to help the client (Edwards, 1966).

All this provides a conveniently justified red herring away from problems of poverty, conflict and power in society.

### The welfare state

One of the shortcomings of much social policy literature and teaching is the focus on isolated problems, on single 'important' authors or reformers. Students are not equipped with broad concepts which enable them to approach their course work, and the social services, critically. The fundamental meaning of the 'welfare state', its relation to capitalism and socialism, its reformist potential, and the interests it serves, are obscured.

Emphasis on individual inadequacy and on social or environmental conditions have always interwoven in social work thinking (see Leonard, 1966, ch. 1; Coates and Silburn, 1970, ch. 1; Stone, n d ). Their relative predominance can be related to more basic social and economic conditions. In the 1950s, the myth that poverty had been abolished, and that capitalism had been tamed was widely disseminated. Those people who remained poor were seen as *individual* failures. This meant a different view of the social services from that held by reformist socialists like the Fabians. Instead of acting as a buffer between the individual and market forces, the social services were now seen as essentially individual oriented. The final triumph of psychiatry and psychology flowered into casework, which saw 'presenting problems' of, for example, financial difficulties or unemployment, as symptoms of latent individual emotional problems. If society was affluent, if the jobs and houses existed in the abundance that was claimed, then the individual must be wrong, not society.

Fifteen to twenty years later, these attitudes are still extremely prevalent among many respected social workers because they continue to provide a world-view which meshes with their job. In the 1950s social work was at last establishing itself as a respectable profession; the concern with psychiatric methods dissociated social work finally from any reformist socialist or political attitudes and tradition, and on the other hand abolished the image of social workers as Lady Bountifuls dispensing charity. These two skeletons in the social worker's cupboard – political reform and charity – were finally banished in the wholesale identification with psychotherapy. So social workers thought they were safe at last, their shady past behind them, their links with socialism severed. In this context casework serves a powerful conservative function, and we see why the emergence of community work arouses so much anxiety in the professional ranks.[1]

In the early 1960s Townsend, Abel-Smith, Titmuss and other reformist Fabians began to make an impression, and it was gradually accepted that not only did poverty exist to a far greater degree than had been imagined, but that it was structurally part of the economy, of the distribution of income,[2] for example in Professor Titmuss's *Income Distribution and Social Change*, published in 1962. Later Titmuss introduced the notion of the welfare state acting not as a provisor of benefits at all, but instead representing 'partial compensations for disservices, for social costs and social insecurities which are the product of a rapidly changing industrial urban society' (1968).

As Peter Sedgwick points out (1969), while in opposition, the Labour Party intellectuals concentrated on structural inequalities, but once in power, they changed the focus to marginal, isolated problems, so they could give an illusion of doing something to remedy these problems while leaving the structure of society intact. The concentration on housing, *or* education, *or* unemployment ignores the fact that these problems coincide within particular sections of the working class. *Class* relations that produce this total situation are ignored, and attention is focused on the patching up of the odd school or house. Coates and Silburn say:

People in the real world, however, cannot live such specialized lives, and it seems only too apparent that the family which lives its life in a Milner–Holland slum,

1. For discussions on Freud which show that 'human nature' is bourgeois man see Deutscher (1967) and Marcuse (1969).

2. For useful discussions of social policy thinking at this time see Wedderburn (1965) and Sedgwick (1969).

may well do so in Abel-Smith–Townsend poverty, while its children are sent to a Plowden school (1970, p. 37).

They suggest that the failure of the welfare state – the retreat into selectivity, the complete absence of real redistribution of income, the abandonment of universalistic principles – coincides with a growing unwillingness to plan and control economic forces. Any real advance in welfare provision requires a corresponding control over the market; welfare legislation has failed because it has failed to confront the economic sector on a fundamental redistribution of income – profits are left untouched, and unchallenged, while only marginal changes are made in income taxes. Similarly a confrontation over the allocation of capital resources is avoided, and it is tacitly accepted that these are the first claim of industry.

Jim Kincaid points to the belief that 'extra resources for welfare should be found, not by redistributive taxation, but out of the proceeds of economic growth'. Here Kincaid is talking about the attitude to welfare under Labour, but what he says is equally applicable to the Conservatives:

Thus repeatedly, the same device has been employed. A general cutback in the social services has been justified by some system of exemptions which it was claimed would give favourable treatment to the most deprived social groups (n.d.).

With the gradual triumph of the market over welfare, the welfare services have now become, not a possible humanizing force putting right the damage done by economic forces, but instead a buttress to them, ensuring that capitalism runs as smoothly as it can. However, the re-emphasis of social and economic anomalies has not removed the teaching of 'Human Growth and Development' from the core of professional social-work training, which continues to orient itself to individual casework. Social work is only beginning to work out strategies for dealing with this threat – for example by designating a separate area for community work, thus leaving most social workers free to continue practising casework.

### Casework and professionalism

It is the clash of meanings and ideas within a discipline that produces growth and stringent theories (see Mills, 1967). A strong consensus makes possible the unqualified, 'common-sense' 'theories' and statements so commonly thrown about in social-work literature. There is no need for rigorous definitions of terms or concepts if there is a basic agreement as to what they mean, and while it is assumed that no one is going to attack on an intellectual or logical level, except in matters of detail. There are no really different 'schools' of social work with different conceptual frameworks and methods of analysis. Instead there are varying strands of thought, for example, the casework–groupwork dilemma, but these debates cannot be fully carried through for the fundamental propositions that form the theories have not been defined. Indeed, the idea that what is taught might *be* 'theory' is often not considered at all, and instead the principles of, for example, ego-psychology, are put forward as how things 'really' are. But because the theoretical basis of casework is not made explicit, it is difficult to find a way to challenge it.

This means that social workers can get away with extremely wishy-washy thinking, saying things like:

When the client is a person who experiences difficulty in his contact with other people, and particularly when this difficulty is combined with emotional immaturity, the development of a good relationship, in which much is given and little is demanded, can provide the sheltered environment necessary for growth and change. *There is a natural tendency in all living things to strive towards wholeness and normality.* As the doctor uses his skill to aid the recuperative powers of the body, so the caseworker uses hers to support and strengthen the client's desire to put right whatever is wrong with his personal or social adjustment [my italics]. (National Institute for Social-Work Training, 1964, p. 25).

This passage is full of completely unjustified beliefs about the characteristics of the 'client', and about the 'natural' order of things. The bland assertions of 'natural tendencies' are simply a crude way of legitimizing the social worker's intervention. Terms like 'immaturity', 'growth', 'adjustment', cannot possibly be said to be value-free, especially since the social-work agency is concerned with the modification of behaviour in the direction of certain (dominant) norms (Leonard, 1965). If the *status quo* is presented as natural and normal, then deviation or criticism is by definition unnatural and abnormal. The definition of abnormality thus depends on one of normality which is never itself questioned or justified.

The belief that the client's behaviour is irrational is common. For example:

The social worker today is more likely to try to discover and understand the reasons for her client's behaviour than to assess his or her moral responsibility, and will make more allowances for unconscious motivation and the irrationality of human behaviour than was done in the past (Hall, 1962, p. 132).

This leads us to a basic contradiction in social work thinking. The social worker states (a) that one of his prime values or principles is the client's right to self-determination; and (b) that the client is behaving irrationally. Or, to put it another way, (a) casework can only work properly if the client has the right to be respected as an individual; and (b) he is a victim of circumstances or unconscious drives and therefore not responsible for his actions. Here is an example:

The individual's right of self-determination stems from the democratic principle of freedom of choice, with its attendant right of non-conformity (*sic*). It is a sign of maturity to want to make one's own decisions, and choose one's way of life, but these rights must be set in the context of the individual's obligations as a member of society. *The individual has the right to make his own decisions, but sometimes he is too young, too unrealistic or too sick to be able to do so; sometimes he is too immature or too lacking in confidence to want to do so; and sometimes he is too anti-social to be allowed to do so.* The social worker must sometimes take some measure of control, guide the client, and set limits to his behaviour. In most socially irresponsible people there is some degree of immaturity which tends to make them dependent on the social worker (National Institute for Social-Work Training, 1964, p. 21).

Because social workers lay such great store by intuition, empathy, insight, support, and so on, they have tended to shy away from cold intellectual reasoning. Peter Leonard (1965) points out that the myth of client self-determination 'has been a powerful and valuable myth, playing an important part in the ideological superstructure of social work, but its continuation unmodified may prevent a realistic appraisal of *what actually happens* in interviews'. The social worker says that the client has the right to self-determination, and mysteriously justifies this by reference to 'British Democracy', but then produces reasons why he is not in fact capable of responsibility in his behaviour.[4]

The question of values, and different, alternative sets of values is not raised. The client is seen as irrationally motivated so he cannot have values or demands that can seriously be considered as alternatives. The nature of the social worker's own values is rarely seen as problematic; while students are encouraged to learn about the cultural background that clients come from – i.e. working-class culture – little is said about the middle-class background that most social workers come from (cf. Bernstein, 1970). Training is in any case seen as neutralizing any bias that social workers might have, so that they are 'freed' from the constraints imposed by values. But the question of whether it is possible to view the world without values in a purely objective way is not discussed, nor is the problem of *overcoming* bias and reaching a true understanding, that is, consciousness, considered.[5]

4. For further discussions of this controversy see Plant (1970) and Halmos (1965).
5. For discussions of the problem of ideology see Berger and Luckmann (1970), Harris (1968) and Lukács (1971).

From denying the validity of the client's behaviour, it is a short step to saying that the client's wants must be respected, but that he doesn't really know what he wants:

The problem that the client brings out initially may not be what is really worrying him ... sometimes the problem which is troubling the client does not seem to the social worker to be the root of the matter, and she is tempted to probe deeper. The client's real need may be hidden alike from himself and from the social worker until it becomes apparent after prolonged discussion (National Institute for Social-Work Training, 1964, p. 32).

Not only does this mean that the practical help demanded is seen as being the symptom of underlying emotional difficulties, but also that the suitability of practical help at all is questioned. Social workers tend to raise the objection that what a client sees as a suitable goal or need for himself is not *realistic*. Being realistic appears to mean that you ask for no more than is offered, so clear pressures are put on clients not to demand their full rights. In this context the emergence of claimants' unions[6] is significant, for they deny that anyone but the client has the right to say what he needs, and they reject the conception of the client as an individual failure. Blame is placed squarely on the capitalist system.[7]

By saying that a client's emotional problems are the prime limitation to his rehabilitation, social workers succeed in *creating* deviant roles, and by controlling these, for example, by arbitrating over what is and is not 'realistic', may add elements to the client's self-conception that he had not experienced before (see Segal, 1971).[8] Although social workers talk of accepting the client as a unique person, in his interaction with the social worker he is forced into the *role* of 'client' which corresponds to the social worker's stereotype. Once seen in terms of this role, certain features of the clients' condition or behaviour, or past history are selected as significant and others recede in importance. The stereotype connotes certain things about the 'client', that he is inadequate in personal relations, that he will become dependent on the social worker, that he has not yet come to terms with his 'real' self, and he will find it difficult to shake these off if he remains in the relationship with the social worker. No attention is paid to the times when he has coped admirably with his problems, let alone the vast majority of his time when he has behaved utterly normally. Handler points out that clients may be persuaded to remain in the relationship by the holding out of material aid as a reward for cooperation (1968).

6. These are the trade unions of people dependent on social security.

7. See for example the literature of the Birmingham Claimants' Union (see bibliography).

8. For discussions on deviant rules see Goffman (1968a; 1968b), Becker (1963).

Many social workers are now pointing out that most clients are unable to understand the process of casework as it uses concepts and methods quite alien to the client's experience – he obviously behaves inadequately when he is mystified as to what is going on.[9] He thus falls into the trap of fulfilling the social worker's expectations of inadequacy (n.d.).

The basic question is what determines the social worker's behaviour, why does he deny the overt, 'presenting' problem, and substitute quite a different framework to explain the client's past and present behaviour, and avoid giving quick material aid which is often all that is demanded in the first place? Casework distinguishes the young untrained social worker from the older experienced, but untrained social worker, it distinguishes social workers from other 'helping' professions and bodies – doctors, churches, psychiatrists, Citizens Advice Bureaux – and gives the trained social worker a feeling of superior insight over social workers of dubious status, like community workers, or voluntary workers. But most importantly it dissociates social work finally from its historical links with reformism, political action, and charity. It legitimates social work as a separate profession by explaining that it provides a very special kind of insight into a problem situation, into what has 'really' happened, and what is 'really' needed. It also declares the sanction of objectivity, and in the next breath of a mystical intuition.

Casework serves the capitalist system admirably since its basic assumption is that there is nothing wrong with society, and that problems are the problems of individuals who cannot 'adjust' in some way. This individual emphasis obscures the situation of clients viewed *collectively*, and the simple recognition of poverty as a *structural* phenomenon, rather than as an individual misfortune. In this way, the practice of casework also serves to prevent the full exploitation by clients of what *is* available in the 'welfare state', as it locates the problems in the individual, not in social organization. Conventional social work then can be said to serve a 'cooling out' function in so far as clients are prevented from seeing the overall contradictions of the rent system, employment and wages. It is in this sense that the social worker may be said to be an agent of social control for he prevents the client from grasping the totality of his situation in social and economic terms, from experiencing solidarity with other clients.

Of course, social workers don't consciously set out to do this. Instead their own attention is not alert to structural problems because of the conceptual framework used in casework, which highlights individual, emo-

9. This is similar to the situation of the patient in hospital – see Silman's article in this book.

tional factors as significant. And when the social worker discovers latent underlying problems, and focuses on emotional relationships, particularly in childhood, and discovers unconscious motives in the client, he is rewarding himself by demonstrating his professional status not only to his colleagues, but also to himself. Not only this, but to avoid conflict with the goals of his social-work agency, the social worker *selects* problems and clients that conform to his image of the kind of problem he has been trained to deal with, and with which he is confident his methods of intervention will produce the desired result.

Alongside professionalism goes a high degree of discretion in handling clients (n.d.). The individual social worker to a large extent is free from control by both superiors *and* clients in dealing with clients, for the professional's authority is justified by his superior knowledge of what the client really wants. It is this superiority of insight and judgement that distinguishes the social worker from a simple administrator, for if the client's needs were what he said they were, then there would be no point in professional training. So the idea of client power threatens the very essence of professional social work.

When conventional social-work thinking attempts to face political issues, we find very unsatisfactory analyses. Thinking on the socio-economic level tends to be unsophisticated, and statements about political formations are usually based on individual psychology. Social work cannot make the transition from individual psychology to sociological thinking, except by basing the social on the psychological – political behaviour, class formations, rules, laws, institutions, are not in themselves problematic, what is problematic are the individuals involved, for each case is unique. So the content and form of social and political institutions are not discussed, except in terms of latent psychological processes.

It is frequently acknowledged that clients come to notice because they fail to measure up to society's rules – a good beginning if the content and purposes of the rules were examined. The question of 'who is the client' might become clearer if social workers asked 'who makes the rules and for whose benefit?' Instead of seeing rules as upholding certain class interests, they see them all too often in the 'social contract' manner, whereby rules are thought necessary, however unpleasant they may be, because they prevent society from falling into anarchy. Thus rules exist to benefit everyone, and the constraints they place on individual behaviour are in the common good in the long run. Here is a glaring example of this:

Reasonably mature and well-adjusted people are able to recognize that just as children need restraint if they are to learn to conform to the requirements of the society in which they live, so the adults in that society must be governed by sets of rules, which, however imperfect, provide the basis for community living. The need for such rules is immediately evident when we think of the relief of drivers in the midst of a traffic jam when a policeman arrives and takes control (Foren and Bailey, 1968, p. 18).

Note that in a traffic jam everyone is stuck, and shares the same interest – to get out of the jam as quickly as possible. In this situation even the policeman is a disinterested figure, who has nothing to gain by not sharing the common interest. In society people do not share similar interests, because society is based essentially on classes defined by their ownership or non-ownership of property. Social-work literature does not discuss the rules or their content, or who they benefit, and so it cannot discuss the true life situation of the client, who is defined by his failure to measure up to these rules.

Social-work thinking is based on an equilibrium, consensus model of society, which means that social control is seen as the limiting of actions in people's own interest, as there is a basic sharing of values. A conflict model would see social control in terms of limiting individuals' behaviour in the interests of dominant groups in society. Thus the idea that the social worker helps the client to achieve 'insight' *himself* mystifies a powerful, controlling relationship (Leonard, 1965).

The consensus conception of society is reinforced in the terminology of social-work literature; for example the term 'community' tends to be preferred to that of 'society', for it connotes fellowship, interlocking of activities and goals, and mutual sympathy among the parts. Sociology has never been very popular among social-work writers; what is tends to be practical and descriptive, rather than theoretical and analytical. The sociologists favoured are predominantly people like Peter Willmott, Michael Young, J. Barron Mays, Elizabeth Bott, all people who place a strong emphasis on community study, rather than on theoretical perspectives (Leonard, 1966; 1968).

### Alternative directions

A critique of social work should consider how radical ideas are 'defused', and how seemingly radical alternatives to casework are made acceptable to establishment social work, and their more progressive elements overshadowed. The use of transaction or labelling theory is becoming increasingly popular among social workers.[10] This is a view which sees social workers, psychiatrists, probation officers and so on as unqualified agents of social control, forcing the rules of the dominant order upon deviants. It doesn't

10. See for example *Anarchy* 98: 'Is there a libertarian criminology?' for discussions on labelling theory.

see anything inherently pathological in a deviant act, which instead is seen as the breaking of a rule, and the incurring of social reactions. The labelling of the rule-breaking act as deviant is what defines the wrongness of the behaviour. Since rules are made and maintained by certain dominant groups in society, those who control rule-breakers are doing so in the interests of those who hold power in society.

Gouldner (1968) shows how this theory can degenerate into an 'underdog' sociology; those who espouse the theory are in danger of falling into sympathy with the underdog as victim, as product of society rather than a rebel against it. He shows that this is basically a liberal (concerned with *particular* reforms) rather than a radical (concerned with *total* change) view, for if the deviant is a 'passive nonentity who is responsible for neither his suffering nor its alleviation', then the conclusion is that he has to be managed, and managed better. The custodial arrangements of society have mismanaged the deviant, they are callous and brutal; this kind of sociology 'has become a component of the new style of social reform which is now engineered through care-taking public bureaucracies'. Thus a radical theory is defused by focusing attention on *local*, middle-level bureaucracies – the housing department, the Ministry of Social Security, the Social Services Department – and by a concentration on the underdog, and not on the power arrangements and ruling class in society.

Radical sociologists want to study 'power elites', the leaders, or masters of men; liberal sociologists focus their efforts upon underdogs and victims and their immediate bureaucratic caretakers (Gouldner, 1968).

This is a criticism that can be made of many community action programmes – the intense concern with grass-roots levels means that the totality of national politics and economics is sacrificed to attempts to reform local bureaucracies' methods of dealing with clients and public.

Young social workers are becoming dissatisfied with traditional methods of social work and with the services they are supposed to be administering (Coates and Silburn, 1970, p. 221). Increasingly they find it inappropriate to identify the causes of clients' problems in personal troubles of the psyche, especially as it is becoming more and more apparent that the 'welfare state' has not revolutionized society, or even secured a marginal redistribution of income (Kincaid, n.d.; Townsend, 1971). But even though 'community development', or 'community work' are terms increasingly in vogue as the new social work, the extent to which social workers can espouse these forms of social work is limited.

As I showed above, the professional social worker has a wide area of control over his relations with individual clients, over his casework skills.

But he has very little control over the other aspects of his work – preventive work to be effective would mean control over the housing and wage situations, control which is obviously not forthcoming. Thus the social worker may be more or less forced to fall back on casework, even though both he and the client feel this to be an inappropriate form of help. Casework at least reduces some of the frustration, for the social worker can feel that in discussing the problems he is playing some part in solving them (Deacon, n.d.). Another barrier to social workers attempting to exert pressure in the appropriate places, the Ministry of Social Security, the Housing Department, and so on, or to thinking that clients' problems may be better dealt with in, for example, a claimants' union, tenants' association, trade union, black-power group, or squatters' association, is of course, the fact that social workers are employed by the local authority in which they work. They risk their jobs and careers if they take their radical critique too far in practice.

Many social workers see community development as a radical alternative to traditional casework, but establishment-sponsored programmes do not differ in their conceptions of society and of problems from those held by caseworkers. The Gulbenkian Report (Calouste Gulbenkian Foundation, 1968) uses the familiar jargon about meeting people's needs in the context of a 'democratic' society, with no attempt to examine what democracy does or should mean. What is even more surprising is the complacent approach to social change. Community work is presented as the real nitty-gritty as it is centrally involved in the turmoil of change and conflict, but the nature of that change is never called into question, so we can assume that no real change at all is envisaged. Again it is assumed that there is a common interest, that wherever the change will be it will benefit everyone; for example:

Community work is essentially concerned with affecting the course of social change through the two processes of analysing social situations and forming relationships with different groups to bring about some desirable change (p. 4).

Community work can be said to be reactionary in so far as it seeks to channel local discontent into legitimate organizations, who are supposed to 'participate' in local affairs.[11] This serves a useful function by preventing illegitimate, militant local action and by identifying what arrangements exist now as 'democracy'.

Community development suffers from two other shortcomings: the spotlighting of particular problem areas at the expense of seeing the whole organization of society as problematic, and the naive belief that local

11. For general discussion of community work see Hodge (1970) and Lapping (n.d.).

groups can in fact control their own destinies. They succeed in drawing attention away from the problems of income distribution in society; the focus on particular problems obscures the view of poverty or bad housing as integral parts of capitalist society. The pretence that local groups can effect some change in the distribution of resources ignores the real power relationships in society which determine the allocation of resources.

Since community work is (with reluctance in some quarters) becoming acceptable, and indeed seen as evidence of 'progressiveness' in the profession, its conservative functions should be stressed. However, this is not to say that it isn't a better alternative to traditional casework, because at least it does indicate people in a common situation, so that a basis for solidarity is set up, that could, under changing circumstances, form a foundation for militant action. Another vital function the community worker could perform is the advising of the public of their rights and how to get them.[12] But community work will only be a useful alternative for radical social workers as long as the basic assumptions are kept in mind, and thus the real limitations and conservative functions openly acknowledged and fought.

But in the final analysis, the community worker can only achieve a radical orientation if he openly takes a *political* stand, and similarly, groups in the community must become political, concerned with what goes on outside the community, at the *top* levels of society. Groups which pretend to be non-political are merely disguising their liberal, middle-class nature, their unwillingness to really get to grips with class relations. If social workers are to become political and to have control over their work, then they must rid themselves of ideas of the 'professional' remaining detached from issues, and of reluctance to take direct action, and should start seeing themselves like other workers who need strength and solidarity in a trade union, not a professional association. In this way, social workers could recognize their *common* interests with clients, dropping the idea of the client–professional relationship, and this could be the first step towards a truly radical social work.

12. For discussions on welfare rights see Brooke (1970) and Fabian Society (1970).

## References

BECKER, H. (1963), *Outsiders*, Free Press.
BERGER, P., and LUCKMANN, T. (1970), *The Social Construction of Reality*, Allen Lane The Penguin Press; Penguin 1972.
BERNSTEIN, B. (1970), 'A critique of the concept of compensatory education', in D. Rubenstein and C. Stoneman (eds.), *Education for Democracy*, Penguin.

BROOKE, R. (1970), 'Civic rights and social service', in W. A. Robson and B. Crick (eds.), *The Future of the Social Services*, Penguin.

CALOUSTE GULBENKIAN FOUNDATION (1968), *Community Work and Social Change: A Report on Tranining*, Longman.

COATES, K., and SILBURN, R. (1970), *Poverty: The Forgotten Englishmen*, Penguin.

DEACON, C. (n.d.), 'Social worker: trade unionist?' *Case Con.* no. 1.

DEUTSCHER, I. (1967), *On Socialist Man*, Merit.

EDWARDS, E. M. (1966), 'A study of the social-work tutor's expectations of fieldwork agencies and his responsibilities towards them', *Social Work*, January.

FABIAN Society (1970), *The Fifth Social Service*.

FOREN, R., and BAILEY, R. (1968), *Authority in Social Casework*, Pergamon.

GOFFMAN, E. (1968a), *Asylums*, Penguin.

GOFFMAN, E. (1968b), *Stigma*, Penguin.

GOLDMAN, L. (n.d.), 'Is there a Marxist sociology', *International Socialism Journal*.

GOULDNER, A. W. (1968), 'The sociologist as partisan: sociology and the welfare state', *American Sociologist*, May.

HALL, M. P. (1962), *The Social Services of Modern England*, Routledge & Kegan Paul.

HALMOS, P. (1965), *The Faith of the Counsellors*, Constable.

HANDLE, J. F. (1968), 'The coercive children's officer', *New Society*, 3 October.

HARRIS, N. (1968), *Beliefs in Society*, Watts.

HODGE, P. (1970), 'The future of community development', in W. A. Robson and B. Crick (eds.), *The Future of the Social Services*, Penguin.

JONES, N. (1970), 'Selection of students for social-work courses', *Social Work*, vol. 27, no. 3.

KENNERY, P. J., and POPPLESTONE, G. (n.d.), 'Child discrimination in social-welfare organizations', *Social Work*, vol. 27, no. 2.

KINCAID, J. (n.d.), 'Social policy and the Labour Government', *International Socialism Journal*, no. 43, p. 22.

KINCAID, J. (n.d.), 'Taxing the poor', *International Socialism Journal*, no. 46.

LAPPING, A. (ed.) (n.d.), *Fabian Tract 400*, Community Action.

LEONARD, P. (1965), 'Social control, class values and social-work practice', *Social Work*, October.

LEONARD, P. (1966), *Sociology in Social Work*, Routledge & Kegan Paul.

LEONARD, P. (1968), 'The application of sociological analysis to social-work training', *British Journal of Sociology*, vol. 19, no. 3.

LUKÁCS, G. (1971), *History and Class Consciousness*, Merlin.

MARCUSE, H. (1969), *Eros and Civilization*, Sphere.

MILLS, C. W. (1959), *The Sociologist Imagination*, Oxford University Press.

MILLS, C. W. (1967), 'The professional ideology of social pathologists', *Power, Politics and People*, Oxford University Press.

National Institute for Social-Work Training (1964), *Introduction to a Social Worker*, Allen & Unwin.

PLANT, R. (1970), *Social and Moral Theory in Casework*, Routledge & Kegan Paul.

ROBINSON, E. (1968), *The New Polytechniques*, Penguin.

SEDGWICK, P. (1969), 'Varieties of socialist thought', *Political Quarterly*, vol. 40, no. 4.

SEGAL, A. (1971), 'Worker's perceptions of mentally disabled clients: effects on service delivery', *Social Work* (USA), July.

STONE, B. (n.d.), *Case Con.* no. 11.

TIMMS, N. (1962), *Casework in Child-Care Service*, Butterworth.

TITMUSS, R. (1962), *Income Distribution and Social Change*, Allen & Unwin.

TITMUSS, R. (1968), *Commitment to Welfare*, Allen & Unwin.

TOWNSEND, P. (1971), 'The problems of social growth', *The Times*, 9, 10, 11 and 12 March.

WEDDERBURN, D. (1965), 'Facts and theories of the welfare state', in R. Miliband and J. Saville (eds.), *Socialist Register 1965*, Merlin.

# Teaching the Medical Student to Become a Doctor
## Robert Silman

Medicine has a privilege. It can be used as a critical test for any revolutionary theory or model of society.

In the arts subjects, there is no reason to suppose the existence of a bulk of information which students require to receive and which teachers are obliged to transmit. It is the characteristic of science, however, that it *imposes* its theories. One can only resist at the expense of being eccentric or suicidal. The flat earth society is eccentric, the man who steps off a high building to demonstrate a direct challenge to the Newtonian laws of gravitation is suicidal. Of course, scientific theory will only impose itself if one accepts its terms of reference. For example, if one is concerned about the problems of thermodynamics, then the laws of thermodynamics will impose themselves. The concern to know about and to apply thermodynamics may be a capitalist or a socialist concern, but the scientific laws that govern the inquiry are themselves indifferent.

If one supposes that there are and will always be certain diseases which are not the expression of social or psychological problems (and that is a supposition), then it is likely that medicine as a science will be the concern of a socialist society. The legitimacy of undertaking any other form of scientific inquiry may be put in question, but medicine is likely to be retained. That is why I say medicine has a privilege.

So we start from the position that medicine is a legitimate subject for practice and research. Now it would be nice to analyse how it would be possible to overcome the problems raised by the accumulation of this medical knowledge or information by an elite group, i.e. those who practise or research in medicine. These are critical problems, since knowledge or information is a form of wealth with its own laws of accumulation and distribution. Not only has information a value which can be exchanged against money, it seems to possess a value which can resist economic devaluation. This ought to be the starting point for a critique of medical education. Unfortunately, medical education is only in tiny part the teaching of medicine. The great bulk of the medical student's course is directed towards the creation of a *doctor*.

Now it is a commonly held illusion that there is a necessary relationship between the concept 'doctor' and the concept 'medicine'. It will be the aim of this article to distinguish the two; and to point out the extent to which the creation of 'doctor' assumes a massive role within the educational system, *even to the point of sacrificing medical knowledge to its ends.*

## The language of doctors

It is in the nature of a science to develop a language which corresponds to concepts that cannot otherwise be articulated or advanced. It is difficult to see how one could, for example, refer to the respiratory enzymes of the mitochondria in a manner which is intelligible to the non-biochemist. It is difficult because, however one expresses it, the respiratory enzymes of the mitochondria only exist for the world of the biochemist. His language is a different language because his world is a different world.

The language of doctors would claim this justification and of course it is true that part of the language of doctors is the language of medical science. But indistinguishably contained within this language is the language of the everyday world translated into the language of medical science.

Most of us have a reasonable idea of what the heart is. Likewise we know what it means to say of someone that his heart has stopped. This is important because if someone drops down, apparently dead, before us, and we are told or we notice that his heart has stopped, our response is likely to be: 'Can we not start it again and, if not, why not?' The concepts that are invoked here are not those that exist outside our world. But a doctor will not say of a patient that his heart has stopped, except in a moment of panic perhaps, when he has lost his professional style. A doctor will say: 'This patient has had a cardiac arrest.'

Why should this be? It is not easier to write: 'cardiac arrest' has thirteen letters, and 'heart stopped' has twelve. It is not easier to say: 'cardiac arrest' has five syllables, 'heart stopped' has two. What is the advantage of the translation? What is the advantage of such a language?

Now these are significant questions. The medical profession has a conscious ethic by which it explains to itself and to others its role in society. We are not interested in giving an account of the doctor's role from the doctor's expressed point of view. We are looking for an alternative model by which we can understand their language and behaviour, a model which will encompass what is at present left silent. So one seeks a foothold from which to undertake the analysis and we can see with this simple example such a foothold. There is nothing within the professional ethic to justify the expression 'cardiac arrest'. For doctors, it is simply there, inexplicable, a fact about the medical profession. For us, it is a sign.

To speak of 'cardiac arrest' is to speak a language that is barely intelligible to most people. Both 'heart' and 'stop' have been translated into less comprehensible equivalents. Consequently, for most people, something has happened which they do not understand. It sounds grand. It sounds like the respiratory enzymes of the mitochondria. It is not part of their world. It is something that doctors understand.

But even if one knows that 'cardiac' means 'heart' and that 'arrest' means 'stop', there is a turn to this expression which takes it even farther away from *our* world. When a heart stops, one is not supposing any reasons for it having stopped. One is not saying that the heart has stopped because there is a disease going on in the heart, or because the patient has bled to death. When a doctor speaks of cardiac arrest, it sounds as if he is referring to a disease – an arrest, which has manifested itself in the heart, like a tumour can manifest itself in a variety of tissues. But a patient cannot *have* a cardiac arrest like he can have a liver (hepatic!) tumour. Yet doctors refer to it that way: and since they are trained in such matters, one wonders if they possess some extra information which permits them to speak of it as if it were a tumour. But this is not so; 'cardiac arrest' means no more than 'heart stopped'. Thus the translation of an ordinary everyday concept into the technical vocabulary of specialized science not only confuses the non-scientist, but confuses the science itself.

When we see that doctors say 'cardiac arrest' in order to create confusion, we have not advanced very far. Obviously they do not wish to cede an inch of their ground. Anything medical is their province. Therefore they create a special language – their language – to cover what is already understood within ordinary language – our language – to the confusion of both. But we still do not know why this is so.

One could say that it is because some doctors are greedy. But this will not do because *all* doctors use this language. An explanation based on the motivation of an individual does not explain the motivation of the group. It is not the language of some doctors, it is the language of *the* doctor, the profession.

Thus we return to the basic distinction between science and its practitioners, between the language of medical science and the language of the medical profession. We will accept that the language of the medical profession includes the language of medical science but, as we have seen, it is *more* than the expression of the science. Our problem is to identify what is being superimposed. We know that confusion is an element of the answer. But what is it that they wish to confuse?

At this point it would be incomprehensible to restrict the analysis to the medical profession alone, because we are indeed characterizing far more. We are attempting to describe the mediators within our society – those who mediate between authority and the world. We can take other examples to illustrate this theme. The lawyer mediates between the authority of the law and its world; the Catholic church mediates between the authority of God and his world; the Communist Party mediates between the authority of Marxist science and its world. In all these examples, we will see a confusion between the role of the authority and the role of those who represent that authority.

Consider the clearest expression of this confusion. When an ordinary soldier salutes an officer, he is told that he is saluting the Queen's Commission. In fact, he is saluting the officer. The officer has become totally confused with the authority he represents; and if we do not obey the officer we are guilty of mutiny.

The mediators demand submission and respect from those not of their class. And they claim that they are not demanding it on their own behalf, but on behalf of the authority they represent. The consequence is that: to challenge the judge is to challenge the law and to disobey the judge is to break the law; to challenge the Pope is to challenge God and not to accept the Pope is to commit heresy; to challenge the Communist Party is to challenge Marxist science and not to follow the Communist Party is to be counter-revolutionary. Thus the mediators create for themselves an identity with their authority such that, if they did not exist, their authorities would no longer exist. They become themselves authority. They are what they mediate. We must behave towards them as we would to the authority itself. Within this perspective, it would be dangerous if the distinction between them and their authority became clear. They would no longer have the authority of their authority.

And yet to challenge the doctor is not to challenge medical science. For the Marxists can create the Marx they serve, the Church can create the God it serves, but doctors must submit to the science they serve. Here is not the place to discuss whether the God of the Church or the Marx of the Communist Party do indeed have a real meaning and authority outside their mediators; but what is clear is that medical science is absolute, unlike God or Marx. It imposes itself in a way that as yet neither God nor Marx have managed to do. To attack the doctor is in no way to attack his authority which is medical science.

Thus the doctor finds himself in a peculiarly vulnerable position amongst his fellow mediators. And it is by recognizing this that we can understand the special nature of the confusion process as it is practised by doctors.

Because the doctor's authority is absolute, in other words because he can never be his authority, he will often reject it. Hence many doctors deny the importance of science. The themes 'medicine is an art', 'intuition' or 'my strong opinion' will often be brought out to downgrade science. There are a great variety of such themes but all with a common link. Instead of the doctor's authority being based on an absolute, a reality outside himself, it is vested in the doctor personally, or rather in all doctors professionally. The mediators thus come to possess within themselves their authority. What is interesting is that this surrogate authority is never capable of definition. It is a 'something', an 'I do not know quite what' to which they will refer. So if we challenge the doctor, we challenge this 'authority' because outside him it has no meaning.

But of course this is not sufficient. The authority of the doctor is real. Therefore to reject it might successfully confuse the doctor and the patient, but it will not *destroy* the authority. A doctor who, by 'intuition' decides to treat a patient in heart failure with a massive blood transfusion, cannot, by his words, prevent his patient from dying.

And so we return to cardiac arrest. If the doctor cannot destroy his authority, he can at least protect it by a special language so that only he knows how to speak to it. A language is created which forces submission on those not instructed in it. We no longer know with what authority the doctor is speaking because we no longer understand what he is saying.

Yet, at the same time, the doctor must serve his authority. He must treat his patients as medical science imposes. But doctors can make mistakes. Doctors often do make mistakes. And there is nothing more likely to separate him from his authority in the eyes of the world than for him to make a mistake. So the special language can serve a double purpose. Not only does it protect the authority, making it the doctor's authority rather than our authority, thereby making the doctor our authority: it also protects the doctor from the charge that he is *not* serving his authority. If we cannot understand his authority, if the authority is speaking a foreign language, we will find it very difficult to know if there has been a mistranslation.

To summarize: anyone can examine a person and notice that his heart has stopped. It takes five years of special training to diagnose a cardiac arrest. To qualify as a doctor, it is not sufficient to know medical science and its corresponding language; one has to learn the language of confusion, the language of the profession, the language that imposes itself by pretending to be science but which is not science because it is the language of the mediator.

## The meaning of doctors

The previous analysis was not undertaken simply to explain the use of 'cardiac arrest' by doctors. If a doctor now decides never to use that term again, he will still be a doctor. We used it as a sign to uncover a meaning. The signs can change yet the meaning remain.

We have so far determined only an element of that meaning – that doctors confuse themselves with their authority. I will now take another example of this confusion process to complete the analysis. It occurred during a ward round conducted by a surgical consultant with a registrar, houseman sister and several students in attendance. We arrived at the bed of a patient who had had an operation a few days before. After discussing her case, the consultant turned to her to ask if she felt all was going well. The patient replied that she felt fine except for the drip attached to her arm. She was agitated about it and asked the consultant imploringly if it could come down.

Now the consultant had a choice of possible answers in this situation, ranging from 'the drip is essential for life' to 'the drip has served its purpose and is due to come down anyway'. I would guess that the consultant decided that the patient's agitation and discomfort were doing her more harm than the drip was doing her good. At any event, he answered good-naturedly, patting her bed: 'Don't worry, the drip will come down right away.' To which the patient replied *naturally*, in other words *as one would expect*, in other words without anyone considering it in the least odd: 'Oh, thank you, Doctor. Thank you so much.' And it was *real* gratitude.

What appeared so natural, what we indeed expected, is of course an absurdity. If a messenger brings me some good news, I can thank the messenger for carrying the news, but it would be absurd for me to thank him for the news itself. If for example I receive a telegram to say I have won a fortune on the football pools, I might exclaim: 'What luck!' 'I'm so happy!', I might even thank God, but I will not thank the messenger boy. He hasn't permitted me to win the pools. All he did was to bring me the news and that is all I will thank him for.

But when the patient thanked the consultant for the news that the drip was to come down, she was not thanking him for carrying the message. She was actually thanking him *for the message itself*.

Hence for the patient there is a confusion on several levels, all hopelessly intermixed. On the one hand, the consultant is the authority and by thanking the consultant, the patient is thanking the authority. On the other, the consultant is not the authority but has perhaps put in a good word for her with the authority and so the patient is thanking the consultant for having persuaded medical science to accord itself with her request. In other words, the consultant has a special relationship with his authority and used it to plead the patient's case. At any event, the consultant did the patient a favour and that is why she thanked him.

Now I am not arguing that the consultant made his decision to take the drip down on the same basis of confusion. But the decision, once taken, was integrated into a whole system of communication whereby the response 'Thank you' was expected and accepted. And again, this is not to argue that the consultant was consciously fooling the patient like some superb confidence trickster. It was all perfectly natural, natural not only for the patient and the consultant but for the other doctors, nurses and students in attendance. One had experienced a trivial, normal and natural exchange between doctor and patient.

However, even supposing that this example has shown us the confusion that exists between the consultant and the authority, why did the patient say 'Thank you'? After all, we argued a propos of a win on the pools that we might exclaim 'What luck!' or 'I'm so happy'! This would mean that we had accepted that the laws of chance are indifferent. However, if we had cried 'Thank God!' and meant it, then we would have seen the result as something determined by God on our behalf and we would be right to thank him. One has no exchange with an indifferent authority. It is there and we simply submit to it. If I am hanging on a cliff edge, I do not address myself to the laws of gravity to plead for them to relax their authority. But if I pray to God, I not only submit to him, but I respect him, and his activities are modified by the degree of my submission and respect. Therefore to thank God is to state my relationship of submission and respect towards him, which will encourage him to go on acting in my favour.

And so we distinguish between an authority which is absolute and indifferent, and an authority which is absolute and sacred. The former imposes its authority indifferently, the latter imposes itself on the basis of our attitude towards it.

We now possess the elements which permit us to understand the meaning of doctor.

The wealth of doctors is the information they possess. Medical science has a value. It is the result of men's labour. The labour involved in learning this science is as nothing compared to the labour of its creation. So medical students pay by five years' study for what has taken millions of man-hours to create. The commodity 'medical science' is bought cheaply.

In the course of this transaction, medical students are taught to camouflage the commodity. They are taught to think of it as their own by right and to conceal their misuse of it. That is what we discussed in the language of doctors.

But that is not enough. Doctors do not say to the world: 'Ha! Ha! I have this knowledge, you haven't, so do as I say.' If they did, the reply might be simple. If one can take the factory out of the hands of the factory owner, one can take medical science out of the hands of the doctor. Of course, it is not as simple as all that, But, at least, as I suggested in the introduction, the accumulation and distribution of information would present itself as a problem to analyse and resolve. To avoid this issue the doctor says instead: 'Ah? Ah! I care for you, I study for you, my aim in life is to serve you. If there are certain social customs that characterize the way we relate to each other, it is my authority that requires them, not me.'

In this way the doctor does not simply confuse himself with an indifferent authority. He simultaneously confuses himself with a sacred authority. What is significant in this distinction is that it is by this sacred authority that social order is imposed. But this sacred authority does not exist. It is a pretence. Medical science is *always* indifferent. As soon as it becomes sacred, as soon as it pretends to impose social relationships, it is no longer medical science.

Thus the meaning of doctors is to confuse for themselves, as well as for others, the knowledge which they have with the social role they enact.

### The rites of doctors

We argue, therefore, that medicine is only sacred when it is pretending to be medicine; otherwise it is indifferent. It is by ritual patterns of behaviour that one can represent that which is sacred. The sections that follow are just some examples of these ritual processes.

They will not be concerned with what doctors do in so far as what they are doing is the application of medical science. For we do not deny that doctors undertake to cure patients by diagnosis and treatment. But as we have seen there is more to it than that, there is the imposition of a social order on the basis of a sacred authority. Our examples are concerned with the rites of this social order – an order that pretends to be determined by sacred medicine; for it creates two ritual social identities, that of 'doctor' and that of 'patient'.

### *The dress of doctors*

On the simplest level, the insistence that medical students should wear ties is an example of a ritual process. It is said that patients expect it. Of course, this is true. Patients have a ritual relationship with doctors of which dress is a part. So by definition a 'patient' is going to expect a 'doctor' to wear a tie. The fact that patients often do not object is not an argument that will carry. This is seen most clearly in the anatomy dissecting-room, where the medical student wears a tie out of 'respect' of the dead. The fact that the body you are dissecting may be that of an anarchist who would most strongly disapprove of such formalism is not at issue. The cadaver has become *entirely* a patient. The cadaver has no individuality. Its only remaining meaning is this last relationship with the potential doctor who is dissecting it. In this sense, the cadaver expects the medical student to wear a tie and, out of respect for its wishes, one does. And in so doing, one learns something of what it means to be a doctor.

When one becomes a doctor, the long white coat is there to clothe the doctor identity. Again, this is not to argue that the white coat has has no utility. Obviously it keeps your clothes clean, and if it is dirty, the dirt is clearly visible. But it is *more* than that. One wears it in situations where it is not required for utility. In this context, the short white coat of the medical student at some teaching hospitals is interesting. He is half-way to becoming a doctor. Not yet fully received into the doctor identity, he is clothed in the style of compromise, half doctor, half non-doctor. At the other extreme, it sometimes happens that the consultant wears no white coat at all. In this case, the doctor identity has been so supremely established that it no longer needs to be emphasized. It has become an implicit quality of the consultant.

Since the long white coat is so much the dress of social hierarchy rather than the dress of medicine itself, it is acceptable for a consultant to demonstrate his relative independence of more basic ritual by forsaking it. However, it may sometimes happen that a surgical consultant during an operation will wear a mask that does not cover his nose. Now one is taught that the mask should cover both mouth and nose in order to prevent the spread of germs on to the patient. (It may be false, but that is what is taught and believed at our present state of knowledge.) Therefore, the consultant who ignores this ruling is contradicting the authority of medical science. It is as if a special dispensation had been issued to him by the sacred side of medicine. But we argued earlier that medicine is only sacred when it is pretending to be medicine, otherwise its authority is indifferent. The wearing of masks relates to the science, not to the sanctity, of medicine. So while the consultant who does not wear a white coat creates no conflict, the consultant who proclaims the sterility of his nose engenders criticism. This again illustrates the peculiarity of doctors in the class of mediators. They are not entirely free to create their authority.

## The bedside manner

The essential requirement here is that it is an exchange between a doctor and a patient. And the rule of this exchange is that a patient requires reassurance and that a doctor bestows it. The style is that of an adult comforting a child.

We suggested earlier that the real problem of medicine as a science is that of the distribution or communication of information. In discussing the bedside manner, we are dealing with what amounts to the communication of no information. Information, as defined within communication theory, only exists in so far as it reduces a condition of uncertainty; and the amount of information communicated is determined by the amount by which the uncertainty has been reduced. For example, in any English word, a 'u' will always follow a 'q'. Thus the 'u' has zero information as there is no uncertainty that it will follow a 'q'. In this context, the bedside manner is an exchange between doctor and patient tending towards the communication of zero information. That it is considered by the profession as the optimum form of communication should alert us to this conclusion. After all, the optimum for the profession is that which creates the professional relationship. And the professional relationship is, as we have argued, that which stabilizes social hierarchy by ritual.

But this relationship can break down if the patient refuses his role and, instead of accepting reassurance, demands information. This presents a serious challenge to the doctor. The patient is refusing to be a patient and is therefore questioning that the doctor is a doctor. In these circumstances the doctor could renounce his role and fully confide in the patient, explaining to him all that he knows about the matter. But in doing this the doctor is exposing himself by arming the patient with his own authority and thus permitting the patient to question his decisions about diagnosis and treatment. A doctor who is a doctor will resist this, and either ignore the quest for information by insisting that the patient be a patient and accept the reassurance because the reassurance is true (even when it is not). Or the doctor can reply in the language of the profession so that the answer is unintelligible anyway.

There is a striking resemblance to the progression 'Good ... bad ... mad' that Laing (1960, chs. 6, 11) describes a propos of the 'schizophrenic'. A good patient is a patient; in other words, someone who trusts his doctor and accepts his reassurance. A bad patient is described by doctors as a 'troublesome' or 'difficult' patient. Now it is interesting that these terms will never be applied if the patient is *medically* troublesome or difficult. The patient will not be criticized if he is seriously ill, demanding great care and attendance on the part of the doctor. The patient becomes troublesome when he refuses to be a patient, in other words when he begins to question the diagnosis and/or the treatment he is receiving. Like the 'schizophrenic', he is seen to be ungrateful and selfish, not appreciating that the doctor is there to help him. The next stage follows swiftly. The patient becomes mad or 'psychotic' or 'pathologically aggressive' because he continues to question the doctor when it would normally be quite clear to any sensible patient that he is not in a position to do so. It takes several years of training for the doctor to understand, so it is a form of madness for the patient to insist on a similar understanding. And if a patient is mad, one is under no obligation to satisfy his absurd requests as they are no longer a challenge, but an expression of a deranged personality.

A confirmation of this was supplied to me by a psychiatrist friend. He told me of a patient, diagnosed as a schizophrenic, who wished to see his casenotes. This was, naturally, refused him The patient replied with a sentence that was interpreted as part of the symptomatology of his schizophrenia. The sentence was: 'By refusing me information, you turn "to heal" into "bringing to heel".' This was labelled a 'clang association' – the random and meaningless association of similar sounding words.

Very rarely, the reverse situation may arise in which there is a patient who is a patient, therefore expecting reassurance, and a doctor who is not a doctor, communicating knowledge in the place of reassurance. But this individual act on the part of the doctor, though it destroys the ritual relationship between himself and the patient, creates only chaos. Because unless the patient joins in this destruction, the patient is left simply as a destroyed patient. There is a famous case of a young doctor, responsible for a ward of dying patients, who went around telling them individually what their situation really was. The result was an epidemic of suicides. It is rather as if the Pope were to curse God before his congregation. This would destroy his congregation, but since it came not from the congregation, it would create nothing but chaos in its place. Or again, if an industrialist gave his factory to his workers, without them demanding it, it would destroy a capitalist relationship to replace it by chaos.

What is interesting is to note the balance of power in these relationships. If the doctor informs his patient or the Pope curses God or the industrialist gives away his factory, the patient, the congregation or the workers will be thrown into chaos. Such acts are not part of the system, they are incomprehensible. But if a patient challenges the doctor, he is troublesome or mad; if a congregation challenges the Pope, they are heretics; if workers challenge the employers, they are socialist troublemakers. In other words, challenge is *expected*. And so the challenge is capable of being resisted because it is integrated into the system. A patient does not know how to deal with a 'troublesome' doctor, but a doctor knows how to deal with a 'difficult patient'.

### The two classes of patient

It is time now to introduce a modification in our characterization of the patient. We have been describing only one patient, what we may call the working-class patient, someone who is mediated not only in his situation as a patient but also in society at large.

It is from this class that one will find most of our 'difficult' patients. The challenge to the doctor comes largely from the working class, giving rise to a grievance on the part of the doctors that they are not properly appreciated and are treated like servants. The doctor's complaint is of course that he is not being treated as a doctor. But the doctor has little to fear. The challenge is impotent in so far as the balance of power reflects a reality. You are finally forced to entrust yourself to a doctor if you are ill because only he may have the knowledge which can save you.

As we find that most members of the working class are not militant socialists, so we find that most working class patients are not 'difficult' patients. The honest, quiet working man is translated into the 'good' patient, the patient who accepts the ritual as a necessary reality, the patient who is *totally confused*.

By a curious circular argument, it is to these patients that a doctor will refer when he attempts to justify the ritual relationship. He will argue his good faith, the fact that he has tried, as an experiment, to inform and explain and then found that the patient understood nothing. This proves, he will argue, that patients are incapable of sharing the doctor's knowledge. But interestingly, these experiments, these proofs, are demonstrated on those patients who do not ask. In other words, the doctor bestows the information as an act of grace, and not in response to a challenge. It is certain that in these circumstances, the 'good' patient will not understand because he is only 'good' in so far as he has renounced his ability to understand. To understand has consequences. It will disturb the respective doctor and patient identities. The 'good' patient has on the contrary fully accepted his identity. So the experiment does not justify the ritual, *it tests its strength*.

But our problem is to determine whether there is a second class of patient. After all, we have already argued that doctors are not the only mediators in our society. We know that some patients are mediators in their own right. The lawyer, the industrialist, the army officer can all fall ill and become patients. We can hardly suppose that society is so fragmented that as patients they will lose all their former rights. It would be simple to argue that there exists a different relationship for these patients which is played out in the intimacy of private practice. This would suppose that it did not exist in the public health service. But it is common to find such mediators on a public ward. Our problem is to decide how the ritual relationship we have described for our working-class patient is modified to include this new class of patient.

It is helpful to state first in what way it is *not* modified. On a public ward, there will be no difference in medical care between the two classes of patient. It is true that doctors sometimes assess their treatment on the basis of the social value of their patient. But although they will recommend that the one available kidney machine should be used for the chairman of ICI in preference to an unmarried immigrant labourer, this is a marginal distinction. For here doctors are forced by a lack of funds in areas of high-cost medicine to make their social philosophy *explicit*. This is distasteful to them. They would prefer to treat all patients equally; and where they can, they do. Nor is there any difference in the bedside manner itself. Doctors are expected to reassure and patients, irrespective of their class, are expected to be reassured. The lawyer does not behave any differently in this respect than the labourer.

So in what way is there a difference? I was several months on the wards before I could arrive at an answer to this. Certainly from the start, I was aware that something was altered when a doctor talked to a lawyer rather than to a labourer, but the difference seemed to escape definition. It was an exaggerated overacted example, played out before me, that finally permitted a solution, a solution that has been confirmed subsequently by the more modest examples that are the custom.

Where we argued that the working-class patient is totally confused, we can say that the mediator–patient is *conditionally confused*. The condition upon which he will accept to be confused is that the doctor should recognize him as a mediator within his own sphere of influence.

This need hardly be spoken. It is the occasional phrase, the consultant turning to the students to tell us that if one had a legal problem, a business problem, a religious problem, a military problem, this is the sort of man on whom one could depend. And what is meant is that: 'As he is a patient for me in this situation, so I would be a patient for him in his.' It is the ritual recognition of one's ritual peer from another tribe, the recognition of territorial rights, an exchange of gifts. It is the statement: 'If you let me be the doctor, I'll let you be the lawyer.'

And so we see that, *on this condition,* the lawyer can become a patient, and in recognizing the doctor he is recognizing himself. Thus those who are most educated, most responsible, are least likely to be 'difficult' patients. They are on the whole 'charming' patients, prepared to confuse the doctor with medical science, on condition that the doctor is prepared to confuse them with their authority.

This interpretation can help us to explain that famous maxim, repeated so often, with a laugh: 'Doctors make the worst patients.' A doctor treating a doctor cannot say: 'If you let me be the doctor, I'll let you be the doctor.' To let the patient be the doctor is to destroy the whole concept of the patient. And alone amongst all mediators, a doctor is not prepared to become a patient, because if he were, he would be no longer a doctor. And so with a smile and a maxim, we have another sign which points to the meaning of the word doctor.

## The medical course

Following the argument that has already been developed, the medical course must impart not only a knowledge of medical science, but also the social role that such a knowledge pretends to impose. The student is taught more than medicine, he is taught the language and rites of the mediator, in other words the social context within which medicine is applied.

But there is one aspect of the medical course which we have not yet discussed, and which is often misinterpreted. After having qualified as a doctor, the graduate cannot register until he has completed a year's house-job in a hospital. This is the notorious compulsory year of underpayment and overwork which has given rise to the complaint that junior doctors are exploited.

Now there is something essentially false in this complaint. A shop-floor worker is not exploited for a year, subsequently to join the managerial class. It is a strange form of exploitation which precedes its elimination, and indeed the improvement in pay has recently removed most of the sting from this charge.

But junior hospital doctors were and still are overworked. They are overworked to the extent that they are obliged to live, eat, relax and sleep within the confines of the hospital. The hospital, with its social structure, becomes the total environment of the doctor.

As a medical student, one has a limited experience of the doctor identity. Of course, one learns to say femur instead of thigh-bone, and on the wards one begins to develop a technique to conceal knowledge from patients. But essentially it is a game. In other words, it is *experienced as a game*. Medical students play doctors carrying stethoscopes and white coats, like children with cap guns play cops and robbers. And so long as one is not a doctor, it can only be a game.

But when one qualifies, one *is* a doctor and the game must be made real. A game is culture and can be altered. Reality is nature and is fixed. The total environment of the hospital removes you from any outside world. One is no longer playing a game because the game has become the real world. It is, I think, the key moment in the creation of the doctor. It is the moment at which cultural play is experienced as necessary reality.

The welfare state is at present under attack from a Conservative government. It is clearly our duty to resist. We must try to prevent the encroachment of private medicine in to the NHS. And we must put forward the argument that a well-financed, adequate service will finally only be established with the outlawing of private capital. For a socialist, this is obvious; it hardly needs to be argued. Unfortunately, it is about all we ever do argue.

What is less obvious is why any ordinary person should accept the arguments of a conservative government. Why is it that they are deceived, manipulated and convinced by an alien ideology to act against their own interests? It is to these questions that I have tried to suggest an answer. And the outline of the answer is that the welfare state is itself deceit, manipulation and ideology.

So the conclusion is that we must do more than simply defend the welfare state. We must also expose it for the ideology it represents. The welfare state is the bureaucracy of care. Thus the 'concern' of a doctor for his patient is essentially false because it does not permit a reciprocal concern on the part of the patient for his doctor. The doctor is *qualified* to aid and comfort his patients; it would be improper for the patient to suggest he might do the same for the doctor. I am not arguing reciprocity as a valid test of whether a system is socialist; but I say that within its own terms the notion of the doctor's concern conceals deceit. These 'personal' relationships are ritual relationships reflecting a power structure. The doctor mediates a care. That means he does not care.

I have tried to indicate that one must be wary of the humanist doctor, the doctor who demonstrates in his white coat for an end to prescription charges, the 'good' doctor. The content of a message may be admirable, but the context from which it is expressed may contradict it. This we see in Eastern Europe, where the message of socialism is betrayed by its context, where the mediators who have as their authority the consciousness of the working class, mediate the working class itself.

It would be nice to finish with a precise and practical conclusion that would change the world. Unfortunately this article lacks authority and will not impose itself. It presents a simple exhortation that when the time for change arrives we do not replace bad doctors by good doctors, but that we destroy all doctors.

*Reference*

LAING, R. D. (1960), *The Divided Self*, Penguin.

# History[1]
## Robbie Gray

I think you like history, just as I did when I was your age, because it is about living men. And everything that is about men, as many men as possible, all the men in the world united among themselves in societies, working and struggling and bettering themselves must please you more than any other thing.

(Antonio Gramsci, letter to his son from prison)

The promise of history is that it may help us to understand ourselves. Our conceptions of the past condition our view of the present, our hopes and aspirations for the future. The question to be asked is whether history achieves its task, helps people to a better understanding of their world.

The reality does not measure up to this promise. This is especially so, when we consider 'history' as experienced by most students. There is a pressure to reduce the study to a series of fragmented 'topics', more or less related to exam questions. This is not surprising, for it is the most likely individual solution to demands made on the student. He is, for example, meant to be learning 'how to use evidence' – but always evidence collected by someone else, then read at second hand, under the pressure of the timetable. The way out of this dilemma is to learn to play the game, to pick a case, and back it with 'quotable quotes', to aim at plausibility rather than conviction. 'One tended to set oneself short-term goals which avoided the fundamental issue, and reduced the syllabus to a set of fragments' (Lee, 1970, p. 327). We must try to understand how this failure comes about, to create alternatives and fulfil the promise of history.

### British historiography: a retrospect

History in Britain grew in a particular way, in a particular social setting.[2] It grew in relative isolation from other social sciences, especially from sociology, which was itself slow to develop and incoherent in Britain

---

1. Geoff Crossick, Anne Gray and Geoff Richman helped me with comments on earlier drafts of this article. My argument (especially in the last section) relates to the general political perspective developed in Geoff Richman's *On Strategy* (1970).

2. Many of the issues raised in this section are more fully analysed in Gareth Stedman Jones's article (1967).

(see on this point Abrams, 1968). The social milieu was that of the late Victorian 'upper class', and its Oxford and Cambridge-centred intellectuals. This group were notable for ties with elite groupings outside the academic world (Abrams, 1968, p. 5).

History, as an institutionalized academic pursuit, was marked by this environment, especially by the dominant empiricist approach to the analysis of society. Thus there emerged a strong emphasis on the empirical study of formal social institutions (politics, law, etc.) and the lives of 'great men'. The teaching of history was part of the education of a future political and administrative elite, with a belief that it would be in some way edifying. This related to the supposed moral lessons of history and to the notion that, like classics, the study of history 'trained the mind', in some unspecified fashion.

History, as it exists today, is the product of a compromise between this tradition and newer ideas and social forces. Factors making for change included the growth of the social sciences, and the proliferation of educational institutions, catering for a less restricted social stratum than Oxford and Cambridge. A focal point was the emergence of 'economic history'. From the 1880s to 1920s this was linked to a questioning of the *laissez-faire* ideology of nineteenth-century liberalism, and an advocacy of more generous welfare provision. The challenge of the working-class movement and growth of socialism helped stimulate this re-thinking of liberal ideology. The early growth of 'economic history' was thus not simply a matter of the application to historiography of orthodox economics. R. H. Tawney, in many ways the central figure, was very much out on a limb, trying to find a synthesizing account of historical change, and analyse 'experience the discipline didn't yet include' (Williams, 1970, p. 208; see also Winter, 1970).

In this context, 'economic history' focused on the study of the conditions of the common people, set in the framework of an appraisal of the origins and consequences of industrial capitalism. This was obviously a challenge to the preoccupations of the established historiography. As well as what we understand by 'economic history', this challenge embraced what is sometimes nowadays distinguished as 'social history'.[3] The importance of Tawney is precisely that he did not separate these two areas. In his work economic change was set in the context of the whole way of life (Tawney, 1912, 1938, 1961).

3. Thus, Thompson pays tribute to the Hammonds' attempt to grasp the total political and cultural context of the working people's experience during the Industrial Revolution (Thompson, 1968, pp. 215–16; for the importance of Tawney and the Hammonds, see also Saville, 1969, p. 247–8).

Academic history assimilated the challenge in a compromise; new approaches were added to the syllabus, but as discrete fragments. The consequence has been to fragment, rather than to advance understanding of the total process of social change. Moreover, as economics has changed, so 'economic history' has been re-oriented, with increasing emphasis on problems of growth, capital formation, etc.; and on techniques of quantification. Wider concerns with social change have been squeezed out, caught in the gap between the specialisms of 'political' and 'economic' history.[4] To cite only one familiar aspect of this situation, the whole issue of the social impact of industrialization was at one time reduced to a narrow economic question, anyhow insoluble for lack of evidence; whether the real wages of most workers rose or fell, 1780–1850.[5] As 'economic history' shifted its focus, it became separated from the understanding of the significance of industrial capitalism, towards which Tawney and the Hammonds were groping.

Without such an analysis we will never manage to understand our society. Yet within historical studies, as they exist at present, it always seems to evade our grasp, lost in the labyrinth of specialisms. The current atmosphere of disquiet in the world of academic history is related to this failure. Historians are often defensive or confused about their discipline. Sociology, in particular, is seen as some sort of vague threat, against which defences are erected by asserting the irreducible uniqueness of the historian's skills – though no one can ever tell us quite what these skills are (for a somewhat extreme version of this, see Elton, 1969). Or else a half-baked version of sociology is swallowed whole, and digested with difficulty.

These uncertainties are communicated to students. As history has expanded – together with higher education in general – it has lost the self-assurance it enjoyed, when it constituted part of the education of an elite, within a homogeneous intellectual culture. The loss of self-assurance has gone hand in hand with the erosion of Victorian notions of 'progress' (the Great War and the Slump being crucial moments in this). No other framework has replaced the Victorian one; all that is left is empiricism, the past has no real meaning, it is all an intellectual game. Even the idea that history 'trains the mind' is less and less com-

4. The syllabus I myself studied as an undergraduate was built around the 'political' and 'economic' history of Britain since Tudor times. Both of these had their own styles and criteria of relevance, which together excluded any discussion of the broader processes of change in British society.

5. 'People may consume more goods and become less happy or less free at the same time' (Thompson, 1968, p. 231). This seems to be the last word on this vexed and over-worked question.

forting. One historian has commented that the traditional history degree 'does not permit the specialized expertise which the modern world seems to demand' (Harrison, 1968, p. 359).

The point here is *not* the merits of history, as compared to rival disciplines, within the existing academic world, but rather the need to understand why the academic world fails to make sense of the development of society. The reasons for this so far considered are themselves historical. Other reasons are to be found in the day to day practice of history.

### History as a 'career': the organization of learning

I begin from the fact that 'history' is a social process (teaching, research) carried on in social institutions (colleges, faculties, departments, access to source material and publication outlets, etc.). We have to consider this neglected fact, to understand how the study of the past becomes fragmented and mystifying.

To see how the intellectual fragmentation of historical knowledge is perpetuated, we have to consider some aspects of 'history as a career'. For we need a portrait of the 'professional historian', the producer of accounts of the past.

I want mainly to discuss the postgraduate stage of the career, leading to the Ph.D., and perhaps to a lecturing job. This is worth discussing, because to evaluate historical knowledge we must know how it is produced. Research means examining 'sources'. Now the historian will have been brought up in some awe of 'sources'. 'The documents had a mystique all their own' (Lee, 1970, p. 332). So much so, indeed, that contact with any particular source can be a disorienting experience, for which under-graduate training is not an adequate preparation. The researcher is thrown in at the deep end. The empirical tone of British historiography means that research students are often encouraged to 'get into the sources', without any clear model or hypothesis to guide them; a pattern is supposed to emerge *ex post facto*, in some mysterious way.

These problems confront the research student in an individualistic, competitive and hierarchic world. The research student's situation is an isolated one; he or she is anyway very much at the mercy of supervisors, who may be assigned in largely fortuitous ways. Research seminars are generally occasions for the competitive display of knowledge and wit (especially the latter) rather than being supportive in a common effort to meet problems encountered. Because the people involved do not really know or trust each other there is a lot of talking at cross purposes. In these circumstances the successful research students are often those who 'play safe' and follow some well mapped line. The better mapped the line, the more defined are the appropriate 'sources' and framework for interpreting them. In this way the historian becomes associated with a special field and a school of thought.

This career pattern perpetuates narrow specialization. It also helps to maintain entrenched procedures of investigation; it defines what evidence will 'count', as well as what questions will be asked. Getting into print – also, of course, important to the academic career – demands slightly different tactics. Unless one is already very prestigious it pays to seem in some way 'original', even to adopt a mildly iconoclastic tone. Hence the numbers of published works (generally rehashed Ph.D.s) which claim to be 'revising accepted views' – but are really only quibbling, engaging in special pleading or talking at cross purposes.

The relevance of this analysis of the 'professional historian' is that it enables us to understand how 'history' becomes and remains fragmented, and is then *experienced in this way by students*.

## History as a 'discipline'– the ideology of historians

History is generally classified as an 'Arts' rather than a 'Social Science' subject. Although this has largely fortuitous origins, there is a real effect on beliefs about the nature of historical knowledge. 'History' is supposedly empirical and intuitive, rather than conceptual; concerned to reconstruct the past, rather than to make systematic generalizations; and so on. I would argue that most of the distinctions implied here are, in fact, false accounts of the process of scientific understanding of human societies.

It is now generally realized that the claim to record 'facts', and reconstruct the past 'as it happened' is not tenable. Carr, who has been influential (at least on those historians who bother to think at all about issues of this kind) argues that 'facts' are defined as worth recording at all, in terms of some model in the historian's mind (Carr, 1964). But although they may follow Carr in this respect, historians rarely take the step of asking: how are models formed in our minds, what factors lead to the use of some conceptual framework, rather than others? The dominance of an empiricist style is an inhibiting factor, working against a consideration of issues of this sort.

The task of conceptual clarification is therefore important. Yet precisely this task is most often under-valued. From undergraduate days onwards, the historian is pulled away from any conceptual critique. As an example take the 'rise of the gentry' debate. At the outset, the *meaning* of the term 'rise of the gentry' is far from self-evident; it raises questions about the nature of the 'gentry' (class, status group, political elite?), about the relation of changing wealth to prestige and political power, and so on. Yet discussion of these matters in general terms is likely to be attacked as 'abstraction', 'waffle', etc. This bias carries through, from undergraduate level to the later stages of the career of the 'professional historian'. Success is defined in terms of working through large amounts of source material. The pressures of 'history as a career' thus perpetuate the anti-conceptual approach.

Related to this is the notion that the historian tries to understand a past society in 'its own terms', with a sort of intuition denied to more abstract sciences. But the distinction is not really valid. On one hand, it is a mystification to suppose that it is possible to recreate a past society. To make sense of the past we always use concepts (whether of everyday speech, or of more technical vocabularies) drawn from our own world. On the other hand, it is equally a mystification to suppose that it is possible to understand any social process (past or present) without also understanding the views of the world held by participants. But their views are never the whole content of our account. Partly because we can never hope to recapture the totality of other people's experiences. And partly because our account is not addressed exclusively to the participants (who, in the case of a historical study, are likely to be dead). Thompson makes this point, in relation to the place of value judgements:

The historian, or the historical sociologist, must in fact be concerned with judgements of value in two forms. In the first instance, he is concerned with the values actually held by those who lived through the Industrial Revolution. . . . In the second instance, he is concerned with making some judgement of value upon the whole process entailed in the Industrial Revolution of which we ourselves are an end-product (Thompson, 1968, pp. 485–6).

As the reference to the 'historian or historical sociologist' implies, any understanding of the central issues in our history will probably transcend the normal disciplinary boundaries. One tradition in sociology has in fact been concerned with the importance of understanding the 'actor's frame of reference' (e.g. Davies, 1968), just as historians have stressed the need to understand a society 'in its own terms'.

It is thus misleading to claim that historical interpretation is a special kind of enterprise, alien to other social sciences. According to this claim, the historian is supposed to 'examine the sources', and thus emerge with an 'interpretation'; whereas the sociologist, psychologist, etc., is supposed to collect 'data', in order to test 'hypotheses', based on 'theory'.

But it is not true that historians never 'test hypotheses'. Often a historian, if asked what he is doing, will reply: 'checking the sources for evidence counter to my interpretation'. Which is surely the testing of hypotheses.

Moreover, if science is an attempt to develop systematic explanations, then the *formulation of theory* is as important as the testing of hypotheses. Properly understood, the interpretation of historical material would be concerned with the formulation of theory. Any understanding of human society will transcend the polarity between 'verification' (= 'Social Sciences') and 'interpretation' (= 'History').

We might conclude from the foregoing that the claim of historians to a distinctive method is not tenable, But it would be a mistake to underestimate the effects of this 'ideology' of historians. These are powerful, and militate against efforts to give an intelligible account of the past.

As a result of the anti-conceptual bias in historical studies we are often at the mercy of particular fragments of information, collected by particular historians, who may use some concept (e.g. of 'class') in a way that is not clear to us – or even, perhaps, to themselves. This gives rise to a deformation of historical knowledge, which I call the 'argument from the persuasive example'. Because history is supposed to be empirical and specific, discussion tends to revolve around particular cases. Thus, to revert to our earlier example, protagonists in the 'gentry' debate cite 'rising' or 'declining' families as typical of the fortune of the stratum.

The quickest way to knock any incipient conceptual critique on the head is to start citing examples, getting the debate back into a safe area of professional expertise and knowledge of the 'sources'. As well as maintaining the corporate identity of historians, as against other disciplines, this procedure helps maintain authoritarian relations between teacher and taught. The ideology, as well as the organization of historical teaching and research, work to reduce 'history' to a series of fragments.

## New trends

In this section I discuss some newer trends in historical scholarship and assess their probable outcome.

### The 'new social history'

Increasing numbers of historians seem to be adopting sociological concepts and methods. To understand why this is the 'new social history' we must retrace our steps a little, and look again at the 'old social history'.

A concern with social change, in its broadest perspective, was one facet of the thought of the founders of 'economic history' in Britain. This concern has since been lost sight of. As modes of thought changed within economics it captured the hitherto 'maverick' discipline of 'economic history'. 'Social history' then became a residual category, often taught together with 'economic history'. It covered such areas as popular living standards, 'social problems', the growth of the Welfare State, and popular movements. This sort of 'rag bag' has become inadequate, with the recent growth of sociology in Britain. A more systematic approach to 'social history' was demanded. Sociological perspectives could, of course, affect the study of virtually the whole range of historical problems. Hence the advent, not of a school of thought, but of a number of individuals and groups moving in parallel directions. It is for this reason difficult to generalize about the 'sociologizing' trend.

The first question I want to raise concerns the precise status of the 'new social history'. Does it claim to reconstitute the theoretical and methodological basis of historical studies generally? Or will it develop mainly as a pragmatic approach to the study of particular fields? At first sight the notion of 'social history' is even more absurd than the other specialized varieties of 'history' currently offered. Professor Perkin (who holds Britain's first 'Chair of Social History') suggests that his subject is '. . . a vertebrate discipline built around a central organizing theme, the history of society *qua* society, of social structure in all its manifold and constantly changing ramifications' (Perkin, 1969, p. ix). It is hard to see how this differs from 'history' in general, properly understood. Since people live in societies, all history is by definition 'social'. But the new trends will probably become institutionalized through setting patterns for the study of certain quite specific fields (e.g. demography for which see Laslett, 1965).

One could also ask whether the adoption of sociological concepts and methodology will give us a more intelligible view of the past. A precondition of this is that the concepts should be properly understood and critically handled. But this is by no means always the case. 'Sociology' is applied without a critical understanding of the implications. The reader is left bewildered, and the introduction of sociological terms appears as so much pretentious verbiage (often having little connection with the substantive empirical content of the work in question).

There is indeed an important way in which sociology can help us make sense of historical experience. Sociology itself first emerged as an attempt to explain the transition to industrial capitalism (partly in response to the challenge of the Marxian explanation). This concern should be central to the study of British history. But it is doubtful if the current importation of sociological concepts and methods will achieve this (quite apart from the fragmentation of sociology itself). The likely outcome of the 'sociologized' history is to add yet another kind of specialized study.

*Marxism*

The impact of Marxism on British historiography was felt from the 1930s, when a number of writers tried to develop Marxist analyses of historical problems. This has been extended and refined since the war – and especially since 1956, under the influence of de-Stalinization and the New Left. Hill, for example, took up, reinterpreted and extended Tawney's inquiry into the significance of Puritanism, and its relation to the emergence of capitalism (Hill, 1958, 1961, 1964).

Yet Marxist writing has not altogether freed itself from the dominant style of British historiography, trying often to meet the established historiography on its own, empiricist, ground. The influence of Marxism has not, by and large, overcome the anti-conceptual bias of the established historiography.

Marxist analysis has perhaps achieved most – and been politically most useful – where it has been located in relation to the national tradition of critical social thought. This tradition is grounded on a literary and aesthetic mode, rather than on that of the social sciences (see Williams, 1961). Yet many of its most important insights parallel those of the Continental sociological tradition.

This current of British social thought conditioned the work of Tawney and the Hammonds; and it is on their work that Marxist historians subsequently built. In his *Making of the English Working Class*, probably the most important historical work to emerge from the Marxist tradition in Britain (Thompson, 1968), Thompson develops the central insight of this 'literary' tradition: that the transition to a new form of society involves losses as well as gains, that cannot be evaluated by uni-dimensional, economistic criteria.

### Towards an alternative: theory and practice

The alternatives discussed in the previous section – despite their significant positive aspects – share one defect. Their challenge is purely intellectual; they offer alternative theories but not alternative practices, an alternative content, but not alternative forms of organization. For this reason their challenge can be absorbed. This will be the fate of any intellectual movement that reduplicates the structures (in teaching and research) of 'official' academic life. The alternative would thus have to be in terms of the *mode of organization*, and of relationship among people. This is as important as any particular intellectual content.

### *The problem of specialization*

One demand made on an alternative is that it should help us to develop a historical consciousness, transcending the division of academic history into specialisms. This consciousness should, indeed, be available to the whole society, not merely to teachers and students. The central task is to make the past intelligible, to explain how the world came to be as it is, and how it might be changed.

There is a real difficulty about specialization which will not be exorcized by references to Marxism as a 'synthesizing theory'; too often this sort of assertion 'serves as an excuse for *not* studying history' (Engels, n.d., page 486). It is not altogether easy to decide to what extent the standards of 'historical scholarship' really matter, and to what extent they are merely fetishes. At a very simple level, it is, for example, important to know whether some purported piece of evidence is or is not genuine. And this question is not always as easy as it sounds, as any competent historian knows. To solve such problems will mean developing a certain degree of technical expertise.

Specialization is legitimate, then – in so far as it is a necessary development of expertise, to answer the questions we ask about the past. In this respect 'learned societies' devoted to specialized fields of historical study are useful – e.g. they survey and preserve material, and so on. Now, it is essential to recognize this, if we are not to substitute dogmatic assertion for investigation of the problem.

Specialization becomes illegitimate, when it is used in a manipulative way, to exert power (either over colleagues or over students). In the competitive and hierarchic world of 'history as a career' specialized knowledge *is* commonly used in this way. One instance of this is the use of superior command of the empirical material to knock any conceptual discussion on the head. The critic is bludgeoned into submission by a massive deployment of the 'argument from the persuasive example'. Criticism is seen as a threat to be countered, rather than as an attempt to further a shared historical understanding. This competitive individualism is one of the most basic, but least discussed ways in which bourgeois social relations deform knowledge.

Another illegitimate use of specialized knowledge is the tendency to evade central issues, by hiding behind the 'specialist' role. Instead of a body of technique, needed to answer certain questions, specialism becomes a means of *not* answering them (or even casting doubt on their legitimacy as questions). Thus Thompson has been attacked on the ground that the growth of class consciousness is an unreal object of study (Currie and Hartwell, 1965). The implication of this type of criticism is that Thompson's attempt to analyse the total process of class exploitation and conflict is a fantasy, inspired by political prejudice; 'objective' study would confine itself to piecemeal, empiricist accounts of particular instances. But this approach is in fact an evasion of the central issues.

Those issues are to do with the conjuncture of economic and social change and popular political mobilization, a world-wide not merely local phenomenon (cf. Moore, 1969; Davies, 1970). In the end this concerns the possibilities and limitations of democracy in a capitalist society, and thus an evaluation of our society today. It is from this sort of issue that historians (and other academics) generally run for the shelter of their specialisms.

The illegitimate use of specialization tends to deform history into a static body of knowledge. Some people have this knowledge, others must passively receive instruction. To teach instead that our historical consciousness rests on a problematic relationship between the past, ourselves as products of the past, and the concepts we use to give meaning to the past is immediately to diminish the authority claimed by the 'professional historian'.

### 'Counter-culture' and the problem of organization

This critique of the existing education process provides a basis for evaluating attempts at 'counter-culture'. So long as they re-duplicate the authoritarian approach (use of superior knowledge to dominate, etc.) such attempts will fail; and the practice of revolutionary groups does often re-duplicate existing practices in this way; the public meeting is modelled on a lecture, the political study-group on a seminar. Most political propaganda work reflects the dominant educational process in society; it is characterized by distance between the 'expert', and an audience that must passively receive instruction.

A critique, in the day-to-day experience of education, must embody alternative types of relationship and organization; collective and equal, rather than individualistic and manipulative. A major theme of this essay has been that the competitive relations of bourgeois society have a distorting effect on historical knowledge. The careerism of 'professional historians' is one aspect of this. In the teaching situation superior knowledge is taken as conferring the right, unilaterally to define the questions asked and the kind of evidence deemed relevant, thus preventing the development of a shared understanding. Mutual isolation aggravates students' feelings of disorientation, stress and oppression (these feelings are not entirely a result of the exam system).

Syllabus reforms will not basically alter this situation, nor will more radical measures, such as the abolition of exams. Desirable though these things are they will not, in themselves, create new kinds of relationships. Nor, necessarily, will the political activity of the student movement. Where their strategy hinges on ephemeral mobilizations and confrontations, revolutionaries become isolated from other students; elitism and sectarianism are both consequences and causes of this isolation. The usual response is to blame others for our failure, instead of analysing it self-critically; to grumble about the volatile nature of student opinion, denounce the 'moderates' for 'selling out', the mass of students for 'apathy', etc. This is elitist, in its implication that we know what to do, and fail only through the shortcomings of other people.

These general tendencies have particular implications for the attempt to criticize the content of courses. The critiques offered by the left may seem as meaningless to most students as their 'official' courses. They are confronted with two kinds of expertise, that of the 'official' discipline and that of its 'Marxist' critics; both may seem equally bewildering and irrelevant. Course criticism should not be a debate between two ideological positions, conducted in a way that many students feel to be outside their own lives. Instead, we must begin from the assumption that there are capacities of creativity and initiative suppressed by the dominant social relations, and seek to find ways of releasing these. Where the student movement has achieved anything, it is in so far as this has happened (as, for example, at Hornsey Art College).

Alternative relationships are needed to underpin the development of *intellectual* alternatives to 'official' historiography. These relationships are defined as collective rather than individualistic and competitive (for the idea of the 'collective' see Richman, 1970). Groups organized in this way would meet the needs of their members, play a generally supportive role and break down the separation of 'work', 'politics' and 'private life'. The work of the group would be an ongoing collective effort, not just a temporary coming together of otherwise separate individuals.

The specific goals of such a group would be self-determining. In the instance of history, they would relate to the legitimate aim of historical knowledge which is to help people understand their situation by making the past intelligible. *To make a historical consciousness available to members of the society* is as much part of this as the further accumulation of specialized knowledge.[6] The rationale of studying the past would have to be re-defined, in terms of the need to help people understand their situation. The norms and practices of academic history would then have to be examined, to decide what is necessary and what is fetishism.

6. 'The creation of a new culture does not only mean individually making some 'original' discoveries. It means also and especially the critical propagation of truths already discovered, 'socializing them' so to speak, and so making them become a basis for live action, an element of coordination, and of intellectual and moral order' (Gramsci, 1957, p. 60).

This alternative is not simply abstract and utopian. It is based on an analysis of existing contradictions. 'Talking at cross purposes', 'pretentiousness', etc. are all aspects of the competitiveness of the 'official' academic world; the effect is bewilderment and trivialization, rather than understanding. Fruitful work often arises, despite the structure, through networks of friends and contacts, people who know, understand and trust each other. The established means for the 'advancement of knowledge' do not help (everyone knows that academic conferences are rituals, that most papers published are written merely to 'get into print', etc ). Knowledge is a social and collective activity. Yet the dominant model of the 'academic career' is individualistic.

The contradiction is felt by students and teachers, as oppression and frustration in their experience of education. The revolutionary left lack a style of work, that can relate to these felt oppressions. They fail to listen to the discontent articulated at some time or other by large numbers of students and teachers, or to see how listening could help develop a correct strategy. Yet – as I have tried to show – there are several respects in which a critique of bourgeois social relations can help students to understand their experience.

## References

ABRAMS, P. (1968), *The Origins of British Sociology*, Chicago University Press.

CARR, E. H. (1964), *What is History?*, Penguin.

CURRIE R., and HARTWELL, R. M. (1965), 'Review of E. P. Thompson. *The Making of the English Working Class*', *Economic History Review*, 2nd series, vol. 18.

DAVIES, I. (1968), 'The poverty of sociology', *Listener*, 7, 14 March.

DAVIES, I. (1970), *Social Mobility and Political Change*, Pall Mall.

ELTON, G. R. (1969), 'Second thoughts on history at the universities', *History*, vol. 54.

ENGELS, F., Letter to Schmidt (5 August 1890), reprinted in K. Marx and F. Engels, *Selected Works* vol. 2, Moscow, n.d., Foreign Languages Publishing House.

GRAMSCI, A. (1957), *The Modern Prince and Other Writings* trans. L. Marks, Lawrence & Wishart.

HARRISON, B. (1968), 'History at the universities', *History*, vol. 53.

HILL, C. (1953), *Puritanism and Revolution*, Secker & Warburg.

HILL, C. (1961), *The Century of Revolution*, Nelson.

HILL, C. (1964), *Society and Puritanism in Pre-revolutionary England*, Secker & Warburg.

JONES, G. STEDMAN (1967), 'The pathology of English history'. *New Left Review* no. 46.

LASLETT, P. (1965), *The World We Have Lost*, Methuen.

LEE, P. J. (1970), 'History at the universities: the consumer view', *History*, vol. 55.

MOORE, B. (1969), *Social Origins of Dictatorship and Democracy*, Penguin.

PERKIN, H. J. (1969), *The Origins of Modern English Society, 1780–1880*, Routledge & Kegan Paul.

RICHMAN, G. (1970), *On Strategy*, available from G. Richman, 138 Fordwych Road, London NW2.

SAVILLE, J. (1969), 'Primitive accumulation and early industrialisation in Britain', in R. Miliband and J. Saville (eds.), *Socialist Register*, Merlin.

TAWNEY, R. H. (1912), *Agrarian Problems in the Sixteenth Century*, Harper & Row.

TAWNEY, R. H. (1938), *Religion and the Rise of Capitalism*, Penguin.

TAWNEY, R. H. (1961), *The Acquisitive Society*, Fontana.

THOMPSON, E. P. (1968), *The Making of the English Working Class*, Penguin.

WILLIAMS, R. (1961), *Culture and Society*, Penguin.

WILLIAMS, R. (1970), 'The teaching relationship', in D. Rubinstein and C. Stoneman (eds.), *Education for Democracy*, Penguin.

WINTER, J. M. (1970), 'R. H. Tawney's early political thought', *Past and Present*, no. 47.

Part Five
**Bibliography**

# Contents

# Introductory Notes

The aim has been to suggest reading on some of the topics that have been of most interest to those sections of the Left in Britain that stress the need for revolutionary social change, and suggest the kind of sources that can be useful in locating further information. The list is not intended to be comprehensive, and only material in English and French has been included (except for 26A). Most of the material is by, and on, writers of radical or revolutionary persuasion; some factual and critical material that is of interest but is not written in any radical perspective is also included. We have tried to exclude three categories of material in particular: works by unsympathetic authors whose criticisms are worthless, e.g. the atrocious books on Marxism produced by some analytical philosophers; uncritical Communist apologetics; and the sectarian polemics of the more insignificant Trotskyist groups. Of course some works in all three categories will unfortunately have slipped through the net.

Many items could be placed under several headings, and because of this, a few works are mentioned several times; but it remains *essential* to make full use of the cross references provided. Publishers of books are given in most cases, and where there is a paperback edition, this is the one given; but as a result of the paperback explosion it is difficult to keep track, and there will be numerous inaccuracies. Bookshops are given for booklets and pamphlets, and for some books, if publishing details are not available; if several bookshops list a pamphlet, the one with the most recent catalogue is the one given. Titles of articles in books and journals have been slightly altered in some cases, to make their content clearer; an article that is actually a review of a book is listed as such. Where known, prices are given for booklets and pamphlets.

To assist in obtaining the material, the list at the end includes the abbreviations used and addresses for the main journals and bookshops. There are also some research guides that can give further advice, such as the NACLA *Research and Methodology Guide*, or Shoenbach's *Power Research Guide* (50p and 12p from Agitprop, who also produce their own lists of new material).

# 1 The Structure of Capitalist Society

## A Class, bureaucracy and technology

Bottomore and Sweezy defend the importance of the concept of class in analysing power relationships, and Goldthorpe and Worsley challenge the common assumption that inequalities are being reduced. Miliband and Poulantzas analyse the role of the state, and the debate between them raises important issues in Marxist methodology. Shachtman was a left-wing exponent of the 'bureaucracy' theses, and Cliff discusses his views critically. Cardan tries to analyse bureaucracy as a basic attribute of modern capitalism. See also 2C, 3A, 6B, 24D, 26A.

R. Miliband, *The State in Capitalist Society*, Weidenfeld & Nicolson.

N. Poulantzas, *Pouvoir Politique et Classes Sociales*, Maspero.

Miliband–Poulantzas debate, *NLR* 58 and 59.

T. Bottomore, *Classes in Modern Society*, Allen & Unwin.

T. Bottomore, *Elites and Society*, Penguin 1966.

P. Sweezy, The Illusion of the Managerial Revolution, in his *The Present as History*, MR Press.

R. Miliband, Critique of Galbraith, *SR* 1968.

J. Goldthorpe, Social Stratification in Industrial Society, in *CS and P*.

P. Worsley, Distribution of Power in Industrial Society, in P. Halmos, ed, *Development of Industrial Societies*, Sociological Review Monograph no. 8.

S. Ossowski, *Class Structure in the Social Consciousness*, Routledge.

M. Shachtman, *The Bureaucratic Revolution*, IS Books.

T. Cliff, Critique of Bureaucratic Collectivism, *IS* 32.

N. Birnbaum, *The Crisis of Modern Industrial Society*, Oxford University Press.

P. Cardan, *Modern Capitalism and Revolution*, Sol 20p.

T. Schroyer, Toward a Critical Theory for Advanced Industrial Society, in H. Dreitzel, ed., *Recent Sociology No. 2*, Macmillan.

J. Habermas, Science and Technology as Ideology, in his *Toward a Rational Society*, Heinemann.

N. Birnbaum, Marx and Weber, in N. Smelser, ed. *Readings on Economic Sociology*, Prentice-Hall.

H. Marcuse, Weber on Capitalism, in *Negations*, Allen Lane, and in *NLR* 30.

S. Wolin, *Politics and Vision*, Allen & Unwin, chapter on Lenin and Organization Theory.

A. Touraine, *Le Mouvement de Mai ou le Communisme Utopique*, Le Seuil, 1968.

## B Inequality in Britain

Blackburn and Westergaard can be used as good general summaries. See also 6B, 8B, 8C and 12B, 3A.

R. Blackburn, The Unequal Society, in *Inc*.

J. Westergaard, The Withering Away of Class: A Contemporary Myth, in *TS*.

M. Barratt Brown, The Controllers, *Universities and Left Review* 1958–9.

T. Nairn, British Political Elite, *NLR* 23.

J. Saville, Labour and Income Distribution, *SR* 1965.

Lydall and Tipping, Distribution of Personal Wealth in Britain, *Oxford Bulletin of Statistics*, 1961.

S. Aaronovitch, *Ruling Class*, Lawrence & Wishart 1961.

R. Titmuss, *Income Distribution and Social Change*, Allen & Unwin 1962.

J. Steve and A. Webb, *Income Distribution and the Welfare State*, Bell 1971.

J. Meade, *Efficiency, Equality and the Ownership of Property*, Allen & Unwin.

J. Goldthorpe and D. Lockwood, Affluence and the British Class Structure, *Sociological Review*, 1963.

A. Brown, *Profits Wages and Wealth*, Central Books.

J. Kincaid, The 1971 Budget and Social Inequality, *IS* 48.

N. Bosanquet, *Pay Prices and Labour in Power*, Fabian 1969.

J. Edmonds and G. Radice, *Low Pay*, Fabian 1968.

A. Hunt, Class Structure in Britain Today, *MT* 1970.

J. Hughes, The Increase in Inequality, *New Statesman* 8.11.68.

E. Morgan, *The Structure of Property Ownership in Great Britain*, Oxford 1960.

C. Feinstein, Changes in the Distribution of National Income in UK since 1860, in A. Marchal and B. Ducros, eds, *Distribution of National Income*, New York 1968.

## C American power structure

See also 2C, 3D, 12C.

G. Kolko, *Wealth and Power in America,* Praeger.

E. Epstein, *The Corporation in American Politics,* Prentice-Hall.

Domhoff, *Who Rules America?*, Prentice-Hall.

C. Wright Mills, *The Causes of World War III*.

C. Wright Mills, *The Power Elite*, Oxford University Press.

Pilisuk and Hayden, Military–Industrial Complex, *Journal of Social Issues* 1965.

Welsh, Building LBJ, *Ramparts* 1967 and Ag 8p.

Welsh and I. Horowitz, Clark Clifford and the Military-Industrial Complex, *Ramparts* 1968.

G. McConnell, *Private Power and American Democracy*, Random House 1964.

D. Matthews, *The Social Background of Political Decision Makers*, Random House 1964.

H. Kariel, *The Decline of American Pluralism*, Oxford University Press.

R. Lampman, *The Share of the Top Wealth Holders in the National Wealth*, U.S. National Bureau of Economic Research 1967.

E. Sutherland, *White Collar Crime*, Holt 1961. (On the corporations)

I. Horowitz, *The War Game*, Ballantine 1963. (The influence of militarism)

## D Political science

The most important works are Playford and McCoy, from 'inside' the discipline, and Chomsky, who attacks the practical application as well as the assumptions of the subject. See also 17C, 24D and 25.

J. Playford and C. McCoy, *Apolitical Politics: A Critique of Behavioralism*, New York 1968. (Includes several of the following articles, including Lukes and Duncan)

N. Chomsky, *American Power and the New Mandarins*, Penguin 1969.

Gitlin and Ono, Critique of Pluralism, *Studies on the Left* 1965.

Duncan and Lukes, The New Democracy, *Political Studies* 1965.

Lichtman, The Facade of Equality in Liberal Democratic Theory, *Inquiry* 1969.

R. Wolff, Critique of Pluralism, in R. Wolff, ed, *Critique of Pure Tolerance*, Cape.

R. Wolff, *The Poverty of Liberalism*, Beacon Press.

B. Moore, ed, *Political Power and Social Theory*, Harper and Row.

Bay, Critique of Behaviourist Approaches, *APSR* 1965.

C. Taylor, Neutrality in Political Science, in P. Laslett and W. Runciman, eds, *Philosophy, Politics and Society*, vol. 3, Blackwell.

T. Lowi, *The End of Liberalism*, Norton.

J. Walker, Critique of the Elitist Theory of Democracy, *APSR* 1966.

B. Nossiter, *The Mythmakers*, Beacon Press. (On pluralism)

P. Bachrach and M. Baratz, *Power and Poverty*, Oxford University Press.

P. Bachrach, *Theory of Democratic Elitism*, University of London Press.

C. MacPherson, The Market Concept in Political Theory, *Canadian Journal of Economic and Political Science* 1961.

### E Sociology

Blackburn's article is a good introductory summary of the whole field of ideological distortion in social science, and Anderson could also be used, although it is more intricate. Atkinson attempts a non-Marxist critique with suggestions for a radical alternative. Baratz, Wilcox and Lévi-Strauss attack racism in social science. Marcuse and Adorno point to the work of the Frankfurt School (26A).

See also 4E, 6A, 2, 8A, 17C, 24D and 26, for critiques of other social sciences and suggestions for a Marxist alternative.

R. Atkinson, *Orthodox Consensus and Radical Alternative*, Heinemann 1971.

R. Blackburn, Guide to Bourgeois Ideology, in *SP* (C and B).

P. Anderson, Components of the National Culture, in *SP* (C and B) and in *NLR* 50.

I. Horowitz, *Project Camelot*, MIT Press. (CIA involvement in social science)

A. Frank, Dialectics and Functionalism, *S and S* 1966.

D. Lockwood, Review of Parsons, *BJS* 1956.

H. Marcuse, *One Dimensional Man*, Sphere, chapters 5–7.

T. Adorno, *Prisms*, Spearman. (First few chapters)

H. Frankel, *Capitalist Society and Modern Sociology*, Lawrence & Wishart.

D. Horowitz, Social Science or Ideology, *Social Policy* 1970.

S. and J. Baratz, Social Science Basic of Institutional Racism, *Harvard Education Review* 1970.

P. Wilcox, Social Policy and White Racism, *Social Policy* 1970.

C. Lévi-Strauss, *Race and History*, UNESCO.

H. Wolpe, Problems Concerning Revolutionary Consciousness, *SR* 1970. (On theories of revolution)

H. Draper, The Mind of Clark Kerr, *NP* 1964. (On the author of *Industrialism and Industrial Man*)

Wrong, The Oversocialized Conception of Man, in L. Coser and B. Rosenberg, eds, *Sociological Theory*, Collier-Macmillan.

Huaco, The Functionalist Theory of Stratification, *Inquiry* 1966.

R. Blackburn, ed, *Reader in Critical Social Theory*, Fontana 1972 (forthcoming).

# 2 The Capitalist Economy

## A Capitalism today

Baran and Sweezy stress the growth of monopoly power, Kidron stresses what he calls the 'permanent arms economy', and Cardan emphasizes the bureaucratic aspects of modern technological capitalism. The critical reviews, particularly of Baran and Sweezy, help to bring out the disagreements. Blackburn summarizes some of the main changes at a more elementary level. See also 3, 12B, 15B and 27.

P. Baran and P. Sweezy, *Monopoly Capital*, Penguin 1968.

J. O'Connor on Baran and Sweezy, *NLR* 40.

N. Harris on Baran and Sweezy, *IS* 30.

M. Kidron, *Western Capitalism since the War*, Penguin 1970.

D. Hallas, Review of Kidron, *IS* 44.

R. Blackburn, The New Capitalism, in *TS*.

E. Mandel, International Capitalism, *SR* 1967.

B. Rowthorn on Shonfield, *NLR* 37.

E. Mandel, Economics of Neo-Capitalism, *SR* 1964.

P. Cardan, *Modern Capitalism and Revolution*, Sol 20p.

M. Dobb, *Capitalism Yesterday and Today*, Lawrence & Wishart.

P. Baran, *The Longer View: Essays towards a Critique of Political Economy*, MR Press.

A. Gorz, Capitalist Relations of Production and the Socially Necessary Labour Force, *ISJ* 1965.

G. Kolko, Power and Capitalism in the Twentieth Century, *Sp* 9, 1971.

O. Cox, *Capitalism as a System*, Lawrence & Wishart.

B. Rowthorn and S. Hymer, *Big Business in the 1960s: an econometric study*, Cambridge University Press.

Tsura, ed, *Has Capitalism Changed*, Tokyo 1961, notably P. Baran, Reflections on Underconsumption.

## B The American and European economic situation

See also 17B, 17C.

J. O'Connor, Contradictions of Advanced U.S. Capitalism, *Social Theory and Practice* 1970.

J. Stein, Locating the American Crisis, *IS* 41.

E. Mandel, Where is America Going, *NLR* 54.

E. Mandel and M. Nicolaus, The Economic and Political Situation in the USA, *NLR* 59

J. O'Connor, The Fiscal Crisis of the State, *Social Revolution* 1970.

A. Glyn and B. Suttcliffe, The Collapse of UK Profits, *NLR* 66.

The Long-Run Decline in Liquidity, *MR* September 1970.

R. Miliband, Galbraith on American Capitalism, *SR* 1968.

E. Mandel, *Europe v. America: Contradictions of Imperialism*, NLB.
I. Birchall, The Common Market and the Working Class, *IS* 27.
M. Barratt Brown, European Capitalism and World Trade, *SR* 1966.
E. Mandel, *Common Market*, REP and Ag 5p.
S. Mallet, Continental Capitalism and the Common Market, *NLR* 19.
*The Common Market*, LRD and Ag 8p.

**C The international corporation**

See also 14C, 17, 18A, 19B, 20A and 1C.
D. Whitehead, *The Dow Story*, McGraw Hill 1968.
S. Melman, *Pentagon Capitalism: The Political Economy of War*, McGraw Hill.
P. Sweezy and H. Magdoff, The Merger Movement, *MR* June 1968 and June 1969, also NEFP and Ag 8p.
J. Ridgeway, *The Closed Corporation*, Random House.
V. Perlo, *Militarism and Industry*, Lawrence & Wishart.
V. Perlo, *Empire of High Finance*, International Publishing Company, New York 1957.
D. Horowitz, *The Corporations and the Cold War*, MR Press.
E. Kefauver, *In a Few Hands*, Penguin 1966.
W. Mennell, *Takeover: The Growth of Monopoly in Britain 1951–61*.
R. Murray, International Corporations and the State, *Sp* 10 and *NLR* 67.
N. Collins and L. Preston, Size Structure of the Largest Firms 1900–58, *American Economic Review* 1961.
*Ramparts* 1969 and 1970, articles on the oil industry.
P. Florence, *The Ownership, Control and Success of Large Companies*, Sweet & Maxwell.
R. Barnet, *Economy of Death*, Atheneum 1969.
R. Engler, *The Politics of Oil*, Macmillan 1961.
F. Cook, *The Warfare State*, Collier, New York, 1964.
A. Hacker, ed, *The Corporations take over*, Anchor 1962.
S. Newens, Mergers and Modern Capitalist Development, *TUR* 1970.
DeMuth, *General Electric: Profile of a Corporation*, NEFP and Ag 5p.
Welsh and Erlich, *Rise of the Conglomerate Corporation*, NEFP and Ag 9p.
Berkley, Corporations and the Vietnam War, *New Republic* 1969.
D. Villarejo, Stock Ownership and the Control of Corporations, *New University Thought* 1961–2, and Ag 18p.
Kayser, The Corporation, in *CS and* P.

# 3 The Worker in Capitalist Society

## A Working-class sociology: the embourgeoisement debate

The Introduction and Conclusion to the third volume of the *Affluent Worker* series, entitled *The Affluent Worker in the Class Structure*, can be used as an introduction to the debate on embourgeoisement; the authors argue that the workers have not become more middle class in political and industrial attitudes, but they are pessimistic about prospects for working-class political action to initiate fundamental changes in society. This conservatism, and the methodological assumptions of the study, are attacked by Blackburn, and a more extensive critique is mounted by Westergaard. Bottomore also argues against the assumption that the 'new' working class is less militant than its forebears. For the historical background to British working-class attitudes, see 11. See also 1A, 1B, 2A, 6B, 24A, 24D.

J. Goldthorpe, D. Lockwood, *et al., The Affluent Worker*, Cambridge University Press, 3 vols.

R. Blackburn, The Unequal Society, in *Inc.*

J. Westergaard, Rediscovery of the Cash Nexus, *SR* 1970.

H. Marcuse and S. Mallet, Nature of the New Working Class, *ISJ* 1965.

T. Bottomore, *Classes in Modern Society*, Allen & Unwin.

Howard, French New Working Class Theories, *Radical American*, March 1969.

J. King, The New Proletariat, *Sol* 6:1 1969.

D. Lockwood, *Blackcoated Worker*, Allen & Unwin.

B. Hindess, *The Decline of Working Class Politics*, Merlin 1971, Paladin.
  (On workers' isolation from Labour politics)

T. Lupton, *On the Shop Floor*, Pergamon.

S. Harkommer, Working Class Political Consciousness, *ISJ* 1965.

*Labour in an Affluent Society*, NEFP and Ag 8p. (Four articles)

S. Mallet, *La Nouvelle Classe Ouvrière*, Editions du Seuil, new edition 1970.

Hamilton and Handel, articles critical of the embourgeoisement thesis, in
  A. Shostak and W. Gomberg, eds, *Blue-Collar World: Studies of the American Worker*, Prentice-Hall 1964.

C. Wright Mills, *White Collar*, Oxford University Press.

Leenhardt, La Nouvelle Classe Ouvrière en Grève, *Sociologie du Travail* 1968.

P. Belleville, *Une Nouvelle Classe Ouvrière*, Paris 1963.

T. Nairn, The English Working Class, *NLR* 24.

D. Lockwood, The New Working Class, *European Journal of Sociology* 1960.

## B Britain: the current struggle

This subsection includes studies of particular strikes, and more general discussions of the newer managerial techniques and appropriate responses (e.g. Cliff and Topham). For coverage of current events, see papers like *Solidarity* and *Socialist*

*Worker*. It is also essential to study the new Industrial Relations Act. See also 12B, 8, 30B.

T. Cliff, *The Employers' Offensive: Productivity Deals and how to fight them*, Pluto Press, and from IS Books 35p.

T. Topham, *Productivity Bargaining*, IWC 8p, and in *TUR* 1969.

T. Topham, New Types of Bargaining, in *Inc*.

R. Collins, Trends in Productivity Bargaining, *TUR* 1970.

P. Foot, The Seamen's Struggle, in *Inc*.

T. Cliff and C. Barker, *Income Policy, Legislation and Shop Stewards*, IS Books.

C. Barker, British Labour Movement: Aspects of Current Experience, *IS* 28.

M. Fore, *The GMWU: Scab Union, Sol* 3p.

V. Allen, *Militant Trade Unionism*, Merlin.

J. Arnison, *The Million Pound Strike*, Lawrence & Wishart. (Roberts Arundel strike 1967–8)

C. Barker, *The Pilkington Strike*, IS Books 13p.

T. Lane and K. Roberts, *Strike at Pilkingtons*, Fontana. (An orthodox sociological approach)

*GEC–EE: The Weinstock Takeover*, IS Books, 10p, and IWC.

*TUR* 1969 and 1970, for surveys of the situation in the ports, teaching, the mines Ford, public services, seamen, etc.

M. Kidron, *Western Capitalism since the War*, Penguin, chapter 7.

M. Barratt Brown, *Opening the Books*, IWC and IS Books, 8p.

Rosser and Barker, The ENV Defeat, *IS* 31.

C. Barker, The Merseyside Building Workers' Movement, *IS* 32.

*The Dockers' Next Step*, IWC and IS Books, 13p.

*The Steel Workers' Next Step*, IWC, 8p.

R. Collins, *Job Evaluation*, IWC, 8p.

K. Coates and T. Topham, *The Law v. The Unions*, IWC 8p.

*Subversive Guide to the Economic League*, LRD and Ag 8p.

*Shop Stewards and Representatives Training Manual*, Workers Educational Association and LL, 60p.

## C The workers' control movement

Coates, Topham and Pannekoek are more general accounts, and Blumberg attacks those industrial sociologists who have doubted the feasibility of workers' control. See also 25D for Gramsci, whose writings on soviets in Italy are important; 15E for the Yugoslav experience, and theoretical issues raised by socialist critics; 14E for workers' soviets in France during the May events; 14A for soviets during the German Revolution of 1918–20; 16B and 16C for the Russian experience. The regular IWC *Bulletin* can be used also.

P. Blumberg, *Industrial Democracy: The Sociology of Participation*, Constable.

A. Pannekoek, *Workers' Councils*, Melbourne 1950.

K. Coates, ed, *Can the Workers Run Industry?*, Sphere.

K. Coates and W. Williams, eds, *How and Why Industry Must Be Democratised*, IWC, 75p, and IS Books.

K. Coates and T. Topham, eds, *Industrial Democracy*, Panther. (Anthology of readings)

A. Gorz, *Strategy for Labour*, Beacon Press.

F. Blum, *Work and Community: the Scott Bader Commonwealth*, Routledge.

H. Scanlon, Workers' Control and International Combines, in *TUR* 1970.

Harrison and Kendall, *Workers' Control and the Motor Industry*, IWC 8p.

K. Coates, ed, *Democracy in the Motor Industry*, IWC 25p.

J. King, Economics of Self-Management, *Sol* 6:4, 1970. (Criticizes blueprints of the IWC kind)

K. Coates, Democracy and Workers' Control, in *TS*.

## D The American working class

See also IC, 2B, 12C 13A.

K. Moody, American Working Class in Transition, *IS* 40. (An up-to-date account)

M. Oppenheimer, White Collar Revisited: Making of a New Working Class, *Social Policy* 1970.

I. Horowitz and P. Mattick, The US Working Class, *S and S* 1969.

M. Glaberman, American Working Class in the 60s, *IS* 21.

*The Class Struggle and the General Motors Strike*, Ag 10p.

Bell, *Subversion of Collective Bargaining*, NEFP and Ag 8p.

Jacobs, *Black Workers Set the Pace in Detroit*, NEFP and Ag 8p.

C. Wright Mills, *White Collar*, Oxford University Press.

S. Lens, *Crisis of American Labour*, Barnes.

# 4 Science and Society

## A General works

Rose is a general survey, and critics like Greenberg, Haberer and Herber provide useful data; Marxist accounts are given by Bernal, Needham, Crowther and Haldane. The last items on the list discuss the historical background, Bernal being the standard account. See also *Red Scientist*, and the work produced by BSSRS. See also 5A, 6A.

D. Greenberg, *The Politics of American Science*, Penguin 1970.

*Socially Responsible Scientists or Soldier Technicians?*, *Sol*, 5p.
  (On BSSRS work)

L. Herber, *Our Synthetic Environment*, Knopf.

D. Greenberg, *The Politics of Pure Science*, New American Library, 1968.

BSSRS, *The Social Impact of Modern Biology*, Routledge 1971. (Especially article by J. Beckwith)

N. Vig, *Science and Technology in British Politics*, Pergamon 1968.

P. Haberer, *Politics and the Community of Science* 1970.

J. Allen, ed, *March 4: Scientists, Students and Society*, MIT Press 1971.

S. Klaw, *The New Brahmins*, Morrow and Co. 1969.

Perl, New Critics in American Science, *New Scientist* April 1970.

P. Handler, ed, *Biology and the Future of Man*, Oxford University Press 1970.

Z. Medvedev, *The Rise and Fall of Lysenko*, Columbia University Press 1969.

D. Joravsky, *Soviet Marxism and Natural Science*, Routledge 1961.

J. Bernal, *The Social Function of Science*, Routledge 1939.

J. Crowther, *The Social Relations of Science*, Cresset 1967.

L. Mumford, *The Myth of the Machine*.

J. Haldane, *Science and Life*, Pemberton 1968.

N. Wiener, *The Human Use of Human Beings*, Sphere.

M. Goldsmith and A. Mackay, eds. *The Science of Science*, Penguin 1966.

N. Calder, *Technopolis: Social Control of the Uses of Science*, Panther 1970.

E. Weil, Science in Modern Culture, *Daedalus* 1965.

Cybernetics, *An* 25 and 31.

Liberatory Technology, *An* 78.

W. Armytage, *Rise of the Technocrats: A Social History*, Routledge.

J. Needham, *The Grand Titration*, Allen & Unwin 1969.

J. Needham, *Science and Civilization in China*, Cambridge University Press 1954–65.

J. Bernal, *Science in History*, Penguin, 4 vols.

L. White, Historical Roots of Our Ecologic Crisis, *Science* 10.3.67.

## B Chemical and biological warfare

The books by Clarke, Hersh and Cookson are up-to-date surveys. See also 21C and 21D for further information on the Vietnam War, discussed by Pfeiffer, Harvey and Whiteside below.

J. Cookson and J. Nottingham, *Survey of Chemical and Biological Warfare*, Sheed & Ward 1969.

S. Hersh, *Chemical and Biological Warfare*, Panther 1970.

R. Clarke, *We All Fall Down: Prospects of Biological and Chemical Warfare*, Penguin 1969.

J. Robinson, Chemical Warfare, *Science Journal*, April 1967.

Biological and Chemical Warfare: Symposium of *Bulletin of Atomic Scientists*, June 1960.

Chemical and Biological Warfare: special issue of *Science and Citizen*, August 1967.

E. Langer, Report on Chemical and Biological Warfare, *Science*, January 1967.

J. Rothschild, *Tomorrow's Weapons*, McGraw Hill 1964.

NARMIC, *Weapons for Counter-Insurgency: Chemical, Biological, Anti-Personnel, and Incendiary*.

UN, *Chemical and Biological Weapons and the Effects of their Possible Use*, from H.

N. Calder, *Unless Peace Comes*, Penguin 1970.

C.-G. Heden, *The Problem of Chemical and Biological Warfare*, International Congress for Microbiology.

E. Pfeiffer, Ecological Effects of the Vietnam War, *Science Journal*, February 1969.

F. Harvey, *Air War: Vietnam*, Bantam.

T. Whiteside, ed, *Defoliation*, Ballantine, New York 1970.

## C The arms race

See also 2C and 1C, for the military-industrial complex, and 21C, 21D, 30B.

G. Thayer, *The War Business*, Paladin.

P. Laurie, *Beneath the City Streets: A Private Enquiry into the Nuclear Preoccupations of Governments*, Allen Lane 1970.

R. Curtis and E. Hogon, *Perils of the Peaceful Atom: The Myth of Safe Nuclear Power*, Gollancz 1969.

R. Barnet, *The Economy of Death*, Atheneum, New York 1970.

*Preventing the Spread of Nuclear Weapons*, Pugwash Monographs, Souvenir Press.

*Implications of Anti-Ballistic Missile Systems*, Pugwash Monographs, Souvenir Press.

P. Alexander, Cost of World Armaments, *Sc Am* October 1969.

G. Rathjens, Dynamics of the Arms Race, *Sc Am* April 1969.

H. York, Military Technology and National Security, *Sc Am* August 1969.

R. Clarke, *Birth of the Bomb*, Phoenix House 1961.

R. Reid, *Tongues of Conscience: War and the Scientists' Dilemma*, Constable 1969.

M. Armacost, *The Politics of Weapons Innovation: The Thor-Jupiter Controversy*, Columbia University Press 1969.

There is also a series of six Praeger books, edited by S. Melman, on the problems of converting military research to civilian uses.

**D Ecology and pollution**

See *The Ecologist* and *Your Environment* also.

J. Barr, ed, *Environmental Handbook: Action Guide for the U.K.*, Pan 1971.

A. and P. Ehrlich, eds, *Population, Resources and Environment*, W. H. Allen 1970.

*The Earth Belongs to the People: Ecology and Power*, Ag 38p.

L. Herber, *Ecology and Revolutionary Thought*, OG and Ag 22p.

P. Ehrlich, Eco-Catastrophe, *Ramparts* 1969.

W. Anderson, ed, *Politics and Environment: Reader in Ecological Crisis.*

R. Arvill, *Man and Environment: Crisis and the Strategy of Choice*, Penguin 1967.

M. Nicholson, *The Environmental Revolution*, Penguin 1970.

B. Commoner, *Science and Survival*, Viking Press.

R. Carson, *Silent Spring*, Penguin 1965.

P. Dansereau, ed, *Challenge for Survival*, Columbia 1970.

P. Helfrich, ed, *Environmental Crisis*, Yale University Press 1970.

H. Rothman, *Pollution*, Hart-Davis.

Special Issue on the Biosphere, *Sc Am*, September 1970.

W. Proxmire, *Report from Wasteland.*

P. Chapman, The Energy Crisis, *New Scientist* 24.9.70.

**E Philosophy of science**

Popper has been the major force in orthodox philosophy of science, and orthodox views about science as constituting an impartial investigation of the nature of objective reality have been attacked by Kuhn and Feyerabend, although the former is himself conservative and the implications of the attack are clearer in Feyerabend's recent work. Capek is perhaps the most thorough survey of the implications of Relativity. In France, Bachelard and Canguilhem have been developing and systematizing the new approaches and have influenced the Structuralists (24C) and the Althusserians (26D). See 24E for the Marxist classics and discussions thereof, and 24A and 26D for the confrontation between Frankfurt and Althusserian views of science. A forthcoming book by P. Binns, *Facts and Theories*, is a very thorough attack, from a Marxist perspective, on the various current philosophies of science.

K. Popper, *Conjectures and Refutations*, Routledge.

T. Kuhn, *Structure of Scientific Revolutions*, Chicago University Press.

P. Feyerabend, Problems of Empiricism, in R. Colodny, ed, *Beyond the Edge of Certainty*, Prentice-Hall 1965.

P. Feyerabend, Classical Empiricism, in R. Butts and J. Davis, eds, *The Methodological Heritage of Newton*, Blackwell.

P. Feyerabend, Against Method, in *Minnesota Studies in the Philosophy of Science*, vol. 4, 1970, and NLB forthcoming.

J. Bernal, *The Word, the Flesh and the Devil*, Cape.

J. Bernal, *The Freedom of Necessity*.

G. Bachelard, *The Philosophy of No*, Orion Press, 1968.

G. Bachelard, The Philosophic Dialectic of the Concept of Relativity, in P. Schilpp, ed, *A. Einstein: Philosopher-Scientist* 1949.

D. Lecourt, *L'Epistemologie Historique de G. Bachelard*, Vrim 1969.

G. Canguilhem, *Le Normale et le Pathologique*, Paris 1966.

P. Macherey, La philosophie de science de G. Canguilhem, *La Pensée*, 1964.

M. Capek, *Philosophical Impact of Contemporary Physics*, Van Nostrand.

A. Koyré, *Newtonian Studies*, Chapman & Hall 1965.

H. Marcuse, *One-Dimensional Man*, Sphere, chapters 5–7.

The following attack standard philosophy, though share too many of its assumptions to be very effective. See also the new journal *Radical Philosophy*.

A. MacIntyre, Breaking the Chains of Reason, in E. Thompson, ed, *Out of Apathy*, New Left Books 1959.

E. Gellner, *Words and Things*, Penguin 1968.

C. Mundle, *A Critique of Linguistic Philosophy*, Oxford 1970.

L. Kolakowski, *Alienation of Reason*, Paladin.

# 5 One-Dimensional Society

## A Repressive tolerance

Marcuse, Laing, Adorno and Henry seek to demonstrate the mechanisms by which socialization serves to conceal the realities of authoritarian domination, and the articles by Mueller, Murray and Habermas discuss the way communication systems are 'loaded'. On the former, see also 26A and 26B, and for the latter, the work of Bernstein on the language of education, 6B.

H. Marcuse, *One-Dimensional Man*, Sphere.

H. Marcuse, Repressive Tolerance, in R. Wolff, ed, *A Critique of Pure Tolerance*, Cape.

D. Cooper, ed, *The Dialectics of Liberation*, especially H. Marcuse, *Liberation from the Affluent Society*, and J. Henry, *Social and Psychological Preparation for War*, Penguin 1968.

J. Henry, *Culture Against Man*, Tavistock.

R. Laing, *The Politics of Experience*, Penguin 1967.

R. Laing, *Knots*, Penguin.

T. Adorno, *et al.*, *The Authoritarian Personality*.

A. Segal, *The Machinery of Conformity*, *An* 94.

R. Murray and T. Wengraf, Political Economy of Communications, *Sp* 5.

R. Williams, *Communications*, Penguin 1968.

C. Mueller, Notes on the Repression of Communicative Behavior, in H. Dreitzel, ed, *Recent Sociology No. 2*, Collier-Macmillan 1970.

J. Habermas, Towards a Theory of Communicative Competence, in *Inquiry* 1970, and in Dreitzel, op. cit.

H. Enzensberger, Towards a Marxist Theory of the Media, *NLR* 64.

## B The critique of the spectacle

In recent years the Situationists have produced far-ranging analyses of the topics covered in subsection A, using the concept of the 'spectacle', the idea that the media and other mechanisms of advanced capitalist society enable revolutionary attacks to be distorted and coopted in ways that cast doubt on the efficacy of traditional modes of revolutionary activity. Some of the material is difficult to obtain; the discussion in Willener can be used as an introduction. See also 3B, 10A (the Yippies) and 14E (the French events).

E. Brau, *Le Situationnisme, ou la Nouvelle Internationale*, Nouvelles Editions Debresse 1968.

G. Debord, *La Societé du Spectacle*, Editions du Champ Libre; Paris 1967, English translation in *Radical American*, 4:5.

R. Vaneigem, *The Totality for Kids*, Sit.

*Ten Days that Shook the University*, Sit, and in French from Gallimard.

*Internationale Situationniste*, Van Gennep 1971. (A complete reprint of the journal of that name)

R. Vienet, *Enragés et Situationnistes dans le Mouvement des Occupations*, Gallimard 1968.

J.-J. Lebel, *Procès du Festival d'Avignon: Supermarché de la Culture*, Pierre Belfond 1968.

A. Willener, *The Action Image of Society*, Tavistock.

## C Sexual repression and the family

The most influential studies are those of Laing and Reich. Brinton is an introduction from a basically Reichian angle. See also 9A and 9E, on the exploitation of women, and also 24F.

M. Brinton, *The Irrational in Politics: Authoritarian Conditioning and Sexual Repression*, Sol, 20p.

R. Laing, *The Politics of the Family*, Tavistock 1971.

H. Marcuse, *Eros and Civilization*, Sphere.

D. Cooper, *The Death of the Family*, Allen Lane 1971.

L. Limpus, *Sexual Repression and the Family*, Ag 5p.

J.-P. Sartre, *Saint Genet*, W. H. Allen.

R. Laing and D. Cooper, *Reason and Violence*, Tavistock, chapter on Sartre on Genet.

N. Brown, *Life against Death*, Sphere.

W. Reich, *What is Class Consciousness?* 1971.

W. Reich, *The Sexual Revolution*, Vision Press.

W. Reich, *Function of the Orgasm*, Panther.

C. Rycroft, *Reich*, Fontana. (A straightforward but very inadequate discussion)

O. Raknes, *W. Reich and Orgonomy*, Pall Mall 1970.

C. Sinelnikoff, *L'Oeuvre de W. Reich*, Maspero 1970. (Scholarly)

Cottier, *La Vie et l'Oeuvre du Docteur W. Reich*, La Cité, Lausanne
*An* 104 on Reich.

A. Comfort, *Sex in Society*, Penguin 1964.

## D The ambiguity of madness

The work of Laing, and his associates Cooper and Esterson, argues that there is necessarily a social and political dimension to the decision to classify someone as insane, and the denial of this by orthodox psychologists results in a legitimation for oppression. See also 10.

R. Laing, *The Divided Self*, Penguin 1964.

R. Laing and A. Esterson, *Sanity, Madness and the Family*, Penguin 1970.

R. Laing, *Self and Others*, Penguin 1971.

A. Esterson, *The Leaves of Spring – A Study in the Dialectics of Madness*, Penguin.
Gillie, Freedom Hall, *NS* 27.2.70.

T. Szasz, *The Myth of Mental Illness*, Harper & Row.

T. Szasz, *Ideology and Insanity*, Doubleday, 1970.

J. Gabel, *La Fausse Conscience*, Minuit. (A comparison of schizophrenia and ideology)

J. Scheff, *Being Mentally Ill*, Weidenfeld & Nicolson.

M. Foucault, *Madness and Civilization*, Tavistock. (A brilliant historical account)

R. Boyers, ed, *Laing and Anti-Psychiatry*, Penguin 1972.

D. Cooper, *Psychiatry and Anti-psychiatry*, Paladin.

# 6 The Role of Education

## A Education and ideology

This subsection considers the general role of education in servicing the system, the complementary roles of 'intellectual' and 'intellect worker' (Baran and Birnbaum), the role of selection procedures in distinguishing them, and the effect of these roles on the content of intellectual activity. On the latter, see also 1D, 1E, 8A, 17C, 17D, and see also 5A, 5B and, for Gramsci, 25D. The role of higher education is covered more specifically in subsection C.

V. Kiernan, Notes on Intellectuals, *SR* 1969.

J. Myrdal, *Confessions of a Disloyal European*, Chatto & Windus.

N. Birnbaum, The Idea of a Political Avant-Garde: Intellectuals and the Technical Intelligentsia, *Praxis* 1969.

P. Baran, *The Commitment of the Intellectual*, in his *The Longer View*, MR Press.

C. O'Brien, Politics and the Morality of Scholarship, in M. Black, ed, *The Morality of Scholarship*, Cornell University Press.

P. Baran and P. Sweezy, *Monopoly Capital*, Penguin 1968, chapter 10.

Q. Hoare, Nature of Education, *NLR* 32.

N. Chomsky, *American Power and the New Mandarins*, Penguin 1969.

P. Blau, Relevance, *Daedalus* 1969.

B. Cuddihy *et al.*, *The Red Paper*, Islander Publications.

On examinations, Fawthrop is best, but probably difficult to find now:

T. Fawthrop, *Education or Education*, Radical Students Alliance.

R. Cox, *Exams and Higher Education: A Survey of the Literature*, Society for Research into Higher Education, London 1967.

*NUS Report on Exams*, NUS 1970, 8p.

B. Simon, *Intelligence, Psychology and Education: A Marxist Critique*, Lawrence & Wishart.

B. Simon, *Studies in the History of Education, 1780–1870*, Lawrence & Wishart 1960.

B. Simon, *Education and the Labour Movement, 1870–1920*, Lawrence & Wishart 1965.

B. and J. Simon, eds, *The Challenge of Marxism*, Lawrence & Wishart.

B. and J. Simon, eds, *Educational Psychology in the USSR*, Lawrence & Wishart.

## B Education and class

See also 1A, 1B, 8B.

J. Westergaard and A. Little, Class Differentials in Education, *BJS* 1964–5.

A. Halsey *et al.*, *Class and Educational Opportunity*, Heinemann 1956.

J. Ford, *Social Class and the Comprehensive School*, Routledge.

G. Taylor, *Born and Bred Unequal*, Humanities Press.

J. Douglas, Unequal Opportunities at School, *Higher Education Journal* 1965.

J. Douglas, *The Home and the School*, Panther.

J. Douglas *et al.*, *All Our Future*, Davies.

B. Jackson and D. Marsden, *Education and the Working Class*, Penguin 1966.

D. Marsden, School Class and the Parents' Dilemma, in R. Mabey, ed, *Class*, Anthony Blond.

Crutchley, Robbins and Newsome, *NLR* 23.

*The Public Schools*, Socialist Education Association.

*Public Schools: Evidence to the Royal Commission*, NUS 13p.

H. Glennerster and R. Pryke, *The Public Schools*, Fabian 1964.

R. Lambert, *The Hothouse Society*, Weidenfeld & Nicolson. (On public schools)

*Guide to Comprehensive Education*, Socialist Education Association.

C. Benn and B. Simon, *Half Way There: Report on British Comprehensive School Reform*, McGraw Hill 1970; Penguin 1972 (forthcoming).

Progress of Comprehensives, *NS* 12–2–70.

Jencks, Social Stratification and Higher Education, *Harvard Education Review* 1968.

Influence of Social Class on Student Performance at University, *Sociological Review Monograph* no. 7.

D. Lawton, *Social Class, Language and Education*, Routledge.

B. Bernstein, *Class Codes and Control*, vol. 1, Routledge 1971.

## C The school

Neill and Lane made important contributions to the progressive education movement, and the books of Wills, Nielsen and van der Eyken discuss these and other educational experiments; Goodman, Henry and Illich have been influential critics abroad; Berg documents an important recent attempt to democratize a school's structure, and the vested interests it encountered; Holt and Hudson discuss psychological aspects of teaching methods. See the previous subsection for life in public schools, and also 5A, 7A. The Schools Action Union journal *Vanguard* and the militant teachers' *Rank and File* are useful for current developments.

*Letter to a Teacher*, by the School of Barbiana, Penguin 1970.

E. Blishen, ed, *The School that I'd Like*, Penguin 1969.

The Schoolkids' Issue of *Oz* 1971.

L. Hudson, *Contrary Imaginations*, Penguin 1968.

J. Holt, *How Children Fail*, Penguin 1969.

J. Henry, *Culture Against Man*, Tavistock, chapter 8.

L. Berg, *Risinghill*, Penguin 1968.

Constable on Berg, *NS* 13.6.68, and subsequent correspondence.

I. Illich, *Deschooling Society*, Harper & Row 1971.

Everett Reiner, *School is Dead*, Penguin 1971.

S. Stuart, *Say: An Experiment in Learning*, Nelson.

S. Hansen, *The Little Red Schoolbook*, Stagel, from LL 30p. (Useful hints for the early years in secondary school)

C. Searle, ed, *Stepney Words*, Reality Press and Ag 1971, 30p.

J. Kozol, *Death at an Early Age*, Penguin 1968.

A. Neill, *Summerhill*, Penguin. (And other books by him, such as *That Dreadful School* and *Problem Child*)

*Neill and Summerhill: A Man and his Work*, pictorial study by John Walmsley, Penguin 1969.

Homer Lane, *Talks to Parents and Teachers*, Allen & Unwin.

E. Bazeley, *Homer Lane and the Little Commonwealth*, Allen & Unwin.

W. D. Wills, *The Barns Experiment*, Allen & Unwin 1945.

W. D. Wills, *The Hawkespur Experiment*, Allen & Unwin 2nd edn 1967.

W. van der Eyken and B. Turner, *Adventures in Education*, Allen Lane 1969.

E. Mason, *Collaborative Learning*, Ward Lock 1970.

P. Goodman, *Compulsory Miseducation*, Penguin 1971.

P. Goodman, *Growing Up Absurd*, Sphere.

*An* 107, on Goodman's views on Education.

The Free School Idea, *An* 73.

B. Massialas and J. Zevin, *Creative Encounters in the Classroom*, Wiley.

H. Kohl, *36 Children*, Penguin 1971. (Teaching in New York)

D. Friedman, Crisis in Schools: Teachers and the Community, IS Books 15p. (From the US)

*Children's Rights*, Elek 1971; also the journal published by Children's Rights Publications Ltd.

### D Higher education

See also 7 for student movements, and for course critiques, 1D, 1E, 2, 3A, 4A, 4E, 8A, 11A, 15A, 17C, 17D, 24–8.

P. Hoch, *Academic Freedom in Action*, Sheed & Ward 1970.

E. Thompson, *Warwick University Ltd*, Penguin 1970.

G. Harman *et al.*, Education, Capitalism and Student Revolt, IS Books 20p.

P. Goodwin, Higher Education in Capitalist Society, *MT* 1970.

D. Adelstein, Crisis in Higher Education, in *SP* (C and B) 1969.

M. Nicolaus, The Iceberg Strategy: *Universities and the Military-Industrial Complex*, REP and Ag.

R. Lichtman, Ideological Functions of the University, *ISJ* 1967.

Cowley, Strange Death of the Liberal University, *SR* 1969.

*Documents on the University–Military Complex*, REP and Ag 50p.

*The University Interlocks: London University–University College Rhodesia*, Ag 3p.

*Ten Days that Shook the University*, Sit.

D. Atkinson, The Academic Situation, in *SP* (N).

*NUS–NCCL Report on Academic Freedom and the Law*, NCCL and NUS 1970 57p.

Articles on the foundations, in *Ramparts* 1967.

T. Nairn and J. Singh-Sandhu, Chaos in Art Colleges, in *SP* (C and B).

*Technical Colleges in a Unitary System of Higher Education*, NUS 1966.

Trow, The Binary Dilemma, *Higher Education Review* 1969.

J. Lukes, The Binary Policy: A Critical Study, *UQ* 1967.

G. Owens, The Module, *UQ* 1971. (On the Trent Poly)

*The Hornsey Affair*, Penguin 1968.

T. Burgess, ed, *Dear Lord James: A Critique of Teacher Education*, Penguin 1970.

# 7 Student Movements

**A General surveys**

Nagel, Cockburn and Harman are good introductory surveys; Franklin, Rowntree and Haberle discuss the 'youth as a class' thesis. See also 5B and 6 (especially 6D).

J. Nagel, ed, *Student Power*, Merlin.

A. Cockburn and R. Blackburn, eds, *Student Power*, Penguin 1969.

Student Movements and Generational Conflict, special issue of *Journal of Contemporary History* 1970.

G. Harman *et al.*, *Education, Capitalism and Student Revolt*, IS Books 20p.

E. Mandel, *The Revolutionary Student Movement*, Red Books.

M. Cohen and D. Hale, eds, *New Student Left*, Beacon Press.

L. Althusser, Problèmes Etudiants, *NC* January 1964.

T. Ali, ed, *New Revolutionaries*, Owen.

S. Lipset and P. Altbach, eds, *Student Politics*. (Documents)

Rowntree, Political Economy of Youth, Ag 9p.

Franklin, Lumpenproletariat and Revolutionary Youth, *MR* 1970.

The Provos, *An* 66.

K. Keniston, *The Young Radicals: Notes on Committed Youth*, Harcourt Brace & World.

R. Haberle, *Social Movements*, Appleton, chapter on political generations.

E. Friedenberg, *The Vanishing Adolescent*, Dell.

D. Cohn-Bendit, *Obsolete Communism: The Left-Wing Alternative*, Penguin 1969.

**B Britain**

See also 6D, 12A, 12B.

P. Hoch and V. Schoenbach, *LSE: The Natives are Restless*, Sheed & Ward.

P. Hoch, *Academic Freedom in Action*, Sheed & Ward. (On LSE in particular)

Shaw, The LSE Sit-in, *IS* 36.

Brewster *et al.*, Student Power and the LSE Sit-in, *NLR* 43.

J. West, *Thugs and Wreckers*, MDM 13p. (On LSE)

*The Hornsey Affair*, Penguin 1969.

A. Arblaster, Student Militancy and the Collapse of Reformism, *SR* 1970.

Payne and Bird, Students in Polytechnics, *NS* 23.10.69.

Special issue on the Revolutionary Socialist Students Federation, *NLR* 53.

Ashby and Anderson, *Rise of the Student Estate in Britain*, Papermac.

**C The United States**

See also 6D, 12C and 13C.

I. Stone, *The Killings at Kent State: How Murder Went Unpunished*, 1971.

Miller and Gilmore, ed, *Revolution at Berkeley*, Dell 1965.

H. Draper, *Berkeley: The New Student Revolt*, Grove Press, 1965.

S. Lipset and S. Wolin, eds, *Student Revolt: Berkeley*, Doubleday.

The Columbia Struggle, *Ramparts* 1968.

*Debate with SDS: RYM v. The Weathermen*, REP and Ag 29p.

*How Harvard Rules*, ARG and Ag 50p. (Links of Harvard with the CIA and the military)

Nicolaus, Blacks, Students and Workers, *NLR* 54. (On the troubles at San Francisco State College)

Stern, The CIA and Student Politics, *Ramparts* 1967.

NACLA, *The University–Military Complex: Military Research in the Universities*, LL 50p.

J. Farber, *The Student as Nigger*, Dell.

J. Ridgeway, *Who Rules the University?*

### D Other countries

See also 14E, for students in France, and 22B for China.

F. Halliday, Students of the World Unite, in *SP* (C and B 1969).

Buddeberg, West German Student Movement, *IS* 33.

Bergmann, R. Dutschke *et al.*, *La Revolte des Etudiants Allemands*.

*The Miracle and After*, MDM 13p. (On Germany)

Weller and Will, German Students, in *SP* (N).

Karl, German Students, *Journal of Contemporary History* 1970.

F. Hunnius, *Student Revolts: New Left in W. Germany*, War Resisters' International, from H, 17½p.

B. and J. Ehrenreich, *Long March Short Spring: Student Movement in US and Europe*, MR Press.

S. Dowsey, ed, *Zengakuren: Japan's Revolutionary Students*, Ishi Press, Berkeley 1970.

G. McCormack, The Student Left in Japan, *NLR* 65.

P. Altbach, Japanese Students, *Comparative Education Review*, 1963.

Sho, Zengakuren, *Japan Quarterly* 1968.

Smith and Isurumi, Japanese Students, *Journal of Contemporary History* 1970.

Mineo, Italian Students, in *SP* (N).

D. Emmerson, ed, *Students and Politics in the Developing Nations*, Pall Mall.

A. Hennessy, University Students in National Politics, in C. Veliz, ed, *The Politics of Conformity in Latin America*, London 1967.

*Mexico 1968: The Students Speak*, Red Books 43p.

P. Altbach, ed, *Turmoil and Transition: Higher Education and Student Politics in India*, Basic Books.

# 8 The Welfare State

## A The ideology of social work

*Case Con* and *Red Rat*, should be consulted for current developments. See also
  5D and 9.
A. Segal, Social Workers' Perception of Mentally Disturbed Clients, *Social Work*,
  USA, 15:3, 1970.
A. Segal, The Machinery of Conformity, *An* 94.
R. Holman, Client Power, *NS* 31.10.68.
Kemeny and Popplestone, Client Discrimination in Social Welfare Organisations,
  in *BQJSW*.
H. Garfinkel, Conditions of Successful Degradation Ceremonies, *American Journal
  of Sociology* 1955.
B. Morris, Thoughts on Participation, *An* 103.
M. Murray, Class and the Welfare State, in R. Mabey, ed, *Class*, Anthony Blond.
A. Gouldner, The Sociologist as Partisan: Sociology and the Welfare State,
  *American Sociologist* May 1968.
C. Wright Mills, The Professional Ideology of Social Pathologists, *American
  Journal of Sociology* 1943.
C. Valentine, *Culture and Poverty: Critique and Counter-Proposals*, Chicago 1968.
  (On the theory and practice of American poverty programmes)
H. Becker, *The Outsiders*, Free Press 1963.
P. Bachrach and M. Baratz, *Power and Poverty: Theory and Practice*.
J. Scheff, ed, *Mental Illness and Social Process,* Harper 1967.
A. Sinfield, *Which Way for Social Work*, Fabian 1969.
R. Laing, Intervention in Social Situations, Association of Family Caseworkers
  and the Philadelphia Association, 1969 (and in *Politics of the Family*)
T. Szasz, The Psychiatric Classification of Behaviour, in L. Brom, ed,
  *The Classification of Behaviour Disorders*.
P. Leonard, Social Control, Class Values and Social Work Practice, *BQJSW*, 1965.
D. Wedderburn, Facts and Theories of the Welfare State, *SR* 1965.

## B Problems of the welfare state

See also the CPAG journal *Poverty*, and 1B, 5D, 9C and 12B, and, for the American
  situation 8A.
K. Coates and R. Silburn, *Poverty: The Forgotten Englishmen*, Penguin 1970.
J. Kincaid, Social Security under Labour, *IS* 25, and 43.
J. Kincaid, Welfare: Means and Ends, *IS* 31.
J. Kincaid, Inequality and Income, *IS* 37.
J. Kincaid, Taxing the Poor, *IS* 46.
D. Piachaud, Taxation and the Poor, *Political Quarterly* 1971.
Survey: Welfare and Pension Plans, *IS* 36.

P. Townsend, *et al.*, *Social Services For All?*, Fabian 1970. (On the argument over selectivity)

A. Harvey, *Casualties of the Welfare State*, Penguin.

B. Abel-Smith and P. Townsend, *The Poor and the Poorest*, OPSA.

P. Townsend *et al.*, *The Fifth Social Service*, Fabian 1970, especially T. Lynes, Welfare Rights. (On Seebohm Report)

R. Holman, ed, *Socially Deprived Families*, Bedford Square Press.

R. Holman, The Wrong Poverty Program, *NS* 20.3.69.

*Supplementary Benefits Handbook*, HMSO 33p.

Critique of Supplementary Benefits Handbook, *Poverty* 15, 1970.

A. Atkinson, *Poverty in Britain and the Reform of Social Security*, Cambridge University Press.

Poverty, *An* 84.

R. Titmuss, *Essays on the Welfare State*, Allen & Unwin.

P. Townsend *et al.*, *Socialism and Affluence*, Fabian.

R. Titmuss and M. Zander, *Equal Rights*, CPAG.

*Guide to the Wages Stop*, LRD and Ag 3p.

*Short Guide to the Redundancy Payments Act 1965*, LRD and Ag 4p.

*Guide to Supplementary Benefits Appeals*, Poverty Leaflets, CPAG 5p.

*Low Wage Employment*, Poverty Leaflets, CPAG 3p.

*Guide to National Welfare Benefits*, Poverty Pamphlets, CPAG 5p.

*Poverty and the Labour Government*, Poverty Pamphlets, CPAG 15p, and in *Sp* 5.

*Policy to Establish Legal Rights of Low Income Families*, Poverty Pamphlets, CPAG 5p.

*Guide to the Social Services*, FWA 50p.

*Unsupported Mothers Handbook*, CU 6p.

P Willmott, *Consumers' Guide to the British Social Services*, Penguin 1967

## C Housing

E. Burney, *Housing On Trial*, Oxford University Press.

J. Kincaid, Housing Fact and Fiction, *IS* 35.

J. Greve, *London's Homeless*, OPSA, 1964.

Glass and Westergaard, *London's Housing Needs*, Centre for Urban Studies, report no. 5, 1965.

H. Rose, *The Housing Problem*, Heinemann.

D. Donnison *et al.*, *Essays on Housing*, OPSA.

Milner Holland Report, *Housing in Greater London*, HMSO. (The appendices are particularly useful)

Notting Hill Housing Service, *Notting Hill Summer Project Report*, 1969.

*Face the Facts*, from Shelter.

J. Greve, *Private Landlords*, OPSA.

O. Marriott, *The Property Boom*, Pan.

Knightley and Milner, Landlords and the Rent Act, *Sunday Times* 8.11.70.

*Tenants Guide to the 1965 Rent Act*, LRD and Ag 5p.

N. Timms, *Rootless in the City*, National Council for the Social Services, 1968.

*Essays in Local Government Enterprise, vol 2: Housing*, Merlin.

**D Tenants and squatters campaigns**

The claimants unions, particularly the Birmingham one, are active in promoting attempts to claim welfare benefits, and publish useful material; the later items in subsection B are also useful for this purpose. Much of the following documentation of struggles on this front will be difficult to find but, as with the section on strikes and the shop-floor struggle (3B), it gives an idea of where to look for current coverage. See also 10A.

T. Woolley, *Housing, Rents and Tenants Struggles in Scotland*, Sol 5p.

C. Lever, Planning and Democracy: St Marylebone Tenants Struggle, *IS* 23.

C. Lever, Tenants Notebook, *IS* 31.

MacDonald, Struggle for Tenants Control, *IS* 33.

Tenants Take Over, *An* 83.

Tenants in Hackney, *IT* 65.

R. Bailey, Squatting, *IT* 66, Penguin forthcoming.

Sims, Squatters, *IS* 41.

Boston, Squatters, *NS* 6–3–69.

*Kent County Council v. The Homeless: The Story of King Hill Hostel*, *Sol* 10p.

*The Ilford Squatters Struggle*, Sol 3p.

Bailey, Mahony and Conn, *Evicted*, 15p from Campaign to Clear Hostels and Slums, 3 Osborn St, E1. (Story of the Redbridge Evictions)

A. Lapping, ed, *Community Action*, Fabian 1970.

# 9 Women's Liberation

## A General works

The first seven works are among the most important of those produced in the last year or two. Reiche is influenced by Freud and Marx; Reich's work is discussed in detail in works in 5C, which should be referred to for works on the family. See also 10.

K. Millett, *Sexual Politics*, Hart-Davis. (Includes discussion of Lawrence, Miller, Mailer and Genet; and see Mailer's counter-attack, *The Prisoner of Sex*.)

S. Firestone, *The Dialectic of Sex*, Cape.

G. Greer, *The Female Eunuch*, Panther 1971.

B. and T. Roszak, *Masculine/Feminine*, Harper & Row. (An anthology of readings)

E. Figes, *Patriarchal Attitudes: Women in Society*, Faber.

R. Morgan, ed, *Sisterhood is Powerful*, Vintage Books.

J. Mitchell, *Women's Estate*, Penguin 1971.

H. Gavron, *The Captive Wife*, Penguin 1968.

B. Friedan, *The Feminine Mystique*, Penguin 1965.

V. Klein, *The Feminine Character: History of an Ideology*, Routledge.

S. de Beauvoir, *The Second Sex*, Four Square.

S. de Beauvoir, *Nature of the Second Sex*, Four Square. (See also her autobiography; *Memoirs of a Dutiful Daughter*, *The Prime of Life* and *Force of Circumstance*, all Penguin)

R. Reiche, *Sexuality and Class Struggle*, NLB. (And see Fernbach's review, *NLR* 64.)

W. Reich, *The Sexual Revolution*, Farrar, Strauss & Giroux.

Also worth studying are novels, like Doris Lessing's *Golden Notebook*, plays, like Ibsen's *Doll's House* and Strindberg's *Dance of Death*, Virginia Woolf's *A Room of One's Own*, Penguin, and poems, e.g., those of Sylvia Plath.

The most influential anti-liberation tradition is that associated with the views of Freud, so it is worth studying his views of female sexuality: see *A Young Girl's Diary*, Allen & Unwin, *Three Essays on the Theory of Sexuality*, Hogarth, and The Psychology of Women, first chapter of *New Introductory Lectures on Psychoanalysis*, Hogarth.

## B History

This subsection includes some of the classic statements on women's rights, e.g. Mill and Wollstonecraft, and studies of the development of the movement, especially the Suffragettes.

J. S. Mill, *The Subjection of Women*, and M. Wollstonecraft, *A Vindication of the Rights of Women*, in one vol. from FP.

M. Wollstonecraft, *Essay on Women*, Everyman.

Marx, Engels and Lenin, *The Women Question*, IS Books, 50p.

F. Engels, *Origins of the Family, Private Property and the State*.

H. Draper, Marx and Engels on Women's Liberation, *IS* 44.
D. Mitchell, *Women on the Warpath*, Cape. (On Suffragettes)
M. Ramelson, *The Petticoat Rebellion: A Century of Struggle*, Lawrence & Wishart.
C. Rover, *Women's Suffrage and Party Politics*, Routledge.
C. Rover, *Love, Morals and the Feminists*, Routledge.
E. Thomas, *Women Incendiaries*, London 1967.
J. and O. Banks, *Feminism and Family Planning in Victorian England*, Liverpool University Press.
W. Neff, *Victorian Working Women*, Cass.
J. Cowley, *Pioneers of Women's Liberation*, IS Books, 10p.
E. Carpenter, *Love's Coming of Age*, Allen & Unwin.
T. Hodgkin, *Love and the Revolutionaries*.
A. Kollontai, *Communism and the Family*, London 1920.

## C Britain: economic, social and legal aspects

See also 5C, 8B, 30B.
J. Blackman, Equal Pay, *TUR* 1969 and 1970.
*Women Workers 1969*, TUC 13p.
V. Klein, *Britain's Married Women Workers*, Routledge.
A. Myrdal and V. Klein, *Women's Two Roles*, Routledge 1968.
M. Rendel, *Equality for Women*, Fabian.
C. Bird, *Born Female*, David McKay & Co. 1968.
S. Yudkin and A. Holme, *Working Mothers and their Children*, Sphere 1969.
R. Holman, *Unsupported Mothers and the Care of their Children*, Mothers in Action 1970.
D. Marsden, *Mothers Alone*, Allen Lane 1969.
P. Ferris, *The Nameless: Abortion in Britain Today*, Penguin 1968.
H. Richardson, *Adolescent Girls in Approved Schools*, Routledge 1969.
P. Pinder, *Women at Work*.
Women in Prison, *An* 113.
S. Gail, The Housewife, in R. Fraser, ed, *Work* vol. 1, Penguin 1968.
A. Cartwright, *Parents and the Family Planning Services*, Routledge 1970.
O. MacGregor, *Divorce in England*, Heinemann 1970.
NCCL, *Women*.
Potts, ed, *A Guide to the Abortion Act*, Abortion Law Reform Association 1967.
Raymond, *Every Woman's Lawyer*, Hutchinson 1965.
A. Reed, *The Woman on the Verge of Divorce*, Nelson 1970.
Sanctuary and Whitehead, *Divorce: And After*, Gollancz 1970.

## D Other cultures

Many of the items in subsections A and B are also relevant to the topics discussed here.
B. Whiting, ed, *Six Cultures: A Study of Child Rearing*, Wiley 1963.
R. Seers *et al.*, *Patterns of Child Rearing*, Harper & Row 1957.
E. Dahlstrom, *The Changing Roles of Man and Women*, Duckworth 1967.
M. Mead, *Male and Female*, Penguin 1962.
E. Evans-Pritchard, *The Position of Women in Primitive Societies and Other Essays*, Faber.
Lisenkova, *Soviet Women at Work*, International Labour Organization 1967.

H. Geiger, *The Family in Soviet Russia*, Harvard 1968.

M. and M. Vaerting, *The Dominant Sex, A study in the Sociology of Sex Differences*, Allen & Unwin, 1923. (A Marxist study of matriarchal societies)

L. Landy, *Women in the Chinese Revolution*, IS Books, 20p.

C. Young, *The Chinese Family in the Communist Revolution*.

W. Hinton, *Fanshen: A Documentary of Revolution in a Chinese Village*, MR Press and Merlin.

E. Reed, *The Myth of Women's Inferiority: Women's Role in Prehistoric Societal Development*, Ag and IS Books 9p.

Saraff and Mitchell, *Women in Revolution*, Socialist Revolution 4. B

**E  The movement**

Women's liberation journals like *Shrew, Socialist Women* and *Women's Newspaper* – the three that get widest circulation in this country – and *Women, a Journal of Liberation* – for the States – need to be consulted for current developments.

J. Mitchell, Women: The Longest Revolution, *NLR* 40, and IS Books and Ag 5p.

S. Rowbotham *Women's Liberation and the New Politics*, MDM and Ag 13p.

Benston and Rowntree, Debate on Women's Liberation, *MR* September 1969, and January 1970, Benston also from Ag 5p.

B. Jones and J. Brown, *Towards a Female Liberation Movement*, NEFP and Ag 5p.

E. Reed, *Problems of Women's Liberation*, IS Books, 43p.

G. Novack, *Revolutionary Dynamics of Women's Liberation*, IS Books, 10p.

Women in Revolution, special issue of *Women, a Journal of Liberation*, 1:4, 1970. (Includes articles on Asia, Cuba, Russian Revolution, Vietnam, French Revolution)

Towards a Rational Bisexuality, *An* 2:1, 1971.

V. Solanas, *SCUM Manifesto*, Olympia Press.

*The Bread and Roses Manifesto*, Ag 5p.

E. Cleaver, The Primeval Mitosis, in *Soul on Ice*, Panther.

A. Oakley, The Myth of Motherhood, *NS* 26.2.70.

D. Densmore, *Sex Roles and Female Oppression*, NEFP.

A. Koedt, *Myth of the Vaginal Orgasm*, NEFP and Ag 8p.

N. Weisstein, *Kinde, Kuche, Kirche as Scientific Law: Psychology Constructs the Female*, NEFP and Ag 5p.

# 10 Underground

## A Life style

Hoffman and Rubin give the Yippie viewpoint, and Quattrocchi represents Situationist influences (see also 5B). Nuttall is useful for the background to the movement in Britain, and Neville's work is a survey of the movement by a participant. Roszak is perhaps the least misleading book on the underground from outside. Mailer's essays have been influential, particularly the early *White Negro*. Berke, Kornbluth, and Hopkins are anthologies of articles, and excerpts from underground journals. See also 8D, 7, 13B, 30B.

A. Trocchi, *The Invisible Insurrection of a Million Minds*, City Lights.

A. Hoffman, *Revolution for the Hell of It*, Dial Press.

J. Rubin, *Do It*, Simon & Schuster and Cape.

J. Gerassi, Living the Revolution, *Oz* 21.

T. Nairn and A. Quattrocchi, *The Beginning of the End*, Panther, section by Quattrocchi. (On the French events)

T. Roszak, *The Making of a Counter-Culture*, Faber.

C. Reich, *The Greening of America*, Penguin 1972.

N. Mailer, *The White Negro*, City Lights, and reprinted with extra material in *Advertisements for Myself*, Panther.

N. Mailer, *Armies of the Night*, Penguin 1970.

*Bitman 3*, from BIT.

R. Neville, *Play power*, Paladin.

Widgery on Neville, *Oz* 26.

J. Nuttall, *Bomb Culture*, Paladin.

J. Berke, ed, *Counter-Culture*, Cape.

J. Hopkins, ed, *The Hippie Papers*, New American Library, Signet 1968.

J. Kornbluth, *Notes from the New Underground*, Viking Press 1968.

N. Polsky, *Hustlers, Beats and Others*, Penguin 1971.

R. Farquharson, *Drop Out*, Penguin 1971.

Mairovitz, ed, *Some of IT*, from IT, especially articles by Ginsberg (also in *IT* 7) and McGrath (also in *IT* 10).

S. Hall, American Hippies, in *SP* (N).

P. Buckman, *Limits of Protest*, Gollancz.

S. Krim, ed, *The Beats*.

T. Wolfe, *The Electric Kool-Aid Acid Test*, Weidenfeld & Nicolson. (On Kesey, the San Francisco Scene, hippies, drugs)

C. Tart, ed, *Altered States of Consciousness*, John Wiley.

*The Directory of Communes*, from BIT, 15p.

W. Hedgepath and D. Stock, *The Alternative*, Collier-Macmillan 1970. (On communes)

C. Gillett, *Sound of the City*, Outerbridge & Dienstfrey 1970.

J. Eisen, ed, *The Age of Rock*, Random House 1969.

D. Laing, *The Sound of Our Times*, Sheed & Ward.

N. Brown, *Love's Body*, Random House.

H. Marcuse on Brown, and reply by Brown, in *Commentary* 1967 and in Marcuse's *Negations*, Allen Lane 1968.

H. Marcuse, The New Sensibility, in his *Essay on Liberation*, Penguin 1972.
The movement has also produced important novels, usually semi-autobiographies, such as: J. Kerouac, *On the Road*, Penguin, and *Lonesome Traveller*, both Deutsch, and *The Dharma Bums*, Mayflower; K. Kesey, *Sometime a Great Notion*, Panther; L. Cohen, *Beautiful Losers*, Bantam; N. Mailer, *Why Are We in Vietnam?*, Weidenfeld & Nicolson. The most important poets are published by City Lights; see especially Ferlinghetti, Corso, Rexroth, McClure and of course Ginsberg, particularly his *Howl*, *America* and *Wichita Vortex Sutra*.

G. Steiner, The Retreat from the Word, in his *Language and Silence*, Penguin 1969.

G. Steiner, The Future of the Book: Classic Culture and Post Culture, *The Times Literary Supplement* 2–10–70.

V. Jasha, Electric Culture, *Oz* 27.

H. Blau, Relevance, *Daedalus* 1969.

Mottram, New Times and Space Structures, *IT* 60 and 62.

**B Drugs**

M. Schofield, *The Strange Case of Pot*, Penguin 1971.

A. Watts, *The Joyous Cosmology: Adventures in the Chemistry of Consciousness*, Panther.

R. DeRopp, *The Master Game: Beyond the Drug Experience*, Allen & Unwin.

D. Ebin, *The Drug Experience*, Grove Press.

R. Lingeman, *Drugs from A to Z: A Dictionary*, Allen Lane 1970.

G. Andrews and S. Vinkenoog, eds, *The Book of Grass*, Peter Owen.

J. Rosevear, *Pot*, Humphrey.

D. Soloway, *The Marijuana Papers*, Panther.

E. Bloomquist, *Marijuana*, Collier-Macmillan.

T. Leary, *The Politics of Ecstasy*, Paladin. (On LSD)

S. Cohen, *Drugs of Hallucination*, Paladin.

P. Stafford and B. Golightly, *LSD: The Problem-Solving Psychedelic*, Tandem Books.

A. Huxley, *The Doors of Perception*, Penguin 1959. (Mescalin)

C. Castaneda, *The Teachings of Don Juan*, Penguin 1970. (Peyote)

W. Burroughs, *Junkie*, New English Library. (Heroin)

C. Coon and R. Harris, *Release Report on Drugs*, Sphere.

P. Newmark, *Out of Your Mind?*, Penguin 1968.

# 11 British History

See also 9B, 12A, 12B, 14, 17A.

## A Background: problems of interpretation

The Anderson-Nairn thesis on the origins and character of the British working-class movement, and the ensuing debate, raised important issues of historical theory, particularly with regard to the relation of ideas to social structure, and the degree of autonomy of levels of the social system; see also 24B for further discussion.

Carr is a good elementary account of the nature of history, and Stedman Jones evaluates his and other English historians' views from a Marxist viewpoint. See also 1E.

P. Anderson, Origins of the Present Crisis, in *TS*.

T. Nairn, The Nature of the Labour Party, in *TS*.

T. Nairn, The English Working Class, *NLR* 24.

E. Thompson, Critique of the Anderson–Nairn Thesis, *SR* 1965.

P. Anderson, Reply to Thompson, *NLR* 35.

N. Poulantzas, The Anderson–Nairn–Thompson Debate, *NLR* 43.

G. Stedman Jones, English Historians, *NLR* 46.

E. Carr, *What is History?*, Penguin 1964.

R. Williams, *The Long Revolution*, Penguin 1965.

Barrington Moore, *Social Origins of Dictatorship and Democracy*, Penguin 1969.

## B Origins and development of the working-class movement

For Chartism, see the Merlin Press series of reprints, as well as the items below; and watch for the Ruskin History Workshop publications of studies of documents, from Ruskin College, Oxford.

E. Thompson, *The Making of the English Working Class*, Penguin 1968.

R. Harrison, *Before the Socialists: Labour and Politics 1861–81*, Routledge.

E. Hobsbawm, *Labouring Men*, Weidenfeld & Nicolson.

E. Hobsbawm and G. Rude, *Captain Swing*, Lawrence & Wishart.

E. Hobsbawm, *The Age of Revolution 1789–1848*, Mentor.

E. Hobsbawm, The Labour Aristocracy, in J. Saville, ed, *Democracy and the Labour Movement*.

E. Hobsbawm, General Labour Unions in Britain, *Economic History Review* 1949.

J. Harrison, *Robert Owen and the Owenites in Britain and America*, Routledge 1969.

M. Dobb, *Studies in the Development of Capitalism*, London 1946.

J. Saville, Primitive Accumulation and Early Industrialization, *SR* 1969.

R. Webb, *The British Working Class Reader, 1790–1848*, Allen & Unwin, 1955.

T. Nairn, Victorian Britain, *NLR* 60.

A. Briggs and J. Saville, eds, *Essays in Labour History*, Macmillan.

H. Collins and C. Abramsky, *Karl Marx and the British Labour Movement.*

F. Engels, *The Condition of the Working Class in 1844*, Panther.

K. Marx and F. Engels, *On Britain*, Moscow 1953.

E. Thompson, Time, Work Discontent and Industrial Capitalism, *P and P* 1967.

P. Thompson, Liberal Radicals and Labour in London, *P and P* 1964.

T. Rothstein, *From Charterism to Labourism.*

G. Lichtheim, *The Origins of Socialism*, Weidenfeld & Nicolson.

S. and B. Webb, *History of Trade Unionism*, Kelley.

R. Gammage, *History of the Chartist Movement*, Merlin. (By a participant)

R. Challinor and B. Ripley, *The Miners' Association, A Trade Union in the Age of the Chartists*, Lawrence & Wishart.

M. Hovell, *The Chartist Movement*, Manchester University Press.

P. Hollis, *The Pauper Press: A Study in Working Class Radicalism in the 1830s*, Oxford University Press.

Symposium on Chartism, *Bulletin of the Society for the Study of Labour History*, Spring 1970.

G. Stedman Jones, *Victorian London*, Oxford University Press 1971.

## C Twentieth century: unions and working-class struggle

Piratin, Murphy, Hannington are accounts by participants.

R. Page Arnot, *The Miners*, 3 vols. London 1949–61.

R. Page Arnot, *The South Wales Miners*, Allen & Unwin.

R. Page Arnot, *History of the Scottish Miners*, Allen & Unwin.

R. Gregory, *The Miners and British Politics 1906–14*, Oxford University Press.

J. Saville, The Background to Taff Vale, in his *Essays in Labour History*, Macmillan.

J. Lovell, *Stevedores and Dockers*, Macmillan. (To the First World War)

Phelps Brown, *The Growth of British Industrial Relations 1906–14*, Macmillan.

H. Clegg, A Fox and E. Thompson, *History of British Trade Unions, vol. 1, 1889–1910*, Oxford University Press.

B. Pribicevic, *The Shop Stewards' Movement and Workers' Control 1916–26*, Blackwell.

The Development of the Trade Union Bureaucracy, *IS* 48.

R. Bagwell, *The Railwaymen*, Allen & Unwin 1963.

R. Groves, *Sharpen the Sickle: History of the Agricultural Workers' Union*, Merlin.

R. Hyman, *The Workers' Union 1898–1929*, Oxford University Press.

J. Jefferies, *The Story of the Engineers.*

J. Symons, *The General Strike*, Cresset, London 1957.

G. Orwell, *The Road to Wigan Pier*, Penguin 1962.

P. Piratin, *Our Flag Stays Red*, Thames 1948.

J. Murphy, *New Horizons*, Lane 1941.

W. Hannington, *Unemployed Struggles*, 1936.

W. Hannington, *Never on our Knees*, Lawrence & Wishart.

V. Allen, The Centenary of the TUC, *SR* 1968.

R. K. Middlemas, *The Clydesiders*, Kelley.

W. Gallacher, *Revolt on the Clyde.*

B. Simon, *Education and the Labour Movement, 1870–1920*, Lawrence & Wishart.

K. Coates and T. Topham, ed, *Workers' Control*, Panther.

## D Twentieth century: political aspects of the labour movement

See also 12A, 12B.

R. Miliband, *Parliamentary Socialism*, Merlin. (An account of the development of the Labour Party and its ideology; the new edition brings it up to date)

W. Kendall, *Revolutionary Movements in Britain 1900–21*, Weidenfeld & Nicolson. (And see the review of it by Perkin, *Bulletin of the Society for the Study of Labour History* 1969)

L. MacFarlane, *The British Communist Party to 1929*, MacGibbon & Kee.

J. Klugman, *History of the Communist Party of Great Britain*, Lawrence & Wishart. (And see the very critical review by Hobsbawm, *NLR* 54)

G. Stedman Jones, The Unsolved 30s, *NLR* 36.

R. Dowse, *Left in the Centre*, Longman. (On the ILP)

P. Stansky, ed, *The Left and War – the British Labour Party and World War I*, Oxford University Press.

R. Page Arnot, *The Impact of the Russian Revolution in Britain*, Lawrence & Wishart.

D. Pritt, *The Labour Government 1945–51*, Lawrence & Wishart.

J. Lewis, *The Left Book Club*, Gollancz 1970.

W. Guttsman, *The British Political Elite*, MacGibbon & Kee.

R. Skidelsky, *Politicians and the Slump: Labour 1929–1931*, Penguin 1970.

Abrams, The Failure of Social Reform 1918–20, *P and P* 24.

M. Foot, *Aneurin Bevan*, vol. 1.

# 12 The British and American New Lefts

## A The British New Left

The first four items below trace the history and ideas of the New Left, and this is followed by two recent political manifestoes that continue the tradition. The last items describe the impact of CND and the reasons for its failure. Nuttall also includes scathing comments on New Left attitudes in general. See also 7A, 7B.

P. Sedgwick, The Two New Lefts, *IS* 17.

P. Anderson, The Left in the 50s, *NLR* 29.

R. Williams, The British Left, *NLR* 30.

Chapter on British New Left in *Rm*.

R. Williams, ed, *May Day Manifesto*, Penguin 1968.

K. Coates, ed, *Future for British Socialism?*, IWC 25p.

C. Driver, *The Disarmers*, Hodder.

P. Parkin, *Middle-Class Radicalism*, Manchester University Press.

J. Nuttall, *Bomb Culture*, Paladin.

## B The experience of Labour Government 1964–70

See also 8B, 19E and 19F (Southern Africa policy), and 1B, 3B, 7B, 11D, 13D, 14C, 14E.

P. Foot, *The Politics of Harold Wilson*, Penguin 1968.

R. Miliband, *Parliamentary Socialism*, Merlin, 1971 edition, last chapter.

T. Nairn, Enoch Powell and the New Right, *NLR* 61.

K. Coates, *The Crisis of British Socialism*, BRPF.

C. Harman, Tribune of the People, *IS* 21 and 24. (Attitudes of the Labour Left)

P. Anderson, Critique of Wilsonism, *NLR* 27.

R. Pryke, *Though Cowards Flinch*, MacGibbon & Kee. (On 1964–5 economic policies)

J. Saville, Labourism and Labour Government, *SR* 1970.

The Neustadt Dossier, *NLR* 51. (British Foreign Policy and its dependence on the US)

Gittings and Singh, *Vietnam Briefing*, CND 8p.

*Labour's Record on S. Africa*, H 13p.

G. Rosie, *The British in Vietnam*, Panther.

M. Christie, *The Simonstown Agreements*, Africa Bureau 15p.

N. Bosanquet, *Pay, Prices and Labour in Power*, Fabian, 1969.

## C The American New Left

The American New Left, and historians associated with it, have contributed to a far-reaching re-evaluation of American history, and the early items on the list are examples of this.

For related historical topics, see 13A, 13B, 17B, 14C.

For the influx of Black Power, see 13; the student movement, 7C; the Yippies, 10A (as well as below) and, for the Vietnam War, 21C and 21D.

W. A. Williams, *Contours of American History*, 1961.

B. Bernstein, ed, *Towards a New Past: Dissenting Essays in American History*, Chatto & Windus 1970.

American Radical History, symposium in *S and S*, Winter 1970.

G. Novack, *Essays in American History*, Merit.

E. Genovese, *Towards a New Past*.

L. Huberman, *We the People*, MR Press.

C. Lienenweber, Is American Socialism Unviable?, *ISJ* 1968.

M. Teodori, ed, *The New Left*, Cape. (Articles and documents)

P. Jacobs and S. Landau, eds, *The New Radicals*, Penguin 1967. (Documents and commentary)

C. Oglesby, ed, *The New Left Reader*, Grove Press.

*Beyond Dissent: Papers from the New Left*, Doubleday 1967.

N. Mailer, *Miami and the Siege of Chicago*, Penguin 1969.

N. Mailer, *Armies of the Night*, Penguin 1970.

Domhoff, *How to Commit Revolution in Corporate America*, Entwhistle-West, Goleta, California 1968.

I. Stone, *In a Time of Torment*, Random House 1968.

Aronson and Cowley, American New Left, *SR* 1967.

J. Newfield, *A Prophetic Minority*, Anthony Blond.

T. Hayden, *Rebellion in Newark*, Random House.

T. Gitlin, Organizing the Poor, in *Beyond Dissent*, Doubleday 1967.

M. Harrington, *The Other America*, Penguin 1963. (On poverty)

C. Wright Mills, Letter to the New Left, in *NLR* 1960 and *Studies on the Left* 1961.

C. Wright Mills, The New Left, in his *Power, Politics and People*, Ballantine 1963.

O'Brien, *Early Years of the New Left 1960–8*, REP and Ag 14p.

R. Stetler, ed, *Selected Writings and Documents of the Weathermen*, from Action Books and Ag.

T. Hayden, *The Trial*, Cape 1971.

# 13 Black Power

**A Exploitation and racism: development of the ghetto**

Included are historical works and analyses of the ghetto situation today. See also 3D, 19A, and for racism in social science, 1E.

E. Genovese, *The Political Economy of Slavery*, MacGibbon & Kee.

E. Genovese, *The World the Slaveholders Made*, Allen Lane 1970.

H. Aptheker, *Essays in the History of the American Negro*, Central Books.

H. Aptheker, *American Negro Slave Revolts*, International Publishers.

M. Duberman, ed, *The Anti-Slavery Vanguard*, Princeton University Press.

O. Cox, *Class, Caste and Race*, MR Press.

J. Davis, ed, *The American Negro Reference Book*, Prentice-Hall.

A. Rose, *The Negro in America*, Harper & Row.

H. Hill, Racial Practices of Organized Labour, *NP* 1965.

J. Kovel, *White Racism*, Allen Lane 1970.

J. Jacobson, ed, *The Negro Worker and the American Labour Movement*, Doubleday 1968.

E. Ofari, *The Myth of Black Capitalism*, MR Press.

P. Baran and P. Sweezy, *Monopoly Capital*, Penguin 1968, chapter 9.

K. Clark, *Dark Ghetto*, Gollancz.

W. Haddad and G. Pugh, eds, *Black Economic Development*, Prentice-Hall.

B. Gilbert, *Ten Blocks from the White House*, Praeger.

F. Halstead, *Harlem Stirs*, Merit.

T. Lowi, *The End of Liberalism*, Norton, chapter on the Ghetto.

R. Vernon, *Black Ghetto*, Red Books 20p.

L. Rainwater, *Behind Ghetto Walls: Black Families in a Federal Slum*, Allen Lane 1971.

The Ghetto, *S and S*, Spring 1969.

*The Kerner–Lindsay Report* on Civil Disorders.

J. Franklin, ed, *Colour and Race*, Beacon Press.

E. Frazier, *Black Bourgeoisie*, Collier-Macmillan.

J. Boggs, *The American Revolution: Pages from a Negro Worker's Notebook*, MR Press.

J. Boggs, *Racism and Class Struggle*, New York and London 1970.

**B Roots of Black Power**

This subsection traces the growth of black self-consciousness since slavery, and includes some outstanding novels, e.g. Styron, Wright, Ellison and the first Baldwin works by black leaders like Garvey, DuBois and Malcolm X, and works on the jazz and blues tradition. (See also 23B, 19A and 17B)

W. Styron, *The Confessions of Nat Turner*, New American Library.

J. Clarke, ed, *Styron's Nat Turner: 10 Black Writers Respond*, Boston 1968.

R. Wright, *Native Son*, Signet.

R. Wright, *Black Boy*, Harper & Row.

R. Ellison, *Invisible Man*, Penguin 1965.

R. Baldwin, *Another Country*, Corgi.

J. Baldwin, *The Fire Next Time*, Penguin 1964.

A. Garvey, ed, *The Philosophy and Opinions of Marcus Garvey*, Cass.

W. E. DuBois, *The Souls of Black Folk*, Fawcett Books.

W. Wilson, ed, *W. E. DuBois: Selected Writings*, Mentor.

H. Wish, ed, *The Negro Since Emancipation*, Prentice-Hall.

Malcolm X, *Autobiography*, Penguin 1968.

G. Breitman, ed, *Malcolm X Speaks*, IS Books 43p.

G. Breitman, *The Last Year of Malcolm X*, Merit.

A. Robinson, *Black Studies in the University*, Yale University Press.

LeRoi Jones, *The System of Dante's Hell*, MacGibbon & Kee. (Autobiography)

W. Grier and P. Cobb, *Black Rage*, Cape.

H. Cruse, *The Crisis of the Negro Intellectual*, Allen Lane.

C. Brown, *Manchild in the Promised Land*, Penguin 1969.

LeRoi Jones, *Blues People*, MacGibbon & Kee.

P. Oliver, *Story of the Blues*, Barrie and Rockcliffe 1969.

F. Kofsky, *Black Nationalism and the Revolution in Music*, Merit.
   (On Coltrane, Shepp, Ayler) (See also 28 H).

LeRoi Jones, *Black Music*, Morrow.

C. Keil, *Urban Blues*, University of Chicago 1968.

J.-P. Sartre, *Black Orpheus*, Gallimard 1963.

A. Cesaire, *Return to my Native Land*, Penguin 1969.

## C The Black Power movement

See also 10A, 12C.

E. Cleaver, *Soul on Ice*, Panther. (The unabridged version)

E. Cleaver, *Post-Prison Writings*, ed, Scheer, Cape.

G. Jackson, *Soledad Brother*, Penguin 1971. (Prison letters)

A. Davies, *If They Come in the Morning*, Orbach & Chambers, 1972.

F. Barbour, ed, *Black Power Revolt*, Collier-Macmillan.

G. Marine, *The Black Panthers: Cleaver, Newton, Seale*, Signet.

T. Cannon, *All Power to the People: Story of the Black Panthers*, Ag 25p.

S. Carmichael and C. Hamilton, *Black Power*, Penguin 1969.

R. Brown, *Die Nigger Die*.

B. Seale, *Seize the Time: A History of the Black Panthers*, Arrow 1970.

J. Lester, *Look Out Whitey, Black Power's Gonna Get Your Mama*,
   Allison & Busby.

R. Allen, *Guide to Black Power in America*.

Black Panther Program, *NLR* 56.

E. Essien-Udom, *Black Nationalism*, Penguin 1967.

Adler, Black Power, *SR* 1968.

A. Conot, *Rivers of Blood*, Bantam.

Marine, Persecution of Black Panthers, *Ramparts* 1968.

Boutelle, *Black Uprisings*, Red Books 15p.

**D Racism in Britain**

See also 8, 12B, 17A. The immigrant journals from the Black Panther Party, and the Black Freedom and Unity Party, such as *Black Voice* (also from Ag), should be used for current developments.

O. Egbuna, *Destroy this Temple*, MacGibbon & Kee.

D. Humphrey and G. John, *Because They're Black*, Penguin 1971.

P. Foot, *Immigration and Race in British Politics*, Penguin 1965.

B. Smithies, ed, *Powell on Immigration*, Sphere. (Powell's speeches)

R. Jenkins, *The Race Relations Industry*, Paladin.

J. Rex and R. Moore, *Race, Community and Conflict*, Oxford University Press. (On Sparkbrook)

N. Harris, Race and Nation, *IS* 34.

B. Hepple, *Race, Jobs and the Law in Britain*, 2nd edn, Penguin 1970.

P. Foot, *The Rise of Enoch Powell*, Penguin 1969.

*How the West Indian Child is made ESN in the British School System*, New Beacon Books and Ag 35p.

*Enoch Powell and West Indian Immigrants*, Afro-American and W. Indian Publications, Ag 40p.

A. Lester and G. Bindman, *Race and Law*, Penguin 1972.

# 14 Western Europe:
## Current Problems and Historical Background

See also 2B, for the Common Market, and 7D, for student movements.

### A History of the internationals

Works on the Commune of 1871 and the German Revolution of 1918–19 are also included. For the relevant works of Marx, see 24A, for Lenin, Luxemburg, Bernstein, Kautsky and their polemics in the 2nd International period, see 25, for Trotsky, 25C; and see also 11, 12C, 16, 29C, 29A.

J. Braunthal, *History of the Internationals*, Praeger.
C. Landauer, *History of European Socialism*, Berkeley and Los Angeles 1959.
F. Borkenau, *World Communism and History of the Communist International*,
Molner, *Le Déclin de la Première Internationale.*, Univ. of Michigan Press.
*Minutes of the General Council of the First International 1868–70*,
    Lawrence & Wishart.
H. Draper, ed, *Writings on the Paris Commune by K. Marx and F. Engels*, MR
    Press 1971.
F. Jellinek, *The Paris Commune of 1871*, Gollancz.
J. Joll, *The Second International*, Harper & Row.
*The Paris Commune of 1871*, University of Sussex.
J. Bruhat and J. Dautry, *La Commune de 1871*, Paris 1970.
A. Dansette, *Les Origines de la Commune de 1871.*
P. Lissagaray, *The Commune of 1871*, MR Press. (By a participant)
W. Abendroth, *Histoire du Mouvement Ouvrier en Europe*, Maspero.
C. Schorske, *German Social Democracy, 1905–17*, Russell.
R. Tökes, *Bela Kun and the Hungarian Soviet Republic*, Praeger.
A. Ryder, *The German Revolution of 1918*, Cambridge University Press.
C. Burdick and R. Lutz, *Political Institutions in the German Revolution, 1918–19*
    Praeger. (Includes documents)
A. Mitchell, *Revolution in Bavaria, 1918–19*, Princeton University Press.
    (On the Munich Soviet)
*From Spartakism to National Bolshevism, the KPD 1918–24*, Sol 10p.
E. Mandel, ed, *Fifty Years of World Revolution*, Merit.
C. James, *World Revolution 1917–36*.

### B Fascism

See also 11D, 29C, 25D, 25C.

L. Trotsky, *Fascism: What it is and how to fight it*, Red Books or IS Books.
L. Trotsky, Fascism, Stalinism and the United Front, 1930–34, *IS* 38–9.
W. Reich, *The Mass Psychology of Fascism*, Farrar, Strauss & Giroux.
J. Gammet, *Communist Theories of Fascism*.
G. Rees, *The Great Slump: Capitalism in Crisis, 1929–33*, Lawrence & Wishart.
    (For origins)

F. Neumann, *Behemoth*, Harper & Row.

E. Nolte, *Three Faces of Fascism*, Weidenfeld & Nicolson.

Q. Hoare, What is Fascism, *NLR* 31.

Symposium on Fascism, *Journal of Contemporary History* 1966.

A. Schweitser, *Big Business in the Third Reich*, Eyre & Spottiswoode.

D. Guerin, *Fascism and Big Business*.

D. Schoenbaum, *Hitler's Social Revolution*, Weidenfeld & Nicolson.

Mason, Labour in the Third Reich, *P and P* 1966.

O'Lessker, Who Voted for Hitler, *American Journal of Sociology* 1968–9.

G. Solverini, *Under the Axe of Fascism*.

F. Chabod, *History of Italian Fascism*, Weidenfeld & Nicolson.

## C NATO and the Cold War

For other material on American Policy, see 12C, 17B, 17C, 18A, 21C and 21D and for Soviet policy in E. Europe, 15C.

D. Horowitz, *From Yalta to Vietnam*, Penguin 1969.

D. Horowitz, ed, *Corporations and the Cold War*, M R Press.

E. Cerquetti, *What is NATO?*, Stage 1, forthcoming.

G. Alperovitz, *Atomic Diplomacy: Hiroshima and Potsdam*, Simon & Schuster.

I. Stone, *The Hidden History of the Korean War*, M R Press.

J. Morray, *From Yalta to Disarmament, The Cold War Debate*, Merlin.

The Neustadt Dossier, *NLR* 51. (The subservience of British foreign policy to American)

G. Kolko, *The Politics of War*, Weidenfeld & Nicolson. (A history of the last thirty years)

T. Draper, *Abuse of Power: U.S. Foreign Policy from Cuba to Vietnam*, Penguin 1969.

A. Fontaine, *History of the Cold War*, Secker & Warburg.

D. Fleming, *The Cold War and its Origins*, Doubleday.

D. Horowitz, ed, *Containment and Revolution*, Anthony Blond, especially article by I. Deutscher, Origins of the Cold War.

I. Deutscher, *Russia, China and the West*, Penguin 1970.

## D Ireland

J. Connolly, *Labour in Irish History*, IS Books 18p.

J. Connolly, *Labour in Ireland*, IS Books.

J. Connolly, *Workers' Republic*, IS Books and Red Books.

E. Strauss, *Irish Nationalism and British Democracy*, 1951. (A Marxist history)

D. O'Connor Lyseaght, *The Republic of Ireland*, 1970. (A Marxist history)

Lynch, The Social Revolution that Never Was, in Williams, ed, *The Irish Struggle 1916–26*.

T. Jackson, *Ireland Her Own*, Lawrence & Wishart. (Historical)

D. Greaves, *The Life and Times of J. Connolly*, London 1961.

*The Working Class in the Irish National Revolution 1916–23*, Ag 13p.

E. Larkin, *James Larkin*, London 1965.

T. Coogan, *The IRA*, London 1970.

F. MacManus, *The Years of the Great Test, 1926–39*.

D. O'Connor Lyseaght, *The Making of N. Ireland*, Red Books 15p.

M. Farrell, *Struggle in the North*, IS Books 10p.

Symposium on Ulster, *NLR* 55.

Gray and Palmer, Ulster, *IS* 36.

Egan and McCormack, *Berntollet*, Ag and Red Books 50p. (The story of the ambush of a civil rights march)

R. Stetler, *The Battle of Bogside*, Sheed & Ward.

A. Boyd, *Holy War in Belfast*, Anvil Books.

L. de Paor, *Divided Ulster*, Penguin 1971.

C. Goulding, The IRA, *NLR* 64.

D. Greaves, *The Irish Question 1971: The Northern Ireland Dictatorship after Fifty Years*, Lawrence & Wishart.

B. Devlin, *Price of My Soul*, rev ed. 1971.

## E The May Events: Paris 1968

Any of the first five or so items could be used as introductions to the issues raised by the French events, but probably Willener is most sensitive to the ideas and activities of the participants. Many of the documents remain untranslated. See also 5B, 7, 10A.

A. Willener, *The Action-Image of Society*, Tavistock.

H. Lefebvre, *The Explosion: Marxism and the French Upheaval*, MR Press.

A. Quattrocchi and T. Nairn, *The Beginning of the End*, Panther.

T. Cliff and I. Birchall, *France: The Struggle Goes On*, IS Books 15p.

D. Singer, *Prelude to Revolution: France in May 1968*, Cape.

H. Bourges, ed, *The Student Revolt*, Panther. (Interviews and documents)

P. Seale and M. McConville, *French Revolution 1968*, Penguin 1968.

J. Gretton, *Students and Workers*, MacDonald.

*Paris May 1968*, Sol 5p. (Eyewitness account)

Symposium on the French Events, *NLR* 52.

C. Posner, ed, *Reflections on the Revolution in France 1968*, Penguin 1970.

*Lessons of May*, MDM 13p.

Coates, French Communist Party, *IS* 32.

The May Events, *An* 89

Gross, The May Events, in *SP* (N).

Hoyles, French Workers, in *TUR* 1969.

Gombin, France 1968, in *Government and Opposition* 5:4. (On Anarchist influences)

J. Pesquet, *Soviets at Saclay?*, Stage 1.

*Renault Strike at Flins*, Stage 1.

Nanterre Documents, *Esprit* May 1968.

S. Zegel, *Les Idées de Mai*, Gallimard 1968.

Y. Guin, *La Commune de Nantes*, Mospero.

A. Barjonet, *La Révolution Trahie de 1968*, Didier 1968.

A. Touraine, *Le Mouvement de Mai ou le Communisme Utopique*, Le Seuil 1968.

E. Morin *et al.*, *Mai 1968: La Brèche*, Fayard.

The Workers in May, *Sociologie du Travail* 12:3, 1969.

Autogestion et la Revolution de Mai, *Autogestion* 5–6, 1968.

D. Bensaid and H. Weber, *Mai 1968: Une Répétition Générale*, Cahiers Libres, Maspero.

Mouvement du 22 Mars, *Ce n'est qu'un Debut: Continuons le Combat*, Cahiers Libres, Maspero 1968.

# 15 The Structure of Eastern European Society

## A Social structure: problems of analysis

Kuron and Modzelewski, and Cliff, analyse these societies in terms of 'state capitalism': Trotsky analysed the Soviet Union as a 'degenerated' workers' state, and this kind of analysis, although amended and extended, is used by Fourth International theorists like Mandel. Analyses in terms of managerialism and bureaucracy, e.g. by Shachtman and Djilas, bring the discussion closer to the debate in orthodox sociology over the 'convergence' of industrial societies; see Weinberg for a review of this, and also Worsley, Goldthorpe, and other material, in 1A. For Trotsky, see 16C and 25C, and for rival analyses of the Russian Revolution, 16B and 16C. Later items in this list include empirical studies of the extent and nature of social stratification in these societies.

Kuron and Modzelewski, *A Revolutionary Communist Manifesto*, IS Books 23p. (An analysis of Polish and Eastern Europe society)

T. Cliff, *Russia: A Marxist Analysis*, IS Books.

H. Marcuse, *Soviet Marxism*, Penguin 1971.

E. Mandel, *The Inconsistencies of State Capitalism*, Red Books 20p.

M. Shachtman, *The Bureaucratic Revolution*, IS Books.

T. Cliff, A Critique of Bureaucratic Collectivism, *IS* 32. (On Shachtman, etc.)

M. Djilas, *The New Class*, Allen & Unwin.

M. Djilas, *The Unperfect Society: Beyond the New Class*, Methuen.

Djordjevic, *Bureaucracy and Bureaucratism*, Belgrade 1962.

S. Mallet, *Bureaucracy and Technocracy in the Socialist Countries*, BRPF 10p, and *Sp* 7–8.

I. Deutscher, Roots of Bureaucracy, *SR* 1969.

Weinberg, Convergence: The State of a Theory, *Comparative Studies in Society and History*, 1969.

Wesolowski, Social Stratification in Socialist Society, *Polish Sociological Bulletin* 1967.

Inkeles, Feldmesser and Bauman, articles on Social Stratification in the USSR and Poland, in *CS and P*.

F. Parkin, *Class, Inequality and the Political Order*, MacGibbon & Kee, chapter 5.

P. Wiles and S. Markowski, Income Distribution under Communism and Capitalism, *Soviet Studies* 1971.

F. Parkin, Class Stratification in Socialist Societies, *BJS* 1969.

## B The planning experience

Lange, Dobb and Horvat outline the theory and practice of planning, from a perspective basically sympathetic to the regimes. For more critical discussions, see Kuron, Cliff and Mandel, above, and Kendall, Sharman and McAuley, below, also subsection E. See also 27 and 16D.

C. Bettelheim, *La Transition vers L'Economie Socialiste*, translation forthcoming from MR Press.

C. Bettelheim and P. Sweezy, Transition between Socialism and Capitalism, *MR* 1969.

B. Horvat, *Towards a Theory of the Planned Economy*, International Arts and Sciences Press.

O. Lange, *On the Economic Theory of Socialism*, McGraw Hill 1964.

O. Lange, *Essays in Economic Planning*, Asia Publishing House.

M. Dobb, *Essay on Economic Growth and Planning*, Routledge.

M. Dobb, *On Economic Theory and Socialism*, Routledge.

Sharman, Marxist Economics and Soviet Planning, *Soviet Studies* 1966–7.

McAuley, Rationality and Central Planning, *Soviet Studies* 1966–7.

J. Wilczynski, *Economics of Socialism*, Allen & Unwin 1970.

W. Kendall, The Breakdown of Stalinist Socialism, *NP* 1970.

O. Sik, Socialist Market Relations and Planning, in C. Feinstein, ed, *Socialism, Capitalism and Economic Growth*, Cambridge University Press. (An analysis by the Czech reform economist)

M. Dobb, *Socialist Planning: Some Problems*, LL 35p.

M. Dobb, Economic Reform in Socialist Countries, *MT* 1969.

J. Felker, *Soviet Economic Controversies: The Emerging Marketing Concept and Changes in Planning, 1960–5*, MIT 1966.

## C Ideology and Soviet imperialism

Included are studies of Soviet ideology and the reality of Soviet domination in Eastern Europe; several works on the Hungarian Revolution are included, Anderson being the most reliable. For the background to the Cold War, see 14C and 16C.

H. Marcuse, *Soviet Marxism*, Penguin 1971.

I. Deutscher, Ideological Trends in the USSR, *SR* 1968.

J.-P. Sartre, *The Spectre of Stalin*, Hamish Hamilton. (On Soviet ideology and the invasion of Hungary)

N. Harris, Soviet Ideology, *Soviet Studies* 1966–7, and chapter 5 of his *Beliefs in Society*, New Thinkers Library.

Chambre, Ideology, *Soviet Studies* 1966–7.

Y. Gluckstein, *Stalin's Satellites in Europe*, Allen & Unwin, 1952.

C. Harman, Stalinist States: Prospects for the 70s, *IS* 42.

Korey, The Brezhnev Doctrine, *PC* 1969.

N. Bethell, *Gomulka: His Poland and His Communism*, Longman.

L. Labedz, ed, *Revisionism*, Library of International Studies, chapters on Eastern Europe.

A. Anderson, *Hungary 1956*, Sol 18p.

P. Fryer, *Hungarian Tragedy*, Dobson 1956.

G. Mikes, *Hungarian Revolution*, Deutsch 1957.

J.-J. Marie, ed, *Pologne-Hongrie 1956*, Etudes et Documentations, Maspero. (Documents)

I. Nagy, *On Communism: In Defence of the New Course*, Thames & Hudson 1957.

## D Czechoslovakia 1968

Included are background works on the crisis, documents from the Czech reformers and from the 'Left Opposition' (some members of which were recently imprisoned), and accounts of the invasion (mainly descriptive).

J. Pelikán, ed, *The Secret Vysocany Congress*, Allen Lane. (The 1968 writers' congress)

D. Hamsik, *Writers Against Rulers*, Hutchinson. (The 1967 writers' congress that precipitated Novotny's fall)

D. Kubat, Social Mobility in Czechoslovakia, *American Sociological Review* 1963.

O. Sik, Czechoslovakia's New System of Economic Planning and Management, *Eastern European Economics*, 1965. (A statement by the Czech reform economist; see also subsection B)

R. Selucky, *Czechoslovakia: The Plan that Failed*.

R. Littell, ed, *The Czech Black Book*, Pall Mall.

Czech Communist Party, *Action Programme of 1968*, BRPF 10p.

H. Lunghi and P. Ello, eds, *Dubcek's Blueprint for Freedom*, Kimber. (His speeches and writings)

Richta and Klein, *Civilisation at the Crossroads*, Czech Academy of Sciences. (Aims and plans of the reformers)

K. Coates, ed, *Czechoslovakia and Socialism*, BRPF.

R. James, ed, *Czech Crisis*, Weidenfeld & Nicolson.

Windsor and Roberts, *Czechoslovakia 1968*, Chatto & Windus.

Z. Zeman, *Prague Spring: Report on Czechoslovakia 1968*, Penguin 1969.

A. Osley, *Free Communism: A Czech Experiment*, Fabian.

M. Johnstone, Czechoslovakia, *SR* 1969.

Golan, Youth and Politics in Czechoslovakia, *Journal of Contemporary History* 1970.

The Czech Crisis, *PC* November 1968, and July 1969.

Krahl, Czechoslovakia, *NLR* 53. (An attempt at class analysis, and includes a student document)

Les Conseils Ouvriers de Tchécoslovaquie, *Autogestion* 11–12, Maspero and LL.

H. Schwartz, *Prague 200 Days*, Pall Mall.

J. Pelikán, ed, *The Czechoslovak Political Trials 1950–4*, Macdonald. *Socialism Lives in Czechoslovakia*, from the Czech Socialist Movement, BRPF 5p.

*Revolutionary Socialist Party Manifesto*, Red Books 4p.

The Piller Document: Show Trials of the 1950s, *Sunday Times* 1–3–70.

**E Yugoslav Workers' Self-Management**

Horvat and Bilandzic give 'official' Yugoslav viewpoints on the nature of the workers' self-management experiment; Mandel, Sweezy, Sayers, and King give criticisms from the left of the theoretical assumptions behind the development, as well as its practice; Riddell is a good general account. On workers' control, see also 3C, 16C, 29C.

B. Horvat, Workers' Management in Yugoslavia, *Journal of Political Economy* 1967. (See also subsection B)

D. Bilandzic, *Management of the Yugoslav Economy 1945–66*, Belgrade.

E. Mandel, Yugoslav Economic Theory, *MR* 1967. (On Horvat)

P. Sweezy and L. Huberman, Peaceful Transition from Socialism to Capitalism?, *MR* 1964.

A. Sayers, Yugoslavia, *IS* 41.

McFarlane, Yugoslavia at the Crossroads, *SR* 1966.

J. King, Economics of Self-Management, *Sol* 6:4, 1970.

F. Singleton, Workers' Self-Management and the Role of the Unions in Yugoslavia, *TUR* 1970.

F. Singleton, Labour Relations in Yugoslavia, *Sp* 1970.

D. Riddell, Social Self-Government: Yugoslav Socialism, *BJS* 1968.

R. Moore, *Self Management in Yugoslavia*, Fabian 1969.

A. Meister, *Socialisme et Autogestion*, Le Seuil 1964.

A. Meister, Diffusion et Concentration du Pouvoir dans une Commune Yougoslave, *Revue Francaise des Sciences Politiques*, 1964.

A. Waterston, Planning in Yugoslavia, Johns Hopkins.

Bajt, Income Distribution under Workers' Self-Management in Yugoslavia, in A. Ross, ed, *Industrial Relations and Economic Development*, Macmillan.

Sefer, Income Distribution in Yugoslavia, *International Labour Review* 1968.

J. Kolaja, *Workers' Councils: The Yugoslav Experience*, Tavistock.

*Workers' Self-Management in Yugoslavia*, International Labour Organization, 1962.

F. Singleton and T. Topham, *Workers' Control in Yugoslavia*, Fabian 1963 10p.

Deleon, Workers' Management, *Annals of Collective Economy*, 1959.

Economic Reform in Yugoslavia, *Planning*, July 1968.

Neal and Fisk, Yugoslavia: Towards a Market Society, *PC* 1966.

# 16 The USSR: History and Current Situation

## A Origins of the Revolution

See also 25A.

V. Lenin, *The Development of Capitalism in Russia*. (His most important work on the topic, but see also 25A)

S. Baron, *Plekhanov and the Origins of Russian Marxism*, Routledge.

F. Venturi, *Roots of Revolution*, Knopf.

D. Lane, *Roots of Russian Communism*, Humanities Press. (A sociological account)

L. Haimson, *Russian Marxists and the Origins of Bolshevism*, Oxford University Press.

J. Keep, *The Rise of Social Democracy in Russia*, Oxford University Press.

G. Robinson, *Rural Russia under the Old Regime*, Macmillan 1949.

A. Yarmolinsky, *Road to Revolution*, Cassell 1957.

von Laue, Legal Marxism and the Fate of Capitalism in Russia, *Review of Politics* 1956.

Rimhinger, Autocracy and the Factory Order in Early Industrialisation, *Journal of Economic History* 1960.

Rimhinger, The Management of Labour Protest 1870–1905, *International Review of Social History* 1960.

A. Avtorkhanov, Lenin and the Bolshevik Rise to Power, *Studies on the Soviet Union* 1970.

## B The Revolution

Many of the disputes over the nature and significance of the Revolution are discussed in the next subsection. Many of Lenin's works of the period are essential reading, such as *The April Theses* and *Will the Bolsheviks Retain State Power?*. See also 25, 28D. Hill, Wolfe or Wilson could be used as introductions, Carr is the main scholarly account. Serge, Trotsky and Lunacharsky are accounts by participants, and Reed is an eyewitness description.

D. Shub, *Lenin*, Penguin 1966.

C. Hill, *Lenin and the Russian Revolution*, Penguin 1971.

E. Carr, *The Bolshevik Revolution 1917–23*, Penguin 1966, 3 vols.

B. Wolfe, *Three Who Made a Revolution*, Penguin 1966.

E. Wilson, *To the Finland Station*, Fontana.

J. Reed, *Ten Days that Shook the World*, Penguin 1966.

L. Trotsky, *History of the Russian Revolution*, Sphere.

A. Lunacharsky, *Revolutionary Silhouettes*, Allen Lane 1967.

V. Serge, *Memoirs of a Revolutionary*, Oxford University Press.

J. Higgins, 1917: Lenin and the Workers, *IS* 30.

W. Chamberlin, *The Russian Revolution*, Grosset & Dunlap.

The Main Groups and Individuals of 1917, *PC* November 1967.
*First Decrees of Soviet Power, 1917–18*, Lawrence & Wishart.
Dossier sur Lénine et les Soviets, *Autogestion* 4, 1967.
R. Luxemburg, *The Russian Revolution*, Ann Arbor 1961.

## C Since the Revolution

The Revolution and later developments such as the Kronstadt rebellion of 1921, the 'Left Opposition', and Stalin's rise to supreme power, are discussed from conflicting points of view: Berkman, Voline, Rosenberg and Mett give anarchist interpretations; Kollontai gives a 'Left Opposition' analysis, Serge is rather closer to the Bolshevik line; Daniels is the best discussion of the Left Opposition; Brinton and Cardan document the dictatorial nature of the Soviet state from the beginning; Trotsky sees the Revolution as 'degenerating' through the ossification of the party elite into a bureaucratic clique, and Harman is quite close to this analysis. See also 25C, for Trotsky.

R. Daniels, *The Conscience of the Revolution*, Oxford University Press.
A. Berkman, The Bolshevik Myth, London 1925, the chapter on Kronstadt is also in I. Horowitz, ed, *Anarchism*, Dell 1967.
Voline, *The Unknown Revolution*, FP 1955.
A. Rosenberg, *History of Bolshevism*, Russell & Russell, 1955.
I. Mett, *Kronstadt*, Sol 13p.
A. Kollontai, *Workers' Opposition*, Sol 15p.
V. Serge, *Kronstadt*, Sol 5p.
M. Brinton, *The Bolsheviks and Workers' Control 1917–21*, Sol 25p.
P. Cardan, *From Bolshevism to the Bureaucracy*, Sol 3p.
C. Harman, How the Revolution Was Lost, *IS* 30 and Ag and IS Books 7p.
L. Trotsky, *The Revolution Betrayed*, New Park.
L. Trotsky, *The New Course*, New Park.
E. Carr, *The Interregnum, 1923–4*, Penguin 1969.
E. Carr, *Socialism in One Country, 1924–6*, Penguin 1970, 2 vols.
E. Carr, *Foundations of the Planned Economy, 1926–9*, Macmillan.
E. Carr, Revolution from Above, *NLR* 46.
I. Deutscher, *Stalin*, Penguin 1966.
I. Deutscher, *The Prophet Outcast: Trotsky*, Oxford University Press.
I. Deutscher, *The Unfinished Revolution 1917–67*, Oxford University Press.
M. Dobb, *Soviet Economic Development since 1917*, Routledge.
A. Erlich, *The Soviet Industrialisation Debate 1924–8*, Harvard University Press.
M. Lewin, *Russian Peasants and Soviet Power*, Allen & Unwin.
M. Dewar, *Labour Policy in the USSR, 1917–28*.
R. and B. Laird, *Soviet Communism and Agrarian Revolution*, Penguin 1970.
L. Huberman and P. Sweezy, eds, *Fifty Years of Soviet Power*, MR Press.
A. Rosmer, *Moscou Sous Lénine*, translation forthcoming from Pluto Press.
E. Mandel, ed, *Fifty Years of World Revolution*, Pathfinder Press.

## D Current economic and political situation

For discussions of Soviet ideology, and policies in Eastern Europe, see 15C and 15D; for more on planning and the economic changes, 15B.
Ellman, Soviet Economic Reforms, *SR* 1968.
Ticktin, Economic Developments in the USSR, *SR* 1968.

Soviet Economic Reforms, *MR* January 1967.

Kabaj, The Evolution of Incentives in Soviet Industry, *International Labour Review* 1966.

Ivanov, Education and Class in the USSR today, *IS* 30.

Armstrong, Party Bifurcation and Elite Interest, *Soviet Studies* 1966–7. (The sociological background to Khruschev's fall)

D. Lane, *Politics and Society in the USSR*, Weidenfeld & Nicolson 1970.

C. Harman, Stalinist States: Prospects for the 70s, *IS* 42.

E. Varga, Political Testament, *NLR* 62. (The view of a Hungarian adviser to the Soviet regime)

### E Protest

Solzhenitsyn, Serge and Tarsis are novels, and Marchenko is an account of prison camp life. Note: some of the material from the underground writers reached the West in ways that cast doubt on its full authenticity, so the material should be used with care. See also 15C, 15D.

A. Solzhenitsyn, *The First Circle*, Collins.

A. Solzhenitsyn, *Cancer Ward*, Penguin 1971.

A. Solzhenitsyn, *One Day in the Life of Ivan Denisovich*, Penguin 1963.

V. Serge, *The Case of Comrade Tulayev*, Penguin 1968.

V. Serge, *Birth of our Power*, Penguin 1970.

V. Tarsis, *Ward 7*, Collins.

A. Marchenko, *My Testimony*, Penguin 1971.

R. Blackburn, Solzhenitsyn's Politics, *NLR* 63.

T. Deutscher, Soviet Fabians, *NLR* 62.

M. Scammell, ed, *Russia's Other Writers*, Longman.

R. Medvedev, *Faut-il Réhabiliter Staline*, Le Seuil 1969.

Protest Documents and Commentary, *PC* 1968, 2 vols.

A. Tertz (= Sinyavsky), *The Trial Begins: On Socialist Realism*, Random House.

E. Ginzburg, *Into the Whirlwind*, Penguin 1968.

L. Labedz, ed, *Solzhenitzsyn: A Documentary Record*, Penguin 1972.

# 17 Imperialism and Underdevelopment

More on the economic background can be found in 2A and 2C. See also 27D for the Marxist theory of imperialism, and 27A and B for Marxist theories of growth and economic planning. See 23A for material on the peasantry.

## A British imperialism

Hobsbawm's book is an introductory historical account, and Barratt Brown looks at the contemporary situation. Hobson is a classic study originally written in 1902. See also 12B, 14D, and 19A, 19B.

E. Hobsbawm, *Industry and Empire*, Penguin 1969.

E. Hobsbawm, Crisis of the Seventeenth Century, *P and P* 5–6. (The old and new colonial systems)

J. Hobson, *Imperialism*, Allen & Unwin 1938.

C. Bodelsen, *Studies in Mid-Victorian Imperialism*, Fertig.

B. Semmel, *Imperialism and Social Reform*, Allen & Unwin. (The Fabians and imperialism)

E. Platt, British Policy during the New Imperialism, *P and P* 39.

Gallagher and Robinson, *Africa and the Victorians*, Macmillan.

T. Rothstein, *British Foreign Policy and its Critics 1830–1950*, Lawrence & Wishart.

E. Williams, *Capitalism and Slavery*, Deutsch.

H. Wright, ed, *The New Imperialism*, in Problems of European Civilization, Heath & Co.

J. Saville, Review of Rostow's *British Economy in the Nineteenth Century*, in *P and P* 6.

M. Dobb, *Studies in the Development of Capitalism*, Routledge.

M. Barratt Brown, *After Imperialism*, Merlin.

J. Strachey, *End of Empire*, Gollancz.

## B American imperialism

These works are mainly by 'New Left' American historians seeking to destroy the conventional myths about America's history and role in the world; the Stedman Jones article is a survey of the discussion. See also 12C, 14C. Wise, Tully and Blackstock give information on CIA activities.

G. Kolko, *Roots of American Foreign Policy*, Beacon 1969.

W. Williams, *The Contours of American History*, M R Press 1961.

W. Williams, *Roots of the Modern American Empire*, Random House.

B. Bernstein, ed, *Towards a New Past: Dissenting Essays in American History*, Chatto & Windus.

G. Stedman Jones, Specificity of American Imperialism, *NLR* 60.

R. van Alstyne, *The Rising American Empire*, Blackwell 1960.

W. LaFeber, *The Empire: An Interpretation of American Expansion 1860–98*, Thomas Allen, Toronto.

T. Draper, *Abuse of Power: US Foreign Policy from Cuba to Vietnam*, Penguin 1969.

C. Oglesby and R. Shaull, *Containment and Change*, Collier-Macmillan.

R. Barnet, *Intervention and Revolution: The US in the Third World*, Meridian Books 1969.

D. Horowitz, ed, *Containment and Revolution*, Anthony Blond.

G. Domhoff, Who Made American Foreign Policy 1945–63 ? in D. Horowitz, ed, *The Corporations and the Cold War*, M R Press.

A. Aguilar, *Pan Americanism from Monroe to the Present*, M R Press.

S. Nearing and J. Freeman, *Origins of Dollar Diplomacy*, M R Press.

V. Perlo, *American Imperialism*, International Publishers 1951.

D. Wise and T. Ross, *Invisible Government*, Random House 1965.

A. Tully, *The CIA: The Inside Story*, Barker.

P. Blackstock, *The Strategy of Subversion*, Quadrangle.

*The CIA as an Equal Opportunity Employer*, A R G and Ag 13p.

R. Gott, *Guevara, Debray and the CIA*, R E P and Ag and L L 9p.

Ray, The CIT and Che, *Ramparts* 1968.

## C Underdevelopment and exploitation

These works describe the operation of imperialism: Magdoff, Jenkins and Jalée present detailed surveys, and Hayter concentrates on exposing the real nature of foreign 'aid'. They also attack the assumptions of the orthodox sociology and economics of underdevelopment; the articles by Frank, Dennon, Rhodes and Abdel-Malek concentrate specifically on this. See also 1E, 2.

H. Magdoff, *The Age of Imperialism*, MR Press, also in several issues of *M R*, vol. 20.

R. Kuper, Review of Magdoff, *IS* 45.

E. Laclau, Feudalism and Capitalism in Latin America, *NLR* 67.

H. Alavi, New Forms of Imperialism, *S R* 1964.

R. Jenkins, *Exploitation*, Paladin 1970.

T. Hayter, *Aid as Imperialism*, Penguin 1971.

R. Rhodes, ed, *Imperialism and Underdevelopment: A Reader*, M R Press.

R. Dumont, *Lands Alive*, M R Press.

D. Horowitz, *Imperialism and Underdevelopment*, Allen Lane.

O'Connor, International Corporations and Underdevelopment, *S and S* 1970.

F. Greene, *The Enemy: Notes on Imperialism and Revolution*, Cape.

P. Jalée, *L'Imperialisme en 1970*.

P. Jalée, *The Pillage of the Third World*, M R Press.

P. Jalée, *The Third World in the World Economy*, M R Press.

R. Mason, *Patterns of Dominance*, Oxford University Press 1970.

J. Woddis, *Introduction to Neo-Colonialism*, London 1967.

A R G, *International Dependency in the 70s*, Ag 30p.

J.-P. Sartre, Introduction to F. Fanon, *The Wretched of the Earth*, Penguin 1967.

*The Rockefeller Empire*, N A C L A and Ag, 50p.

A. Frank, The Sociology of Development and the Underdevelopment of Sociology, in *Catalyst* 1967, and in his *Latin America: Underdevelopment or Revolution*, M R Press, and from Pluto Press, 20p.

Dennon, Political Science and Development, *S and S* 1969.

A. Abdel-Malek, Orientalism in Crisis, *Diogenes* 1963.

R. Rhodes, Disguised Conservatism in Evolutionary Development Theory, *S and S* 1968.

M. Dobb, *Economic Growth and the Underdeveloped Countries*, International Publishers.

G. Myrdal, *Economic Theory and the Underdeveloped Regions*, Duckworth 1957.

### D Anthropology

These works criticize the methods and assumptions of anthropologists. For works on Structuralism, and the Asiatic mode of production, see 24B and 24D. See also 1E.

D. Goddard, Limits of British Anthropology, *NLR* 58.

J. Banaji, Crisis of British Anthropology, *NLR* 64.

K. Gough, World Revolution and the Science of Man, in *DA*, and in *MR* 1968, in modified form.

E. Leach, The Epistemological Background to Malinowski's Empiricism, in R. Firth, ed, *Man and Culture*, Routledge 1957.

P. Worsley, The Analysis of Rebellion and Revolution in British Social Anthropology, *S and S* 1961.

C. Lévi-Strauss, *Race and History*, UNESCO.

C. Lévi-Strauss, *Structural Anthropology*, Allen Lane 1968, chapters 1, 15, 16.

C. Lévi-Strauss, *World on the Wane*, London 1961. (The destruction of primitive cultures by Western imperialism)

P. Worsley, *The Trumpet Shall Sound*, Paladin. (Cargo cults as a reaction to the incursion of colonial power)

E. Leach, Virgin Birth, in his *Genesis as Myth and Other Essays*, Cape.

# 18 Latin America

## A General analyses

These works document the effects of American economic penetration in the continent; Frank and Petras are thorough recent studies. Gott provides the most comprehensive survey of the revolutionary movements. See also 17B, 17C, 2, 23D, 7D.

A. Frank, *Latin America: Underdevelopment or Revolution*, MR Press 1970.

J. Petras, *Politics and Social Structure in Latin America*, MR Press 1970.

R. Gott, Guerrilla Movements in Latin America.

I. Horowitz *et al.*, *Latin American Radicalism*. (Documents)

J. Petras and M. Zeitlin, eds, *Latin America: Reform of Revolution*, Fawcett World Library.

A. Aguilar, *Latin America and the Alliance for Progress*, MR Press.

C. Furtado, *Development and Underdevelopment*, California University Press.

C. Fuentes *et al. Whither Latin America?*, MR Press.

J. Gerassi, *Imperialism and Revolution in Latin America*.

I. Davies and S. Miranda, Working Class in Latin America, *SR* 1967.

S. May, *The United Fruit Company in Latin America*.

E. Hobsbawm, Guerrillas in Latin America, *SR* 1970.

Black, *A New Look at UR Investments in Latin America*, NEFP and Ag 5p.

Revolution in Latin America, *MR* February 1967.

J. Petras, Class Struggle in Latin America, *SR* 1969.

Smith, *Social Revolution in Latin America: Role of US Policy*, NEFP and Ag 7p.

J. Nun, *Latin America: Hegemonic Crisis and Military Coups.*

E. Aguilar, ed, *Marxism in Latin America*, Knopf.

H. Landsberger, ed, *Latin American Peasant Movements*, Cornell University Press.

V. Alba, *Politics and the Labour Movement in Latin America*, Stanford University Press.

L. Vega, *Guerrillas in Latin America*, Pall Mall.

M. Niedergang, *The Twenty Latin Americas*, 2 vols, Penguin 1971.

A. G. Frank, *Capitalism and Underdevelopment in Latin America*, Penguin 1971.

C. Marighela, *For the Liberation of Brazil*, Penguin 1971.

## B Central America

These works document the American interventions in Guatemala, Dominica and Cuba. See also 17B, 7D.

E. Galeano, *Guatemala: Occupied Country*, MR Press.

Tobis, Foreign Aid to Guatemala, *MR* 1968.

*Turcios Lima: Guatemalan Revolutionary*, Ag 40p.

R. Ramirez, *Lettres du Front Guatemaltèque*, LL 80p.

J. Petras, Dominican Republic, *NLR* 40.

L. Huberman and P. Sweezy, *Revolution and Counter-Revolution in the Dominican Republic*, NEFP and Ag 7p.

Draper, The Dominican Crisis, *Commentary*, December 1965.

E. Abel, *Missiles of October*, MacGibbon & Kee. (The Cuban missile crisis)

R. Smith, *The US and Cuba: Business and Diplomacy 1917–60*, Bookman Associates, 1960.

R. Scheer and M. Zeitlin, *Cuba: An American Tragedy*, Penguin 1964.

W. Williams, *The US, Cuba and Castro*, MR Press 1962.

O. Paz, *The Labyrinth of Solitude*, Allen Lane 1967.

J. Reed, *Insurgent Mexico*.

R. Dumont, Mexico: Sabotage of Agrarian Reform, *NLR* 17.

*Mexico: A Study in Domination and Repression*, REP and Ag 50p.

C. Jagan, *The West on Trial*.

## C South America

See also 17B, 17C.

A. Frank, *Capitalism and Underdevelopment in Latin America: The Case of Chile and Brazil*, MR Press.

J. Quartim, *Dictatorship and Armed Struggle in Brazil*, NLB.

O. Ianni, *Crisis in Brazil*.

C. Furtado, *Diagnosis of the Brazilian Crisis*.

*Carlos Marighela: Brazilian Revolutionary*, Ag 30p.

A. Frank, *Mechanisms of Imperialism: The Case of Brazil*, LL and Ag 10p, or MR vol. 16.

R. Debray, *Revolution in Chile? – Conversations with Allende*, NLB.

J. Petras and M. Zeitlin, Agrarian Radicalism in Chile, *BJS* 1968.

J. Petras, *Politics and Social Forces in Chilean Development*, California University Press 1969.

Wolpin, The Left in Chile, *SR* 1969.

P. Cannebrava, *Militarism and Imperialism in Brazil*, Stage 1.

*Camilo Torres, Priest and Revolutionary*, LL and H 50p.

H. Bejar, *Notes on a Guerrilla Struggle: Peru 1965*, LL.

L. Whitehead, *The US and Bolivia*, Ag and LL 13p.

D. Bravo, *Guerrilla War in Venezuela*, Stage 1.

E. Laclau, Argentina, *NLR* 62.

J. Gerassi, Uruguay's Urban Guerrillas, *NLR* 62.

## D Cuba

See subsection B for US policy, and 23D for Castro, Guevara, Debray and their theories of revolution.

R. Blackburn, Sociology of the Cuban Revolution, *NLR* 21.

J. O'Connor, *Origins of Socialism in Cuba*.

R. Smith, ed, *Background to Revolution*, Knopf.

J. le Riverend, *Economic History of Cuba*.

P. Sweezy and L. Huberman, *Cuba: Anatomy of a Revolution*, MR Press 1961.

J. O'Connor, The Working Class in the Cuban Revolution, *Studies on the Left* 1966.

M. Zeitlin, *Revolutionary Politics and the Cuban Working Class*, Oxford University Press.

B. Goldenberg, *The Cuban Revolution and Latin America*, Allen & Unwin.

H. Thomas, Middle-Class Politics of the Cuban Revolution, in C. Veliz, ed, *The Politics of Conformity in Latin America*, Oxford University Press.

E. Boorstein, *The Economic Transformation of Cuba*, M R Press.

S. Tutino, *L'Octobre Cubain*, LL 1968.

E. Sutherland, *The Youngest Revolution*, LL and IS Books 1970.

G. Green, *Revolution Cuban Style*, 1970.

M. Gutelman, *L'Agriculture socialisée à Cuba*, Maspero.

L. Huberman and P. Sweezy, *Socialism in Cuba*, M R Press 1969.

J. Yglesias, *In the Fist of the Revolution*, Penguin 1970. (Life in a Cuban country town)

R. Dumont, *Cuba: Socialisme et Développement*.

I. Horowitz, ed, *Cuban Communism*, Aldine, Chicago 1970.

J. Morray, *The Second Revolution in Cuba*, M R Press 1962.

H. Thomas, *Cuba – Or the Pursuit of Freedom*, Eyre and Spottiswoode 1971.

L. Lockwood, *Castro's Cuba, Cuba's Fidel*, Vintage 1969.

J. North, *Cuba – Hope of a Hemisphere*, IS Books 50p.

K. Karol, *The Guerrillas in Power*.

Wood, Cuba: The Long Revolution, *S and S* 1970.

Cuba: End of a Road, *IS* 45, 1970.

Works by F. Castro on the progress of the Cuban revolution include *Cuba's Agrarian Reform*, and *A New Stage in the Advance of Cuban Socialism*, from Red Books.

# 19 Africa

## A Historical background

See 17A for more on Britain in Africa, 13A and 13B, and 23B for the work of Fanon.

B. Davidson, *The African Past*, Penguin 1967.

B. Davidson, *Old Africa Rediscovered*, Gollancz 1958.

B. Davidson, *Black Mother*, Gollancz 1961.

E. Morel, *Black Man's Burden*, MR Press. (White Man in Africa, Fifteenth Century of First World War)

C. James, *History of Pan-African Revolt*, Drum and Spear Press, Washington 1969.

L. Gann and P. Duignan, eds, *Colonialism in Africa*, 2 vols.

K. Ankomah, The Colonial Legacy and African Unrest, *S and S* 1970.

J. Woddis, *Africa: Roots of Revolt*, Lawrence & Wishart 1960.

J. Woddis, *The Lion Awakes*, Lawrence & Wishart 1962.

Gallagher and Robinson, *Africa and the Victorians*.

E. Sik, *The History of Black Africa*.

## B Africa today

See 17C and 17D for more general works on imperialism and underdevelopment, and 23B for Fanon's works.

B. Davidson, *Which Way Africa*, Penguin 1964.

K. Nkrumah, *Neo-Colonialism: Last Stage of Imperialism*, Nelson 1965.

K. Nkrumah, *Class Struggle in Africa*, Panaf 1970.

K. Grundy, Nkrumah's Theory of Underdevelopment, *World Politics* 1963.

Mohan, African Socialism, *SR* 1966.

G. Arrighi and J. Saul, African Nationalism, *SR* 1969.

R. Dumont, *False Start in Africa*, Sphere. (An important influence on Nyerere's policies in Tanzania)

Ledda, Classes in Africa, *ISJ* 1967, and NEFP.

J. Woddis, Military Coups in Africa, *MT* 1968.

K. Grundy, Class Struggle in Africa, *JMAS* 1964.

S. Amin, *Class Struggles in Africa*, ARG and Ag 11p.

*The Extended Family*, ARG and Ag 25p. (On the CIA, the corporations, and the 'African experts')

B. Davidson, African Prospects, *SR* 1970.

F. Helleiner, New Forms of Foreign Investment in Africa, *JMAS* 1968.

J. Saul, African Populism, in E. Gellner and G. Ionoescu, eds, *Populism*.

I. Potekhin, Land Relations in African Countries, *JMAS* 1963.

G. Arrighi and J. Saul, Socialism and Economic Development in Tropical Africa, *JMAS* 1968.

B. Magubane, Pluralism and the Conflict Situation in Africa, *Africa Social Research* 1969. (Critique of pluralism)

R. Green and A. Seidman, *Unity or Poverty: The Economics of Pan-Africanism*, Penguin.

C. Andrain, Patterns of African Socialist Thought, *Africa Forum* 1966.

W. Friedland and C. Rosberg, eds, *African Socialism*, Oxford University Press 1964.

I. Cox, *Socialist Ideas in Africa*, Lawrence and Wishart.

## C East Africa and Portuguese Africa

Works on Kenya, Tanzania, Zambia, Malawi are included, and the independence struggle in the territories still held by Portugal.

D. Barnett and K. Njama, *Mau Mau from Within*, M R Press.

J. Kariuki, *Mau Mau Detainee*, Penguin 1965.

O. Odinga, *Not Yet Uhuru*, Heinemann 1967.

I. Resnick, *Tanzania: Revolution by Education*, Longman 1968.

J. Nyerere, *Ujamaa: Essays on Socialism*, Oxford University Press. (Includes the Arusha Declaration)

J. Nyerere, *Freedom and Unity*, Oxford University Press 1967.

B. van Arkadie and D. Shai, The Economy of E. Africa, in P. Robson and D. Lury, eds, *The Economy of Africa*, Allen & Unwin 1968.

A. Ross, Malawi, *NLR* 45.

M. Faber, *Towards Economic Independence: Papers on the Political Economy of Zambia 1964–9*.

E. Mondlane, *The Struggle for Mozambique*, Penguin 1969.

B. Davidson, *The Liberation of Guine*, Penguin 1969.

A. Cabral, *Revolution in Guinea*, Stage 1.

G. Chaliand, *Armed Struggle in Africa*, M R Press. (On Guinea)

J. Duffy, *Portugal in Africa*, Penguin 1962.

*Portugal and Colonial War*, Ag 10p.

D. Barnett, Angolan Revolutionaries, *Ramparts* 1969.

## D West Africa and the Congo

Two topics are documented here: the nature of the UN intervention in the Congo, and subsequent developments; and the coup against Nkrumah in Ghana, and its repercussions.

C. O'Brien, *To Katanga and Back*, Simon and Schuster 1962.

C. O'Brien, The Congo, *NLR* 31.

J. van Lierde, ed, La Pensée Politique de Patrice Lumumba, *Présence Africaine* 1963, introduction by J.-P. Sartre.

Gérard-Libois, The Congo, *SR* 1966.

K. Nkrumah, *Challenge of the Congo*, LL.

K. Gott, *Mobutu's Congo*, Fabian 1968.

J. Mohan, Nkrumahism, *SR* 1967.

B. Fitch and M. Oppenheimer, *Ghana: End of an Illusion*, MR Press.

R. Murray, Review of Fitch and Oppenheimer, *NLR* 42.

K. Nkrumah, *Dark Days in Ghana*, Panaf 63p.

## E Rhodesia

See also 12B and the next subsection.

G. Arrighi, *The Political Economy of Rhodesia*, Humanities Press.

G. Arrighi, Rhodesia: Class and Power, *NLR* 39.

R. Austin, *Character and Legislation of the Rhodesian Front since UDI*, Ag 10p.

Symonds, *Background to the Rhodesian Crisis*, H 25p.

*Rhodesia: Why Minority Rule Survives*, Ag 12p.

*Rhodesian and S. African Subsidiaries of U.K. Companies*, Anti-Apartheid and Ag, 18p.

J. Rasmussen, Effects of Sanctions on Rhodesia, in *Studies in Progress*, 1969.

K. Nkrumah, *Rhodesia*, Panaf.

N. Sithole, *African Nationalism*, Oxford University Press.

G. Arrighi and J. Saul, Nationalism and Revolution in Sub-Saharan Africa, *SR* 1969.

## F South Africa

See also 2C, 12B, 17.

B. Bunting, *The Rise of the South African Reich*, Penguin 1964.

H. and R. Simons, *Class and Colour in South Africa 1850–1950*, Penguin 1969.

G. Mbeki, *South Africa: The Peasants' Revolt*, Penguin 1964.

E. Roux, *Time Longer than Rope: History of the Struggle of the Black Man in S. Africa*, Wisconsin 1964.

N. Mandela, *No Easy Walk to Freedom*, Heinemann 1965.

M. Benson, *South Africa: South Africa: Struggle for a Birthright*, Penguin 1966.

R. Segal, ed, *Sanctions against South Africa*, Penguin 1964.

P. Rensburg, *Guilty Land*, Penguin 1962.

Ainslie and Robinson, *The Collaboration*, Ag 10p. (UK companies in South Africa)

A. Mintz, *S. African Military Strategy*, Ag and LL 13p.

Asheron, Race and Politics in South Africa, *NLR* 53.

A. Hepple, *S. Africa: Workers under Apartheid*, International Defence and Aid Fund, and Ag 30p.

W. Hutt, *The Economics of the Colour Bar*, Deutsch 1964.

M. Christie, *The Simonstown Agreements*, Africa Bureau 15p.

Southern Africa, *An* 112.

A. Sachs, *S. Africa – The Violence of Apartheid*, International Defence and Aid Fund, and Ag 23p.

S. Africa: '*Resettlement*', *the New Violence to Africans*, International Defence and Aid Fund, and Ag.

P. Brauerman, Trade Union Apartheid, *African Communist* 1967.

P. Duncan, *S. Africa's Rule of Violence*, Methuen 1964.

Z. Nkosi, S. African Imperialism, *African Communist* 1967.

Kuper, *Passive Resistance in S. Africa*, H.

C. Mutwa, *My People*, Penguin 1971. (A witch doctor's view)

# 20 Middle East

## A General analyses

See also 2C and 17B.

M. Rodinson, *Islam et Capitalisme*.

A. Laroui, *L'Idéologie Arabe Contemporaine*, Maspero.

A. El Kodsy, Nationalism and Class Struggle in the Arab World, *MR* 1970.

A. Abdel-Malik, *Egypt: Military Society*, Random House.

M. Hussein, *Les Luttes de Classe en Egypte 1945–68*, Maspero 1970.

H. Ayrout, *The Egyptian Peasant*, Beacon 1968.

H. Riad, *L'Egypte Nasserienne*, 1964.

P. Mansfield, *Nasser's Egypt*, Penguin 1965.

A. Abdel-Malik, Nasserism and Socialism, *SR* 1964.

A. Abdel-Malik, Crisis in Nasser's Egypt, *NLR* 45.

M. Kerr, *The Arab Cold War*, Oxford University Press 1970. (Egypt–Ba'ath relations)

K. Jaber, *The Arab Ba'ath Socialist Party*, 1966.

E. Rouleau, Syria, *NLR* 45.

B. Nirumand, *Iran: The New Imperialism in Action*, MR Press.

S. Zabih, *The Communist Movement in Iran*, Cambridge University Press 1966.

M. Pablo, *The Arab Revolution*.

G. Harris, *The Origins of Communism in Turkey*, Stanford University Hoover Institute on War and Peace, 1967.

M. Ben Barka, *Option Révolutionnaire au Maroc*, 1965.

Jeanson and Fletcher, Algeria, *SR* 1965.

H. O'Connor, *World Crisis in Oil*, MR Press.

H. O'Connor, *Empire of Oil*, MR Press. (An older work)

R. Engler, *The Politics of Oil*, University of Chicago Press.

S. Longrigg, *Oil in the Middle East*, Oxford University Press.

G. Lenczowski, *Oil and State in the Middle East*, Cornell University Press.

## B The Arabs and Israel

M. Rodinson, *Israel and the Arabs*, Penguin 1969.

H. Hanegbi *et al.*, The Class Nature of Israeli Society, *NLR* 65.

F. Trabulsi, Palestine, *NLR* 57.

I. Deutscher, The Arab–Israel War, *NLR* 44.

W. Laqueur, ed, *The Israel–Arab Reader*, Penguin.

W. Laqueur, *Struggle in the Middle East*, Penguin 1972.

J. Parkes, *Whose Land? A History of the Peoples of Palestine*, Penguin 1970.

A. El Kodsy and E. Lobel, *The Arab World and Israel*.

S. Jiryis, *Les Arabes en Israel, 1948–67*, LL.

D. Horowitz, *The Economics of Israel*, Pergamon, 1967.

N. Weinstock, *Le Sionisme Contre Israel*, 1969.

N. Israeli, Israel and Imperialism, *IS* 32.

Matzpen, *The Other Israel*, Ag 14p.

Jones and Liebman, articles on Israel and the Arabs, *SR* 1970.

*Palestine: Crisis and Liberation*, LL and Ag 50p.

Buch, *Zionism and Arab Revolution*, Red Books 18p.

D. Leon, *The Kibbutz*, Pergamon 1969.

H. Darin-Drabkin, *The Other Society*, Gollancz. (On the kibbutz)

## C The Arab peninsula

These items document the little-known liberation struggles in the
southern Arabian states.

S. el-Attar, *Le Sous-Développement économiqueet social du Yemen*, Algiers 1964.

D. Schmidt, *Yemen: The Unknown War*, London 1968.

M. Wenner, *Modern Yemen 1918–66*, Baltimore 1967.

F. Halliday, Counter-Revolution in the Yemen, *NLR* 63.

P. Nizan, *Aden Arabie*, MR Press. (A travel account, useful as background)

F. Halliday and F. Trabulsi, *Revolution in Arabia*, Penguin.

F. Halliday, Class Struggle in the Gulf, *NLR* 58.

The Workers' Movement in Bahrein, *Tricontinental* 43.

A. Humaidan, *Les Princes de l'Or Noir*, Paris 1968.

D. Holden, *Farewell to Arabia*, Walker & Co. 1966.

T. Little, *South Arabia*, Pall Mall 1968.

# 21 South-East Asia

## A General analyses

See also 7D, 17B, 17C.

M. Caldwell, Oil Imperialism in East Asia, *Journal of Contemporary Asia*, Spring 1971.

J. Montgomery, *The Politics of Foreign Aid: The Case of S.E. Asia*, Praeger.

E. Jacoby, *Agrarian Unrest in South-East Asia*, London 1961.

R. Scalapino, ed, *Communism in Asia*, 1965.

H. d'Encausse and S. Schram, *Marxism and Asia*, Allen Lane 1969. (Readings and commentary)

I. Stone, *The Hidden History of the Korean War*, MR Press.

E. Friedman and M. Seldon, eds, *America's Asia*, Pantheon 1971.

W. Pomeroy, *American Neo-Colonialism*, Lawrence and Wishart. (Mainly on Asia)

J. Halliday, Asian Capitalism, *NLR* 44.

H. Bix, The Security Treaty System and the Japanese Military-Industrial Complex, *BCAS* January 1970.

## B North Vietnam

G. Chaliand, *The Peasants of North Vietnam*, Penguin 1969.

S. Seltzer, Land Reform in North Vietnam, *Viet Report* June–July 1967.

M. Selden, The NLF and the Transformation of Vietnamese Society, *BCAS* October 1969.

M. Selden, People's War and the Transformation of Peasant Society: China and Vietnam, in E. Friedman and M. Selden, eds, *America's Asia*, Pantheon 1971.

J. Gerassi, *N. Vietnam: A Documentary*, Allen & Unwin.

J. Lacouture, *Ho Chi Minh*, Penguin 1970.

W. Warbey, *Ho Chi Minh*, Merlin.

W. Burchett, *Vietnam North*, Lawrence & Wishart.

H. Salisbury, *Behind the Lines: Hanoi*, Harper & Row.

F. Kofsky, Vietnam and Social Revolution, *MR* 1967.

G. Kolko, *Vietnam: Three Documents of the NLF*, BRPF 10p.

Ho Chi Minh, *On Revolution*, Pall Mall.

B. Fall, ed, *Ho on Revolution*, Signet.

Ho Chi Minh, *Selected Articles and Speeches*, LL 55p.

V. Giap, *Banner of People's War, Party's Military Line*, Pall Mall.

V. Giap, *The Military Art of People's War*, MR Press.

Le Duan, *On the Socialist Revolution in Vietnam*.

## C The War: Vietnam

This includes works on the historical background, the development of the war, and American war crimes. For the latter, see also 4B; see also 12B, 17B, and the next subsection.

M. Gettleman, ed, *Vietnam: History, Documents and Opinions*, Penguin, 1966.

T. Cannon, *Vietnam: One Thousand Years of Struggle*, Ag 25p.

J. McAlister, *Vietnam: Origins of Revolution*, Knopf.

McDermott, *Vietnam Profile*, CND 1965, 10p.

*Vietnam Read-In*, H 25p.

P. Sweezy *et al. Vietnam: The Endless War*, MR Press.

B. Potter, *Rape of Vietnam, Sol* 10p.

D. Pike, *Vietcong*, MIT.

W. Burchett, *Vietnam Will Win!* MR Press.

G. Therborn, From Petrograd to Saigon, *NLR* 48.

Morrock, Revolution and Intervention in Vietnam, in D. Horowitz, ed, *Containment and Revolution*, Anthony Blond.

N. Chomsky, *American Power and the New Mandarins*, Penguin 1969.

R. Scheer, *How the U.S. Got Involved in Vietnam*, Santa Barbara, California, 1965, and Red Books 33p.

Scheer and Hinckle, Vietnam Lobby, *Ramparts* 1965.

F. Schurman *et al.*, *The Politics of Escalation in Vietnam*, Fawcett World Library.

B. Fall and M. Raskin, eds, *Vietnam Reader*, Vintage 1965.

B. Fall, *Vietnam Witness*, Praeger 1966.

J. Schell, *The Military Half*, Vintage 1968. (The war in the provinces)

G. Kahin and J. Lewis, *The U.S. in Vietnam*, Dial Press 1967.

G. Rosie, *The British in Vietnam*, Panther.

A. Hassler, *Saigon U.S.A.*, Baron Press 1970.

G. Hammer, *One Morning in the War: The Tragedy of Pinkville*, Hart-Davis.

J. Schell, *The Village of Ben Suc*, Cape.

K. Coates *et al. Prevent the Crime of Silence*, Allen Lane. (The Russell War Crimes Tribunal documents)

Norden, *American Atrocities in Vietnam*, Red Books 10p.

S. Melman, ed, *In the Name of America*, Turnpike Press 1968.

E. Herman, *Atrocities in Vietnam*, Pilgrim Press 1970.

T. Taylor, *Nuremberg and Vietnam: An American Tragedy*, Quadrangle 1970.

## D The War: the involvement of Cambodia and Laos

N. Chomsky, *At War With Asia*, Fontana.

N. Chomsky, *Three Essays on Cambodia*, BRPF 20p.

M. Caldwell and L. Tan, *Cambodia in the South East Asian War*, MR Press 1971.

L. Boramy and M. Caldwell, Behind the Cambodian Coup, *Sp* 5.

M. Leifer, Rebellion or Subversion in Cambodia?, *Current History* 1969.

W. Burchett, *The Second Indo-China War: Cambodia and Laos Today*, Lorrimer 1970.

N. Adams and A. McCoy, eds, *Laos: War and Revolution*.

H. Toye, *Laos: Buffer State or Battleground*.

P. Scott, Air America: Flying the US into Laos, *Ramparts* 1970. (Prentice-Hall)

B. Fall, The Pathet Lao, in R. Scalapino, ed, *Communist Revolution in Asia*, *Laos, Cambodia: Victory of People's War*, Pacific Studies Center and Ag 1970, 25p.

P. Vongvichit, *Laos and the Victorious Struggle of the Lao People against U.S. Neo-Colonialism*, Neo Lao Hak Sat Editions, 1969.

**E India and Pakistan**

See also 17A.

C. Bettelheim, *India Independent*, M R Press.

R. Segal, *The Crisis of India*, Penguin 1965.

M. Kidron, *Foreign Investment in India*, Oxford University Press.

N. Harris, India, *IS* 17–18, 1964.

S. Melman, *Foreign Monolopy Capital in the Indian Economy*, New Delhi 1963.

V. Pavlov, *India: Economic Freedom versus Imperialism*, New Delhi 1963.

R. Hazari, *The Corporate Private Sector: Concentration, Ownership and Control*, Asia Publishing House, London 1966.

P. Chattopadhay, State Capitalism in India, *M R* 1970.

G. Appa, The Naxalites, *NLR* 61.

M. Desai, Vortex in India, *NLR* 61.

V. Pavlov, *The India Capitalist Class, a Historical Study*, New Delhi 1964.

V. Kiernan, Marx and India, *S R* 1967.

R. Palme Dutt, *India Today*, Gollancz 1940. (Includes a Marxist analysis of the caste system)

T. Ali, *Pakistan: Military Rule or People's War*, Cape.

T. Ali, Class Struggles in Pakistan, *NLR* 63.

H. Alavi, Army and Bureaucracy in Pakistan, *ISJ* 14.

H. Alavi, *Pakistan: The Burden of U.S. Aid*, N E F P and Ag 10p.

Pakistan and Bangla Desh, *NLR* 68.

N. Harris, *Struggle in Bangladesh*, Pluto Press.

**F Indonesia**

M. Caldwell, *Indonesia*, Oxford University Press 1968.

B. Grant, *Indonesia*, Penguin 1967.

R. McVey, *Origins of Indonesian Communism*, Cornell University Press, 1965.

W. Wertheim, *Indonesian Society in Transition*, Van Hoeve 1956.

J. Pluvier, *Confrontations*, Oxford University Press 1965. (An analysis of class structure)

R. Mortimer, Indonesia: Emigré Post-Mortems on the P K I, *Australian Outlook*, December 1968.

W. Wertheim, Suharto and the Untung Coup, *Journal of Contemporary Asia*, winter 1970.

L. Rey, The Massacre of the P K I, *NLR* 36.

Soedarso, *Catastrophe in Indonesia*, Red Books 20p.

# 22 China

See 23C for the works of Mao and discussion of his theory of war and revolution.

## A Origins and development of Chinese Communism

F. Schurmann and O. Schell, eds, *China Readings*. Penguin 1968.

J. Ch'en, *Mao and the Chinese Revolution*, Oxford University Press.

E. Snow, *Red Star Over China*, Penguin.

M. Roy, *A Marxist Interpretation of Chinese History*, NEFP and Ag 10p.

S. Schram, *Mao*, Penguin.

M. Meisner, *Li Ta-chao and the Origins of Chinese Marxism*, Oxford University Press.

J. Gittings, Origins of China's Foreign Policy, in D. Horowitz, ed, *Containment and Revolution*, Anthony Blond.

T. Chen, *The Chinese Communist Regime: Documents and Commentaries*, Pall Mall.

A. Smedley, *The Great Road: The Life and Times of Chu Teh*, MR Press.

C. Bettelheim, *La Construction du Socialisme en Chine*, Maspero.

B. Schwartz, *Chinese Communism and the Rise of Mao*, Cambridge Massachusetts 1952.

K. Karol, *China: The Other Communism*, Heinemann.

S. Griffith, *The Chinese People's Liberation Army*, Weidenfeld & Nicolson.

J. Gittings, *The Role of the Chinese Army*, Oxford University Press.

N. Harris, China, *IS* 35.

T. Bernstein, Leadership and Mass Mobilisation in Soviet and Chinese Collectivisation Drives, *China Quarterly* 1967.

F. Greene, *The Wall Has Two Sides*, Cape.

N. Harris, *Beliefs in Society*, New Thinkers Library, chapter 6.

W. Hinton, *Fanshen: A Documentary of Revolution in a Chinese Village*, Merlin.

W. Hinton, *Iron Oxen: A Documentary of Revolution in Chinese Farming*, MR Press.

J. Lewis, ed, *Party Leadership and Revolutionary Power in China*.

J. Myrdal, *Report from a Chinese Village*, Penguin 1967.

S. Burki, *A Study of Chinese Communes*, Harvard University Press.

## B The Cultural Revolution

K. Fan, *Chinese Cultural Revolution: Documents*, MR Press.

K. Karol, Two Years of Cultural Revolution, *SR* 1968.

J. Robinson, *The Cultural Revolution in China*, Penguin 1969.

J. Gray and P. Cavendish, *Chinese Communism in Crisis*, Pall Mall. (Includes documents)

V. Nee, *Cultural Revolution at Peking*, MR Press.

T. Cliff, The Sheng Wu Lien Faction, *IS* 37. (On the extreme left group in the Cultural Revolution)

J. Gittings, The Red Guards Now, *NS* 20-2-69.

Collier, The Cultural Revolution in Canton, *NLR* 48 and 50.

Jenner, China Now, *NLR* 53.

China Today and the Position of the Military, *PC* November 1969.

E. Snow, *Red China Today: The Other Side of the River*, Penguin 1970.

P. Shu-tse, *Behind China's Great Cultural Revolution*, Red Books 33p.

W. Hinton, *Fanshen Reconsidered in the Light of the Cultural Revolution*, NEFP and Ag 10p.

J. Daubier, *Histoire de la Révolution Culturelle en Chine*, Maspero 1970.

E. Wheelwright and B. McFarlane, *The Chinese Road to Socialism: Economics of the Cultural Revolution*, MR Press.

C. Brendel, *Theses on the Chinese Revolution*, Sol 13p.

D. Wilson, ed, *China After the Cultural Revolution*, Random House 1969, especially Gray, Economics of Maoism.

W. Hinton, *China's Continuing Revolution*.

A. Macciochi, *De la Chine*, Le Seuil 1971.

# 23 Third-World Revolution

This section considers the analyses of revolution, guerrilla warfare, and military strategy of the most influential Third-World theorists; but see also 21B for the Vietnamese theorists, and 19B, 19C for other African views. For connected issues, see 17, 24D, 27D, and 30. For current coverage of revolutionary movements, see *Tricontinental* and *Monthly Review*.

## A Guerrilla warfare and the peasant question

The twin, interconnected issues are whether the peasantry can supplant the proletariat as the revolutionary class, and the degree to which guerrilla warfare is an adequate means to revolution. Harris and Sweezy, writing in the Lenin-Trotsky tradition, see the peasantry as a counter-revolutionary force, or at best the proletariat's reluctant ally; Caldwell, Alavi and Wolf are closer to the Mao-Guevara view. Shanin and Oppenheimer criticize both positions. Pomeroy is a reader that contains varied viewpoints on guerrilla warfare; Taber is a favourable account, Oppenheimer is hostile. See also 18A, 19B, 21A, 22A.

N. Harris and M. Caldwell, Debate on the Revolutionary Role of Peasants, *IS* 41.

N. Harris, The Third World: Prospects for the 70s, *IS* 42.

P. Sweezy, Proletariat in Today's World, *Tricontinental* 9, 1968.

M. Caldwell, Role of the Peasantry in S.E. Asia, *Afrasian* 1969.

T. Shanin, Workers and Peasants in Revolution, *Sp* 10, 1971.

T. Shanin, *Peasants and Peasant Societies*, Penguin 1971.

T. Shanin, Peasantry as a Political Factor in his *Peasants and Peasant Societies*, Penguin 1971.

E. Wolf, On Peasant Rebellions, *International Social Science Journal* 1969, and in T. Shanin, *Peasants and Peasant Societies*, Penguin 1971.

H. Alavi, Peasants and Revolution, *SR* 1965.

V. Kiernan, Peasant Revolution, *SR* 1970.

Barrington Moore, *Social Origins of Dictatorship and Democracy*, Penguin 1969, chapter 9.

J. Gerassi, *Towards Revolution*, Weidenfeld & Nicolson, 2 vols.

M. Oppenheimer, *Urban Guerrilla*, Penguin 1970, chapters 2 and 3.

E. Hobsbawm, *Primitive Rebels*, Manchester University Press.

T. Cliff, Marxism and the Collectivisation of Agriculture, *IS* 19.

W. Pomeroy, ed, *Guerilla Warfare and Marxism*, Lawrence & Wishart.

D. Girling, *People's War*, Allen & Unwin.

K. Nkrumah, *Handbook of Revolutionary Warfare*, Panaf.

M. Lewin, *Russian Peasants and Soviet Power*, Allen & Unwin.

J. Woddis, *New Theories of Revolution*, Lawrence & Wishart.

R. Taber, *War of the Flea*, Paladin.

Two of the most important discussions of the peasantry in the major works of
   Marx and Engels are Marx's *Eighteenth Brumaire of Louis Napoleon*, and
   Engels's *The Peasant War in Germany*. A useful anthology is: S. Avineri, ed,
   *Marx on Colonialism and Modernization*.

## B Fanon and the African Revolution

Frantz Fanon's works on the effects of colonialism on African society have made
him the most influential African theorist. His main works are: *Black Skin White
Masks*, Paladin; *A Dying Colonialism*, Penguin 1970; *Toward the African
Revolution*, Penguin 1970; and *The Wretched of the Earth*, Penguin 1967, with an
introduction by J.-P. Sartre. The following discuss aspects of his work; see also 19B.
D. Caute, *Fanon*, Fontana.
Geismar and Worsley, Fanon, *M R* 1969.
Thompson, Fanon, *M T* 1968.
Stambouli, Fanon Face aux Problèmes de la Décolonisation et de la Construction
   Nationale, *Revue de l'Institut de Sociologie* 1967.
Staniland, Fanon and the African Political Class, *African Affairs* 1969.
Gottheil, Fanon and the Economics of Colonialism, *Review of Economics and
   Business* 1967.
Grohs, Fanon and the African Revolution, *J M A S* 1968.

## C Mao: political and military thought

Mao's philosophical ideas are stated most clearly in his *On Practice*, his *On
Contradiction*, and his *Combat Liberalism*. For general problems of strategy and
tactics, see *Strategic Problems of Revolutionary War*, and *On the Correct Handling
of Contradictions Among the People*. More sociological in emphasis are *The Peasant
Movement in Hunan* and *Analysis of Classes in Chinese Society*. These can all be
found in the four-volume *Selected Works*, and most are reproduced in Fremantle
below; they can also be obtained separately, published by the Foreign Languages
Press, Peking, as can Lin Piao's main work, *Long Live the Victory of People's
War*, a summary of Maoist military theory. See also 22A.
A. Fremantle, ed, *Writings of Mao*, New English Library.
M. Rejai, ed, *Mao on Revolution and War*, Doubleday.
W. Chai, ed, *Essential Works of Chinese Communism*.
   (Includes Peng Ch'en, Shao-chi and Lin Piao)
J. Ch'en, *Mao Papers: Anthology and Bibliography*, Oxford University Press 1970.
   (Includes Cultural Revolution documents)
S. Schram, *The Political Thought of Mao Tse-Tung*, Penguin 1969. (Includes a selection
   from his work)
A. Glucksmann, Mao on Politics and War, *N L R* 49.
N. Harris, Marx–Lenin–Stalin–Mao, *I S* 26.
I. Deutscher, Maoism, *S R* 1964.
Masi, Le Marxisme de Mao et le Gauche Européen, *T M* 1970.
Swi Tse, *The Art of War*, Clarendon Press.

**D The Cuban model: Castro, Guevara, Debray**

The most important works of Che Guevara are: *Guerrilla Warfare*, Penguin 1969; *Socialism and Man*, Stage 1; *Reminiscences of the Cuban Revolutionary War*, Penguin 1969; *Bolivian Diaries*, Red Books; and *On Vietnam and World Revolution*, Red Books. The relevance of the Cuban experience, and the general conclusions drawn from it in the work of Debray, are discussed in later items on the list. See also 18A, 18D.

M. Kenner and J. Petras, eds, *Fidel Castro Speaks*, Allen Lane.

F. Castro, *Major Speeches*, Stage 1.

F. Castro, *History Will Absolve Me*, Cape.

F. Castro *et al.*, *Viva Che*.

J. Gerassi, ed, *Venceremos*, London 1968. (Readings from Guevara)

R. Debray, *Revolution in the Revolution*, Penguin 1968.

R. Debray, *Strategy for Revolution*, Cape.

Moreno, Che's Theory of Guerrilla Warfare, *Comparative Studies in Society and History* 1970.

R. Lamberg, Che in Bolivia, *P C* July 1970.

L. Huberman and P. Sweezy, eds, *Debray and the Latin American Revolution*, M R Press, and *M R* July 1968.

J. Quartim, Relevance of Debray to Brazil, *N L R* 59.

J. Petras, *Politics and Social Structure in Latin America*, M R Press, chapters on Debray.

# 24 Marxism

This section contains discussions of the works of Marx and of the problems that stem from it; but the main contributions of the more important Marxist theorists will be found in 25 and 26, and discussions of Marxist economics in 27. Subsection B considers the major disputes in contemporary Marxist theory and could therefore be used as a focus for studying these problems. It precedes the subsection that contains works on Marx's thought, as these works usually fail to state their basic assumptions and can be misleading without an awareness of the theoretical issues; but of course the general reader might prefer to omit B and go straight to C.

## A The works of Marx and Engels

These works, with exceptions noted below, are published by Lawrence & Wishart in Britain. Those marked with an asterisk are also available in the one-volume *Selected Works*, which also includes important correspondence. See 27A for Marx's economics. Marx's first substantial work is his *Critique of Hegel's Philosophy of Right* (Cambridge University Press 1970, ed. J. O'Malley), which includes important comments on the role of the state and the nature of bureaucracy. The 1844 *Economic and Philosophic Manuscripts* comprises the first statements on economics and an analysis of Hegel's dialectic. *The German Ideology* (with Engels) is a polemic against the various neo-Hegelian phiosophers of the time, and *The Holy Family* (with Engels) continues this; the section on Feuerbach, in particular, repays careful reading. The most concise statement of Marx's perspective in the early period is the brilliant *Theses on Feuerbach\**. *The Poverty of Philosophy* is a polemic against Proudhon's economic and philosophical theories; chapter 2, section 1 includes an account of the dialectic. By the late 1850s the main outline of Marx's later views is apparent; unfortunately the vast work of the period, the so-called *Grundrisse*, is untranslated. (There is a French translation, as *Fondements de la critique de l'economie politique*, Anthropos, but it is in some ways inaccurate: an English translation is due for about 1973.) Excerpts have been translated as *Marx's Grundrisse*, Macmillan 1971, by D. McLellan. The most important part of this work is probably the part referred to as the *Introduction* to the *Contribution to a Critique of Political Economy*, which states the methodological and theoretical assumptions underlying his later theory of capitalism. (This Introduction is available in the Lawrence & Wishart edition as an appendix, and is also in McLellan.) The *Preface\** to this *Contribution* includes Marx's summary of the evolution of his views. Another part of the *Grundrisse* is translated as *Pre-Capitalist Economic Formations*, with a useful introduction by E. Hobsbawm. In *Capital*, vol. 1, see especially chapter 1, section 4 on the fetishism of commodities, and the last chapters on the historical development of capitalism. Marx's other works are important for their contributions to analysing problems of revolutionary struggle in concrete historical situations: see particularly *The Communist Manifesto\** (with Engels), also available as a Penguin; *The Eighteenth Brumaire of Louis Napoleon*\* (includes discussion of the peasantry); *Class Struggles in France 1848–50; Civil War in France*\* (important for Marx's analysis of the state); and *The Critique of the Gotha Programme*\* (the role of the party, the nature of the revolution and the transition to communism).

Engels' main independent works are his early *Condition of the Working Class in England in 1844* (available as a Panther or in Marx and Engels, *On Britain*, which includes other useful material), and the later *Origin of the Family, Private Property and the State*\*, *Ludwig Feuerbach and the End of Classical German Philosophy*\*, *Socialism Utopian and Scientific*\* (a history of previous socialist thinkers), *The Peasant Question in France and Germany*\* and *Anti-Dühring* and the *Dialectics of Nature* (both important for his views on science and dialectics). The following are some of the more useful of the numerous anthologies; Bottomore and Caute are good introductory surveys, McLellan and Easton contain material not easily available elsewhere:

T. Bottomore and M. Rubel, *K. Marx: Selected Writings in Sociology and Social Philosophy*, Penguin 1963. (And a helpful introduction)

D. Caute, *Essential Writings of K. Marx*, Panther.

L. Easton and K. Guddat, *Writings of the Young Marx on Philosophy and Society*, Anchor.

D. McLellan, *K. Marx: Early Texts*, Blackwell.

L. Feuer, *K. Marx: Basic Writings on Politics and Philosophy*, Fontana.

W. Henderson, *Engels: Selected Writings*, Penguin 1967.

R. Freedman, *Marx on Economics*, Penguin 1962.

S. Avineri, *Marx on Colonialism and Modernization*, Doubleday Anchor.

## B Marxist theory: basic controversies

The basic issue is the nature of the Marxist claim to have produced a science of human society: one tradition sees the object of this science, man, as implying a different conception of science from that prevailing in the natural sciences, one that stresses history as the project of a human subject and dialectic rather than objectivity as characterizing the relation between the social scientist and his object of study (Sartre, Goldmann, Lukács, Hegelians, humanists); the other tradition denies this distinction, either because the natural science method is held to be *the* method of science (positivism and its variants), or because a new conception of science can make the distinction irrelevant (some forms of structuralism, Althusser). Goldmann's work is an unstable synthesis that remains basically historicist, and as it is quite readable it could serve as an introduction (see also his sociology of literature, 28B). Sartre *v.* Lévi-Strauss on the relative claims of history and structure raises many of the issues. Gorz provides background on Sartre (see also 26C), and as structuralism is still fairly unknown in this country, some works to introduce it are included: Foucault and Lévi-Strauss are leading practitioners, Leach is an introduction to Lévi-Strauss, and Benoist is an excellent summary of their work. Other discussions of these issues and their relevance to Marxism follow. Godelier presents a reading of *Capital* heavily influenced by structuralism, and the ensuing debate discusses the relation of structure to dialectic. Althusser's work is a major attempt to use the insights of structuralism while preserving a conception of history as the object of social science (see 26D). See also the debate on British history, 11A, and the discussion of Frankfurt critiques of science, 26A, and 26B, as other ways into the controversies. See also 4E.

L. Goldmann, *The Human Sciences and Philosophy*, Cape.

M. Glucksmann, Critique of Goldmann, *NLR* 56.

J.-P. Sartre, *The Problem of Method*, Methuen.

C. Lévi-Strauss, *The Savage Mind*, Weidenfeld & Nicolson, chapter 9.

A. Gorz. Sartre and Marx, *NLR* 37.

C. Lévi-Strauss, Overture to *The Raw and the Cooked*, Cape.

C. Lévi-Strauss, *Structural Anthropology*, Allen Lane 1968, chapter 1.

M. Foucault, *The Order of Things*, Tavistock.

E. Leach, *Lévi-Strauss*, Fontana.

J.-M. Benoist, The End of Structuralism, *Twentieth-Century Studies*, May 1970.

L. Sebag, *Marxisme et structuralisme*, Payot 1964.

M. Foucault, Introduction to the Archaeology of Knowledge, *Social Science Information* 1970. (See also *Theoretical Practice*, 3–4)

M. Gaboriau, Structural Anthropology and History, in M. Lane, ed, *Structuralism*, Cape.

M. Godelier, System Structure and Contradiction in *Capital*, in *SR* 1967 and in M. Lane, ed, *Structuralism*, Cape.

L. Sève, Méthode structurale et méthode dialectique, *La Pensée* 1967.

M. Godelier, Logique dialectique et analyse des structures, *La Pensée* 1970.

P. Vilar *et al.* Dialectique marxiste et pensée structurale, *C du C d'ES* 1968.

L. Althusser, *For Marx*, Allen Lane 1970.

L. Althusser, *Reading Capital*, NLB.

## C The development of Marx's ideas

This subsection includes general works on Marx and Engels, on Hegel and his effect on Marx, and on the compatibility of the early (neo-Hegelian) Marx with the later Marx (with his stress on the scientific nature of his work). See also the discussions in subsection B (particularly Althusser). Mehring is a biography; Avineri is becoming the most widely-read book on Marx (its 'continuity' emphasis is criticized by Fernbach); Lefebvre, Fischer and Korsch are also useful; Garaudy and Berlin are simpler introductions. For background on Hegel, Marcuse is probably best. Nicolaus discusses the significance of the *Grundrisse*. On Engels, Hodges is useful, but see Sedgwick's comment.

F. Mehring, *Karl Marx: The Story of His Life*, Ann Arbor.

S. Avineri, *The Social and Political Thought of Karl Marx*, Cambridge University Press. (And review by Fernbach, *NLR* 56)

H. Lefebvre, *Sociology of Marx*, Allen Lane 1968.

E. Fischer, *Marx in His Own Words*, Allen Lane 1970.

K. Korsch, *Karl Marx*, Russell & Russell 1963.

I. Berlin, *Karl Marx*, Home University Library.

E. Mandel, *La Formation de la pensée économique de Karl Marx*, Maspero.

R. Garaudy, *Karl Marx: The Evolution of His Thought*, Lawrence & Wishart.

D. McLellan, *The Thought of Karl Marx*, London 1971.

D. McLellan, *The Young Hegelians and Marx*, Macmillan.

D. McLellan, *Marx Before Marxism*, Penguin 1972.

H. Marcuse, *Reason and Revolution*, Routledge.

J. Hyppolite, *Studies on Marx and Hegel*, Heinemann.

A. Kojève, *Introduction to the Reading of Hegel*, New York 1969. (A much abridged version of the French original)

A. Cornu, *Origins of Marxian Thought*, Thomas, Springfield Illinois 1957.

S. Avineri, Hegel and the Origins of Marx's Thought, *Review of Metaphysics* 1967.

S. Hook, *From Hegel to Marx*, Ann Arbor.

Mueller, The Hegel Legend of Thesis-Antithesis-Synthesis, *Journal of the History of Ideas* 1958.

J. Texier, Un Marx ou deux, *TM* 1967.

M. Nicolaus, The Unknown Marx, in *NLR* 48, and in C. Oglesby, ed, *New Left Reader*, Grove Press.

G. Mayer, *F. Engels: A Biography*, London 1936.

F. Nova, *F. Engels: His Contribution to Political Theory*, Vision Press.

Gustafson on Engels, *S and S* 1966.

Hodges on Engels, *SR* 1965. (And comment by P. Sedgwick, *SR* 1966, p. 190–91)

### D Marxist social theory: particular topics

Topics covered here include alienation, the state, social class, the relation of Marxism to sociology, and discussions of the Asiatic Mode of production. See also 1A, 1E, 5A, 11A, 15A, 17C, 17D, for discussions of bourgeois social theory; and 25 and 26, for the major Marxist contributions.

L. Goldmann, La réification, in his *Recherches dialectiques*, Gallimard.

I. Meszaros, *Marx's Theory of Alienation*, Merlin 1970.

E. Mandel and G. Novack, *Marxist Theory of Alienation*, Leader Books 43p.

N. Geras, Fetishism in Marx's *Capital*, *NLR* 65.

Berger and Pullberg, Reification, *NLR* 35, and in *History and Theory* 1965. (And see Brewster's comments in *NLR* 35)

O'Neill, Concept of Estrangement in Early and Later Marx, *Philosophy and Phenomenological Research* 1964.

E. Hobsbawm, Marx's Historiography, *Diogenes*, 1968.

H. Draper, Death of the State in Marx and Engels, *SR* 1970.

R. Miliband, Marx and the State, *SR* 1965.

H. Lefebvre *et al.*, Les marxistes et la notion de l'état, *C du C d'ES* 1963.

M. Johnstone, Marx, Engels and the Party, *SR* 1967.

M. Rubel, Marx's Concept of Democracy, *NP* 1962.

M. Nicolaus, Proletariat and Middle Class in Marx, *Studies on the Left* 1967.

Timofeef, Marx and the Development of the Working Class, *Social Science Information* 1968.

D. Hodges, Intermediate Classes in Marxist Theory, *Social Research* 1961.

Marxism and Sociology, symposium in *Praxis* 1968.

L. Goldmann, Is there a Marxist Sociology?, *IS* 34.

Marx et la sociologie, *H and S* 10, 1968.

R. Bastide *et al.*, *Contribution à la Sociologie de la Connaissance*, Anthropos.

J. Lojkine, Pour une theorie marxiste des ideologies, *Cahiers du Centre d'Etude et de Recherche marxistes*, 1969.

A. Schmidt, *The Concept of Nature in Marx*, NLB.

M. Godelier, Mode de production asiatique, *TM* 1965.

M. Rodinson, Marx and Ancient Societies, *NLR* 35.

G. Lichtheim, Marx and the Asiatic Mode of Production, *St Anthony's Papers* 1963.

E. Terray, *Le Marxisme devant les sociétés primitives*, Maspero.

K. Wittfogel, *Oriental Despotism*, Yale.

Vidal-Naquet on Wittfogel, *Annales* 1964.

### E Marxist philosophy: particular topics

Topics discussed include the nature of dialectic, the relation of thought and action and the concept of praxis, and the relation of Marxism to science. Lefebvre's work is difficult but thorough. See also discussions of the relation of Engels to Marx in subsection C, works on the philosophy of science, 4E, Lenin's philosophical works, 25A, Althusser, 26D, and the Frankfurt School, 26A, B.

H. Lefebvre, *Dialectical Materialism*, Cape.

H. Lefebvre, *Logique formelle, logique dialectique*, Maspero.

K. Kosik, *Dialectique du concret*, Maspero.

K. Korsch, *Marxism and Philosophy*, NLB.

N. Rotenstreich, *Basic Problems of Marx's Philosophy*, Bobbs-Merrill.

L. Dupré, *Philosophical Foundations of Marxism*, New York 1966.

N. Lobkowicz, Abstraction and Dialectics, *Review of Metaphysics* 1967–8.

N. Lobkowicz, *Theory and Practice from Aristotle to Marx*, Notre Dame 1967.

L. Kolakowski, Marx and the Classical Definition of Truth, in his *Marxism and Beyond*, Paladin.

G. Cohen, Criticisms of Historical Materialism, *Proceedings of the Aristotelian Society*, 1970, supp. vol.

M. Cornforth, *Dialectical Materialism*, 1961–3, 3 vols, Lawrence & Wishart.

G. Petrovic, Dialectical Materialism and Praxis, *Boston Studies in the Philosophy of Science*, vol 4.

G. Petrovic, Man as economic animal and man as praxis, *Inquiry* 1963.

Sohn-Pethel, Historical Materialist Theory of Knowledge, *MT* 1965.

D. Hodges, Dual Character of Marxian Social Science, *Philosophy of Science* 1962.

J. Hyppolite, Science and Ideology in a Marxist Perspective, *Diogenes* 1968.

Schaff, Marxist Dialectics and the Principle of Contradiction, *Journal of Philosophy* 1960.

J. Bernal, *Marx and Science*.

J. Crowther, Lenin and Science, *New Scientist* April 1970.

D. Struik, Marx and Mathematics, *S and S* 1948.

Mao, *Four Essays on Philosophy*, Peking 1963.

G. Dean, Mao and Science, *New Scientist* vol. 45.

### F Marxism and psychoanalysis

Some Marxists are hostile to psychoanalysis, Baran for example; but most tendencies in Marxism have tried to develop a common ground. Marcuse and Adorno give Frankfurt approaches (see also 26A, B); for works on the influential Reich, see 5C and 10; for Laing see 5C, D. The work of Lacan is an attempt to reinterpret the theories of Freud in a structuralist perspective.

H. Marcuse, *Eros and Civilisation*, Sphere.

H. Marcuse. *Five Lectures*, Allen Lane 1970.

T. Adorno, Sociology and Psychology, *NLR* 46–7.

W. Reich, *The Sexual Revolution*, Vision Press.

P. Baran, Marxism and Psychoanalysis, *MR* 1959, and in his *The Longer View*, MR Press.

I. Deutscher, *Socialist Man*, Merit 1967.

E. Fromm, *Beyond the Chains of Illusion: Marx and Freud*, Pocket Books.

J.-P. Sartre, *Being and Nothingness*, Methuen, chapter on Existential Psychoanalysis.

J.-P. Sartre, Interview, *NLR* 58. (Present views on psychoanalysis)

R. Osborn, *Marxism and Psychoanalysis*, Barrie & Rockcliff.

J. Gabel, *La Fausse Conscience*, Paris 1969, 3rd edn.

J. Lacan, *The Language of the Self*, Johns Hopkins 1968.

J. Lacan, *Ecrits*, Le Seuil 1966.

J. Lacan, The Mirror-phase as Formative of the Function of the I, *NLR* 51.

J. Lacan, The Insistence of the Letter, *Yale French Studies* 36–7.

J. Roussel, Introduction to Lacan, *NLR* 51.

L. Althusser, Freud and Lacan, *NLR* 55 (and in *Lenin and Philosophy*, NLB).

A. Rifflet, *Jacques Lacan*, Dessart 1970.

# 25 The Marxist Tradition

## A Lenin

There is a 45-volume *Collected Works*, and a one-volume *Selected Works*, all published in this country by Lawrence & Wishart. Most of the more important works are also available seperately, in paperback. Lenin's most influential statement is probably *The State and Revolution*, and this needs to be read in conjunction with *Questions of the Socialist Organization of the Economy* and *Will the Bolsheviks Retain State Power?* to get a fair picture of his contribution to the Marxist theory of the state. Strategy and tactics are discussed in his *One Step Forward, Two Steps Back, What is To Be Done, Socialism and Anarchism*, and *Left Wing Communism, An Infantile Disorder*. His general view of the importance of Marxism is summarized in *On Utopian and Scientific Socialism*. See also his writings on Russia, 16A and 16B, and on imperialism, 27D. On the peasantry, see *The Agrarian Question*. For his philosophy, compare the early *Materialism and Empirio-Criticism* with the later *Philosophical Notebooks*. Note that the Althusserians have initiated a reassessment of his contribution to Marxist science, so see 26D and the journal *Theoretical Practice*.

N. Krupskaya, *Memories of Lenin*, Panther (by his wife) 1966.
D. Shub, *Lenin*, Penguin 1966.
G. Lukács, *Lenin*, NLB.
L. Colletti, The Leninist State, *NLR* 56.
R. Miliband, Lenin's *State and Revolution*, *SR* 1970.
Symposium on Lenin, *MR* 11:6.
M. Lewin, *Lenin's Last Struggle*.
J. Higgins, Lenin, *IS* 30.
H. Selsam, Lenin's Philosophical Notebooks, *Studies on the Left* 1963.
L. Althusser, *Lenin and Philosophy*, NLB.
J.-M. Benoist, *Marx est Mort*, Gallimard, chapter on Lenin.

## B Luxemburg

Luxemburg defended the concept of a libertarian revolutionary movement against both Leninist and reformist tendencies. Her main works are *The Russian Revolution* and *Leninism or Marxism*, available as one book from Ann Arbor, and *The Spartacus Programme, The Junius Pamphlet*, and *The Mass Strike*, all from Merlin. See also her works on economics, 27A and 27C. See also 30A.

P. Frolich, *Rosa Luxemburg*, Gollancz 1940, and Pluto Press.
T. Cliff, *Rosa Luxemburg*, IS Books 25p.
J. Nettl, *Rosa Luxemburg*, Oxford University Press, 2 vols.
D. Howard, *Selected Political Writings of Rosa Luxemburg*, MR Press 1971.
L. Basso, Luxemburg: Theory and Practice, *ISJ* 1966.
Articles on Luxemburg, *International Socialist Review*, January 1969.
Carsten, Luxemburg, in *Rm*.

## C Trotsky

For Trotsky's most important work on Russia in the 1920s and 1930s, analysing it as a workers' state deformed by Stalinist bureaucracy, see 16C, and for his work on Fascism, see 14B. See 28A for his work on the arts and revolution. His other works include *In Defence of Marxism, The Third International After Lenin, The Platform of the Left Opposition, The Death Agony of Capitalism and the Tasks of the 4th International, Strategy and Tactics in the Imperialist Epoch*, and *Permanent Revolution*, all from Red Books, IS Books, Leader Books, and New Park Publications, and *Terrorism and Communism*, Ann Arbor. See also 14A, 30A.

I. Howe, ed, *Basic Writings of Trotsky*, Mercury.

I. Deutscher, ed, *The Age of Permanent Revolution: A Trotsky Anthology*, Dell.

I. Deutscher, *The Prophet Armed, The Prophet Unarmed*, and *The Prophet Outcast*, all Oxford University Press. (Biography)

*Trotsky: The Man and His Works*, Merit.

Schurer, Trotsky, in *Rm*.

N. Krasso and E. Mandel, Debate on Trotsky, *NLR* 44, 47, 48, 56. (Discussion of his basic perspective, theory of permanent revolution, etc.)

M. Johnstone, Trotsky and the Debate on Socialism in One Country, *NLR* 50.

T. Cliff, *et al., Party and Class*, IS Books 36p.

J.-J. Marie, *Le trotskysme*, Paris 1970.

B. Wolfe, *Three Who Made a Revolution*, Penguin 1966.

## D Gramsci

Gramsci's work is largely on the relation of the intellectuals to the working class, and the relation between ideology and action generally. He also wrote useful analyses of the Italian factory soviets. Some of his writings are included in Q. Hoare and G. Nowell-Smith, eds, *Gramsci's Prison Notebooks*, Lawrence & Wishart, and in his *The Modern Prince and Other Essays*, London 1957.

See also the following articles of his:

Soviets in Italy, *NLR* 51.

*Factory Councils*, and *Two Revolutions*, IWC Bulletin 1968.

*Ten Essays*, IWC 1969.

*Turin 1920*, IS Books and Collets, 25p.

La science et les idéologies scientifiques, *H and S* 1969.

Books and articles on Gramsci:

A. Pozzolini, *Gramsci: An Introduction to His Thought*, Pluto Press.

G. Fiori, *A. Gramsci: Life of a Revolutionary*, NLB.

J. Cammett, *Gramsci and the Origins of Italian Communism*, Stanford University Press.

J. Merrington, Gramsci's Marxism, *SR* 1968.

Q. Williams, 'Egemonia' in Gramsci, *Journal of the History of Ideas* 1960.

L. Colletti, Gramsci and Revolution, *NLR* 65.

P. Anderson, Introduction to Gramsci, *NLR* 51.

J. Texier, *Gramsci*, Paris 1966.

A. Davidson, *Gramsci's Marxism*, Australia 1968.

Symposium on Gramsci, *Praxis* 1967.

C. Harman, Party and Class, *IS* 35.

**E Lukács**

Lukács has mainly written in the field of aesthetics and literary criticism, see 28B.
His work of the early 1920s is an attempt to reinvigorate Marxism by reconsidering
its Hegelian foundations; this resulted in a historicist conception that frequently
degenerated into Stalinist apologetics. His most important work is *History and Class
Consciousness*, Merlin. A book of articles on this is I. Meszaros, ed, *Aspects of
History and Class Consciousness*, Routledge. Lukács has also written a critique
of Existentialism, see 26C, and a critique of Bukharin, in *NLR* 39. Works on
Lukács:

J. Revai, Review of *History and Class Consciousness*, in *Theoretical Practice* 1, 1971.

G. Abendroth, *Entretiens avec G. Lukács*, Maspero 1969.

H. Arvon, *Lukács*, Paris 1968.

L. Goldmann, Introduction aux premiers écrits de Lukács, *TM* 1962–3.

J. Hyppolite, *Studies on Marx and Hegel*, Heinemann, chapter 4. (On Lukács'
interpretation of Hegel)

M. Merleau-Ponty, *Aventures de la dialectique*, chapter 3.

G. Lichtheim, *Lukács*, Fontana.

Watnick, Lukács, in *Soviet Survey* 1958–9, and in *Rm* (abbreviated).

V. Zitta, *Lukács' Marxism*, Nijhoff, The Hague 1964. (Very hostile, but includes
quotes from relatively unknown material)

G. Parkinson, ed, *Lukács*, Weidenfeld & Nicolson.

Morawski, Lukács, *S and S* 1968.

W. Runciman, *Social Science and Political Theory*, chapter 8, Cambridge
University Press.

# 26 Contemporary Marxist Theorists

## A The Frankfurt school

Theorists associated with the Institute of Social Research at Frankfurt since the 1930s have developed a total critique of contemporary society, emphasizing in particular the manipulative and authoritarian nature of advanced technological culture, and attacking sociology for its subservience to these trends. Their work owes much to Hegelian influences; and recently, through the work of the rather conservative Habermas, their ideas have begun to be absorbed into the sociological consensus, although their critique of science remains of value.

T. Adorno, Sociology and Psychology, *NLR* 46 and 47.

T. Adorno, *Prisms*, Spearman. (On sociology, knowledge, aesthetics)

T. Adorno, Rapport entre la théorie et l'empirique en sociologie, *H and S* 1969.

T. Adorno, Scientific experiences of a European scholar in America, in *Perspectives in American History*, vol. 2, Harvard 1968.

T. Adorno *et al., The Authoritarian Personality*, Harper & Row.

T. Adorno, *Negative Dialektik*, Suhrkampf.

T. Adorno and M. Horkheimer, *Dialektik der Aufklarung*.

M. Horkheimer, *Eclipse of Reason*, O UP, New York 1947.

M. Horkheimer, *Kritische Theorie*, ed, Schmidt Suhrkampf.

W. Benjamin, *Illuminations*, Cape. (Essays in history and aesthetics)

W. Benjamin, *Schriften*, ed. Adorno, 2 vols, Suhrkampf.

H. Schweppenhauser, Critical Reason and Scientific Thought, in L. Dencik, ed, *Scientific Research and Politics*, Lund 1968.

J. Habermas, Knowledge and Interest, *Inquiry* 1966.

J. Habermas, *Toward a Rational Society*, Heinemann 1971.

J. Habermas, *Theory and Practice*, Beacon Press.

J. Habermas, *Cognition and Human Interests*, Beacon Press.

J. Habermas, Towards a Theory of Communicative Competence, in *Inquiry* 1970 and in H. Dreitzel, ed, *Recent Sociology no. 2*, Collier-Macmillan.

T. Schroyer, Toward a Critical Theory for Advanced Industrial Society, in Dreitzel.

G. Therborn, Frankfurt Marxism: A Critique, *NLR* 63 and 67.

Articles on Habermas and the Frankfurt School, *Continuum*, Chicago 1970.

The Frankfurt School, *Times Literary Supplement* 5.6.69.

Wohlfarth on Adorno, *NLR* 46.

Brewster on Benjamin, *NLR* 48.

## B Marcuse

Marcuse has been the most influential of those associated with the Frankfurt School; his critique of capitalism is based on a synthesis of Marx and Freud. His most important works are *One-Dimensional Man* and *Eros and Civilization*

Allen Lane, both Sphere, but more accessible are his *Essay on Liberation*, Penguin 1972 and his *Five Lectures* 1970, both Allen Lane. His other books are *Reason and Revolution*, Routledge (on Hegel and Marx), *Soviet Marxism*, Penguin 1971, and *Negations* 1968, Allen Lane (early essays). Other essays of his include:
Repressive Tolerance, in R. Wolff, ed, *Critique of Pure Tolerance*, Cape.
Liberation from the Affluent Society, in *D of L*.
Science and Phenomenology, in *Boston Studies in the Philosophy of Science*, vol. 2.
Ethics of Revolution, in T. deGeorge, ed, *Ethics and Society*, Macmillan.
On Revolution, *NLR* 45 and *NLR* 56.
On Socialist Humanism, in E. Fromm, ed, *Socialist Humanism*, Allen Lane 1967.
Definition of Culture, in *Daedalus* 1965.
Realm of Freedom and the Realm of Necessity, *Praxis* 1969.
On Existentialism, in G. Novack, ed, *Existentialism v. Marxism*, Dell.
Works on Marcuse:
R. Wolff and Barrington Moore, eds, *The Critical Spirit* (with bibliography).
P. Sedgwick, Natural Science and Social Theory: Critique of Marcuse, *SR* 1966.
G. Cohen, Marcuse's Philsophy, *NLR* 57.
A. MacIntyre, *Marcuse*, Fontana.
E. Fromm, Instinctivistic Radicalism, in *Voices of Dissent*, Grove Press 1959.
Breines, *Critical Interruptions*, 1970.

## C Sartre

The early Existentialism of Sartre implied a radical subjectivism; his later work is an attempt to reconcile the valid parts of this with Marxism, and thereby remove the totalitarian strains in the latter. His work is therefore distinct from both the Hegelian tradition (Lukács and the Frankfurt School) and the scientific perspectives of the Althusserians. An anthology of extracts from both periods is R. Cumming, ed, *The Philosophy of J.-P. Sartre*, Methuen. For Sartre's present views on many topics, and a survey of his career, see the useful interview in *NLR* 58. Of his earlier work, see especially his major philosophical statement of the period, *Being and Nothingness*, also *Existentialism and Humanism*, *Sketch for a Theory of the Emotions*, and *Psychology of the Imagination*, all Methuen. The key statement for his later position is *The Problem of Method*, Methuen, a part of the *Critique de la Raison Dialectique*, Gallimard. See also his *Saint Genet*, Allen; *Spectre of Stalin*, Hamish Hamilton; *Black Orpheus*, Gallimard; and *Sartre on Cuba*, Ballantine. Essays of his include his introduction to F. Fanon, *The Wretched of the Earth*, Penguin 1967, and to P. Nizan, *Aden Arabie*, and his essay, Mass-Spontaneity-Party in *SR* 1970. For his work on aesthetics and literature, and his novels, see 28B.
Critical work concentrating on his earlier period:
R. Garaudy *et al.*, *Marxisme et Existentialisme*. Plon 1962.
G. Lukács, *Existentialisme ou Marxisme*, Paris 1946.
D. Cooper, Two Types of Rationality, *NLR* 29.
G. Novack, ed, *Existentialism v. Marxism*, Dell.
Krieger, History and Existentialism in Sartre, in R. Wolff and Barrington Moore, eds, *The Critical Spirit*.
A. Manser, *Sartre*, Athlone Press.
General discussions follow – Desan, Laing and Gorz are accounts of his later views:
M. Merleau-Ponty, *Aventures de la Dialectique*, Gallimard.
W. Desan, *The Marxism of J.-P. Sartre*, Doubleday Anchor.

R. Laing and D. Cooper, *Reason and Violence*, Tavistock.

Lichtheim, Sartre Marxism and History, *History and Theory* 1963–4.

Blakeley, Sartre, *Studies in Soviet Thought* 1968.

Gorz, Sartre and Marx, *NLR* 37

Lessing, Marxist Existentialism, *Review of Metaphysics* 1966–7.

Symposium on Sartre, *NC* 173–4, 1966.

C. Lévi-Strauss, *The Savage Mind*, Weidenfeld & Nicolson, chapter 9.

Pouillon, Sartre et Lévi-Strauss, *L'Arc* 26, 1965.

H. Lefebvre, Critique de la Critique, *Nouvelle Revue Marxiste de Metaphilosophie* 2, 1961.

## D 'Scientific' Marxism

Some trends in postwar French and Italian Marxism have resisted humanist, Hegelian and Existentialist interpretations, demanding that Marxism should be rigorously scientific, and stressing the importance of Marx's later work. Althusser is the most important of these thinkers, and there is considerable disagreement among them over the nature of scientific method, the Italians being close to a conventional positivist interpretation. For Althusser's relation to structuralism see 24B. See also 4E.

L. Althusser, *Reading Capital*, NLB.

L. Althusser, *Lenin and Philosophy and Other Essays*, NLB.

L. Althusser, *For Marx*, Allen Lane 1970.

L. Althusser, Politics and Philosophy, *NLR* 64.

B. Brewster on Althusser, *NLR* 41.

N. Poulantzas *et al.*, Symposium on Althusser, *TM* 1966.

A. Glucksmann, Un structuralisme ventriloque, *TM* 1967. (On Althusser)

H. Lefebvre, Althusser, *H and S* 1969.

J.-C. Forquin, Lecture d'Althusser, in *C du C d'ES* February 1968.

P. Hirst, Althusser and Philosophy, *Theoretical Practice* 2, 1971.

M. Gane, Althusser in English, *Theoretical Practice* 1, 1971.

A. Badiou, Le recommencement du matérialisme dialectique, *Critique* 1967.

N. Poulantzas, Political Ideology and Scientific Research, in L. Dencik, ed, *Scientific Research and Politics*, Lund 1968.

N. Poulantzas, *Pouvoir politique et classes sociales*, Maspero (translation forthcoming).

N. Poulantzas, The State in Capitalist Society, *NLR* 58.

N. Poulantzas, *Fascisme et dictature*, Maspero 1970.

N. Poulantzas, Marxism in Great Britain, *NLR* 43.

A. Glucksmann, Discours de la guèrre, Editions de l'Herne, 1968.

B. Brewster on Glucksmann, *NLR* 49.

Little of the Italian material is translated, but see:

U. Cerroni, Italian Marxism, *Social Research* 1967.

S. Bodington, The Il Manifesto group, *Sp* 5.

G. della Volpe, Marx and Rousseau, *NLR* 59.

L. Colletti, The Leninist State, *NLR* 56.

# 27 Marxist Economics

## A General works

The most thorough exposition of Marx's theory is found in vol. 1 of *Capital*,
the earlier sections of which discuss the production of surplus value and the
tendency of capitalist accumulation, and the concluding sections analyse the
historical development of capitalism. Freedman, below, includes excerpts.
*Wages, Price and Profit**\* is a short presentation of the foundation of the theory
of surplus value (see section VI especially), and a general statement of Marx's
economic theory. *Wage Labour and Capital**\* is a short popular exposition of the
nature of exploitation. Further development of the theory is given in vols. 2 and 3
of *Capital*, and in *Theories of Surplus Value; Capital* vol. 3 is where Marx drops
his restrictive assumption about the uniform organic composition of capital and
thereby engenders the difficulties for the theory of value discussed in subsection B.
(These works are available from Lawrence & Wishart; those marked with an
asterisk are in the one-volume *Selected Works*.)
McLellan's book of translations from the *Grundrisse* is essential, especially sections
18–22; section 19 is vital for the theory of capitalist breakdown. (For this book,
and Marx's other works, see 24A.)
Of the following general accounts by Marxists, the books of Mandel and Sweezy
are the most influential and comprehensive; the Mandel booklet, Eaton are shorter
expositions. Comparisons of Marx and Keynes are included as a useful way
to understand the differences between the traditions. Most general discussions by
non-Marxists are misleading, but Robinson, Blaug, are included as being among
the more interesting. See also 2A, 15B.

R. Freedman, ed, *Marx on Economics*, Penguin 1962.
P. Sweezy, *Theory of Capitalist Development*, Dobson 1946.
E. Mandel, *Marxist Economic Theory*, Merlin, 2 vols.
E. Mandel, *Introduction to Marxist Economic Theory*, Red Books 45p.
Critical articles on Mandel: Kidron, *IS* 36; Harman, *IS* 41.
R. Luxemburg, *What is Economics*, Merlin 25p.
J. Eaton, *Political Economy: A Marxist Text*, Lawrence & Wishart.
L. Althusser, *Reading Capital*, NLB. (And see 26D)
M. Godelier, *Rationalité et Irrationalité en Economie*, Maspero.
Symposium on *Capital*, *MR* December 1967.
Symposium on Marxist Economics, *S and S*, autumn 1967.
P. Mattick, *Marx and Keynes: Limits of the Mixed Economy*, Boston 1969.
O. Lange, *On the Economic Theory of Socialism*, McGraw-Hill 1964.
M. Dobb, *On Economic Theory and Socialism*, Routledge.
M. Dobb, *Political Economy and Capitalism*, Routledge.
J. Robinson, *An Essay on Marxian Economics*, Macmillan.
M. Blaug, *Economic Theory in Retrospect*. (Section on *Capital*)

## B The labour theory of value and the transformation problem

The labour theory of value, on which the concept of exploitation is based, is the heart of Marx's economics; his attempt to make its assumptions more realistic, in vol. 3 of *Capital*, led to the 'transformation problem', how to convert values into prices. In the early years of the century, Böhm-Bawerk argued that this revealed a basic contradiction; Hilferding attempted a defence, but it was left to the neo-Ricardians Bortkiewicz and (in our time) Sraffa, to develop a solution, which however, leads to further difficulties in that it implies that there is no inherent tendency for capitalism to generate worsening crises; for the resulting discussion of the falling rate of profit, and capitalist breakdown, and relevant empirical data, see subsection C. Meek and Kidron can be used as summaries or introductions to the problem.

P. Sweezy, ed, *Böhm-Bawerk, Karl Marx and the Close of his System*, and *Hilferding, Böhm-Bawerk's Criticism of Marx*, Kelley, New York 1966. (Also includes L. von Bortkiewicz, On the Correction of Marx's Theoretical Construction, which is also in *International Economic Papers* 1952)

M. Kidron, Marx's Theory of Value, *IS* 32.

D. Hallas on Kidron, *IS* 44.

E. Mandel, The Labour Theory of Value and Monopoly Capital, *International Socialist Review* 1969.

P. Mattick, Value Theory and Capitalist Accumulation, *S and S* 1959.

H. Sherman, Marxist Theory of Value Revisited, *S and S* 1970.

J. Duffield, Value in *Capital, S and S* 1970.

R. Meek, *Economics and Ideology*, Chapman & Hall 1967. (Transformation problem, immiserisation, falling rate of profit, and discussion of Sraffa)

R. Meek, *Studies in the Labour Theory of Value*, Lawrence & Wishart 1956.

J. Robinson, Value and Price, in *Marx and Contemporary Scientific Thought*, Unesco, Mouton, The Hague 1969.

Johansen, Labour Theory of Value and Marginal Utilities, *Economics of Planning*, no. 2, Oslo 1963.

P. Sraffa, *Production of Commodities*, Cambridge 1960.

J. Robinson, Sraffa and the Rate of Exploitation, *NLR* 31.

F. Seton, The Transformation Problem, *Review of Economic Studies* 1957.

J. Winternitz, Values and Prices: A Solution of the Transformation Problem, *Economic Journal* 1948.

## C Other topics

Topics discussed here include the falling rate of profit, the controversy over the breakdown of capitalism the immiserisation thesis, and the relevance of Marxist economics to the theory of growth and economic development. For the latter, see also 2, 15B, 17C (particularly Lange and Dobb in 15B). Fellner, Samuelson, Dickinson, Gillman and Gottheil discuss the empirical data and its significance for Marx's theory; Baran and Bettelheim outline Marxist approaches to growth; and the models of Robinson and Kalecki are included as non-Marxist approaches that nevertheless owe a considerable amount to Marxist influences.

D. Horowitz, ed, *Marx and Modern Economics*, MacGibbon & Kee 1968. (Articles by Bronfenbrenner, Blaug, Tsuru, Lange, Sweezy, etc.)

W. Fellner, Marxian Hypotheses and Observable Trends under Capitalism, *Economic Journal* 1957.

P. Samuelson, Wages and Interest, *American Economic Review* 1957. (And further discussion by Gottheil and Samuelson, 1960)

J. Gillman, *The Falling Rate of Profit*, Dobson 1957.

H. Dickinson, The Falling Rate of Profit in Marxian Economics, *Review of Economic Studies* 1957.

F. Gottheil, *Marx's Economic Predictions*, Evanston 1966.

F. Gottheil, Increasing Misery of the Proletariat: An Analysis of Marxian Wage and Employment Theory, *Canadian Journal of Economic and Political Science* 1962.

Erlich, Bronfenbrenner and Samuelson, *Kapital:* A Centenary Appreciation, *American Economic Review* 1967.

N. Georgescu-Roegan, *Analytical Economics*, Harvard 1966. (Attacks mathematical proofs of the breakdown of capitalism)

F. Gottheil, Marx's Mehrwert Concept and Pure Capitalism, *Review of Economic Studies* 1951.

Meek on Gottheil, *Review of Economic Studies* 1951-2.

J. Robinson, *Accumulation of Capital*, Macmillan 1966.

Articles on Robinson: Bronfenbrenner, *Journal of Political Economy* 1957; Findlay, *Economica* 1963.

R. Luxemburg, *Accumulation of Capital*, 1951. (And see Robinson's introduction)

M. Dobb, *Welfare Economics and the Economics of Socialism*, Cambridge University Press.

P. Baran, *The Political Economy of Growth*, M R Press. (See also Sweezy in 27A)

M. Kalecki, *Theory of Economic Dynamics*, M R Press.

M. Kalecki, *Introduction to the Theory of Growth in a Socialist Economy*, Blackwell.

C. Bettelheim, *Planification et croissance accélérée*, Maspero.

C. Furtado, Marx's Model and the Analysis of Underdeveloped Economic Structures, in *Marx and Contemporary Scientific Thought*, Unesco, Mouton, The Hague 1969. (See also articles by Kalecki, Tsuru, Milejkovskij)

K. Naqvi, Marxian Model of Growth and Underdeveloped Economies, in B. and V. Singh, eds, *Social and Economic Change*, Bombay 1967.

**D Theory of imperialism**

Kemp gives a summary of the theories. Lenin, Hobson and Bukharin are classic statements, Baran, Dobb, Mandel are recent contributions, and Fieldhouse is critical of Marxist approaches generally. See also 17.

V. Lenin, *Imperialism, Highest Stage of Capitalism*, 1916; Lawrence & Wishart.

J. Hobson, *Imperialism*, 1902; Allen & Unwin 1938.

N. Bukharin, *Imperialism and the World Economy*, 1917; Lawrence & Wishart 1930.

E. Varga and L. Mendelsohn, *New Data on Lenin's Imperialism*, International Publishing Co. 1940.

T. Kemp, *Theories of Imperialism*, Dobson.

E. Mandel, *Marxist Economic Theory*, Merlin, chapter 13.

P. Baran, *Political Economy of Growth*, M R Press, chapters 5-7.

M. Dobb, *Studies in the Development of Capitalism*, Routledge.

D. Fieldhouse, Imperialism, *Economic History Review* 1961.

Symposium on Imperialism, *American Economic Review*, May 1970.

P. Baran and P. Sweezy, *Monopoly Capital*, Penguin 1968, chapter 7.

# 28 The Arts and Revolution

## A General works

Fischer presents a Marxist approach to the arts in general; Trotsky, Castro and Mao give Marxist views on the relation of the artist to society (see also Gramsci, 25D); Adorno, Benjamin and Marcuse write from a Frankfurt School perspective (see 26A, 26B); Laing is influenced by psychoanalysis and Sartre (see subsection B). For underground approaches, see 10; see also 3B, 5A, 6A.

L. Trotsky, *Literature and Revolution*, Ann Arbor.

L. Trotsky, *Art and Revolution*, IS Books.

*Marx and Engels on Literature and Art*, Lawrence & Wishart.

Mao, *On Art and Revolution*, Foreign Language Press, Peking.

F. Castro, Address to Artists and Intellectuals, in J. Cohen, ed, *Writers in the New Cuba*, Penguin 1967.

E. Fischer, *The Necessity of Art*, Penguin 1963.

E. Fischer, *Art Against Ideology*, Allen Lane 1969.

H. Marcuse, The Affirmative Character of Culture, in his *Negations*, Allen Lane 1968.

T. Adorno, *Prisms*, Spearman. (On sociology and cultural criticism)

W. Benjamin, *Illuminations*, Cape.

W. Benjamin, The Author as Producer, *NLR* 62.

G. Steiner, *Language and Silence*, Penguin 1969, section on Marxist criticism.

R. Laing, *Self and Others*, Penguin 1971.

A. Bold, ed, *Socialist Verse*, Penguin 1970.

S. Giedion, *Space, Time and Architecture*, Oxford University Press.

S. Giedion, *Mechanization Takes Command*.

F. Klingender, *Art and the Industrial Revolution*.

## B Current approaches: Lukács, Goldmann, Sartre

For discussion of the general perspective of Lukács, see 25E, and for Sartre, 26C. Goldmann has worked particularly in the sociology of literature, and his work is heavily influenced by Lukács' Hegelianism and Piaget's structuralism; he therefore has some affinities with the tendencies in the next subsection, although his approach remains firmly Marxist.

Lukács' works include the early *Theory of the Novel*, and the later *Meaning of Contemporary Realism*, *The Historical Novel* (Penguin 1969), *Goethe and His Age*, *Essays on Thomas Mann*, *Selected Essays*, *Writer and Critic* and *Solzhenitsyn*, all from Merlin. See also the following discussions:

L. Goldmann, *Recherches Dialectiques*, Gallimard, part 3.

I. Birchall, Lukács as Literary Critic, *IS* 36.

Agnes, Lukács' Aesthetic, *New Hungarian Quarterly* 1966.

MacIntyre on Lukács, *Encounter* 1963 and 1965.

P. Demetz, ed, *Marx, Engels and the Poets*, University of Chicago Press, chapter on Lukács.

Megill, Lukács as Ontologist, *Studies in Soviet Thought* 1969.

Sartre's works include *What is Literature?*, Methuen, *Essays in Aesthetics*, Owen, *Literary and Philosophical Essays*, Criterion, *Baudelaire*, Hamish Hamilton, and *Saint Genet*, Allen. See also his two volume *Flaubert*, Gallimard. His early novels and plays, such as *Nausea* and the *Roads to Freedom* trilogy, all Penguin, are also useful. See also:

R. Cumming, Sartre's aesthetics and politics, in M. Philipson, ed, *Aesthetics Today*, Meridian 1961.

P. Thody, *J.-P. Sartre, a Literary and Political Study*, Hamish Hamilton.

Goldmann's books include *The Hidden God*, Routledge, *Pour une Sociologie du Roman*, Paris 1964, and *Recherches dialectiques*, Gallimard. The following are some of his articles, and a critique of his work:

L. Goldmann, Criticism and Dogmatism in Literature, in *D of L*.

L. Goldmann, Sociology of Literature, *International Social Science Journal* 1967.

L. Goldmann, Subject of Cultural Creation, *Boston Studies in the Philosophy of Science*, vol. 4.

M. Glucksmann, Critique of Goldmann, *NLR* 56. (And reply by Birchall, *NLR* 59)

## C Current approaches: influence of structuralism

Barthes is the most important figure in the field; anyone seriously interested should also consult the structuralist journals, e.g. *Tel Quel*, *Communications* and *Poétique*. Macherey attempts in his book to develop an Althusserian approach. On the general background to structuralism, see 24B, and see subsection D for the Russian Formalists.

R. Barthes, *Writing Degree Zero*, Cape.

R. Barthes, *Elements of Semiology*, Cape.

R. Barthes, *Racine*, Hill & Wang.

T. Todorov, *Littérature et Idéologies* special number of *La Nouvelle Critique*, 1970.

G. Charbonnier, *Conversations with Lévi-Strauss*, Cape.

P. Macherey, *Pour une théorie de la production littéraire*.

P. Wollen, *Signs and Meaning in the Cinema*, Secker & Warburg.

C. Metz, *Essais sur la signification au cinéma*, Klincksieck, Paris 1968.

R. Macksey and E. Donato, eds, *The Languages of Criticism and the Sciences of Man*.

Special issue of *Twentieth-Century Studies*, May 1970.

## D Art in revolution: the Russian experiment 1917-20s

See also subsection A for Trotsky.

C. Gray, *The Great Experiment: Russian Art 1863-1922*, Thames & Hudson.

S. Fitzpatrick, *The Commissariat of Enlightenment: Soviet Organization of Education and the Arts under Lunacharsky 1917-21*, Cambridge University Press 1971.

Soviet Decrees on the Reorganization of Art Education, *NLR* 51.

A. Kopp, *Soviet Architecture and City Planning 1917-35*, Thames & Hudson.

El Lissitsky, *Russia: An Architecture for World Revolution*, Lund Humphries 1970.

*El Lissitsky: Life, Letters, Texts*, Thames & Hudson.

Jacobson and Tynyanov, Theses on Formalism, *NLR* 37.

T. Todorov, ed, *Théorie de la littérature*, Le Seuil. (Texts of Russian Formalists)

V. Markov, *Russian Futurism*, London 1969.

K. Malevich, *Essays on Art*, Rapp & Whiting.
V. Mayakovsky, *How Are Verses Made*, Cape.
M. Gorky, *Untimely Thoughts*, Garnstone Press.
*Autobiography of M. Gorky: My Childhood, In the World, My University*, London 1953.
S. Eisenstein, *The Film Sense*, Faber.
P. Wollen on Eisenstein, in his *Signs and Meaning in the Cinema*, Secker & Warburg.
E. Braun, ed, *Meyerhold on Theatre*, Methuen 1969.

### E Painting

M. Raphael, *The Demands of Art*, Routledge.
J. Berger, *The Moment of Cubism and Other Essays*, Weidenfeld & Nicolson.
J. Berger, *The Success and Failure of Picasso*, Penguin 1965.
J. Berger, *Permanent Red*, Methuen.
J. Berger, *Art and Revolution*, Penguin 1969. (On Neizvestny)
A. Hauser, *The Social History of Art*, Routledge.
F. Antal, *Florentine Painting and Its Social Background*, Routledge.
F. Antal, The Method of Art History, *Burlington Magazine* 1948.
F. Alquié, *The Philosophy of Surrealism*, University of Michigan Press.
P. Waldberg, ed, *Surrealism*, Thames & Hudson. (Includes Breton's *First and Second Surrealist Manifestoes*, Artaud's *Letter to the Chancellors of the European Universities* and *Dinner is Served*, etc.)
M. Nadeau, *History of Surrealism*, Cape.
T. Tzara, *Les manifestes dada*, Pauvert, Paris 1968.
M. Carrouges, *André Breton et les données fondamentales du surréalisme*, Gallimard.

### F Theatre and cinema

Other subsections are also relevant: D for Meyerhold and Eisenstein, C for structuralist approaches to the cinema, and E for surrealism.
A. Artaud, *The Theatre and Its Double*, Evergreen 1958.
J. Hirschman, ed, *Artaud Anthology*, City Lights.
A. Artaud, *Collected Works*, Calder & Boyars.
E. Sellin, *The Dramatic Concepts of A. Artaud*, Chicago 1968.
J. Grotowski, *Towards a Poor Theatre*, Methuen.
V. Spolin, *Improvisation for Theatre*, Northwestern University Press 1963.
J. Willett, ed, *Brecht on Theatre*, London 1964.
F. Ewen, *Bertolt Brecht: His Life, His Art and His Times*, London 1970.
L. Althusser, Bertolazzi and Brecht, in *For Marx*, Allen Lane.
S. Tretyakov, Brecht, *Sp* 1, 1970.
B. Brecht, *The Messingkauf Dialogues*, London 1965.
W. Benjamin, *Essais sur Bertolt Brecht*, Maspero.
E. Copfermann, *Le Théâtre populaire pourquoi?*, Maspero.
P. Biner, *Le Living théâtre*, Maspero.
D. Caute, *The Illusion*, Deutsch. (On ideology in drama)
P. Feyerabend, The Theatre as an Instrument for the Criticism of Ideologies, *Inquiry* 1967.
R. Williams, *Modern Tragedy*, London 1966.
A. Glucksmann, Violence on the Screen, British Film Institute 1971.
S. Renan, *The Underground Film*, Studio Vista. (Documents)
R. Roud, *Jean-Luc Godard*, Secker & Warburg.

A. Willener, *The Action Image of Society*, Tavistock, chapter on Godard.
Wood and Russell on Godard, *NLR* 39.

## G English literature

R. Williams, *Culture and Society 1780–1950*, Penguin 1961.

R. Williams, *The Long Revolution*, Penguin 1965.

C. Caudwell, *Studies in a Dying Culture*, M R Press.

C. Caudwell, *Further Studies in a Dying Culture*, M R Press. (On Shaw, Wells, Lawrence, etc.)

C. Caudwell, *Illusion and Reality*, Lawrence & Wishart. (On poetry)

D. Margolies, *The Function of Literature: A Study of Caudwell's Aesthetics?*, Lawrence & Wishart.

G. Orwell, *Inside the Whale*, Penguin 1957.

E. Thompson, Outside the Whale, in his *Out of Apathy*, New Left Books 1960. (On Orwell)

P. Sedgwick, Orwell – International Socialist?, *IS* 37.

R. Williams, *Orwell*, Fontana.

P. Anderson, Components of the National Culture, in *SP* (C and B), section on Leavis.

E. Thompson, *William Morris*, Lawrence & Wishart.

W. Morris, *Selected Writings and Designs*, Penguin 1963.

A. Morton, *The English Utopia*, London 1969.

I. Watt, *The Rise of the Novel*, Penguin 1963.

J. Goode, Character and the Novel, *NLR* 40.

A. Kettle, *Introduction to the English Novel*, Hutchinson.

A. Kettle, ed, *Shakespeare in a Changing World*, London 1964.

D. Horowitz, *Shakespeare: An Existential View*, London 1965.

P. Demetz, ed, *Marx, Engels and the Poets*, University of Chicago Press.

G. Thompson, *Marxism and Poetry*, Lawrence & Wishart.

## H Oral tradition and popular culture

A. L. Lloyd, *Folk Song in England*, Panther.
(Bibliography of Song Collections)

John Aston, *Humour, Wit and Satire of the Seventeenth Century*, Dover; Seven Dials.

Charles Hindley, *Curiosities of Street Literature*, Seven Dials.

B. A. Botkin, *A Treasury of American Folklore*, Crown.

G. Leghorn, *Rationale of the Dirty Joke*, Grove Press.

Jan Vansina; *Oral Tradition*, Routledge & Kegan Paul.

C. M. Bowra, *Primitive Song*, Weidenfeld & Nicolson.

Katherine M. Briggs, *Dictionary of British Folk Tales* (4 vols.), Routledge.

John Ashton, *Chapbooks of the Eighteenth Century*, Seven Dials.

A. V. Judges, *The Elizabethan Underworld*, Routledge.

Peter and Iona Opie, *The Language and Lore of Schoolchildren*, Oxford University Press.

Ken Boynes *et al.*, *Art and Society* (4 vols: – War, Work, Worship, Sex), Lund Humphries.

Tom Hopkinson ed, *Picture Post 1938–50*, Penguin.

Studs Terkel, *Hard Times*, Allen Lane.

Alan Lomax, *Folk Songs of North America*, Doubleday.

Rossell Hope Robbins ed, *Secular Lyrics of the Fourteenth and Fifteenth centuries*, Oxford University Press.

Joseph Strutt and J. C. Cox, *The Sports and Pastimes of the People of England*.

E. K. Chambers, *The Folk Play*, Oxford University Press.

E. K. Chambers, *The Medieval Stage*, Oxford University Press.

Peter Drouke, *The Medieval Lyric*, Hutchinson.

Roman Jakobson, 'On Russian Fairy Tales' in M. Lane, ed, *Structuralism*, Cape.

George Ewart Evans, *Where Beards Wag All*, Faber.

Paul Oliver, *Blues Fell This Morning etc.*, Cassell.

Williams Ferris Jr, *Blues from the Delta*, Studio Vista.

John Wardrope, *Jest Upon Jest*, Routledge.

A. B. Lord; *The Singer of Tales*, Harvard University Press, Atheneum.

Francis Magoun Jr, 'The Oral Formulaic Character of Anglo-Saxon' in Lewis E. Nicholson, ed, *An Anthology of Beowulf Criticism*, University of Notre Dame Press.

Ed. M. and J. Raven, *Folklore and Songs of the Black Country*, Wolverhampton Folksong Club.

Samuel McKechnie, *Popular Entertainments Through the Ages*, Sampson Low, Marston.

*New City Songsters* (6 vols.) MacColl & Seeger.

Richard Dorson, ed, *Folktales of the World* (17 vols.), Routledge.

*Brewer's Dictionary of Phrase and Fable*, Cassell.

Dell Hymes, *Language in Culture and Society* (Part VI 'Speech Play and Verbal Art), Harper & Row.

For records of traditional singers, 'revival' singers and political singers the following lists should be consulted: Topic, Xtra, Folkways, Leader and Argo.
A selected list of singers and writers of revolutionary song material would include:
Ewan MacColl, Peggy Seeger, Woody Guthrie, Huddie Leadbetter (Leadbelly), The Critics Group, Pete Seeger, Big Bill Broonzy, Joe Hill, Sonny Terry and Brownie McGhee, Cisco Houston, Dominic Behan, Ian Campbell, The Exiles, The High Level Ranters.

# 29 Anarchism

## A The development of anarchist ideas

This includes anthologies, and works on and by the main anarchist thinkers.
See 14A for the Internationals, and 16C for anarchist interpretations of the Russian Revolution.

I. Horowitz, ed, *The Anarchists*, Dell. (Anthology)

P. Eltzbacher, ed, *Anarchism*, FP 1960.

G. Woodcock, *Anarchism*, Penguin 1963.

J. Joll, *The Anarchists*, Methuen.

A. Camus, *The Rebel*, Penguin 1962.

E. Malatesta, *Anarchy*, FP.

V. Richards, *Malatesta: His Life and Ideas*, FP.

M. Bakunin, *Marxism, Freedom and the State*.

G. Maximoff, ed, *The Political Philosophy of Bakunin*, Collier-Macmillan.

Aldred, *Bakunin: Selected Writings*, FP 23p.

Kenafick, *Bakunin and Marx*, FP.

E. Carr, *Bakunin*.

P. Kropotkin, *The State: Its Historical Role*, FP 20p.

Woodcock and Avakumovic, *Anarchist Prince: Biography of Kropotkin*, FP.

M. Miller, ed, *Kropotkin: Selected Writings on Anarchism and Revolution*, MIT 1971.

R. Baldwin, ed, *Kropotkin's Revolutionary Pamphlets*, Constable 1971.

E. Fraser, ed, *Selected Writings of Proudhon*, Macmillan.

S. Edwards, ed, *Proudhon: Selected Writings*, Macmillan.

Jackson, *Marx, Proudhon, and European Socialism*, FP.

Ansart, *Marx et l'anarchisme, Essai sur les sociologies de Saint-Simon, Proudhon et Marx*, Anthropos 1969.

M. Stirner, *The Ego and His Own*, Cape.

W. Morris, *News from Nowhere*, Lawrence & Wishart.

W. Godwin, *Essay on Property*, FP 50p.

E. Carr, *Romantic Exiles*, Penguin 1968. (On Herzen, Bakunin, etc.)

P. Avrich, *The Russian Anarchists*, Princeton 1962.

Yaroslavsky, *History of Anarchism in Russia*, FP.

## B Contemporary anarchist viewpoints

Analyses of particular topics will usually be found in the appropriate section.
See also 5B (Situationists), and 10A (Yippies), and *Anarchy* for current coverage.

D. Guérin, *Anarchism: From Theory to Practice*, MR Press 1971. (Includes discussion of Russian Revolution, Spanish Civil War, factory soviets, etc.)

N. Chomsky on Anarchism, *An* 116.

N. Chomsky versus E. Hobsbawm on Anarchism, *Sp* 6 and 7, 1970.

S. Christie and A. Malzer, *Floodgates of Anarchy*, Kahn & Averill.

D. Cohn-Bendit, *Obsolete Communism: The Left-Wing Alternative*, Penguin 1969.

N. Hentoff, ed, *Essays of A. J. Muste*, Bobbs-Merrill 1967.

H. Read, *Anarchy and Order*, Faber.

N. Walter on Anarchism, *An* 100.

G. Ionescu, ed, Anarchism Today, special issue of *Government and Opposition*, 5:4.

Berkman, *ABC of Anarchism*, FP.

Goldman and Berkman, *An* 114.

W. Powell, *The Anarchist Cook Book*, 1970.

A. Comfort, *Authority and Delinquency in the Modern State*, Routledge.

P. Goodman, *Persons or Personnel: Decentralising and the Mixed System*, Random House 1965.

P. Goodman, *Communitas*.

A. Carter, *The Political Theory of Anarchism*, Routledge 1971.

G. Baldelli, *Social Anarchism*, Penguin 1972.

## C Anarchism in practice: the Spanish Experience 1936–9

H. Thomas, Anarchist Agrarian Collectives in the Spanish Civil War, in M. Gilbert, ed, *Century of Conflict 1850–1950*, Hamish Hamilton 1967.

V. Richards, *Lessons of the Spanish Revolution*, FP 1953.

P. Broué and M. Témime, *La Révolution et la Guerre d'Espagne*, Editions de Minuit.

N. Chomsky, Objectivity and Liberal Scholarship, in his *American Power and the New Mandarins*, Penguin 1969.

G. Leval, *Social Reconstruction in Spain*.

B. Bolloten, *The Grand Camouflage*, Praeger. (On the Communist Party role)

G. Orwell, *Homage to Catalonia*, Penguin 1962.

F. Morrow, *Revolution and Counter-Revolution in Spain*, New Park.

F. Borkenau, *Spanish Cockpit*, University of Michigan Press.

Maura, Spanish Anarchism, *Government and Opposition* 5:4.

# 30 Tactics and Strategy

Many relevant topics are discussed in other sections: for anarchist views, see 29; for underground and Yippies, 10A; for Situationist views, 5B; for the Third World theorists, see 23; and 23A for discussions of guerrilla warfare. See also 3D, 8D, 12D, 16C.

## A The revolutionary party

This subsection includes works on the Marxist conception of the party and its role in revolutionary activity, and general problems of strategy and tactics. The Lenin–Luxemburg debate on the nature of revolutionary organization is perhaps the best introduction to the issues. Lenin's views changed their emphasis over time: compare the early *What Is To Be Done?* and *One Step Forward, Two Steps Back* with the later *State and Revolution*. See also 25A. For Luxemburg's views, see 25B (especially *Leninism or Marxism*). For Gramsci on the relation of ideas to action, see 25D. Trotsky's views on the logic of transitional demands and revolutionary tactics generally can be found in *Strategy and Tactics in the Imperialist Epoch*, *The Tasks of the Fourth International*, and other works in 25C. For the theory of the state in Marx and Lenin, see 24D and 25A. The following articles by Johnstone, Magri and Wolpe are surveys of the problems.

M. Johnstone, Marx, Engels and the Party, *SR* 1967.
L. Magri, Marxist Theory of the Revolutionary Party, *NLR* 60.
H. Wolpe, Revolutionary Consciousness, *SR* 1970.
J.-P. Sartre, Party, Mass, Spontaneity, *SR* 1970.
R. Rossanda, Class and Party, *SR* 1970.
T. Cliff *et al.*, *Party and Class*, Pluto Press 35p.
J. Higgins, Lenin and Luxemburg, *IS* 27.
A. Gorz, Reform and Revolution, *SR* 1968.
H. Marcuse on Revolution, *NLR* 45 and 56.
*Revolutionary Organization*, Sol 6p.
P. Buckman, *Limits of Protest*, Gollancz.
L. Magri, Revolution in the West, *SR* 1969.
B. Brewster, Fighting to Win, *NLR* 58. (On the relevance of Clausewitz and games theory)
E. Mandel, *Socialist Strategy for Western Europe*, IWC and Red Books, 8p.
A. Neuberg, *Armed Insurrection*, NLB. (A Comintern statement from Tukhachevsky, Ho Chi Minh, etc.)
A. Glucksmann, *Le Discours de la guèrre*, Editions de l'Herne 1968. (Analyses the theory of war from Clausewitz)
J. Connolly, *Revolutionary Warfare*, IS Books 8p.

## B Self-defence and direct action

This subsection includes works on direct action, demonstrations and urban guerrilla activities, and items on the law and what to do in the event of a bust. In an

emergency, the following organizations can be contacted for advice and assistance: Release, Street Aid, and the National Council for Civil Liberties. Also able to give useful information: Agitprop, BIT Information Service.
See also 8B, 8D.

C. Marighela, *Mini-Manual of the Urban Guerrilla*, Ag 20p.

M. Oppenheimer and G. Lakey, *Manual for Direct Action*, Quadrangle, Chicago 1965, and H.

A. Carter, *Direct Action*, H 13p.

W. Powell, *The Anarchist Cook Book*, 1970. (How to make bombs, etc.)

M. Oppenheimer, *Urban Guerrilla*, Penguin 1970. (Critical)

R. Howard, *The Hooligans' Handbook*, Action Books and Ag.

Berger, The Nature of Demonstrations, *NS* 23.5.68, and *IS* 34.

*How To . . . Manuals*, on posters, street theatre, local journals, films, all from Ag, 8p each.

*Which? Contraceptives Supplement*, Consumers Association 1970.

N. Saunders, *Alternative London*, from Ag or 65 Edith Grove SW 10, 34p. (A very wide range of useful information: pads, communes, politics, bookshops, organizations, sex, drugs)

R. Neville, *Playpower*, Paladin, appendices. (Information on living cheaply)

*Bust Book*, Ag 27p. (What to do, and what to expect)

*Handbook of Citizens' Rights*, NCCL 29p. (The best short summary)

*Arrest*, NCCL 10p.

*Drugs and Civil Liberties*, NCCL 25p.

C. Coon and R. Harris, *Release Report on Drugs and the Law*, Sphere.

*Privacy under Attack*, NCCL 18p.

*Picketing: Your Rights Explained*, LRD and Ag 2p. (But see Industrial Relations Act)

Picciotto and Davies, Sit-ins and the law, *NS* 16.4.70.

S. Bowes, *The Police and Civil Liberties*, Lawrence & Wishart.

D. Pritt, *Law, Class and Society*, Lawrence & Wishart.

R. Jackson, *Enforcing the Law*, London 1967. (A conventional account of the law)

*Bitman 3*, from BIT. (General alternative society information)

A. Coote and L. Grant, *Civil Liberty: The NCCL Guide*, Penguin 1972.

# Abbreviations and Addresses

Note that the addresses of small bookshops and left-wing groups tend to change frequently; if there is difficulty in locating one, try one of the information centres like Agitprop (Ag) or BIT, or a current copy of one of the underground or revolutionary papers. Addresses are not given for standard academic journals as they can be consulted easily in libraries.

|  |  |
|---|---|
|  | Advise: 313 Upper St, N1. 01–226 9365. |
|  | Africa Bureau: 2 Arundel St, WC2R 3DA. |
| ARG | Africa Research Group: PO Box 213, Cambridge, Mass, USA. |
| ANC | African National Congress: 49 Rathbone St, W1. |
| Ag | Agitprop: 248 Bethnal Green Rd, E2, 01–739 1704. |
| *APSR* | *American Political Science Review.* |
| *An* | *Anarchy*: 84B Whitechapel High St, E1. |
|  | Anti-Apartheid: 89 Charlotte St, W1. |
|  | *ARse*: 20 Chalcot Rd, NW1. |
|  | Association for Radical E. Asian Studies: 22 Chepstow Crescent, W11. |
| BRPF | Bertrand Russell Peace Foundation: 45 Gamble St, Forest Rd West, Nottingham NG7 4ET. |
|  | Better Books: 92 Charing Cross Rd, WC2. |
|  | BIT, and *Bitman*: 141 Westbourne Park Rd, W11. 01–229 8219. |
|  | Black Panthers: 3 Hornsey Rise Gdns, N19. |
|  | Black Unity and Freedom Party: 115A Stoke Newington Rd, N16. |
|  | Bookshop 85: 85 Regents Park Rd, NW1. |
| *BJS* | *British Journal of Sociology.* |
| *BQJSW* | *British Quarterly Journal of Social Work.* |
| BSSRS | British Society for Social Responsibility in Science: 42 Great Russell St, WC1. |
| *BCAS* | *Bulletin of Concerned Asian Scholars*: 1737 Cambridge St, Cambridge, Mass 02138, USA. |
| *C du C d'ES* | *Cahiers du Centre d'Etudes socialistes.* |
| CND | Campaign for Nuclear Disarmament: 14 Grays Inn Rd, WC1. |
|  | *Case Con*: 19 Lidfield Rd, N16. |
|  | Central Books: 37 Grays Inn Rd, WC1X 8PS. |
|  | *Character and Energy*: David Boadella, Abbotsbury, Dorset. |
|  | Chemical and Biological Warfare Action Group: 77 High St, Penge, SE20. |

CPAG  Child Poverty Action Group: 1 Macklin St, Drury Lane, WC2B 5NH.

*Cinemantics Magazine*: 117 Hartfield Rd, SW19.

*CS and P*  *Class Status and Power*, R. Bendix and S. Lipset, eds, Routledge.

CU  Claimants Unions: 74A Stratford Rd, Birmingham B11 1AH.

Collets: 66 Charing Cross Rd, WC1.

Committee against Dictatorship in Greece: 60 Tottenham Court Rd, W1.

Communist Party: 16 King St, WC2.

Communist Party of Great Britain (Marxist-Leninist): 155 Fortress Rd, NW5.

Compendium Books: 240 Camden High St, NW1.

*D of L*  *Dialectics of Liberation*, D. Cooper, ed, Penguin 1968.

Dillons University Bokshop: 1 Malet St, WC1.

*DA*  *The Dissenting Academy*, T. Roszak, ed, Penguin 1969.

Economists' Bookshop: Clare Market, Portugal St, WC2.

Europe–Africa Research Project: 103 Gower St, WC1.

Fabian  Fabian booklets and research series: 11 Dartmouth St, SW1.

FWA  Family Welfare Association: Denison House, 296 Vauxhall Bridge Rd, SW1.

Fifth Estate Press: 64 Muswell Hill Rd, N10.

Free Communications Group: 30 Craven St, WC2.

FP  Freedom Press: see *Anarchy*.

Frelimo: 531 Caledonian Rd, N1.

Guideline Publications: Whole Earth, 2813 Telegraph Ave, Berkeley, California, USA.

Help International: 10 South Wharf Rd, W2.

*H and S*  *Homme et Société*.

H  Housmans Bookshop: 5 Caledonian Rd, N1.

*Inc*  *The Incompatibles: Trade Union Militancy and the Consensus*, R. Blackburn and C. Cockburn, eds, Penguin 1967.

IWC  Institute for Workers Control: see BRPF.

International Defence and Aid Fund: 104 Newgate St, EC1.

International Marxist Group: 182 Pentonville Rd, N1.

*IS*  *International Socialism*: 6 Cottons Gdns, E2 8DN. (And IS Books)

*ISJ*  *International Socialist Journal*: now ceased publication.

*IT*  *International Times*: 11A Berwick St, W1.

*Journal of Contemporary Asia*: PO Box 49010, Stockholm 49, Sweden.

*JCH*  *Journal of Contemporary History*.

*JMAS*  *Journal of Modern African Studies*.

LRD  Labour Research Department: 78 Blackfriars Rd, SE1.

LASITOC: c/o Peter Harper, 17 Brunswick Place, Hove BN3 1ND, Sussex.

Leader Books: 28 Poland St, W1V 3DB.

|  |  |
|---|---|
|  | League for Democracy in Greece: 26 Goodge St, W1. |
|  | Liberation News Service: 160 Claremont Ave, New York, USA. |
|  | *Libertarian Teacher*: 36 Devonshire St, NW7. |
| LL | Libro Libre: 21 Theobalds Rd, WC1X 8SL. |
| *MT* | *Marxism Today.* |
| MDM | May Day Manifesto Group: 6A Vernon Terrace, Brighton, BN1 3JG. |
| *MDM* | *May Day Manifesto*, R. Williams, ed, Penguin 1968. |
|  | *Militant*: 197 Kings Cross Rd, WC2. |
| *MR* | *Monthly Review*: 33–7 Moreland St, EC1. (And MR Press) |
| NARMIC | National Action/Research on Military–Industrial Complex; 160 N. 15th St, Philadelphia, Penn, USA. |
| NCCL | National Council for Civil Liberties: 4 Camden High St, NW1. 01–485 9497. |
| NUS | National Union of Students: 3 Endsleigh St, WC1. |
| NEFP | New England Free Press: 791 Fremont St, Boston, Mass 02118, USA. |
| NLB | New Left Books: 7 Carlisle St, W1V 6NL. |
| *NLR* | *New Left Review*: see NLB. |
| *NP* | *New Politics*: 507 5th Ave, New York 10017, USA. |
| NACLA | N. American Congress on Latin America: PO Box 57, New York 10025, USA. |
| *NC* | *La Nouvelle Critique.* |
| OPSA | Occasional Papers in Social Administration: published by Bell. |
|  | *Oz*: 52 Princedale Rd, W11. |
|  | Pacific Studies Center: 1963 University Ave, E. Palo Alto, California, USA. |
| Panaf | Panaf Books: 89 Fleet St, EC4Y 1DU. |
| *P and P* | *Past and Present.* |
|  | Pluto Press: see *IS*. |
| *PC* | *Problems of Communism:* US Information Service. |
| REP | Radical Education Project: Box 625, Ann Arbor, Michigan 48107, USA. |
|  | *Radical American*: 1237 Spaight St, Madison, Wisconsin 53703, USA. |
|  | *Radical Philosophy* S. Sayres, University of Kent, Canterbury. |
|  | *Ramparts*: 495 Beach St, San Francisco, California 94133, USA. |
|  | *Rank and File*: 58 Allerton Rd, N16. |
|  | *Realtime*: 66 Hargrave Park, N19 5JN. |
|  | Red Books: 182 Pentonville Rd, N1. |
|  | *Red Mole*: see Red Books. |
|  | *Red Rat*: 42 Essendine Mansions, Essendine Rd, W9. |
|  | *Red Scientist:* c/o Martin Thomas, 88 Princes Rd, Harteshill, Newcastle-under-Lyme. |
|  | Release: 70 Princedale Rd, W11. 01–603 8654 (emergency) and 01–229 4717 or 5959. |

| | |
|---|---|
| *Rm* | *Revisionism*, L. Labedz, ed, Library of International Studies. |
| SAU | Schools Action Union: 160 N. Gower St, NW1. |
| *Sc Am* | *Scientific American*. |
| *S and S* | *Science and Society*. |
| | *Seven Days*. |
| | Shelter: 86 Strand, WC2. |
| | *Shrew*: 27 Albany Mansions, Albert Bridge Rd, SW11. |
| Sit | Situationist International: BCM King Mob, SW1. |
| SLL | Socialist Labour League: 186A Clapham High St, SW4. |
| *SR* | *Socialist Register*, R. Miliband and J. Savile, eds, Merlin, annually since 1964. |
| | *Socialist Woman*: 16 Elia Rd, West Bridgeford, Nottingham NG2 5GW. |
| *Sol* | *Solidarity*: 27 Sandringham Road, NW11. |
| *SS* | *Soviet Studies*. |
| *Sp* | *The Spokesman*: see BRPF. |
| | Stage 1: see LL. |
| | Street Aid: 35 Southampton St, WC2. |
| *SP*(C and B) | *Student Power*, A. Cockburn and R. Blackburn, eds, Penguin. |
| *SP* (N) | *Student Power*, J. Nagel, ed, Merlin. |
| *TM* | *Les Temps Modernes*. |
| | *Theoretical Practice*: 13 Grosvenor Ave, N5. |
| *TS* | *Towards Socialism*, P. Anderson, ed, Fontana. |
| *TUR* | *Trade Union Register*, K. Coates *et al.*, Merlin, annually since 1969. |
| | Underground Press Syndicate: Box 26, Village St, New York 10014, USA. |
| *UQ* | *Universities Quarterly*. |
| | US Directory Services: c/o Laird Wilcox, PO Box 1832, Kansas City. |
| | *Vanguard*: see SAU. |
| | *Viet-Report*: 133 W. 72nd St, New York 10023, USA. |
| *Voice* | *Voice of the Unions*: 73 Ridgway Place, SW19. |
| | War Resisters International: 3 Caledonian Rd, N1. |
| | *Women, a Journal of Liberation*: 3028 Greenmount Ave, Baltimore, Maryland 21218, USA. |
| | Women's Liberation Workshop: see *Shrew*. |
| | *Women's Newspaper*: 12/13 Little Newport St, WC2. |
| | Your Environment: 10 Roderick Rd, NW3. |

# Some other Penguins

**Demonstrations and Communication**
A Case Study

*James D. Halloran, Philip Elliott and Graham Murdock*

The demonstration against the Vietnam war on 27 October 1968 was overwhelmingly peaceful. Yet the press and television coverage concentrated on the tiny violent minority. The authors have analysed the way in which the newsmen predetermined the quality of the event and were then compelled to find incidents to fulfil their prophecies. The analysis is a study of the structure of our understanding of 'news', of what counts as news and why all the media are committed to reporting not what happens but what they think should happen.

The importance of this study lies also in the pioneering nature of the work. The authors work in the Centre for Mass Communications Research in the University of Leicester and have brought their knowledge to bear on a particular subject to which expert consideration has not been given before.

**Education for Democracy**
Second Edition

*Edited by David Rubenstein and Colin Stoneman*

Since its publication at the very beginning of the decade, *Education for Democracy* has established itself as a key manifesto for any debate on education in Britain. Originally written as a radical reply to the Black Papers, most of the essays have now been updated or completely revised. In addition new essays have been added, covering further education, the government of universities and colleges, and the highly topical issue of intelligence, race and education. The new edition appears at a timely moment, as the educational requirements of a privileged minority are once again being favoured, to the detriment of the needs of the majority.

'essential reading' *The Times Educational Supplement*

'the egalitarian passion of these writers is a passion that relies in the main on hard, cold, realistic scholarship' John Vaizey, *Listener*

'The range of topics covered . . . and the depth and authority of each contribution, combine to make this a definitive work on the aims of education' Clyde Chitty, *Morning Star*

**The Incompatibles**
Trade Union Militancy and the Consensus

*Edited by Robin Blackburn and Alexander Cockburn*

Britain is in economic crisis, and the unions are more and more being nailed as the culprits. They are accused of pricing Britain out of world markets with their inflationary claims and restrictive habits: costs are forced up, but production pegged. As unemployment rises, the unions seem to be busy bickering over trivialities like demarcation.

How much truth and how much prejudice is there in this picture? Have the unions, like the rhinoceros, outlived their age? And what about shop stewards and wildcat strikes? And the 'go-it-alone' strike of the seamen – was that engineered by Communists, as the Prime Minister suggested?

The contributors to *The Incompatibles* include Philip Toynbee, Jack Jones (Assistant Secretary of the T G W U), Ken Coates, Michael Frayn, Perry Anderson, Paul Foot and Clive Jenkins (General Secretary of ASSET). From varying standpoints they re-examine the roots of trade unionism, and their appraisal of the present functions and purposes of unions and of their relationship with the Labour movement raises fundamental questions concerning the unions and socialism.

**The Learning Society**

*Robert M. Hutchins*

With the establishment of the Open University, which could cater for
millions where the University of California is merely projecting a student
population of 300,000, it is time to examine the basic purpose of
education at all levels.

Dr Hutchins, the well-known American educationist and chairman of
the editorial board of the *Encyclopaedia Britannica*, defines education
as 'the deliberate, organized effort to help people to become intelligent'.
Its aim, he contends, must be the fuller realization of manhood, not
manpower. He argues that if universities merely process students for
success in industrial society, then the technology which has freed man
from drudgery in many societies may leave him fit only for 'bread and
circuses' or 'lollipops and Cup Ties'.

In this Pelican he discusses the major issues which are already
emerging in the educational field and looks forward to the next century,
when it is possible to foresee a 'learning society', in which everyone of
every age would have the chance to continue his education as long as
possible. For, as Dr Hutchins comments: 'The way to stay human is to
keep on learning.'

**Obsolete Communism**
The Left-Wing Alternative

*Gabriel and Daniel Cohn-Bendit*

Written by Gabriel and his brother Daniel ('Red' Danny), this is more than just an account of what happened in Paris in May 1968. It is also a passionate statement by a young leader (who is anything but Communist) of a left radical alternative to the encrusted beliefs of revolutionaries and reactionaries of East and West alike. A comment on power, on bureaucracy, and on the paths to liberation. A youthful 'manifesto' addressed from the barricades to students all over the world, to the Negroes of America, the Czechs, the Vietnamese . . . and (if you have a heart) to you.

**Student Power**
Problems, Diagnoses, Action

*Edited by Alexander Cockburn and Robin Blackburn*

American students paralyse the world's largest university. Italian students put their professors on public trial; in Britain the LSE is occupied, free universities operate within our oldest academic institutions and the art colleges make a pattern of creative revolt; and in France students lead a dramatic national revolution which is still to find fulfilment. All industrial societies are now facing a pattern of increasingly effective student revolt, directed in the Communist bloc against authoritarian bureaucracy and in the West against the bland illusions of the liberal academic establishment. Students are today's news. But could they be the revolutionary vanguard of tomorrow's social order?

This Penguin Special, published in cooperation with *New Left Review*, examines the real nature and international implications of student activism in Britain. Students have piecemeal grievances over discipline, examinations and grants – but do they amount to a coherent structural critique of modern society? What is wrong with established student organizations? How does the student situation differ in the established universities, in art colleges and in teacher training colleges? And most important (since students are often accused of fomenting anarchy) what is the strategy for the future?